'Donald Maclean was arguably the most valuable, and certainly the most troubled, of the Cambridge spies. Roland Philipps knows the world that formed him and has given us the fullest account we've yet had not only of his treason but of the conflicted man who committed it'
Joseph Kanon

'In his biography of Maclean, Roland Philipps illuminates, in both broad and subtle strokes, a life lived on the razor edge of discovery by his colleagues and recurring suspicion on the part of his Soviet masters'
Financial Times

'What great storytelling . . . I couldn't put it down'
Peter Snow

'Philipps's telling of the tale is masterly . . . A wonderfully fluent, coherent and compelling narrative'
Standpoint

'A masterpiece . . . Picture Erik Larson meets John le Carré and you have only begun to scratch the surface of this absolutely gripping book'
Brad Thor

'Hugely impressive – by an historian who is a master of storytelling and empathy. A rare combination'
Carmen Callil

'An adroit, deeply researched and richly embroidered portrait'
Ferdinand Mount, *Prospect*

ROLAND PHILIPPS

Roland Philipps went into publishing on graduating from Cambridge and until recently was Publisher at John Murray. He has edited leading novelists, politicians, historians, travellers and biographers. *A Spy Named Orphan*, his first book, arises from lifelong connections to Donald Maclean and his story.

ROLAND PHILIPPS

A Spy Named Orphan

The Enigma of Donald Maclean

VINTAGE

1 3 5 7 9 10 8 6 4 2

Vintage
20 Vauxhall Bridge Road,
London SW1V 2SA

Vintage is part of the Penguin Random House group of companies
whose addresses can be found at global.penguinrandomhouse.com

Penguin
Random House
UK

Copyright © Roland Philipps 2018

Roland Philipps has asserted his right to be identified as the
author of this Work in accordance with the Copyright,
Designs and Patents Act 1988

Front cover image: Westminster © Nat Farbman/Time
& Life Pictures/Getty Images. Spine images: © Archive
Photos/Stringer/Getty Images; figure © Getty Images.
Back cover image: Donald Maclean © Getty Images.

First published in Vintage in 2019
First published in hardback by The Bodley Head in 2018

penguin.co.uk/vintage

A CIP catalogue record for this book is available from the British Library

ISBN 9781784703578

Printed and bound in Great Britain by Clays Ltd, Elcograf S.p.A.

Penguin Random House is committed to a sustainable future
for our business, our readers and our planet. This book is made
from Forest Stewardship Council® certified paper.

For Felicity

Contents

Prologue

Donald Maclean awoke on 25 May 1951 at his house in the quiet Kent village of Tatsfield to a beautiful late-spring day, a welcome change in the weather. That Friday morning would be his last in England; it was his thirty-eighth birthday. He ate his breakfast of bacon and eggs with two cups of tea in his usual haste. The housekeeper and nanny to his sons Fergus and young Donald (known as 'Beany') entered the comfortable Victorian villa to see him rush upstairs to kiss his American wife Melinda goodbye. Remarkably, given the traumatic year they had just had, Melinda was now eight months pregnant with their third child. Donald came back downstairs, quickly watered the cyclamen that Melinda had bought him, bent his long frame into his car and set off for Oxted station and the commuter train to London's Victoria. When he arrived in London the tall, slender, elegantly pinstriped diplomat with his trademark bow-tie, his good looks now with an air of distinction about them as his blond hair was starting to grey, walked briskly from the station through St James's Park, which was in full flower, to the Foreign Office. The man with the trilby and unnecessary raincoat had to adopt an undignified scurry to keep pace with Maclean's stride; it was almost as if the taller man were taunting him. Maclean was at his desk as head of the American Department by 10.00 as usual. He was young for such a prestigious job, the latest promotion in what had so far been, with one setback, a remarkably successful career. He was on track to reach the heights of his profession, the major ambassadorships certainly, perhaps even ending up as Permanent Secretary. His friends were already calling him 'Sir Donald Maclean, OHMS', in recognition of his work On His Majesty's Service. Here was a cultivated, laconic mandarin who was also a highly experienced Soviet agent, and MI5, Britain's domestic intelligence service, were on to him.

Maclean's employers had been exceptionally loyal. They had not only brought him back into the fold the previous winter but they had promoted him to his influential new post. Less than a year before he had been in the throes of paranoid alcoholism and had come close to bringing disgrace upon British diplomacy. When one of his oldest friends had picked him up at the station on his way to stay with her in Wiltshire, she had been so alarmed by his appearance that she took him first to a friend's garden to relax before driving him home. As he lay on piled-up cushions beneath a beech tree, he was seized by an attack of *delirium tremens* so violent that he kept jumping up to fight the branches above him. An acquaintance saw him soon afterwards and described him as looking 'as if he had spent the night sitting up in a tunnel'. A year on, and a delicious lunch in Soho seemed a fitting celebration both of his birthday and of his recovery.

*

The Foreign Office had been constructed on a regal scale in keeping with the majesty of the British Empire in the mid-1860s. That Empire was now shrinking fast, although the outlook of the politicians and diplomats was not always keeping pace with the decline. The great ideological struggle of the twentieth century between Communism and capitalism was now being fought as a cold war between the superpowers of America and the Soviet Union; Britain's most potent contribution to the struggle had ended with the Second World War, when Donald Maclean had held a prime ringside seat in Washington DC. The grandest office in the Whitehall building was that of the Foreign Secretary, and there Herbert Morrison had the previous day signed the order for Maclean to be brought in for questioning. Although the extent of his betrayal was barely understood, the trap was about to snap shut on one of the most influential spies of the century.

*

Maclean's lunch date, who had helped him through his crisis the previous year, drove her jeep into the palatial Foreign Office courtyard just before noon. She noticed he was wearing a jaunty bow-tie, always a sign that he was in good spirits. Gone was the shaky wreck of the previous summer. They chatted about his family over preprandial oysters and a half-bottle of champagne in Wheeler's fish restaurant, then made their way through Soho's bustle and sunny spirits to Schmidt's where they were meeting the friend's husband for an unseasonably heavy German lunch. En route they bumped into a writer they knew, who noted that Maclean seemed 'calm and genial', a welcome change from the gate-crasher who had appeared late in the evening at his Regent's Park home a couple of weeks earlier and passed out in the hallway so that the departing dinner guests had to step over him.

As Maclean had insisted on paying for their lunch he needed to refill his wallet so he walked back to Whitehall, his watcher trotting not far behind, via the Travellers Club in Pall Mall to cash a cheque for £10. He was back at his desk by 3.00 for the only planned meeting of the day, a dull one which he despatched with his usual efficiency. He left his office for the last time around 5.45, reminded a colleague that he would not be at work the following morning, Saturday, and ran into his boss, Sir Roger Makins, in the grand courtyard with its marble pavements and arched colonnades. Makins thought highly of Maclean and had given him his current job after being impressed by him when they worked together on top-secret atomic matters in Washington at the end of the war. Makins had been as astonished as all the other senior men in the Foreign Office when he had learned of Maclean's crimes, but had been assured that there was no danger that he would be able to leave the country, so he acted in his normal friendly manner. The tail followed Maclean to Victoria, where he caught the 6.10 train, carrying a cardboard box and a few small parcels, but without his briefcase. Makins was the last civil servant to see him. Donald Maclean was now invisible to official eyes.

*

That same afternoon, Guy Burgess, an acquaintance of Maclean's from their days in Cambridge and someone he had seen on several occasions in the past couple of weeks, was in his flat in New Bond Street preparing for a journey. He carefully packed a tweed suit, some shirts, shoes, socks, a dinner jacket, shaving kit, £300 and the novels of Jane Austen in a one-volume collected edition ('I never travel without it') and put the case into the back of a cream Austin A40 he had hired that afternoon. Tickets had been booked for the midnight sailing of a ship, the *Falaise*, on the advice of Anthony Blunt, Surveyor of the King's Pictures and Director of the Courtauld Institute, an establishment figure soon to be recognised with a knighthood. Blunt, Burgess and Maclean were all three members of the Cambridge spy ring, known to their Soviet controllers as the 'Magnificent Five'. Now, after decades of brilliant espionage that meant no government had ever been as comprehensively penetrated as Britain's, the ring was about to come apart.

*

Melinda Maclean later claimed that she had spent the day baking her husband a birthday cake and preparing a 'special dinner' and that she was therefore understandably upset when he got back to announce that not only would Roger Styles, a friend of his she had never heard of, be joining them but the pair had to go somewhere on business immediately after dinner and might even have to spend the night away. He started to go upstairs to pack and they argued – not only was it 'too bad' that he had invited an 'unknown guest' home for his birthday which they could have spent as a family, but now he was not even staying with her and their boys, both of whom were in bed with measles. She would now be alone as she prepared the house for his high-maintenance sister Nancy and Nancy's new husband who were arriving on the following day. She begged him not to go, but he insisted. The argument woke up their son Fergus, aged seven, who asked 'Why are you going away, Daddy? Can I stand at the window and watch you go?' His father said: 'Get back into bed, you little scamp; I'm not going far; I'll be back soon.'

Roger Styles, dark and thickish-set, turned up half an hour after his host and was introduced to Melinda, who found him 'charming and easy to talk to'. Dinner was in the end a chatty, 'normal' meal, with nobody showing any sign of strain. After dinner, Maclean announced that they had to be on their way smartly, and went out to stoke the boiler for the night, leaving Styles talking to his wife. They did indeed have to hurry, and only just covered the ninety miles to Southampton in time to embark at 11.45. They left the car on the dockside as they jumped aboard. 'We'll be back for it on Monday!' they shouted to a waiting sailor.

The following morning, they stayed on the boat for too long, drinking beer, before disembarking in Saint Malo, leaving their luggage and some 'disorder' in their shared cabin. Although a few days earlier a general instruction had been put out for UK police and passport control to watch for Maclean, the British had chosen not to share this warning with continental police or ports for fear of leaks, so the pair were free to have a leisurely cooked breakfast. They were so leisurely that they missed the 11.20 boat-train to Paris and ended up hiring a taxi to drive them the forty-three miles to Rennes where they caught up with the train.

*

The Foreign Office was shut from Saturday afternoon until Monday morning, in common with the rest of the country, so, as she later explained, Melinda could not do anything to contact her husband until Monday at 10.00 when she rang his office to say that she had lost track of him. Makins thought he might have given Maclean that day off as well, so it was not until she called again and mentioned his hurried departure with Roger Styles that anyone became worried, and then, in a very controlled and mandarin way, panic-stricken. Word went out to all the diplomatic and consular posts on the continent to look out for the two men and to report back on a 'clear the line' basis direct to the Prime Minister.

*

The charming, well-connected and brilliant enigma that was Donald Maclean had made his choice. The events of that day provoked a sea-change within the British establishment, destroyed much of the carefully built trust between Britain and America and damaged the great nation's standing in the eyes of the world. The Cold War was about to get very much colder. This is the story of a scandal still reverberating today, although the man at its centre has, until now, largely remained a mystery.

1

Purity in Thought

By any standards Donald Maclean was a very successful schoolboy. He had risen to the highest rank in his school's Officer Training Corps, was a prefect, the editor of the school magazine, secretary of its League of Nations Union and a successful all-round sportsman with colours in cricket, rugby and hockey. His contemporaries regarded him as 'way ahead of others' at a time when the 'others' included those who were to become some of the leading figures in British political, public and intellectual life. He left his centuries-old school as the holder of an exhibition to Cambridge, at the summit of the first generation of Macleans to go to university, the hopes of his ambitious parents and teachers intact, a glittering future lying before him. The reference later provided by his school for the Foreign Office seems to bask in shared triumph as it enumerates his achievements and acclaims his 'moral character' as 'exceptionally good'. He was the ultimate insider at the school, liberal and not too showy, high-achieving without being seen to try too hard.

Yet although a combination of his devout family upbringing and his school's unique disciplinary code enabled him to appear as a 'reliable person of integrity … who would not let you down', this young paragon was already morally primed to be 'the cat that walked alone', the outsider with 'an open invitation to betray one's friends'. And to betray his country even as he was its most diligent servant. He needed to find a cause and an opportunity.

*

Donald Maclean was born in 1913, when the British Empire was at its zenith, before the Great War and the Russian Revolution undermined the assumptions that upheld it. His father, also Donald, was a successful Member of Parliament and a leading member of that exalted establishment that sustained the Empire. He was of strong non-conformist stock, a stern and austere patriot who was able to love and serve his country while applying his highly developed conscience to every decision he took in its service. Of his five children, his namesake was the one who turned out simultaneously most to resemble him and yet most to go against the grain. The roots of their beliefs were planted firmly in the soil of the barren, windswept Hebridean island of Tiree.

Sir Fitzroy Maclean, 26th Chief of the Clan Maclean, summoned his clansmen from all over the world to Duart Castle on the far northern Isle of Mull, Tiree's neighbour, for 24 August 1912. All were loyal members of one of the oldest and fiercest families of Argyll and the Hebrides, families that had for the most part been scattered in the Highland Clearances of the previous century as the landowners ejected the crofters to make way for their vast flocks of sheep. The devout and hard-working Liberal Member of Parliament, now being celebrated as a prominent member of the clan, was just a generation away from his father's subsistence on the soil, on part-time work as a fisherman and on meagre earnings as a shoemaker in their tiny home. His obedience to the summons was a demonstration of the pride he felt in his small branch of the vast clan tree, in their rise from their centuries-old, back-breaking and diligent Hebridean life to middle-class Edwardian comfort and national respectability. He kept the invitation to the gathering at Duart Castle among his papers for the rest of his life. His third son and middle child, born nine months later on 25 May, was named Donald Duart, binding the infant to his own success and the newly attained family standing. From then on, Duart became the middle name of all his male descendants.

Donald instilled in his children, young Donald especially, a powerful moral impulse. When he died, Stanley Baldwin paid tribute to him in the House of Commons: 'In Donald Maclean

I see a soul as clean as the West wind that blows over Tiree, where
he was born.' In fact, Donald senior had been born in Lancashire
in 1868 as his father John had come south with his wife, Agnes
Macmellin, to look for work. No more successful in the north of
England, John continued moving down the country until he
reached Haverfordwest, in the south-west corner of Wales, and
later nearby Carmarthen, where his cordwaining skills could
flourish. But the former Prime Minister correctly identified the
defining characteristic of Sir Donald – the purity of his soul, the
clarity of conscience which throughout his life drove him to act as
that conscience dictated, not for personal gain but for the greater
good as he and his religion saw it.

   Both Donald and his younger brother Ewen received a gram-
mar school education in South Wales. Donald moved to Cardiff at
the age of nineteen to train as a solicitor, soon forming his own
firm with a partner. The Welsh non-conformist, Methodist tradition, known locally as 'Chapel' and resistant to the established
Anglican Church, suited a man with his upbringing and reinforced his certainty that the writ of God could not be transgressed
for fear of damnation, his conviction that others must be helped
on to the right paths. Non-conformity ran deep within the family
in both action and reaction. The religion emphasised temperance:
Sir Donald was a lifelong teetotaller who banned alcohol and
tobacco in his houses, although his friend, neighbour and fellow
Scot J. M. Barrie, author of *Peter Pan*, noted that 'at times he lit a
cigarette to please me, and I have almost as nobly looked the other
way while he got rid of it. On a special occasion I have also seen a
ginger-beer bottle in his hand.' Among his other early appointments, Maclean was a director of a life assurance company, the
United Kingdom Temperance and General Provident Institution,
a founder of the National Society for the Prevention of Cruelty to
Children, secretary of the Cardiff Chamber of Commerce and
vice-president of the Cardiff Free Church Council, advocating
tolerance for all beliefs in conscience as well as in the debate over
free trade. C.P. Scott of the *Manchester Guardian* wrote in his
diary that Maclean had 'Liberalism in his bones', and all this

activity in the Welsh Liberal heartland brought him to the attention of the leader of the Party, Herbert Asquith. Maclean entered Parliament at his second attempt as MP for Bath in 1906, glad to support the new Prime Minister, a man 'he loved as few men are loved by another'.

Donald Maclean worked hard, 'and quickly made his mark in Parliament by modesty, sincerity and industry', concentrating on domestic issues that would improve the lot of the working or unemployed man – labour exchanges, old-age pensions and National Insurance. In 1907 he opened an office in London, and in that year married Gwendolen Devitt, the daughter of a Surrey magistrate and colonial rubber broker.

In her only daughter's eyes, Gwendolen was 'an exceptionally good-looking woman but very difficult to live with' as she reinforced, in a less biblically stern way, the pattern of parental dominance over her children. Although her parenting style was sweeping, unethical and, to modern thinking, wrong, the family doctor described her as 'that type of strong personality you often do get as the parent of episodic drinkers' – a judgement made at a time when young Donald was finding it impossible to stick to his father's temperate path. Gwendolen was a forthright product of her age and her own upbringing. Like almost all girls of her generation, she was not well educated, yet she was never afraid to speak her mind, the more so as she got older. She was imperious to the point where her family gave her the affectionate nickname the 'Queen Bee', abbreviated in speech and correspondence to 'Queenie'. The Macleans 'made a handsome couple: he had a florid complexion and since his late twenties his hair had been white. She was a fine-looking woman with a lively manner. When Asquith invited them to dinner to meet the Prince of Wales, [Asquith] described her as "young and quite good-looking ... with glowing cheeks and glittering eyes".' Donald remained strongly attached to his mother all his life, but she was no more privy to the most important parts of his mind than anyone else. She in turn remained devoted to her son and to the memory of her husband and his principles. When young Donald was being splashed across the front pages of every newspaper, it was Lloyd George who was 'that traitor' for splitting the Liberal Party half a century earlier. In her eyes, constancy was the key to both Donalds.

Ian Maclean was born in 1908, followed by Andrew in 1910, then Donald Duart (known by his parents as 'Teento', for 'Teeny Don') in 1913, Nancy in 1918 and, when Sir Donald (as he had become for his work in the House of Commons during the First World War) was sixty and Lady Maclean forty-four, their fourth son, Alan Duart, in 1924. The expanding family and their cook, parlourmaid, housemaid, nanny and nursery-maid moved into a stuccoed five-storey house at 6 Southwick Place, Bayswater. The house, with its porticoed entrance and gloomy interiors, was just on the north side of Hyde Park, close to Paddington Station for Sir Donald's visits to his business in Cardiff and to his constituency, which by then was North Cornwall.

The Macleans also bought Elm Cottage in the village of Penn, in Buckinghamshire's Chiltern Hills. The largely eighteenth-century house had three-quarters of an acre of land, an orchard, a vegetable garden and rosebeds, which the children weeded and pruned during their weekends there. Penn, about twenty-five miles from London, was true to the Quaker foundation that had sent William Penn from there to found the state of Pennsylvania in the seventeenth century; whether or not this influenced the Macleans in their choice of country retreat, Sir Donald did not relax his religious principles there: Ian got into very hot water with his father when he saw 'God First' painted on the wall and told villagers that it was announcing the result of a bicycle race. Their summer holidays were spent in Cornwall and carried on the same routine of daily prayers and healthy endeavour.

The senior Macleans (Sir Donald's mother, speaking Gaelic as her first language, also lived with them until her death in 1924) led blameless lives. He worked 'soundly and sweet-temperedly' in Parliament, promoting free trade and improving the lot of his less fortunate countrymen. In the occasional periods when he did not have a seat, Sir Donald was a diligent solicitor, charity campaigner and committee man, as well as a lay preacher.

Religion was always at the centre of family life, claustrophobic-
ally so for his children. Sir Donald, in his frock coat and grey silk
hat, led his family every Sunday to the Presbyterian church in
Marylebone to hear about grace through faith and the absolute
sovereignty of God. J. M. Barrie wrote in *The Times* after Sir
Donald's death that 'You did not know him at all unless you knew
his religion. He was in London as much a Scotch Presbyterian as
though he had never left his native Tiree. He was an elder of the
Church and in his home held that "family exercise" in which a
Scottish household is seen at its best.' These family prayers were
one of young Donald's strongest memories: enforced daily service
to a God one could not believe in would be a good working discipline for when he had formed his own views.

Donald saw his father as a 'middle-aged martinet' and 'a harsh
man'. He was fixed in his ways, Victorian in style and unbending in
his outlook, insisting on the highest and purest standards of probity.
He was clear that his sons' privileged start in life meant the offices
where they could do most good were easily attainable by them if
they worked hard and looked to their morals. There were rows when
Ian and Andrew crashed back into the 'teetotal fold' in the small
hours after late-night parties. Drinking was a source of deep shame
in Sir Donald's eyes. His middle son took this in at an impressionable age, and made increasingly vain attempts to keep his
consumption under control until it became mired in his own profound shame and ultimately overwhelmed him. When Sir Donald
had reached the peak of his career towards the end of his life he
became a 'doting old parent' to his two youngest children. Teento
was in the middle of these two groups, able to forge his own beliefs
unseen behind the paired older boys and their battles, neither the
girl nor the baby of the family; the clever one they did not have to
worry about, but also the one who had to feel his way, watchful
without drawing attention to himself, finding his own outlets for
his inherited conscience. Paradoxically, young Donald, who found
his father and 'his principles daunting', absorbed so thoroughly 'his
passionate belief that you did what you thought was right at all costs'
that he too became 'a genuine political animal'.

The two Donalds felt the same 'vehement sense of rectitude' and saw the world in terms of clearly defined certainties which they both acted upon consistently. When Alan and young Donald were sharing a bedroom and recovering from flu, they spent hours playing soldiers together on the floor of their room, the five-year-old Alan trying to ensure that the glorious Highlanders always beat the ragged sepoys ranged against them, the teenage Donald playing for the opposite result. When the younger boy complained that this did not seem to be the way things were in real life, his elder brother said, 'Why shouldn't the Indians win? After all. It's their country.' Even as a pillar of the diplomatic corps, Donald could be provoked to unstatesmanlike rage by a chance derogatory remark that violated his personal moral codes and the rights of those without a voice. He carried his father's moral imprint deep within him for the rest of his life.

*

After a few years at St Mary's College in Lancaster Gate, near the family's London home, Maclean went at the age of ten to Gresham's School, Holt, isolated just outside a picturesque Georgian town on the far eastern edge of England. The great and misnamed 'public' schools that nurtured the British elite – Eton, Harrow, Winchester, Marlborough and the rest – tended to be within easy reach of London. Alongside this geographical difference, the school had developed a unique ethos that set it even further apart from its rivals, and made it the perfect psychological training-ground for a nascent spy.

W. H. Auden wrote shortly after leaving Gresham's that he thought its disciplinary code had been the most 'potent engine' for turning his schoolmates into 'remote introverts, for perpetuating those very faults of character which it was intended to cure'. It meant that 'the whole of our moral life was based on fear, on fear of the community, not to mention the temptation it offered to the natural informer, and fear is not a healthy basis'. If Maclean had absorbed from his home life the need to follow his conscience, but not its spiritual corollary of openness, his education at the same school as Auden gave him the ability to turn himself inwards, to live as a high achiever for both the country that he loved and the country with the system he would crave. He turned out to be such a natural keeper and supplier of secrets himself that he was able to maintain his two lives in balance for decades, until the division between them, and not being sufficiently recognised in one of them, became too much for him to bear.

*

Most of the schools of the time emphasised sport and the classics, promoted Christianity of the Anglican sort and produced men to run the country and Empire that were theirs by inheritance. These attributes did not fit with the more radically non-conformist outlook of the Macleans, and when the time came to choose a school for their eldest son Ian, they took the advice of Dr Gillie, the minister of the Presbyterian church in Marylebone, to send him to Gresham's. Until 1900 the sixteenth-century foundation had mainly served the sons of local clergymen and merchants in the prosperous farmlands of East Anglia, under the motto 'All worship be God'. In one measure used to judge a school's academic standing, between 1858 and 1900 it had sent a mere twenty-four pupils to Cambridge, and three to further-off Oxford. In 1900, by which time the number of pupils had fallen to an unsustainable fifty and the fabric of the school was in disrepair, a new headmaster, G. W. S. Howson, took charge.

Howson and his successor from 1919, J. R. Eccles, changed Gresham's into a forward-looking school that would attract the sons and grandsons of some of the leading liberal thinkers of the time, including those of C. P. Scott of the *Guardian*, Walter Layton of the *Economist*, the Presbyterian John Reith, first Director General of the BBC, the Liberal MP and future Chairman of the BBC Ernest Simon, Erskine Childers, executed Irish nationalist and author of *The Riddle of the Sands*, and Sir Donald Maclean, MP. The school also fostered a remarkable artistic roll-call of alumni in this period that included Stephen and Humphrey Spender, W. H. Auden and Benjamin Britten; and some notable scientists and engineers, among them the future Nobel laureate Alan Hodgkin and the inventor of the hovercraft, Christopher Cockerell. In 1932 alone, the year after Donald Maclean left the school, fifty-seven former pupils went to Cambridge and twenty-one to Oxford. By the time of Donald's arrival in 1923, it was the school of choice for those of a progressive outlook who recognised the educational needs of a changing world. Ian had passed through the school in exemplary fashion, becoming head boy before going to Cambridge and eventually starting work without much enthusiasm in their father's law firm. The next brother, Andy, had difficulty adjusting to the school, and was withdrawn after a bout of pneumonia just as Donald, his junior by three years, started to outshine him.

The curriculum was modernised to concentrate on the sciences and modern languages rather than the classics, and Greek was abandoned altogether. Caning was abolished far ahead of most schools, and punishments instead involved the more wholesome essays, being 'off jam' or runs of three or four miles. After the First World War the school was the first of the public schools to become a member of the League of Nations Union, reflecting a more modern outlook that valued negotiation over conflict and debate over bloodshed – lessons the future diplomat took to heart. Gresham's developed a culture far removed from the hierarchical outlook of the more traditional schools, in effect creating an environment in which pupils were able to work out their own beliefs and were more inclined to join the professions or, a significant attraction to the liberal parents of the new pupils, become committed public servants. Charles Trevelyan, the first Labour Minister of Education, gave the Speech Day address in 1924, and the hidebound Master of Magdalene College, Cambridge, A. C. Benson, reported that 'he made a vulgar attack on the old Public Schools – and rejoiced that the blue-blooded land-owning aristocratic product was down in the market … He spoke idealistically and with some passion and impressed the boys …'

But what really set Gresham's apart from its competitors, other than geography, was the 'Honour System'. The headmaster spoke to new pupils 'of truth, and frankness, and honour; of purity in thought, and word, and deed; of the value and importance of hard work and honest work'. Each boy then took a private oath to him and separately to his housemaster by which he promised:

1. Always to avoid impurity.
2. Always to confess the truth to the Headmaster.
3. Always to refrain from smoking.

'Impurity' in this context meant 'dirty talk or masturbation', impracticable in the extreme in a school of teenage boys, particularly those brought up in a rigid environment focused on the suppression of 'vices' such as alcohol and tobacco. To help promote purity in deed, all the boys' trouser pockets were sewn up; purity in thought was a different matter altogether. The notion behind the system was 'liberty based on loyalty or freedom founded upon trust', but the most troubling rider to the oath encouraged anything but loyalty and trust: if you didn't turn yourself in, or couldn't be persuaded to do so by your schoolfellows, one of them could do it for you.

Gresham's was proud of its Honour System. Bullying and homosexuality (and presumably swearing, smoking and smut) were rarer than in other public schools as a result of the system's strictures, but the consequences of its imposition are psychologically troubling, as Auden made clear – not least in encouraging the betrayal of one's schoolmates. The gap between the rules and the way boys actually are meant that the official morality was unworkable. It led to a high rate of anxiety and often breakdown among the pupils, to an obsession with secrecy, to the burying of true and open selves and to the repression of emotions. For a boy who kept himself to himself as much as young Donald did, a third son with two brothers to draw the heat, able to keep his head below the parapet, the system was a continuation of his home life under Sir Donald: he could adhere to strict codes without subscribing to them himself, and hide any duplicity and resentment behind successful conformity. He made the transition to boarding school effortlessly.

Even in those earliest days of psychological study, the consequences of the repression of sexual exploration inculcated through such a process of tale-telling as the Honour System, particularly for those coming at an impressionable age to such an unnatural school environment from more old-fashioned homes, were disregarded. Such shame and confusion as Maclean may later in his life have felt in his attitudes to sex and to the secrecy surrounding his drinking are as deeply embedded in his schooldays as in his home life.

Eric Berthoud was at Gresham's before Maclean. As Sir Eric, a distinguished ambassador, he wrote from his posting to highlight the danger of the Honour System for boys emerging into adulthood. Berthoud claimed that he had always 'felt that the psychological background for Maclean's ultimate mental disequilibrium', as his actions were seen by the fearful, incredulous establishment of the 1950s, 'should be sought in his school background … It might be worth someone discussing Maclean's evolution at the school with J. R. Eccles … a bachelor of very rigid views.' Berthoud described how he had been beaten in front of the whole school for an unspecified 'breach of trust and honour' and carried the scars throughout his outwardly successful life. An earlier alumnus than Berthoud, John Reith, said that the system 'upset his relations with women for years afterwards'. Keeping oneself hidden, learning to bury one's natural urges, could only have repercussions in later life.

*

The galvanic political event of Maclean's schooldays was the General Strike of 1926, with its accompanying excitement and hope for the left, and fear of revolution for the right. Mine owners' proposals to reduce miners' pay (which had almost halved in the previous seven years) and impose longer hours of work led to protracted negotiations between the government and the unions; final talks broke down when the printers of the *Daily Mail* refused to print an editorial condemning the strike as 'a revolutionary movement intended to inflict suffering upon the great mass of innocent persons in the community and thereby to put forcible constraint upon the Government'. The Trades Union Congress, in support of the miners, called a General Strike. For nine days there was no transport and no press; local committees of trade unionists controlled the distribution of food and power. The army was patrolling the streets, with armoured cars in London's main shopping artery, Oxford Street. Upper-class volunteers registered for work at their Mayfair clubs, manned soup kitchens, enlisted as special constables and helped out in the docks. Some members of this 'thug militia of St James's Street', comprising 'bands of young, steel-helmeted clubmen', went on to have Damascene conversions to socialism as their eyes were opened for the first time to the conditions in which most of their countrymen worked. These included the artist Wogan Philipps, who was moved towards Communism by the plight of the strikers he met while working as a special mounted constable in the London docks. Sir Donald, a strong advocate for freedom of both thought and trade, spoke strenuously against the strike in the House of Commons, just as he consistently voted against loans for Soviet Russia. His two eldest sons, both still at Gresham's, volunteered: Ian Maclean took a job as a railway porter, Andrew as a delivery boy.

The Communist Party saw the strike as 'the greatest revolutionary advance in Britain since the days of Chartism, and the sure prelude to a new revolutionary era', although ultimately it did little more than preserve the status quo and banish the spectre of a Bolshevik revolution in Britain. But the sight of the strikers, the alarming news coverage of the parts of the country that came to a standstill and the divisions between workers and masters all impressed themselves upon the minds of the young and inquisitive. It prepared the way for Communism to flourish in the radical political decade to come and, for a boy searching for a banner to follow, signalled the first notes of the call to arms.

*

Maclean's closest friendship during his time at the school was not based on his games prowess or mutual sexual attraction but on academic compatibility. Above all, he was searching for the peg on

which to fix his conscience, formed largely by his father, for he
sensed that the Honour System had no workable morality. He was
not easily given to making friends at any stage in his life, but at the
age of twelve, the cat that was already walking alone, he was gangly
and awkward, and had not yet developed his polished good looks.
His height and shyness sometimes made him appear 'supercilious
and reserved' to others. His school friendship with James
Klugmann, his first exposure to an ideologically kindred spirit,
was the most formative of his life, even though it would last less
than a decade.

Norman John (known as James from his teens) Klugmann was
in his last term at the Hall School in Hampstead at the time of the
strike, heading for Gresham's the following September. He wrote a
poem, 'On the Lower Fourth Debating Society', which satirised
those who spoke against the unions:

A diminutive child
Then steps out to speak
On the strike. And he talks
Of the TUC's cheek
In calling a strike –
Mr Baldwin he says,
Is only the Prime Minister.
He is not sinister.
But Ramsay MacDonald
He never would like.

Baldwin was the Conservative Prime Minister, MacDonald the
Labour leader. The Klugmann family were leading Jewish
Hampstead liberals: James's father Samuel had been born in
Bavaria and now ran Klugmann & Co., Rope and Twine Merchants,
in the City of London. In common with Sir Donald's, 'his liberalism was rooted in the idea of self-improvement and individual
responsibility … it was a liberalism which sought a wider civic
duty, to use the advantages of privilege to aid the common good'.
James was a natural candidate for Gresham's, which he entered on

a scholarship. Even at the age of thirteen he was showing many of the characteristics that brought him to Moscow's attention as a potential recruit. He was 'quiet and thoughtful, modest, conscientious, industrious and serious'. Above all, 'he exercises great influence over people', and through his quiet persuasiveness was later called upon when a good turn-out was needed from the Cambridge socialists at demonstrations and marches. He was certainly to influence Donald Maclean's intellectual and political development profoundly: the latter, an outwardly unformed boy hidden under the weight of family beliefs and the Honour System, was ready to go into his adolescent cocoon and emerge fully formed.

*

The Svengali-like teacher of the questing, conscientious young minds of Gresham's was a young French master, Frank McEachran. Maclean and Klugmann were his best students at the time. Auden 'looked up to him … as a father figure', and McEachran encouraged each new pupil to arrive at the 'basic literary and philosophical framework of his lifetime's enquiry while still at Gresham's'. He ranged far beyond his own subject across literature, history, philosophy and poetry, a thrilling and inspirational combination to a thirsty young mind.* He believed passionately in the unity of Europe and its peoples, brought about through common culture, and wrote two books in response to the darkening situation in the wake of the economic collapse of the Depression and the growing fascist sentiment in Germany. He warned in 1932 that 'the fever of nationalism which now rages around the world has not only shattered into fragments what little common feeling it once possessed but has also nearly destroyed the unity of Europe, the focus in modern times of human civilisation'.

---

* McEachran was to be the model for Hector, the eccentric teacher who instils excitingly varied knowledge into his pupils rather than slavishly following the curriculum, in Alan Bennett's play about a class preparing for Oxbridge entrance, *The History Boys*.

Klugmann credited McEachran with the ability to open his 'eyes to new horizons of ideas, new excitements, to rouse imagination in books and theories and liberalism and languages'. Although not a Marxist himself, McEachran urged Maclean and Klugmann to read Marx, and imbibe 'the core ideas on the state, class struggle and historical materialism'. Both boys served on the school's library committee and spoke regularly at the Debating Society, itself founded by McEachran in 1930. In February 1931, Maclean opposed the motion that 'This House condemns Socialism both in theory and practice'. In words that picked up on his own unacknowledged tug of moralities, he 'deplored the distinction between public and private morality. Socialism would carry into a wider sphere the domestic virtues of service, liberty and justice.' The motion was narrowly defeated.

Another McEachran innovation at the school, from 1929, was *The Grasshopper* magazine, for which Maclean wrote a strikingly dreamlike short story in 1931. 'The Sandwichmen' are shuffling through the West End of London, 'a bedraggled lot, with their ramshackle bowlers, their greeny-black overcoats all worn at the shoulders, their sagging, muddy trousers and then their boots that oozed mud as they slumped along the gutter. Their faces were studies in abject misery; dirty hair hung over their coat collars.' Shades of the General Strike and the early hunger marchers. In their degraded state the Sandwichmen are not even worthy of names. 'Number Seven' looks up at a house in Wimpole Street 'with a vague sort of interest'. We then cut to an operating theatre being prepared for an emergency night-time operation on a 'famous society hostess'. The surgeon who is driven up for the surgery is 'a very popular young man in town, for he had a rare charm of manner and a quick smile that made him many friends; but more than just being popular, he stood high on the esteem of the whole medical world, not only for his undisputed brilliance, but for his unstinting generosity with his talents'. He has come from 'Lady Marsham's reception' and 'his face was flushed, his eyes bright and his manner slightly aggressive'. His blade slips, the patient's blood wells up into the fatal wound, 'the fumes left his fuddled brain, and he could see all too clearly now'. The surgeon flees into the night and the final sentence takes us back to the Sandwichmen as they leave Wimpole Street with 'Number Seven'. The fall from brilliant young man to Sandwichman is painful, as Maclean imagines the narrow divide between fame and success. There is the background guilt associated with the ruinous effects of drink which he had absorbed from his Temperance Society father and the sermons both religious and secular at home; there is also a tension between desire and duty that was to run through-out the teenage author's life, and the painful awareness of class differences and the dispossessed poor. The detail employed in the description of the men contrasts with the almost callous brittle-ness in the prose evoking the upper-crust society and the bright cleanliness of the operating theatre.

'The Sandwichmen' is eerily prophetic of many of Maclean's own experiences in life. He rehearses the gaps between what we seem to be and what we are, between society life where conform-ity is important and 'real' life. He subconsciously offers some of the key themes of his maturity, including the effects of drink and its potential for damage as instilled into him by his father, in fic-tional form.

Maclean and Klugmann saw each other in London during the holidays. While Maclean was a welcome guest in the free-speaking openness of the Klugmann household, he was careful to keep the self-styled 'clever oddity' out of Southwick Place for fear of Sir Donald finding out about his burgeoning political philosophy. They went instead to socialist or avant-garde films or met in pubs. The school careers of the two boys in many ways mirrored their subsequent outward revelation of themselves to the world. Klugmann, who happily called himself 'The Communist' while still at Gresham's and went on to become one of the most overt and active members of the British Party, was 'chubby, bespectacled and hopeless at games'. He hated the very idea of the Officer Training Corps, and did not become a prefect. Maclean, by contrast, excelled in these areas and had now become a good-looking young man, although his full lips and smooth face beneath his high cheekbones, combined with his rather mincing walk and naturally high-pitched voice, gave him an effeminate demeanour until he was well into his twenties. By that time his politics were completely covert.

*

When Sir Donald came to the school in November 1930, his son's last year, to give a talk about the League of Nations, he was shortly to attain Cabinet office. The rise from crofter-shoemaker's son to public figure was a triumph of hard work, faith in God and standing by his principles. He had chosen to send his first three sons to Gresham's for the school's liberal thinking and ethos, upholding the attributes that had served him so well. But his most brilliant and successful child shared Auden's open loathing of the school's 'Fascist state' as created by the Honour System,* 'a recipe for grief and anger', for betraying pointless rules rather than adhering to any true morality – and in Maclean's case, duplicity to hide that grief and anger. A few weeks before his father's visit, young Donald spoke in a school debate to say that 'man was at last beginning to "know himself"' ... and to realise that true liberty was to be found in social service'. The model schoolboy, moulded by Presbyterianism and his school's codes, needed to find the expression of 'true liberty' that could satisfy his upbringing and the inner cravings that it engendered. He had come through a morally challenging childhood and adolescence without a stain on his character; he was the pride of his parents and teachers.

Above all, he had learned the spy's most essential art of keeping himself hidden while remaining a model of conformity in plain sight. He was the right man in the right times, and about to go to the right university.

---

* The poet's final rejection of the Gresham's oath comes in his 1936 poem 'Last Will and Testament', written with Louis MacNeice: MacNeice's school bequest is 'To Marlborough College I leave a lavatory / With chromium gadgets and a Parthenon frieze', and Auden bleakly completes the stanza with an abstract bequest: 'And Holt three broken promises from me'.

2

Dared to Question

Donald Maclean gave voice to the radically different selves that both brought him to establishment pre-eminence and nearly destroyed him. In the first month of his last year at Cambridge, October 1933, the student magazine *Granta* started a new column, 'The Undergraduate in the Witness Box', a question-and-answer format which explored the beliefs and personalities of its subjects. First up was Roualeyn Cumming-Bruce, who is clear and open about his politics: 'I am a Communist ... when I left the Labour Party and took up my stand with the Communists it was after as complete an examination as possible of the theory.' Cumming-Bruce, who ended a distinguished legal career as a Lord Justice of Appeal unaffected by his earlier political affiliations, takes all the questions put to him head-on. The witnesses in the following issues of *Granta* are similarly frank: the next talks about his controversial views on art, the third about mathematics, in which she is much more interested than in being one of the few woman undergraduates of the time.

The fourth undergraduate 'in the box' was Maclean, and the tone of the series shifts dramatically. On being asked by 'Q' (for 'Questioner') whether he would be embarrassed if his 'undergraduate personality' was examined, Maclean replies, 'Not a bit. But which one? I have three dear little fellows. Here comes Cecil. Perhaps you would like to begin with him.' Cecil, a camp aesthete, is somewhat startled to be called upon, as he 'was just slipping into my velvet trousers when I heard you call ... You must come to my next party. I am going to have real Passion flowers, and everybody is going to dress up as a Poem of Today.' He would be better suited to the Oxford of Evelyn Waugh's *Brideshead Revisited*, with Anthony Blanche reciting poetry through a megaphone from his window while less privileged undergraduates are ducked in college fountains, than to the more austere and high-minded world of 1930s Cambridge, the university of choice for the next generation of the intellectually modern Bloomsbury Group.

Maclean takes over asking the questions as well as introducing alter egos to answer them. He dismisses Cecil ('Now run along and get on with your tapestry work') and produces the hearty Jack: 'I just crack around. Buy a few club ties here and smash up a flick there. Bloody marvellous.' Jack is sent off to 'oil his rugger boots' (Maclean had played the game for his college the previous year) and Fred, the swot, appears. 'Everybody ought to work. That's what I am here for. I want to get on. Take Shakespeare or Henry Ford – they knew what was what.' Fred belongs to 'eleven societies and three lunch clubs', and has read 'a paper on Lessing's *Laokoon* (in German, of course)' to one of the societies. He hopes to leave the university the following year with a first-class degree, as Maclean was to do.

Maclean is striving to mediate between his uncomfortably competing selves as he becomes adult. Even the voices that do not ring as true as others, Jack and to an extent Cecil, are an effective blurring device, a tidy evasion. However, towards the end of the piece the fun, the campness and the heartiness disappear. Instead, we have a direct, slightly peeved, slightly pompous appeal for the parts to be allowed to coexist, a plea for the three characters to be seen as a whole: 'I like them all equally. I see no standard against which to set them, no hierarchy in which to put them – they are all of the same value to me … Cambridge expects one to be either Cecil, or Jack, or Fred. If one isn't, Cambridge is annoyed.' Although he was already becoming more outspoken, often violently so, in his socialism – by that time he was serving on the committee of the Cambridge University Socialist Society (CUSS) – Maclean avoids being seen intimately as he throws his characters up in the air. He was publicly announcing a pattern that was to continue throughout his life: he was the outsider who sought roles and poses that are at odds with his upright social and professional standing, all the while concealing his most cherished beliefs.

Yet very shortly after leaving university he had worked out how to combine his different selves into what felt to him and looked to others like a confident, integrated man. Cambridge was to be his personal and political proving ground.

*

Maclean was at Cambridge at the key moment. Historically non-conformist and anti-establishment from the time of Oliver Cromwell, the university in the 1920s had shown few signs of being a political Petri dish and was firmly conservative. Britain had recognised the Soviet Union diplomatically only in 1924 (ten years before the United States opened an embassy there) and undergraduates' 'main political enthusiasms [in the 1920s] were hostility to Bolshevism, suspicion of the motives of trade unions and Labour politicians and a belief in the continuing utility and virtues of the British Empire'. Cambridge men had helped break the General Strike, with over half the undergraduate body taking up emergency positions on trains, trams, buses and soup kitchens rather than side with the strikers. In the same year, the Bishop of Nyasaland, the Right Reverend T. C. Fisher, preached a sermon in the University Church in which he told his audience (who were presumably quite startled even then) that 'some years previously a writer had been a good deal criticised for saying he wished to try to train the African native as he trained his dog, but that he himself [the Right Reverend] did not feel inclined to criticise the sentence so sharply as he knew both the writer and the dog'. The students who came up after the 'war to end all wars' were clinging to this old order, and the Union debates and student politics of the time reflected that.

The poet and Bloomsbury scion Julian Bell, soon to die for his left-wing convictions, wrote that when he first came to know Cambridge in 1930 'the central subject of ordinary intelligent conversation was poetry. As far as I can remember we hardly ever talked or thought about politics. For one thing, we almost all of us had implicit confidence in Maynard Keynes's rosy prophecies of increasing capitalist prosperity.' As the world changed, by the end of 1933 'almost the only subject of discussion is contemporary politics, in which a very large majority of the more intelligent undergraduates are Communists, or almost Communists'.

Anthony Blunt, then a languid and elegant research fellow at Trinity, was aware of the same moment of change: 'Quite suddenly, in the autumn term of 1933, Marxism hit Cambridge ... I had sabbatical leave for that term, and when I came back in January, I found that almost all my younger friends had become Marxist and joined the Party; and Cambridge was literally transformed overnight.'

A political metamorphosis was the only solution to the despair of the times. David Bensusan-Butt was a year younger than Maclean at Gresham's and Cambridge, where he was a disciple of Keynes. He found the early 1930s 'blackly depressing ... It was not merely that there were millions of unemployed whose festering boredom and misery were all around ... it was not only that for ten to fifteen years governments had been continuously impotent and silly.' Worse, 'the foundations of ordered society in Europe, the ordinary decencies of peaceful civilisation seemed to be breaking up'. The only hope was 'of some new treatment for the multiplying diseases of a dying capitalism in the shortening list of countries still civilised'.

The *Cambridge Review* of January 1934 noted that 'the Russian experiment has aroused very great interest ... It is felt to be bold and constructive, and youth, which is always impatient of the cautious delays and obstruction of its elders, is disposed to regard sympathetically ... this attempt to found a new social and political order.' Communism, and its more acceptable sibling socialism, was a clear rallying point for those desperate for change from the Victorians who had landed their generation with the war, the Depression, mass unemployment and poverty, thereby enabling the rise of fascism in Europe. Hitler had become Chancellor of Germany in January 1933, a development which tightened Mussolini's fascist grip on Italy, and a move to the left was the only way out for level-headed people. John Strachey, nephew of Lytton, exaggeratedly summed up the view of many when he characterised Communism, from the point of view of the young people of Britain, as having mutated from something barbaric to representing 'the eternal course of human culture, of science and of civilisation'.

The most notable Communist don was Maurice Dobb of Trinity, a pupil of Maynard Keynes. Dobb was a decade older than Maclean, had joined the Communist Party on its foundation in 1920 and became a member of its central committee. With his 'fair hair, bright red face and infectious, warm personality', he shared a Presbyterian upbringing with Maclean. He had become a fervent Marxist as an undergraduate shortly after the war, as a result suffering frequent dunkings in the River Cam at the hands of the conservative, mostly less intellectual, hearties, the more sporty men from the private schools who were not as reliant on scholarships (nor as keen on attending lectures). He had a 'unique ability to portray the inconsistencies of communism as consistent and to make unfathomable Marxist mysteries appear logical'. He visited Moscow from time to time and paraded his opinions openly at the Union, the public crucible for political debate; in November 1925 he claimed there that 'an aristocracy of intellect was more likely to rule in Russia than any other country and that science and art were prospering [there] as never before'. This intellectual consistency enabled him to defend himself against criticism of his views, as when King George V, after simmering as usual over Scotland Yard's annual reports about subversion in Britain, wrote to the Chancellor of the university in 1925 demanding to know why such a well-known Marxist was permitted to indoctrinate undergraduates. It was not until 1938 that there was even a lecture on Marxist theories.

*

Maclean arrived at Trinity Hall for his first term in October 1931 to find Cambridge in the grip of this political ferment, which seemed to demonstrate, as Klugmann put it, 'the total bankruptcy of the capitalist system' and evoked 'a very strong feeling of doom, doom that was not very far off'. By contrast, Stalin's Five-Year Plan seemed to be yielding more benefits for the lowest of Soviet citizens and building a society free of snobbery, at least to the credulous. Visitors to Russia were given carefully curated tours of model farms and factories. Malcolm Muggeridge, living in Moscow, thought 'the delight' these admirers took 'in all they saw and were told, and the expression they gave to this delight, constitute unquestionably one of the wonders of the age'.

Klugmann already had strong connections to the political life of the university as his sister, five years older and a Girton pupil, had married Maurice Cornforth, himself a former student of the philosopher Ludwig Wittgenstein at Trinity. Wittgenstein rejected Marxism but was pro the Soviet Union and had a wide influence. Another disciple was David Haden Guest of Trinity, who moved very far left after spending a fortnight in a Nazi cell in Brunswick in 1931 as a consequence of joining a Communist demonstration. He was released only when he threatened to go on hunger strike – and on his return to Trinity he marched into college hall wearing a hammer-and-sickle emblem, telling of the horrors of Nazism and its anti-semitism and preaching that only Communists understood the real threat posed by the Nazis. Guest and Cornforth both joined the Communist Party in the summer of 1931, just before Maclean and Klugmann came up.

Keynes's 'rosy prophecies' of continued growth in Western economies as they rebuilt in the decade after the First World War had collapsed with the Wall Street Crash of 1929 and the triggering of the worldwide Depression. Unemployment was rocketing, and would reach a peak of three million in January 1933. In some communities it ran as high as 70 per cent, with huge gaps between rich and poor, and between north and south. Membership of the Communist Party of Great Britain (CPGB) continued to rise from its 1920 base of 2,500 to 6,000 in 1930; it would peak at 16,000 in 1939. Labour had won the first full election following universal suffrage in 1929, but without a majority of seats in the House of Commons could not survive in the crisis engulfing the capitalist world. On 24 August 1931, after a further general election, the first all-party coalition National Government was formed under Labour's Ramsay MacDonald in an attempt to deal with the downward spiral. Labour was now the official opposition, despite achieving an all-time low of fifty-two seats. At last Sir Donald Maclean, representing the largely superannuated Liberals, reached the summit of his ambitions as he was appointed to the Cabinet as President of the Board of Education.

*

Cambridge University was made up of twenty-six colleges of varying size, opulence and architecture, ranging from the medieval to the high Victorian, with gated entrances managed by porters in bowler hats. All bar two of the colleges were male preserves, the undergraduates cycling between them and around the town in college scarves, tweed jackets and Oxford 'bags' with turn-ups, regardless of social standing. Each college consisted of a series of quadrangles, known as 'courts', each with a manicured lawn and surrounded by a series of staircases leading to the rooms that housed the academic body of the college. To find a bathroom, one often had to walk around the edge of the court in East Anglia's chilly climate; each staircase was looked after by a 'bedder', who cleaned and washed up after the young gentlemen.

Maclean's first choice of college had been Trinity, with Trinity Hall second, but it was the smaller college that offered him the exhibition, with its annual value of £40, that determined his decision. He was reading Modern Languages, his strong suit at Gresham's and one which perhaps prefigured a potential profession on the world stage. Trinity Hall is one of the most intimate colleges in Cambridge, situated between the vast grandeur of Trinity and the soaring majesty of King's College Chapel and with an annual intake in the 1930s of around a hundred undergraduates. Maclean's rooms in his first two years were in Latham Court, close by the River Cam. The court had neatly tended borders of spring bulbs, delphiniums and foxgloves, and magnificent magnolia and purple beech trees. It was a peaceful setting, developed over six centuries, in which to cultivate his own future.

Klugmann, with his 'birdlike head and manner', went up at the same time to the grander neighbouring college of Trinity, where he joined Anthony Blunt on his staircase in New Court. Blunt's erstwhile and future lover, Guy Burgess, was in the same college. Kim Philby was two years above Maclean and also at Trinity. The Cambridge Spy Ring, as they came to be known, was all but completed when Maclean arrived at the university, with only John Cairncross, yet another Trinity man, still to arrive.

*

Maclean did not pay much attention to his French and German studies in his first year. He was awarded a 2.2 in German and a 2.1 in French in the first part of his degree in the summer of 1932, and was given a sharp warning that if he was to keep his exhibition he would have to improve. He still muted any burgeoning political views, out of pride in and loyalty to his father and his ministerial post as well as out of fear of what the older man's reaction might be to his developing godless creed. While Sir Donald was alive, being the model son and conforming was more important than standing out at a time when even the National Government, with its Conservative bias, was despised. Maclean 'complained bitterly of the betrayal of the Labour rank and file through the perfidy of their leader', but he did not disclose these feelings outside his Cambridge circle. That circle was coming to the view that more radical action was needed on the left, that 'only the Soviet Union seemed to have all the answers'. As a result, an active branch of the Communist Party had recently been founded in the university.

This Communist cell started in Trinity College. In June 1931, Clemens Palme Dutt, who had recently served in the Comintern in Paris and India and was a proselytising ideologue, paid a visit to Dobb. From that meeting, at which Guest and Cornforth were present, the cell sprang into being. The Comintern (an abbreviation for Communist International) was the organisation that advocated world Communism 'by all available means, including armed force, for the overthrow of the international bourgeoisie' without directly serving the Soviet state. Guest assumed responsibility for the cell, which was a relief for Dobb and the other two dons present as it would compromise their positions as teaching fellows if they were openly fronting controversial organisations; undergraduates had licence to proselytise on the extremes by their very youth. Klugmann knew about the cell from his sister Kitty and her fiancé, and had discussed it with Maclean. Maclean acknowledged his schoolfriend and mentor's political generosity: 'Verily, James Klugmann, you are the universal provider.' He joined the CUSS, the replacement for the Labour Club, amid the disillusionment aroused by the MacDonald administration in his first year. He and Klugmann were soon on the committee, with the latter, employing his 'easy wit and debonair manner' to influence and convert waverers, in charge of publicity. Maclean's election to the committee took place at a rowdily excited meeting at which 'members created a precedent in Cambridge by singing the Internationale and other songs vociferously'. The exuberant youth of Cambridge were riding their wave.

By 1934 the CUSS had some 200 members, of whom about a quarter were also card-carrying members of the Communist Party. The meetings were held in rooms in Trinity with 'little furniture and only a bare lightbulb', the undergraduates puffing on pipes and sustained by 'mugs of disgustingly strong tea and large hunks of bread and jam'; sometimes they gathered in cafés in the town on a Sunday afternoon. These were chaotic and passionate affairs. Members talked much of 'the world situation … showing the increasing rottenness of the capitalist system', without necessarily being able to do much about it. The society was active in getting up petitions and writing letters for its causes. It wrote to the Japanese government about its policies towards China; closer to home it petitioned the Cambridge bus companies when employees' wages were cut. It got cut-price admission to the university Film Society for left-wing screenings and raised funds for suitable causes. Its most successful activity was persuading students to attend marches in London: opposing cuts in education and most particularly supporting the hunger marches, when the unemployed of the north of England came to the capital to protest about their anguish.

Maclean joined a march in the spring of 1932 which clashed with police near Hyde Park. 'Helmets rolled' and inevitably the tall, blond Maclean stood out among the cloth-capped, shorter, older and shabbier marchers; he was taken to the nearest police station. His mother came to spring him and he was not charged. He was relieved to get back to Southwick Place, on the edge of the park, and find his father absent on Parliamentary business.

Maclean kept himself withdrawn from public political expression in his first year and flexed his debating muscles at the Union only once. The motion in May 1932 was that 'This house sees more hope in Moscow than in Detroit', the latter being the heart of American industrialisation and capitalism, home of its now Depression-scarred motor industry. Dobb spoke for the motion, presenting America as 'a land of despair, with no hope and no faith in the future; its chief enemies being robotization, gangsterism and over-production'. Russia, on the other hand, was not in decline; it had 'no share in the world's crisis, no unemployment and increasing production'. Culture and internationalism were spreading, 'embracing different races and tongues'. Russia had 'a new faith, a new spiritual hope'. Maclean spoke from the floor, saying that 'bloodshed was inevitable, either by an imperialist war or by a communist revolution'. He believed 'the only ultimate solution was the victory of the propertyless classes'. Unlike Dobb, Maclean had turned his back on the language of 'faith' and 'spiritual hope' that was such a feature of his boyhood and was airing what was to become a lifelong theme, central to some of his later actions: the desire to avoid war at all costs. Communism was the only vehicle for peace. Maclean's intellectual questing and need for a cause had brought him to that realisation in the vanguard of his fellow undergraduates. *Granta*, reviewing the debate (the motion was carried), suggested that 'Mr McLean [*sic*] should speak more often.' He did not, but by the time he left Cambridge two years later, his political views were formed and entrenched and available for all to see.

*

Through the CUSS, Maclean was to meet the man who was to dictate the course of his life at its two most critical and most secret turning-points, as well as the man with whom his name was ever after to be linked.

H. A. R. Philby, fittingly known from his birth in India as Kim after Kipling's character in the eponymous novel about the Great Game between Britain and Russia in Asia, was a Trinity economist studying under and profoundly influenced by Dobb. Kim was the son of St John Philby, a noted Arabist and tough explorer who rarely saw his son owing to his travels (and to his eventual decision to live in the Middle East). He was such an authoritarian that he kept the birch twigs until his death which he had used to flog small boys during his time as head boy of Westminster School. St John, like his son, was a divided figure: he railed all his life 'against the perfidy, deceit and moral decline' of Britain, abandoned Christianity to become a Muslim and took a Saudi slave-girl to become his second wife; yet he remained a member of the Athenaeum Club in Pall Mall, tried never to miss a Test Match and stood twice for Parliament. Kim himself was handsome, charming, worldly and cynical, his soft blue eyes belying a ruthlessly calculating mind. He was as self-contained, watchful and heterosexual as his colourful Trinity friend Guy Francis de Moncy Burgess was socially reckless and homosexual. What they shared, and in this they differed from Maclean, was a total lack of morality.

Burgess was 'outrageous, loud, talkative, irreverent, overtly rebellious', Maclean's opposite in every respect when they first met. Cherubic-featured, manically beguiling, conversationally gifted where Maclean was more shy in his charm, Burgess had been educated at Dartmouth Naval College and Eton and was about to get his first-class degree in history. In his charm and energy, he seemed at first sight to have been favoured by the gods. Even drinking – and alcohol was starting to become a recreational pastime for both of them – was more flamboyantly indulged in by Burgess. He 'drank … like some Rabelaisian bottle-swiper whose thirst was unquenchable'. By comparison, Maclean was 'introverted and diffident, an idealist and a dreamer given to sudden outbursts of aggression'. He was less sure of himself than the Trinity man, drowning his uncertainties in his 'feckless undergraduate' binge-drinking. Another way in which the two men differed was in their sexuality.

Burgess 'conducted a very active, very promiscuous, and somewhat sordid sexual life' as his close friend Goronwy Rees put it. 'He was very attractive to his own sex and had none of the kind of inhibitions which usually afflict young men of his own age and upbringing,' inhibitions which certainly affected Maclean. Burgess went to bed 'with any man who was willing to do so and was not positively repulsive and by doing so he released them from many of their frustrations and inhibitions'. He broadcast his seductions throughout his life and one of his boasts at Cambridge was that he had seduced Maclean; he certainly told Rees that he had done so. Later, expediently, he would deny the deed, saying that the thought of touching Maclean's 'large, flabby, white, whale-like body' nauseated him. Maclean was then undeniably plump; but he was also, with his rather feminine good looks and shy intensity, undeniably attractive. With their political views in common it seems that Burgess rose to the challenge and succeeded in the conquest of Maclean, who was finding the last steps into adulthood difficult and confusing. Cecil jostled with Jack and Maclean seemed to find certainty only with the simpler Fred, who just had to work hard without giving himself away. Maclean's sexuality was to remain a point of confusion for him, one of the most complex aspects of his personality that he struggled to pull into line with his conformist side. The date of Maclean's seduction is unknown, and possibly coincided with his wholehearted political commitment. But whether or not it occurred in his first year at Cambridge, at the end of that year a momentous change in his life played the largest part in allowing his inhibitions to be released.

*

At the start of the first Long Vacation in May 1932 Parliament was sitting, and the National Government, made up as it was mainly of 'hard-faced Tories and a few renegade Socialists', was not a congenial environment for an uncompromisingly principled Liberal such as Sir Donald. The economy was still in the doldrums, and the Cabinet was split over whether to pursue free trade or impose tariffs. The Imperial Conference in Ottawa, set up to resolve these matters, would take place in September and that would decide whether Sir Donald, 'old and grey with worry and overwork', would stay in government or resign. An 'impenitent Free Trader', he was prepared to sacrifice his career and standing for something his son thought 'tawdry and meaningless'. Perhaps later in life Maclean reflected on the matters of conscience that were so agitating his father. At the time, as always, he kept his views from the hard-working and important minister: clan loyalty and the need not to upset a man he both admired and in many ways feared triumphed over frankness and honesty.

In the end, the dilemma resolved itself and young Donald was freed from the rigidity of the old man's presence when after a brief period of illness Sir Donald suffered a fatal heart attack on 15 June, at the age of sixty-eight. He was buried at Penn following a near-farcical funeral in which the family accidentally shut themselves in the dining-room of the London house after closing its door in order not to see or hear the coffin bumping down the narrow staircase. They had to be rescued by the London Fire Brigade before the cortège could move off to the Chilterns.

Dr Gillie spoke at the funeral and described a time when in his youth Sir Donald had suffered a crisis of faith:

He locked himself in his study, and spent a whole night at his desk, wrestling with the doubts that crowded his mind. At one point he got up and paced the room, after drawing an imaginary line down the centre: 'On this side,' he told himself, 'I walk with Christ. One step across that line, and I shall turn away for ever from him.' The pacing continued, on the right side of the line, until daylight. He did not falter or stumble again, once that anguished night lay behind him, but clung tenaciously to the truth as he saw it.

It is possible that Donald the younger picked up a reference to Calvin's inner turmoil exactly 400 years before. Certainly as a man well down the road towards cementing his own secular faith outside church or chapel, he would have been responsive to Gillie's words. Tenacity of belief, remaining true to his value systems and not being seen to allow doubt to creep in whatever the provocations were bred in the bone. So too were other qualities which served him well throughout his official life – reasonableness, conscientiousness, an extraordinary capacity for hard work and attention to detail. He was now free to go further, with less guilt and distracted loyalty, into his own causes and philosophy.

Stanley Baldwin's tribute in the House of Commons echoed Gillie's eulogy. He said that he saw in Sir Donald 'a courage and a love of justice' and 'a soul that could not be deflected from the straight course'. The ability to stick to a straight course ran deep in the family. Whatever guilt young Donald may have felt over rejecting his father's religion could now be eased by his open adherence to the conscience of socialism.

The death of Sir Donald enabled his son to be 'cheerfully open about his unreserved allegiance to the Communist cause'. He returned to Cambridge in October a man unleashed, liberated from the oppressive presence of his father into full-throated political engagement (and probably sexual experimentation). His father's absence made him an immediately different figure. Jocelyn Simon, a family friend who used to play cricket and skate with the Maclean boys in Holland Park, was at Trinity Hall two years above Donald. Simon remembered the younger man as 'a perfectly normal undergraduate' who played cricket in the college side in his first year and who became its secretary in his second. When Simon came back to visit, Maclean had resigned the secretaryship, 'had ceased to be a normal undergraduate and become a Communist', a conversion that 'was based on genuine humanitarian interest in the underdog'.

Maclean had 'identified himself so much with the masses that he had sold all his clothes and was wearing clothes bought second-hand and going about in a generally scruffy way, especially as regards his fingernails'. The unhygienic state of Guy Burgess's fingernails was much remarked upon throughout his life (as was the stench of garlic which accompanied him from breakfast onwards as he often stirred it into his porridge); there seem to be no other references to Maclean's cuticles, a metaphor perhaps for one man to keep himself hidden, the other to announce himself all too grubbily.

Maclean's new openness meant that he became much more visible, and at times vociferous. His newfound freedom came at the cost of moderation. It was a foretaste of the volatility that was to shake him at moments of stress in the years to come.

*

World events gathered pace in Maclean's second and third years, increasing CUSS attendance to a record of ninety in December 1933, and the commitment of its members. After the Nazi Party had come to power Hitler swiftly introduced the Enabling Act which meant he could constitutionally exercise dictatorial power: the subsequent witch-hunt in pursuit of the once-powerful German communists (including a young scientist named Klaus Fuchs) at last precipitated Maclean into joining the Communist Party that spring; Klugmann did so too. Guy Burgess followed suit in the winter, according to Anthony Blunt. Blunt was a fellow of Trinity, bonded to Burgess not only through their having slept together but also through their membership of the elite conversation society, the Apostles, whose members included at the time the historian G. M. Trevelyan, the novelist E. M. Forster, the economist John Maynard Keynes, Ludwig Wittgenstein, Victor Rothschild and another of Blunt's lovers, Julian Bell.

One of the demonstrations the CUSS helped organise became significant in the steady emergence of Maclean as a political figure. In the week that the issue of *Granta* was published in which Cecil, Jack and Fred came into public view, there were clashes between the Cambridge undergraduate left and the more traditionalist hearties. The first involved the socialists walking out of a showing at the Tivoli cinema of *Our Fighting Navy* which they deemed full of 'militaristic propaganda'. A crowd of 'patriotic' students waited outside to 'rag the cads' as they emerged, 'complete with Union Jacks and a brass band'. In the ensuing free-for-all, had both sides not been dressed indistinguishably there would have been far more injuries than the wounded pride suffered by a left-winger who was debagged. Finally 'the band struck up and "tough" Cambridge, having dealt with the cranks in time-worn manner, marched back '. The Tivoli management withdrew the film.

The scuffle encouraged the left to turn out in greater numbers a few days later for the anti-war march on Armistice Day, 11 November. The march was organised by the CUSS and the Student Christian Movement as a protest against the growing militarism of the Cenotaph celebrations in London. The CUSS put an inscription on their wreath to be laid at the town's war memorial that read: 'To the victims of the Great War, from those who are determined to prevent similar crimes of imperialism'.

When it was known that the pacifists, under the slogan 'Against War and Imperialism', were to march to the memorial near the station – the 'town' rather than 'gown' end of the city – the hearties of the Tivoli punch-up rallied their friends from rugger and boat clubs across the university and intercepted the march on Parker's Piece, the patch of parkland between the memorial and the university. The police had to draw their batons in the ensuing running battles, in which both Julian Bell and Guy Burgess played a prominent part: they used Bell's beaten-up Morris, armoured with mattresses, as a battering-ram to break through a barricade outside Peterhouse. The hearties pelted them with tomatoes, eggs and flour, but the left's wreath was eventually laid after Bell had driven around the back of the mêlée to reach the war memorial from the other direction.

Maclean, who did not play quite as conspicuous a part in the day as Bell or Burgess, expressed his feelings in a savage poem in the Trinity Hall magazine *Silver Crescent*.

Dare Doggerel. Nov. 11

Rugger toughs and boat club guys
In little brown coats and old school ties.
Tempers be up and fore-arms bared
Down in the gutter with those who've dared.
Dared to think war-causes out,
Dared to know what they're shouting about,
Dared to leave a herd they hate,
Dared to question the church and state;
Dared to ask what poppies are for,
Dared to say we'll fight no more,
Unless it be for a cause we know
And not for the sake of *status quo*.
Not for the sake of Armstrong Vickers,
Not for the sake of khaki knickers,
But for the sake of the class which bled,
But for the sake of daily bread.
Rugger toughs and boat club guys
Panic-herd with frightened eyes,
Sodden straws on a rising tide,
They know they've chosen the losing side.

The anger of the poem contrasts sharply in style with the 'bespectacled, soft-voiced' and demurely witty Klugmann, living his 'monastic existence' and quietly laying out his persuasive philosophy. The change in a few months from the withdrawn son of the minister to public scourge of the hearties is dramatic.

Maclean's next appearance in print was in *Cambridge Left*, a magazine that began publishing in the summer of 1933, catching the new political voices. His only contribution to the journal was a review of R. D. Charques's *Contemporary Literature and Social Revolution*, where he unleashes another passionate diatribe, revealing the almost indiscriminate range of the fury he was now experiencing in his new freedom after a lifetime of keeping his emotions in check. 'The economic situation, the unemployed, vulgarity in the cinema, rubbish on the bookstalls, the public school, snobbery in the suburbs, more battleships, lower wages' were all intolerable and the 'cracked-brained economic mess' would soon collapse. In more measured but equally sweeping tones he then dismisses the work of Galsworthy, Huxley, Eliot, Waugh, Joyce and Woolf, denigrating even the great modern authors who do not fit his politics, while lamenting the non-inclusion in Charques's book of the politically admirable Auden and Dos Passos. He finds some hope in the sexual liberation of D. H. Lawrence's *Sons and Lovers* and E. M. Forster's *Passage to India* and praises Charques for hinting at 'a Marxian conception of literature' and for saying that literature has 'become the unconscious propaganda of ruling-class culture', The magazine did not outlast Maclean's time at Cambridge; its timing exactly caught the wave which determined his political future.

In the Lent term of 1934, in his final year, Maclean was editor of *Silver Crescent*, and he wrote an editorial stemming from what had become known as 'the Armistice Day Riots' on 'The whole question of the student's relations to the outside world and to the authorities'. His call was for undergraduates, with the capitalist world mired in Depression, to take a full and active part in politics: 'the student finds that his College bill is too large ... that good jobs are difficult to find, that his lectures are meaningless, that he is faced with the prospect of being killed in a new Imperialist war ... [Those who say students should not get involved] are totally out of touch with the real position of the student during the present stage of capitalist decline, characterised as it is by "new rounds of revolutions and wars".' The same issue carried a snippet on its jokey gossip page, 'Cambridge Goes Red', which included the unyielding image of 'The Tomb of Donald Maclenin in red Bakelite in Market Square'. Maclean's Communism was briefly on display for everyone to see. Later in this hectic term with Finals and decisions about a career looming, he started to rein himself in and wrote a carefully reasoned, politically sound letter to *Granta* on behalf of the CUSS setting out the need for a student council. His ten 'specific and immediate demands for Cambridge' included 'Complete freedom of thought and action', 'The right to have public discussion on lectures' and 'A share in the control of tutorial fees'. The left-wing man of reason appeared to be replacing the firebrand as Maclean endeavoured – for the time being – to conform to the role of being his father's privileged, cleverest son.

*

Throughout his life, Maclean was able to show a rigorous intellectual focus and an immense capacity for hard work, which left little time for human relations outside politics and his studies. His friend Christopher Gillie, son of the Marylebone Presbyterian minister whose sermons Maclean had sat through so often, describes him at the end of his time in Cambridge as not only playing a lot of cricket and tennis, but pacing himself 'to a nicety' in his revision to 'romp home with the expected First'. Gillie took in Maclean's essential solitariness and shyness, particularly around women, that could be covered up by the certainties of political discourse. 'I have no recollections of his having any girl friends at all … He did show me a postcard once inviting one or two Newnham or Girton undergraduates to a Party meeting. The card mentioned the date and the place, followed by the quotation [from Shakespeare's *Othello*]: "It is the cause! Let me not name it to you, you chaste stars, it is the cause!"'

Maclean's rooms in his last year were decorated with 'large red banners with slogans in one corner of the room and a lot of Marxist books and tracts'. Perhaps it is hardly surprising that his political obsession meant that Donald, never known for the gift of small talk when there were so many weighty matters to consider, had few real friends of either sex to communicate with on a non-political level. His tutor picked up on the guarded young man's lack of intimacy, and noticed he had 'no friends, although he had many acquaintances'. He 'could recall none of them as being of any particular significance'. An addictive life and the need to have a hidden life often march together. Maclean's widowed mother also observed her prodigiously talented son's essential private solitariness: 'He is completely ungregarious and has never enjoyed social activities.' As his time at Cambridge approached its end, the outspoken undergraduate had retreated into himself. Cecil and Jack, the aesthete and the hearty, had gone, leaving a gap that would need filling by someone who fitted more comfortably into Maclean's interior gallery.

*

Donald Maclean, Bachelor of Arts (with Honours), left Cambridge in early June 1934 with a first-class degree in French and German and a burning certainty that socialism was the only way to combat the capitalism that was now moving Europe towards another crisis, this time an avoidable one. Beatrice and Sidney Webb's last major work, *Soviet Communism: A New Civilisation?*, dropped its question mark for its second edition in a telling symbol of the moment. Maclean had spent his last Christmas vacation at Hawarden Castle in North Wales with the Gladstone family, descendants of the greatest Victorian Liberal, both Chancellor of the Exchequer and Prime Minister four times. At the family seat Maclean had been reading Mikhail Pokrovsky's *Brief History of Russia*, with its congratulatory foreword from Lenin. He underlined a passage and initialled and dated it in the margin 'Hawarden Dec. 25, 1933' as a memento of a notable moment in his political journey:

> For we repeat that, like the bourgeoisie, the intelligentsia lived on the surplus product that was extracted by force from the peasant and the workman. A Communist Revolution would mean that it would have to give up all its advantages, renounce all its privileges and join the ranks of manual labour. And this prospect could be accepted by only a small number of the most sincere and devoted revolutionaries of the intelligentsia.

Maclean, a prime exemplar of the bourgeois intelligentsia, was planning to live in Russia after his graduation and to work as a teacher of English, the closest thing to 'manual labour' available to him as he renounced his British 'privileges'. He was sure that 'world revolution will be accomplished in English', so 'the Russians must know the English language'. His mother, who saw that at Cambridge he had got 'mixed up in a set who came to the conclusion that there was perhaps something in Communism', was puzzled but outwardly accepting of his decision, which would not have been contemplated had his father, with his spur to public service and strength of personality, lived. Alongside teaching in Russia, Maclean was also toying with the idea of embarking on a PhD. His subject was a Marxist analysis of John Calvin and the rise of the bourgeoisie, a rich yoking of his political views and his religiously strict upbringing.

In July 1934 Tony Blake rented a small house at Saint Jacut, on the northern French coast. Blake was a former secretary of the CUSS, and he asked Maclean and Cumming-Bruce, the self-professed Communist of the first *Granta* 'Undergraduate in the Witness Box', to join him. Lady Maclean's hopes of a more conventional career for her favourite son were raised when he 'took [her] fully into his confidence' to say he was going on holiday with some left-wing friends to 'talk themselves into an understanding as to what their attitude would be to his newish creed, Communism'. She hoped that he would 'resolve his difficulties', as she saw left-wing politics, 'for it had always been intended that he should enter the Diplomatic Service'.

However, as Blake later reported, there was no political talk on the holiday, in spite of the three men being bound by their ideology; rather, 'they merely played cricket on the sands and lazed, generally taking what they believed to be a well-earned holiday'. Cumming-Bruce was to give a much less discreet account. Maclean had fallen for a local, married woman called Marie, whose husband was away with the Garde Mobile. Cumming-Bruce, meantime, was frolicking with her sister Francine. For Cumming-Bruce it was 'a holiday diversion', but Maclean, who throughout his life threw himself full-heartedly into his few relationships and almost certainly lost his heterosexual virginity to Marie, 'was seriously in love with the married sister'.

Cumming-Bruce remembered the daytime's activities in much the same way as Blake, with the addition of a visit to their girlfriends and a lot to drink at lunchtime. Like Blake, Cumming-Bruce did not recall any 'animated discussions' about politics, maybe not surprisingly with all this to occupy them. There was also the added distraction of Francine and Marie's 'imbecile' brother, whom the girls used to 'carry everywhere'; he would 'frequently lapse into an epileptic fit, sometimes at the most embarrassing moments, but the girls would say, "Pay no heed, he's always doing that"'. In the early evening there would be more drinking, and when the villagers went off fishing for lobsters and crabs the holidaymakers would join them. Once they had reached the rocks where the fishing took place, Donald and Marie would disappear behind one rock and Cumming-Bruce with Francine would find somewhere else to make love. Unfortunately Marie's husband got word of his wife's dalliance and was coming home 'seeking explanations and possibly satisfaction', so the Englishmen cut the holiday short and crossed the Channel back to safety. It was Maclean's first sensation of needing to get away before he was caught in a betrayal.

*

At some point between graduation and August, perhaps in the immediate afterglow of his sybaritic holiday, faced with the prospect of forgoing the comforts of home that enabled so many university socialists to revert to type after graduation, Maclean decided that he was neither going to Russia nor returning to Cambridge to research his thesis on Calvinism and Marxism. He was going to apply to the Foreign Office. He wrote with the news that he was abandoning his PhD to Owen Wansbrough-Jones, Fellow of Trinity Hall and himself a former Gresham's pupil, who replied that he thought the decision 'a wise one. It may seem a little dull at first sight, but from what I have seen of people who went into the Foreign Office I gather that they have a very interesting time, and I am not sure that you will not find you have considerable talents in that direction.'

Maclean's mother, who had moved to a smaller house in Kensington and opened a knitwear shop called The Bee after her family nickname, was delighted when he returned from France to confirm that he was going into the conventional, familiar public service that his father would have wished for him. Her aspirations were now centred on Donald, the most brilliant of her children, the one most like his late father. As she later recounted, he 'came to her somewhat pink-faced to admit that he had changed his mind, and suggested that she would accuse him of failing to know his own mind'. Her response was that the whole point of university was to 'find one's own mind'. Donald had wrestled with his beliefs in Brittany just as her husband had in his Welsh study and had achieved a similar resolution. When she ventured to ask whether his now lapsed Communist views might be an issue for his Foreign Office application, he replied, 'You must think I turn like a weathercock; but the fact is I've rather gone off all that lately.' Far from turning like a weathercock, Maclean was now very single-minded about his future. Whether or not espionage was in his mind, if he succeeded in his application he was going to have a 'very interesting time' indeed in the Foreign Office, right from the start, as he continued his fight for peace in a turbulent world.

3

Orphan

In the middle of August 1934 two recent graduates sat down to supper in a flat in Acol Road, a quiet residential street in Kilburn, on the genteel borders of St John's Wood and Hampstead. The supper invitation was unexpected. Kim Philby and Donald Maclean knew each other through the CUSS. This was the encounter that changed everything for Donald Maclean.

The carefully calculating Philby, with his powerful charm and attractive stutter, claimed that he had gone to Vienna the previous summer to improve his German before applying to the Foreign Office. His real intention was to work for the International Workers Relief Organisation and to observe the left-wing opposition to the dictator Dollfuss's suspension of the constitution and suppression of the socialists. He announced that henceforward 'My life must be devoted to Communism.' While in Vienna, Philby had fallen in love with a 'tremendous little sexpot', Litzi Kohlmann, the daughter of his landlord; he lost his virginity to her while they were out for a walk in the snow, which sounded 'impossible, but it was actually quite warm once you got used to it'. The couple married in February 1934 to facilitate Litzi's visa out of a country that had turned dangerous for her as it swung ever further to the right. Litzi was already in contact with Soviet intelligence through her friend Edith Suschitzky, another Viennese who had moved to London to marry Alex Tudor-Hart: both the Tudor-Harts were already spying for Moscow under the one code-name 'Arrow' (Edith's spinster code-name had been the unimaginative and not altogether watertight 'Edith'). Arrow was being run by Arnold Deutsch, a spy recruiter of genius, the first and most effective guide to the world of espionage for the Cambridge spy ring. In June the newly married Philby found himself on a bench in Regent's Park being captivated by the power and charisma of Deutsch – although he, in common with the other Cambridge men, was to know him only as 'Otto' in that freedom that espionage anonymity bestows. He did not hesitate to sign up as a Soviet agent, at once seeing the romance and purpose of the role; after all, 'one does not look twice at an offer of enrolment in an elite force'.

*

Arnold Deutsch was thirty-two, 'a stout man, with blue eyes and light curly hair'. He had arrived in England after a glittering academic career in Vienna that had taken him from undergraduate to PhD in only five years: his combination of subjects – his doctorate was in chemistry, though he had also studied philosophy and psychology – was a compellingly useful mix of the coolly analytic and the persuasively sympathetic, ideal for his work both as a recruiter and as a tutor of newly minted agents. He was also an accomplished linguist, speaking German, French, Italian, Dutch, Russian and English. Deutsch had been an observant Jew, but his religious fervour had been replaced by an ardent commitment to the Communist International's vision of 'a new world order which would free the human race from exploitation and alienation'.

After leaving Vienna Deutsch started working as a courier for the Comintern, travelling to Romania, Greece, Palestine and Syria. He collaborated with the German psychologist Wilhelm Reich, who was attempting to bring together the work of Marx and Freud and gained a reputation as 'the prophet of the better orgasm'. The 'sex-pol' movement, as it was known, held that if marriage and family, the bourgeois building-blocks of society, were broken up, all inhibitions would be released and the Revolution would surely follow. Reich propounded the startling theory that 'a man's poor sexual performance led him to fascism'. Deutsch was running Münster Verlag, a publishing house which published Reich's work and other 'sex-pol' literature; not surprisingly, by April 1934 he was under surveillance by the Viennese vice squad as a pornographer and it was time for him to leave the country.

Arnold Deutsch's cousin Oscar was already living in London. The millionaire founder of the hugely successful cinema chain Odeon (an acronym for 'Oscar Deutsch Entertains Our Nation') backed his Viennese cousin's application to do a further degree in phonetics and psychology at University College, London. Deutsch settled into British life in some style, renting a flat in the modern Lawn Road Flats in Hampstead, where his neighbours included Walter Gropius and Agatha Christie. Lawn Road Flats was the first building to have outside walkways and staircases, although Deutsch made sure his front door was hidden by a stairwell so that his visitors could not be seen entering or leaving. Once installed he began the work that would make him the most successful Soviet recruiter of all time: his KGB files credit him with twenty agents, of whom by far the most important and longest lasting were those from Cambridge, known to Moscow as 'the Magnificent Five'. Deutsch inspired an intense loyalty in all of them but particularly so in Maclean. He played a central role in his life and replaced the late Sir Donald as a mentor, in this case a political as well as a moral one.

Deutsch came up with the strategy of picking young radicals from the universities before they became influential in the careers he hoped they would enter:

Given that the Communist movement in these universities is on a mass scale and that there is a constant turnover of students, it follows that individual Communists whom we pluck out of the Party will pass unnoticed, both by the Party itself and by the outside world. People forget about them. And if at some point they do remember that they were once Communists, this will be put down to a passing fancy of youth, especially as those concerned are scions of the bourgeoisie.

He was a subtle man, as John Cairncross, the Scottish Marxist recruited in 1937 at the suggestion of his former tutor Anthony Blunt, acknowledged: Deutsch 'would never have been so successful' were it not for his 'skill, flexibility and cosmopolitan ways'. Once these young men were out of the cosseted and self-regarding world of Cambridge and faced with the choice between driving a tractor on a collective farm or entering into a comfortable life in the professions or civil service, it was a good bet that in most cases the socialist 'passing fancy of youth' would be just that. Deutsch proved himself to be a superb picker of young talent as he set about building the most effective spy network ever seen.

His sheer personality and psychological acuity were overwhelming. Kim Philby said of their first meeting:

It was an amazing conversation. And he was a marvellous man. Simply marvellous … I felt that immediately … He knew Marx and Lenin brilliantly … He spoke of the Revolution with enthusiasm … You could talk on any topic with him … The first thing you noticed about him were his eyes. He looked at you as if nothing more important in his life than you and talking to you existed at that moment.

The first task for Philby – code-named 'Söhnchen' ('Synok' in Russian), meaning 'Sonny' – was to break off all contact with his Communist friends and cultivate those with pro-German views to find out what they knew. His steps towards this were so bold as to appear beyond any possible bluff: he became a sub-editor on the *Anglo-German Trade Gazette*, a journal partly financed by the Nazi government, and joined the Anglo-German Fellowship, known by Winston Churchill as the 'Heil Hitler Brigade'. The other tasks suggested by Deutsch were to spy upon his own father, an astute psychotherapeutical loyalty test for a trainee agent; and above all to practise his observational skills by writing character sketches of prominent people he met as well as of his contemporaries, always with an eye to recruiting the cream of the next generation.

At the top of Philby's list was Donald Maclean, then just graduated and 'the most serious of anyone' he had met at Cambridge, the one who was 'convinced of the righteousness of socialism'. Better still, Maclean stood a good chance of passing the punishing Foreign Office exams to give the Soviets their badly needed mole there. Philby himself had failed in his application because his chosen referee, a fellow of Trinity, had refused to give 'a radical socialist' a reference; such people should not become civil servants in the don's view. The enmeshment with Kim Philby, the man Maclean barely saw over the next quarter of a century, but which was to last for the rest of his life and involve his marriage as well as espionage, was under way.

*

In late June or early July 1934, when Maclean was first mooting the idea of working in the Foreign Office, he was still freely professing his political leanings, especially after a drink. Fitzroy Maclean, who was then in his first year in the service, was introduced to his namesake at a party as someone 'who also hoped to become a diplomat'. Fitzroy, a relation only in the clan sense, 'made conversation with a tall, rather droopy, good-looking, golden-haired young man in faultless white tie and tails who caused me no more than momentary astonishment by announcing (it was almost the first thing he said) that he was a member of the Communist party'. Donald's 'clearly adoring mother', to whom he was sticking close even at a party, was listening to their conversation and said, 'Donald is even more of a radical than his dear father was.' To Lady Maclean, Communism was simply an extension of the Liberalism she had shared with her late husband.

The Foreign Office had obvious appeal both to Maclean and to Moscow. After his own failure, Philby had told Moscow that 'the FO would be hard put to find a formal excuse for rejecting Maclean'. Maclean's application form left the boxes blank for political clubs and societies and Dr Wansbrough-Jones did not share the scruples of Philby's referee when, either by accident (unlikely in an eminent scientist), ignorance (unlikely in such a small college) or design (possibly at Maclean's request), he glossed over the political side of Maclean's undergraduate life in his reference the following March:

> I have no hesitation at all in saying that on the scores of intellect, personality and ability [Mr Maclean] is in every way suitable for selection in the Foreign Office and Diplomatic Service. He is a man both possessing quite unusual personal charm and distinction of mind … He always took a prominent part in College and University affairs and he had particularly in his last year rather pronounced political views. Without allowing his work to suffer he spent a good deal of his time assisting various political associations both in Cambridge and, I think, elsewhere. I have always found him a man who had the courage of his convictions and able to make up his own mind firmly and decisively after hearing various points of view.

Wansbrough-Jones had followed up with an important further testimonial at the end of May 1935 to boost his former pupil's chance of success, adding that Maclean had won his school and college colours in rugby, cricket and hockey. The applicant himself did not hold back in his choice of second referee: he first of all put forward Lord Gladstone, son of the Victorian Prime Minister, but on the old man's death at the age of eighty-three replaced him with another liberal grandee a decade younger, Lord Rhayader. At a time when name mattered more than exploration of character and past, all the referees had to do was vouch for the health and honesty of the applicant, and state that he was free from 'pecuniary embarrassment'. This application was the first of many occasions in Maclean's life when an Englishman's background and his ambiguous words mattered more than official scrutiny.

*

Maclean told Philby his plans when they met over his 'modest table' at the Acol Road flat. Philby was confident of his man and became direct in his approach on getting this news: 'If you are going to sell the *Daily Worker* [in the Foreign Office], you're not going to be there very long. But you can carry out special work there for us.' Maclean's response was quick and equally blunt as a hunger for secrecy and belonging surged through him. It was as if he was hoping for exactly this result from the supper invitation. Would he be working for Soviet intelligence or the Comintern? The distinction was a very important one: it would be one thing to spy for a foreign government while in the employ of his own; quite another to belong to an international organisation pledged to create an 'international Soviet republic'. Maclean was a patriot as well as holding firm to an ideology which allowed room for actions based on his essential moral compass. The Comintern felt very comfortable for those who were 'intoxicated by the rhetoric of international proletarian revolution' in those smoky Cambridge rooms; they could still believe at that time, before they knew of Stalin's Terror, that it stood for peaceful progress in spite of its declared readiness to use armed force to achieve its goals. James Klugmann was working as an academic in Paris and was already a member of the secretariat of a Comintern front organisation (which he was to head from 1936), the Rassemblement Mondial des Etudiants. It seemed as if the Comintern was the fulfilment of a dream for Maclean – even if he was not planning to make his participation in the organisation public.

Philby was stunned by the speed of Maclean's reply to his opening gambit. He 'still had an arsenal of arguments and approaches. It was a shame to leave them unused.' He hedged his bets. 'The people I could introduce you to are very serious, they work in a very serious anti-fascist organisation, which may be tied to Moscow.' Maclean asked somewhat naively if he could discuss the matter with Klugmann, his guide through the machinery of the Communist world, but Philby said that if he did so, this discussion over supper had never taken place. It was essential tradecraft to keep the circles as small as possible. Ignace Reif, NKVD* *rezident*, or chief of the London espionage station, sent a telegram to his masters in Moscow on 26 August: 'Söhnchen has contacted his friend, the latter has agreed to work, and wants to come into direct contact with us.' Kim Philby, the future master-spy, had deftly identified and easily played the eager Maclean to get him over the initial recruitment hurdle.

Two days later Donald Maclean walked into a north London café carrying a book with a bright yellow cover presumably from Victor Gollancz's Left Book Club, a strong visual symbol of political discourse at the time, as a prearranged identification signal for the first of his many meetings with Arnold Deutsch, Otto. He did not need to be seduced by the recruiter's compelling personality to commit himself wholeheartedly to the cause and to secrecy. Philby's first recommendation was landed. A few months after leaving Cambridge, where he had been broadcasting his youthful idealism, Maclean was now embarking on a life where he would have to balance the betrayal that fulfilling his convictions entailed and performing the public service that was the other half of his family legacy. It was a double belonging. His early conditioning was to prove invaluable in both his careers.

*

Donald Maclean was given the code-name 'Waise' in German, 'Sirota' in Russian, both meaning 'Orphan', which not only highlighted Maclean's fatherless state but also captured his essential solitariness. It was another telling psychological insight from Deutsch. He had worked out four desirable characteristics of a successful agent: 'an inherent class resentfulness, a predilection for secretiveness, a yearning to belong, and an infantile appetite for praise and reassurance'. In Deutsch's report to Moscow

---

* The Cheka, the original Soviet intelligence agency, had by 1934 evolved into the NKVD, which became the NKGB (February 1941), NKVD again (July 1941), NKGB again (1943), MGB (1946), MVD (1953) and KGB the following year.

following their meeting, it was clear how well his new recruit fitted these criteria:

> Waise is a very different person to Synok [Philby]. He is much simpler and more sure of himself. He is a tall, handsome fellow with a striking presence. He knows this but does not make too much of it because he is too serious … He came to us out of sincere motivation, namely that the intellectual emptiness and aimlessness of the bourgeois class to which he belonged antagonised him. He is well-read, clever, but not as profound as Synok. He is honest, and at home became accustomed to a modest life-style because, even though his father was a minister, he was not a rich man. He dresses carelessly and is involved … in the Bohemian life. He takes an interest in painting and music. Like Synok, he is reserved and secretive, seldom displaying his enthusiasms or admiration. This to a large degree is explainable from his upbringing in the English bourgeois world, which is first and foremost conditioned always to display a reserved appearance. He lives without a wife, although it would not be difficult for him to find someone. He explained it to me by the fact that he had an aversion to girls of his own class and so could only live with a woman who is also a comrade … Waise is ambitious and does not like anyone telling him he has made a mistake … He likes to be praised for our work, since it provides him with the acknowledgement that he is doing something useful for us.

The volatile undergraduate emerged as focused, serious and reserved, but still immature when compared to the more contemplative and 'profound' Philby. Deutsch noted the over-arching importance of politics even in the excited recruit's sex life.

The direct focus that Philby also experienced in his first meeting with Deutsch was a new sensation for the previously scattergun Maclean of Cambridge days. 'The infantile need for praise and reassurance' identified by Deutsch is revealing when one considers the relations between fathers and sons in the recruitment of the

Cambridge Five: Maclean's feelings towards his own 'imposing but distant' father lay somewhere between idolatry and frustration. Burgess's father had died when he was young, before he had a chance to be a role model. St John Philby was peculiar and difficult. Cairncross's father 'was old enough to be my grandfather' and, as with Maclean, 'a Scots restraint made for a lack of intimacy between us'.* Cairncross too had had a strict Calvinist upbringing. Anthony Blunt was the agnostic youngest son of a clergyman 'who held to the stiff Victorian values that had been instilled in him'. Maclean's austere (and now dead) father who was not able to give him the necessary reassurances in his choices seems to be reflected in Deutsch's assessment of the son. Maclean passed for a paid-up member of a class to which he could not truly belong thanks to his father's humble origins and his own lack of a private income. In class-conscious Britain, he felt both keenly. Adoring mothers played their own part in forming these spies, even if they had no relevance in the Soviet recruiting mindset: to the end of her life Lady Maclean did not believe that Donald had done anything wrong; Guy Burgess's mother could not understand why her son was not allowed home.

Even after their first meeting, Deutsch's assessment of Orphan's character and skills is astonishingly good. Maclean's readiness to spy, to fulfil both sides of himself, meant that there were no ideological sticking-points, no qualms about legality, no final pricks of his conscience. One cannot but wonder how different the course of his life and career might have been had his Russian recruiter not been so gifted, and what the differences might have been in the history of international relations in the middle years of the century. Maclean would have risen, as he very nearly did, to the top of the ambassadorial ladder; possibly a career as a politician might have beckoned. He would have retired full of honour, a second Sir Donald and a figure in the history books – yet not as

---

* Cairncross, who displayed 'sex-pol' traits in his writings more than in his actions, wrote a history of polygamy, on which his friend Graham Greene commented, 'This is a book which will appeal strongly to all polygamists.'

prominent as the one he became. The events he would influence were, of course, unknowable at this point; the Soviets could not have dreamed what a valuable catch they had so easily landed at exactly the right moment.

*

In spite of his outstanding degree, Maclean still had to cram for the Diplomatic Service exams. As young men had done for sixty years, he went to Scoones, a school in a gloomy townhouse near the British Museum. Scoones was run by André Turquet, 'stout, with a florid complexion ... [who] simulated outbursts of rage, provoked usually by an error of French syntax'. Turquet, the son-in-law of the school's founder, 'once said that no man could be a diplomat unless he knew the history of the last three centuries' and at least two languages. As well as French and German, in both of which Maclean was proficient, modern history and economics were also taught. Maclean admired the economics tutor who 'expounded the frailties of the capitalist system in a way that tended to convince his hearers that it was doomed'.

In the evenings, in the world beyond Scoones, 'the Season' – the dinners and dances that introduced that year's crop of well-born adults to each other and to society – was in full swing. Maclean conformed to his instructions from Deutsch in suppressing his political views from now on. Wearing the regulation white tie and tails, with his silk-lined opera cloak draped around his tall figure, he escorted Asquith's granddaughters Laura and Cressida to dances (the daughters of his father's old friend Lady Violet Bonham Carter). He made friends with the Oxford-educated sons of two ambassadors, Tony (later Sir Anthony) Rumbold, whose best man he was to be in 1937, and Robin Campbell, under whose father he was to serve abroad. He was confident in intellectual matters, but at this stage 'had yet to lose his public-school *gaucherie*'. He had little success with women: despite his height, his understated charm and his 'nice, quiet sense of humour', he could still appear uncertain and was often described as 'flabby' (as Burgess put it) and other words suggesting chubbiness. He was most often to be seen hovering on the edge of the dance floor rather than taking part in the entertainment, sometimes talking to his mother. The literary critic Cyril Connolly saw 'both amiability and weakness' in Maclean. He was 'an outsize Cherubino intent on amorous experience but too shy and clumsy to succeed … charming, clever and affectionate, he was just too unformed'. Connolly said that he thought Maclean could be 'set right' by an older woman. Presumably word had not reached Connolly, even with his enthusiastic knowledge of other people's sex lives, of the previous summer's Brittany affair with Marie; nor had he taken Burgess's boasting into account.

While Guy Burgess continued to cut his homosexual swathe through London, Maclean rather ineffectually courted the independently minded and sweet-faced Mary Ormsby-Gore, daughter of Lord Harlech, for a brief period accompanying her to dinners and dances. Even if he never got quite as far as proposing to her, she had already decided that she could not marry him as the highly political Ormsby-Gores were 'strong Conservatives' and he was of 'Liberal stock'; she married Robin Campbell instead, his assiduous courtship causing him to fail his Foreign Office exams. In her second marriage to another diplomat who was a close friend of Maclean's, Mary became an appalled witness to the exposure of her erstwhile admirer's tragic fall from grace. She could not have regretted her decision.

Maclean was also attracted to one of the Bonham Carter sisters he escorted, the clever and funny Laura. Laura, whom he had known all his life, had the pale skin of her family and a sweet smile that belied her reputation as 'a great mocker' who 'rotted people and had nicknames for them all', as a more serious suitor, Jeremy Hutchinson, described her. She was, like Maclean, 'a difficult person to get to know … very independent'. There was no sign that she returned his crush, not responding in any way to his tentative moves towards a kiss in a taxi. Even if she had been interested, her powerful mother was 'very keen that her daughters should make *proper* marriages', and the grandson of a Highland cordwainer, however much in the true Liberal tradition of her father, might not have constituted a proper marriage in the eyes of the 'extraordinarily formidable' Lady Violet. Hutchinson, who became a fêted barrister, felt he had been rejected because he was not rich enough. Laura was to marry the rising star Jo Grimond, who fulfilled Lady Violet's criteria of being 'brainy, rich, good-looking and Liberal'.

*

At this point Maclean met a man who was to be the closest he had to a male confidant. Philip Toynbee was to be at his side at some of the most emotionally fraught moments of his life. Toynbee was 'tall and muscular with a sallow, long-jawed face and a sardonic twist to his mouth', simultaneously both 'wild and warm'. He had been the first Communist president of the Oxford Union and a close friend of the radical Romilly brothers who had demonstrated against Sir Oswald Mosley's fascist Blackshirts in London. He slept with both men and women, most recently Julia Strachey, niece of Lytton Strachey, and he too had been infatuated with Laura Bonham Carter, writing woundedly of 'making tiny attempts to hold Laura's arm – always repulsed to my fury'.

Toynbee was captivated by his first encounter at a debutante ball in 1936 with 'Donald Maclane [*sic*]. He was beautifully clothed and seemed a perfect bourgeois. I was quite drunk and thought at first he was being rude to me so I went off.' Later on, attracted by what he knew of Toynbee's Communist past and by what he had heard from the Bonham Carters, Maclean 'buttonholed me and we sat out together. He's in love with Laura! He'd heard *all* about me from Lady V (a bad woman we agreed) and thought highly of me ... It was very good to meet someone who thought highly of Laura ... he really was a very nice man.' Even though he was addressing a committed Communist (according to Toynbee, Communism gave 'humanity the possibility of happiness'), Maclean spread the word that he had moved away from his past beliefs: 'He accepted the Marxist analysis but had definitely decided he was on the losing side. A hopeless position and I didn't argue.' Maclean told him that 'his interests now lay with the ruling classes'.

The two men got progressively drunker, as they sat on the edge of the dance floor while the band played 'Smoke Gets in Your Eyes' and 'Body and Soul'. Maclean confided to Toynbee that 'he may also fall in love with [Jasper Ridley] and I encouraged him'. As Ridley, more familiarly known as 'Bubbles' and later to be killed in the war, was shortly to marry Cressida Bonham Carter, that kept the circle very tight. To a like-minded man Maclean was still content to display his sexual ambivalence; in this instance it is mixed with a yearning to be cherished within a small group. As the debauched night wore on the pair went 'very drunk in a taxi to a night-club called the Nest. DM ordered a bottle of gin most of which he drank; niggers danced and I wanted D cuddle [*sic*] but didn't ... ' After that, 'More taxis ... I woke E [Esmond Romilly] up and tried to persuade him to come to bathe in the Serpentine. He wouldn't but we did. It was extraordinary bathing blind tight.' Not only were they 'blind tight', they were both fully clothed in their white tie and tailcoats, the dress for society balls. They went to Maclean's house, where Toynbee finally passed out and Maclean, 'poor bugger', went to work, not for the last time after an all-night bender with his new friend. Toynbee was smitten, 'shocked and fascinated by this ingenious monster, but charmed, above all, by his lazy wit and sophisticated good humour' – and unaware that the 'ingenious monster' was covering up political passions that ran deeper underground than this.

Acting on Deutsch's instructions, Maclean never mentioned Burgess or Philby or spoke to them on the rare occasions when their paths crossed at parties. Peter Pollock, a very close friend of Burgess's in the late 1930s and 1940s, did not remember Maclean's name coming up at all; it was against Soviet tradecraft to allow social contact between agents, a policy that was proved disastrously right when Burgess and Philby went against the rules by living together in 1950. Even in November 1955, when Philby gave the press conference in his mother's flat that rehabilitated him for a while and is now used as a training tool by MI6, Britain's overseas intelligence agency, as 'a master-class in mendacity', he got away with saying, 'The last time I spoke to a communist, knowing him to be a communist, was some time in 1934.'

Alongside ditching his friends, Otto also ordered Maclean, as he had Philby, to cut loose from and deny his Communist past. To carry on as he had been in his last year at Cambridge would certainly cause a problem with his Foreign Office application, particularly with the rise of fascism in Europe. Maclean would utter enigmatic conversation-stoppers such as 'my future lies with the oppressors rather than the oppressed'. Toynbee, who 'would have considered it the highest honour to perform any service at all for Soviet Russia' and on paper would have seemed ideal for the job, was not approached to be a spy, maybe because with his supportive father and self-esteem intact he did not fit Deutsch's psychological profile. Maclean said to Laura Bonham Carter, 'I'm on *your* side of the barricades now,' at which she felt a great relief because the 'distemper' of the Marxist politics of his student years 'had made him such a boring companion', to the further detriment of their prospects together. Jocelyn Simon, who had minded that Maclean's Communism had led to his giving up his post as secretary of the Trinity Hall Cricket Club, lunched with him in Mayfair soon after he had joined the Foreign Office and discussed his political views: 'Maclean said that he had ceased to be a Communist as he found that he could not accept the Communist doctrine intellectually, and gave the impression that he was now in the centre politically, i.e. back to the traditions of his parents.' When Mary Ormsby-Gore and her younger sisters met him at their parents' house, they thought he was 'simply on the left wing of the Liberal Party'.

Alan Maclean, the youngest of the five children and eleven years Donald's junior, remembered the softer brother who emerged at this time now that he had been given fulfilment and purpose by Deutsch: Donald was 'gentle, tolerant, funny and understanding', and 'the fact that he'd given up being a Communist didn't seem to surprise anyone'. Their mother said 'that she hadn't minded him being a Communist at the time but that it hadn't seemed to her to be very "useful" ... She was delighted by his change of heart and at the prospect of his being a diplomat instead of a Communist. It just hadn't occurred to her that he could be both at the same time.'

Donald had fully and swiftly covered his traces to family and friends with the remarkable efficiency in both action and deceit that was to stand him in such good stead in later life.

*

Donald Maclean was now in the game as a Soviet agent. He was still ignorant of tradecraft and of what the role might fully involve, and he was without regular contact with a controller, still waiting to be activated. Burgess, because of his wildly extrovert nature, was a far riskier proposition to Moscow. But such was his love of gossip that he could not fail to notice how Maclean had distanced himself and become quiet where he used to be strident. At the very end of 1934, a few months after the newly graduated Maclean had been enlisted, Philby passed on to Deutsch his concern that the promising new secret ring might be broken before it had begun to be useful:

> [Burgess] had convinced himself that Maclean and I had not undergone a sudden change of views, and that he was being excluded from something esoteric and exciting. So he started to badger us, and nobody could badger more effectively than Burgess. He went for Maclean and he went for me ... Otto became increasingly worried that, if he got nowhere, he might try some trick – perhaps talk about us to people outside our circle. He might well be more dangerous outside than inside. So the decision was taken to recruit him. He must have been one of the very few people to have forced themselves into the Soviet special service.

Burgess, having got his own trouble-making way as usual, was given the code-name 'Mädchen' ('Little Girl'). His first act as an agent was to produce a list of potential contacts: the list was 'mad and enthusiastic ... four pages long and included just about everyone he'd ever met, from G. M. Trevelyan [Regius Professor of History at Cambridge] and Maynard Keynes to London prostitutes'. It also included the name of his former lover Anthony Blunt, most likely recruited in 1937 as a useful talent-spotter at Cambridge (puzzlingly and disappointingly given the code-name 'Tony'). Like Philby, Burgess reinvented his politics and resigned from the Communist Party, much to the disgust of his former Cambridge comrades, who saw him as 'a traitor, because he took care to advertise his alleged conversion to right-wing views as soon as he had gone down'. The man whose name was to be linked for posterity with Maclean's, the loosest wheel in the Magnificent Five, was now attached.

*

The examinations for the Foreign Office took place in April 1935 in Burlington Gardens, behind the Royal Academy of Arts in Piccadilly, in a 'shadowy hangar (smelling of varnish and rubber and freshly poured ink) with unsightly pipes as its sole decoration'. The exams were meant to test a candidate's ability to synthesise and repackage information, to think on his (all the candidates were male) feet, and to look at any given situation tangentially, as well as to assess languages and literacy. Maclean's Foreign Office contemporary Valentine Lawford described some of the questions for which they had been cramming for months: 'assess the influence of Descartes or the importance of Jansenism ... Even the Everyday Science paper included the old chestnut about sewage disposal, for which one was naturally well prepared – an acquaintance with sewage being as everyone knew a prerequisite for success for employment under the Crown.' The English paper involved précising a 'Letter to a Young Friend Thinking of a Mercantile Career' to test the candidates' powers of condensing information, and for the rest a 'meagre choice between interpreting statistics about Welsh tin-plates and writing a Congratulatory Ode to the Gas Light and Coke Company on the completion of a new 250-ft. gas-holder'. The competition was intense, with only six or seven of the most brilliant and suitable Oxbridge graduates out of a field of seventy-five to a hundred being offered a place each year.

The interview was crucial, and Maclean found a panel that was well disposed towards him and prepared to take him on trust. It included Tony Rumbold's father, Sir Horace, the anti-Nazi Ambassador in Berlin when Hitler came to power, Lady Violet Bonham Carter, Clement Attlee, the future Labour Prime Minister, Sir John Cadman and Edgar Granville MP; three Foreign Office representatives made up the rest. In the clubby atmosphere of the Foreign Office in the 1930s questions of security did not enter anyone's mind and it was not an issue that two of the interviewers were personally known to Maclean, that others had worked with his father or that possibly all of them thought well of the late minister. It would have been hard to put together a panel where any candidate was not known to some of them. Inevitably Maclean's political views would be raised; even if his reference from Wansbrough-Jones did not overplay them, his vociferousness at Cambridge would have stood a good chance of reaching the panel. He told his friends afterwards:

> All went well, and I got on famously with the examiners at the *viva*. I thought they'd finished when one of them suddenly said: 'By the way, Mr Maclean. We understand that you, like other young men, held strong Communist views when you were at Cambridge. Do you still hold those views?' I'm afraid I did an instant double-take. Shall I deny the truth, or shall I brazen it out? I decided to brazen it out. 'Yes,' I said. 'I did have such views – and I haven't entirely shaken them off.' I think they must have liked my honesty because they nodded, looked at each other and smiled. Then the chairman said: 'Thank you, that will be all, Mr Maclean.'

In that more socially blinkered age when who you were rather than what you were counted, before any deeper enquiries were made, let alone the 'positive vetting' that his career eventually brought about, Donald Maclean, with the emerging display of confidence that disarms the innocent questioner, crossed the last line at which he could have redeemed himself and was admitted into the Foreign Office. John Cairncross, without the social and political advantages that the Maclean family held, was in no doubt that if his left-wing past had come out in his own application to the Foreign Office two years later, he would not have been given the same 'exoneration' for his frankness; his 'student activities would then be viewed in a much more sinister light'. The difference between them, he believed, was that Maclean passed effortlessly as 'a member of the élite, whereas I was the son of a modest Scottish shopkeeper'. Five applicants were successful that year and Maclean scored highest in English and elementary economics, surprisingly lowest in French and German, earning him fourth place. He got an outstanding 285 out of 300 marks in his *viva voce* interview – the rest scored 220 – despite splitting the panel to the extent that the two surviving pencilled notes made at the time are 'Pleasant and quiet. Attractive' and 'B+. Rather weak face.' A candidate who scored highly in exams but came across as 'weak' might seem useful in the Foreign Office, where conformity and malleability allied to brains and connections made for a sound civil servant.

It was just over a year since Donald Maclean had left Cambridge. He was about to start his conventional British career and at the same time his unconventional, hidden one. The life of the insider was opening before him at last, yet the perpetual outsider could be simultaneously nourished. Orphan was ready for the 'special work' Philby had mentioned to him at his kitchen table. The brilliant student who had been uncertain of where his true self lay was now setting out in the world to fulfil the destiny expected of him, yet with his ideals intact. He could have no inkling of where his choices of the past year would lead him, nor how quickly his secret life was to be activated, and fulfilled.

4

Lyric

Maclean's entire Foreign Office career was one of treachery along-side immensely hard work. He had been recruited as a 'sleeper', encouraged to learn his tradecraft and not expected to pass any-thing on from his lowly post as Third Secretary in the League of Nations and Western Department. Deutsch was clear that his real value to Moscow would come as he climbed the ladder and became privy to ever more important secrets. As he arrived for his first day at work on 11 October 1935 his nervous excitement was about the insights he would get on the worsening world situation rather than about the prospect of immediately nourishing his secret soul. Yet nothing about Donald Maclean's life as a diplomat was ever con-ventional, and before long his speed of mind, his impatience to serve and belong and the opportunities that came his way meant he was soon producing prodigious amounts of valuable intelli-gence. He made such an impression on Moscow Centre, the NKVD headquarters, that his spying career could have been brought to a humiliating end almost before it began, and he even needed to be allocated his own handler – with whom he promptly fell in love.

*

The ambitious new Third Secretary, smartly dressed in his 'black coat and striped trousers', could not have failed to be impressed by his new office as he arrived on that first day. The Italianate build-ing with its grandest rooms looking across Horse Guards to St James's Park, a brief walk from the Palace of Westminster, is the most impressive in Whitehall. With the British Empire still remarkably intact amid the uncertainty of the 1930s, the Foreign Office lived up to its purpose of symbolising and endorsing British power in the world. The most remarkable part of the building is perhaps the Durbar Court of the old India Office, a vast granite and marble courtyard three storeys high complete with pillars and curved arches.

Maclean's own office was a humbler affair, down several long and defiantly unornate corridors. The Western Department consisted of three rooms, one occupied by the head of department, a smaller one for his secretary, and a large one shared by the three or four junior officials. The juniors' room was miserably furnished, according to Valentine Lawford:

> the mahogany Office of Works hat-stand hung with unclaimed umbrellas and unattractive 'office coats' with *glacé* elbows, the screen with its gruesome pin-ups of Himmler, Streicher and Roehm, the jaundice-coloured distempered walls, hanging light-bulbs under China shades, and generically threadbare, grey-blue-bistre carpet of the kind that one had dismissed at one's private school as 'probably made by convicts out of coconut fibre in the Andaman Islands'.

Even as he was learning how to handle the telegrams that flooded into the department, Maclean saw their, and his, importance at a critical period for Europe and the world. His arrival coincided with the first major test for the League of Nations since its foundation in 1920 as Benito Mussolini, keen to restore Italian pride and power by creating an empire, had invaded Abyssinia on 3 October 1935. The League imposed sanctions on Italy, but Britain stopped short of embargoing supplies of oil for fear that Il Duce would attack British territories in Africa.

The latest Nuremberg Rally and its display of determined Nazi might had been held the previous month. The vital coal-producing region of the Saar, taken from Germany after the Great War and awarded to France, had just voted overwhelmingly to return to the Fatherland. Hitler saw the League's reaction to the

Abyssinian crisis as evidence of pusillanimity and was encouraged to invade the Rhineland in March 1936. At a meeting of the League Council in London, only the Soviet Union delegate, Maxim Litvinov, proposed sanctions against Germany, and found his proposal rejected. Hitler countered with an offer of 'a twenty-five-year non-aggression pact' in Europe, yet he did not clarify what he meant by that. Mussolini summed up his contempt for the League on which their opponents had pinned their hopes when he declared that it was 'very well when sparrows shout, but no good at all when eagles fall out'.

As Maclean saw the telegrams coming in and going out while the fascist dictators ran roughshod over world diplomacy, he was painfully aware that the League on which he, and British politicians including his father, had pinned such hope was being shown up as toothless. His faith in Communism was not only cemented, but was increasingly shared in the most unlikely official quarters. King George V told his former wartime Prime Minister Lloyd George that he 'would go to Trafalgar Square and wave a Red Flag myself' in protest if there was a question of war over the Abyssinian crisis. The monarch died the following year before he could fulfil his promise. Anthony Blunt justified his own impending recruitment when he said that 'the Communist Party and Russia constituted the only firm bulwark against fascism' in the mid-1930s, as 'the Western democracies were taking an uncertain and compromising attitude towards Germany'. The rapid events of the 'dark valley' of the 1930s were a similar spur to action for Maclean, action that did not feel like betrayal because he was helping Britain's cause in the fight against fascism, lessening his frustration with his government. The sleeper was awakened early through the fast-moving diplomacy he was immediately engaged in. At the age of only twenty-two, Donald Maclean found his prolific espionage career taking off.

*

The Third Secretaries saw all the incoming telegrams from the embassies and would pass them up to the Second Secretaries for sifting and sending further up the chain. Rarely was anything locked in the safe of the head of department, and even those documents marked 'Secret' could be taken home by employees without checking them in or out. Security was an alien subject until the Second World War broke out, and even then it was administered by one officer rather than by a department. When it became apparent that there was a major leak from the Rome Embassy in 1937, Colonel Valentine Vivian of MI6 was called in. He quickly identified the source as a Chancery servant called Secondo Constantini, yet the Ambassador refused to believe that such a thing could happen and made sure that both Signor Constantini and his wife were asked later that same year to the coronation of King George VI as a reward for his long service.[*]

Nobody questioned the hard-working Maclean as he took papers with him to his small flat in Oakley Street, between Chelsea's King's Road and the River Thames, to work on at night. The more he was able to familiarise himself with the rapidly shifting events in Western Europe and the British response to them, the greater his efficiency in the office. As his anxiety grew in line with the worsening international situation, his briefcase bulged more and more each evening. Deutsch would meet him on the way home, take the files to his photographer and then meet Maclean again in Chelsea late in the evening so that he could give the documents back for their return to the office.

As well as these near-daily encounters, Maclean had lengthier meetings with Deutsch most weeks. Deutsch was an 'illegal', not on any diplomatic or trade delegation lists, and free to use a variety of aliases but unable to plead diplomatic immunity to avoid prosecution should he be caught doing anything wrong – should he be discovered in discussion with anyone from the Foreign Office, for example. He was quite relaxed about sitting on a park bench in one of London's 'remoter open spaces' such as Hampstead Heath with

---

[*] It later transpired that more than a hundred of Constantini's leaks in 1935 alone were deemed important enough to be 'sent to Comrade Stalin' for his personal attention.

his charge, or to have Maclean visit him in his Lawn Road flat near by. But Deutsch's own preparations were much more elaborate and NKVD-textbook: he would be driven out of town, both he and the driver checking to see that they were not being followed, before Deutsch came back by at least two forms of public transport. He would be careful to ensure that the film of the documents was concealed in the false backs of items such as hairbrushes or household utensils that he might legitimately have in a briefcase or about his person. These films, and letters written in secret ink, would be sent on to Moscow via the Copenhagen diplomatic pouch.

The sheer quantity of material coming from the eager young diplomat, the only one of the Cambridge recruits to have penetrated the citadels of power, was overwhelming. Deutsch also had Philby and Burgess (completing the trio known to Moscow as 'the Three Musketeers' until Blunt and Cairncross joined their ranks to make them 'the Magnificent Five') to keep in play. He begged Maclean to slow down, to bring more material out on a Friday night and less on other days so that his sleepless photographer had more time over the weekend to take it away and record it efficiently somewhere more conducive to the production of good images.

Deutsch sent a memo to Moscow asking for help in sharing the load: 'Taking into consideration the importance of the above-mentioned material … in addition to the importance of other cultivations and recruitments … I consider the question of the Foreign Department's assigning an experienced and talented underground *rezident* to head the field station in the British Isles to be extremely pressing.' Moscow did not send a *rezident*, who would have had official cover and diplomatic immunity, but one of their greatest illegals, Teodor Maly.

*

Maly, born in 1894, was as tall as Maclean at six feet four inches, his gold front teeth shining between a dark moustache on his 'short upper lip' and a 'slightly cleft chin' and with the 'typical shiny grey complexion of some Russians and Germans'. Inevitably, most of those with whom he came into contact remembered him quite clearly, so that if his own side had not taken against him first he might not have survived long at liberty to weave his spell over the still-raw and enthusiastic agent from the Foreign Office. Maly, code-named 'Man', approached his Communism as a spiritual matter. Like Deutsch, he came to strong political beliefs from religious ones. Although his passport said he was born in Austria, he was in fact a Hungarian who had entered a Catholic monastery after leaving school and become a priest. He had been called up as a chaplain in the Austro-Hungarian army, and been taken prisoner in the Carpathians on the Russian front in June 1916. As a result of the horrors he had seen and the indoctrination he received from his captors, he lost his faith in his old God and emerged from captivity a revolutionary Communist who then fought for the Bolsheviks in the Russian Civil War until 1921.

After working in Crimea and Moscow in various intelligence roles, Maly and his wife Lydia arrived in London as Paul and Lydia Hardt, representatives of the Amsterdam textile company Gada, in the business of exporting rags to Poland. The cover for the business was poor, especially considering the sums of money Gada brought into the country, £4,700 in eighteen months into one account alone at a time when the salary of a Third Secretary in the Foreign Office was £144 a year. When Gada was investigated long after Maly had left the country, 'all the persons interviewed said Hardt did not know anything about the business ... or the intricacies of the rag trade ... None of the firms had heard of "Gada" before February 1936.' Notwithstanding this dodgy but successful piece of tradecraft, Maly was a forward-thinking planner to the extent that before he left Britain 'he had recruited fishermen off the coast of France, Belgium and the Netherlands in order for the Russians to have access to radio transmission in the event of war'.

Maly exerted a calming influence on Maclean and was credited in Moscow with teaching the frenetic diplomat 'patience'. He tried to bring focus to Maclean's productivity, exhaustedly reporting in May 1936 that 'tonight Waise arrived with an enormous bundle of dispatches ... Only a part of them has been photographed ... because we have run out of film and today is Sunday – and night-time at that. We wanted [Maclean] to take out a military intelligence bulletin but he did not succeed in doing this.' When these films were developed in Moscow the results were greeted with delight as Orphan had been able to send a report which showed 'the state of German ordnance factories with exact figures of armaments production of each plant given separately', and another 'describing the mobilization plans of various countries, Germany, Italy, France and the Soviet Union'.

The Committee of Imperial Defence was at the heart of government policy in the making of preparations for war. Maclean's greatest early coup was to supply its minutes which summarised the contingency plans throughout the still-extensive Empire and former colonies. These constituted such welcome intelligence that Maclean's feat in sending them on was celebrated in NKVD circles.

Prime Minister Baldwin frequently attended the sittings of the committee. Plans being made about the 'organisation of British industry for war purposes … about procurement for government arsenals and plants, and about the adaptation of private industry and transport companies for a smooth transfer of the country in the event of war' in Europe were discussed; there was even a strategy for 'British army procurement in the event of war with the USSR'. On 20 December 1936 the committee deliberated on such matters as broadcasting and the defence of government buildings in wartime, and the lack of oil for both the British and the Australian navies. The secrecy of such deliberations was stressed: it was decided that 'the shortage of fuel should be kept absolutely secret, since its disclosure would lead to serious political complications', but no steps were taken beyond assuming that all those present were gentlemen who would keep their word to ensure confidentiality. The issue of fuel might have been unimportant anyway as the number of 'Cruisers available for service … is likely for some years … to be below the number required'. Another document picked out for special attention in Moscow contained the minutes of a conversation between Hitler and the British Ambassador in Berlin about a secret pact for exchanging technical air force data between Britain, Germany and France. The British report said

Hitler had been adamant about not sharing with the French because 'if France were trusted with these materials, they would immediately fall into the hands of the Soviet Union'. The references to the state of German and British war-readiness run through the files sent to Moscow as a commentary on the urgency of the times, including the thoroughgoing minutes of the 1937 Imperial Defence Conference 'to review current problems and liabilities'. The references to the fledgling Government Code and Cypher School, later GCHQ, and the steps it was taking to crack the codes of overseas powers, especially Soviet, was a harbinger of future machinations, but at that time a leak from within the ranks seemed unthinkable. In a very short time, this trust was to mean that the first of Donald Maclean's many charmed lives in espionage was used up.

*

If politics had started to become an urgent business at the time of Maclean's arrival in Whitehall, the outbreak of the Spanish Civil War was the defining event, the rehearsal for what was to follow from 1939, and the drama on to which all could project their concerns. It unassailably put the left-wingers on the side of decency in a country where Oswald Mosley's British Union of Fascists, the Blackshirts, was starting to gain some traction. Maclean's position in the department responsible for Spain in a war where Soviet interests were closely involved was a bonanza for Russian interests. A few months into his first job, the war also introduced the first moment of tension between government policy, where he had to be an impartial observer and toe the line, and his core beliefs. This was to be a test for what was to come as the divisions within him grew ever greater.

The roots of the war lay buried deep, and were bound up in the global crisis as well as in more local issues, such as the poverty of many of Spain's citizens, and the power of the clergy, who sometimes banned the teaching of reading in schools to prevent the children being 'corrupted' by Marxist texts. In July 1936 General Franco led the right-wing Nationalist uprising against the left-leaning government, and what was meant to be a swift coup became a bloody three-year struggle. Across the world, idealists of the left flocked to join the International Brigade, on behalf of the Republicans, including many of the Cambridge Communists well known to Maclean. David Haden Guest, John Cornford and Julian Bell were all killed alongside 500 British volunteers, from Oxbridge intellectuals to miners. An estimated 2,500 joined the International Brigade from Britain, over 5,000 from the United States under the name of the Abraham Lincoln Battalion, a total of 32,000 from around the world. The passion felt by these people for the cause ran deeper than the patriotism of the Great War; this was about saving the world for the freedom of future generations. Wogan Philipps, driving an ambulance for the Republicans, wrote to his wife, whom he had abandoned in England with their two young children, to say that he was doing 'a tiny bit to make the world better for them. If you saw women and children bombed to pieces night after night as I have you would be enraged, and think as I do. If you saw these young Spanish boys fighting to keep their liberty – they are so young, so gay, lively, friendly – just children.' Kim Philby was still under his right-wing cover when he went to Spain as a reporter, first freelance and later for *The Times*, in January 1937 – a good disguise should he have succeeded in getting near enough to carry out his orders from Moscow to assassinate Franco. He returned in May, somewhat depressed, without having come close to fulfilling his suicidal mission.

The war galvanised political debate in Britain: the publisher Victor Gollancz's Left Book Club soon had 57,000 members and 1,500 discussion groups in offices, factories and community centres. Titles in the distinctive yellow livery included George Orwell's *Road to Wigan Pier*, *Spanish Testament* by Arthur Koestler and *Days of Contempt* by André Malraux. Maclean, who wherever he was throughout his life kept up with the latest literary movements, subscribed to the club. On the far right, in the London County Council elections of 1937 the British Union of Fascists polled up to a quarter of the vote in the wards in which its candidates stood. But as the debate sparked into life, the establishment worked hard to steer a passive course that maintained the values, not to say the patrician condescension, that had served it until now. Walter Greenwood wrote the widely noticed *Love on the Dole*, a powerful novel of unemployment in Salford, outside Manchester, set between the General Strike in 1926 and 1931. A stage adaptation was produced in 1934, but the British Board of Film Censors twice refused a film version to be shown on moral (swearing) and political (the unemployed fighting the police) grounds. They said it was 'a very sordid story in very sordid surroundings'. The film was not released until 1941, when fascism had acquired a more universal hue.

As Maclean's Foreign Office contemporary Robert Cecil put it, Spain was 'the last chance to hold back fascism in Europe ... In Italy and Germany nothing could be done; but in Spain history was being made under our eyes.' Nancy Maclean, who had not had the same moral and political clarity as Donald drilled into her by her parents, came back from a prolonged stay in Dresden in July 1936 and was surprised to be quizzed by her elder brother on what she had seen and heard. She had gone to Germany to enjoy herself, 'not to keep copious notes on the state of the economy and the size of the military'. Her brother was building up his spy muscles at the same time as exercising his powerful, policy-based mind on behalf of his government. 'The beautiful and irredeemably heterosexual' Louis MacNeice wrote in his poem of the times, *Autumn Journal*, that:

> Spain would soon denote
> Our grief, our aspirations;
> ... our blunt
> Ideals would find their whetstone ... our spirit
> Would find its frontier on the Spanish front ...

The British government, determined not to get involved in the war, set up a Non-Intervention Committee, bringing in the French. The committee effectively proposed that Germany, Italy and the USSR should play no part in the Spanish conflict, which was a distraction from Britain's effort to maintain the balance of power within Europe. Sir Orme Sargent, supervisor of the Western Department, wrote, 'If the principle of non-intervention in the affairs of Spain breaks down ... it may well be that the first step will have been taken in dividing Europe into two *blocs* each based on a rival ideology ... horrible development.' Sir Orme's blocs did indeed come into being, but only after a war in which non-intervention was not an option. At the time, only Churchill, out of fashion as the prophet of war and champion of the need to rearm, saw the committee for what it was, 'an elaborate system of official humbug'. Lord Halifax encapsulated Britain's official aims for Spain in minimalist fashion when he stood in for Foreign Secretary Eden who was on holiday and did not consider this a sufficient crisis to warrant an early return: the government's policy was 'to localise the disturbance ... and prevent outside assistance from prolonging the war'. Baldwin, who loathed extremes of any kind and had a 'deep fear of ideas', summed up the ostrich-like position of the government and his belief that the status quo would reassert itself around the world on the basis of British values when he said: 'We English hate fascism, but we loathe bolshevism as much. So, if there is somewhere that fascists and bolshevists can kill each other off, so much the better.'

In a dual career of such importance as Maclean's, ironies will abound. In November 1936 the Third Secretary was entrusted by the Non-Intervention Committee with compiling 'a summary of Soviet infringements of the Non-Intervention agreement', in effect to identify the Soviet Union's attempts to provide resources to Spain in order to prevent them. This was at a time when the Royal Navy was ordered to send supplies to the Nationalists through Gibraltar, and Shell-Standard Oil in the US neatly sidestepped President Roosevelt's embargo on arms sales by supplying them with oil and raw materials on credit. Franco remarked that FDR had 'behaved like a true gentleman'. Maclean commented privately much later in his life that he had achieved much more 'underground' than he could have done 'overground' during the Spanish Civil War. He felt that in transmitting British policy, such as it was, he was 'acting, without their knowing it, as an intelligence officer for my own friends who had gone to fight … for the International Brigade'.

As a straight ideological arrow, unlike some of his coevals spying for personal glory or for the pleasure of troublemaking, Maclean could not always disguise the strain he was under in his hard-working double life. He did not always fully engage with the office, a remoteness attributed to his 'somewhat diffident manner' which the mandarins suggested 'will probably be corrected as he acquires greater confidence in himself'. A colleague's comment that what his superiors dismissed as 'the tiresome and ticklish work' of dealing with the refugees from Spain left Maclean 'often very nervy … his ashtray always piled high with cigarette ends'. It was an indication of the addictive stress that was in time to wreak such devastation. He was among the first to see the British Ambassador's telegram informing the Foreign Office that the Luftwaffe 'had bombed [the 'Basque spiritual capital'] Guernica to smithereens', before sitting through the Imperial Conference in London in May 1937 to learn that Germany was apparently co-operating 'loyally, efficiently and zealously' in non-intervention. By smoking, and by passing on all he could in the hope that it would help the embattled Republicans, he could at least find some release.

John Cairncross, the Marxist 'Fiery Cross' of Cambridge, shortly to be recruited by Deutsch, arrived at the Foreign Office at the end of 1936. In best Soviet practice, he did not know that Maclean was already working for Moscow, and viewed his 'new colleague and immediate superior' in the Spanish section as 'a tall, mild-mannered figure … highly efficient, most competent in his work and always friendly, though he never expressed strong views either in conversation or on paper'. Maclean passed on a clumsily coded warning, to a man he knew held similar views, about the need for restraint and the presentation of a covering nonchalance when he said to Cairncross that he 'did not make the right impression' through being 'too spontaneous and oblivious of conventional behaviour: it was not so much a question of having the wrong views, though this was noted, as not coming from the right background'. Behind the social arrogance there is a chilling acknowledgement of the need to suppress true feelings, as Maclean had been taught to do when benefiting from his own 'right background'. A few months later, when Cairncross was safely within the fold, he was reported by his handler as believing that 'although Orphan has become a complete snob, he nevertheless retains a "healthy line" in his work which shows that he has retained Marxist principles in his subconscious. What is more, he is of the opinion that Orphan has the best brains in the Foreign Office.' Cairncross, with his 'prickly personality and lack of social graces', found it much harder to dissemble without the Gresham's training, and it was a relief to the social outsider, as well as a boon to Moscow's desire to spread their agents throughout the corridors of power, when he was transferred to the more meritocratic Treasury in December 1938.

The gauche young Maclean who had been standing at the edge of the debutante balls was now on firmer ground, growing into himself as he became more purposeful and felt more needed. The earlier 'amiability and weakness' pointed out by Connolly had gone now and he 'seemed suddenly to have acquired a backbone, morally and physically' through the work he was doing for both his masters. Although he could be 'priggish' in the presentation of his Marxist views, in the pubs and bars of bohemian Chelsea where he used to spend his evenings with Mark Culme-Seymour, another boon companion, as well as other friends, he was at least able to drop some of his office stiffness, helped by large amounts of whisky. Yet he was also able to move back into official mode: 'he could switch to a magisterial defence of Chamberlain's foreign policy and seemed able to hold the two self-righteous points of view simultaneously'. Holding the establishment line while not letting go of his principles was still possible, and was serving him well.

*

Maclean's fluency and supply were rewarded and echoed, wittingly or not, in the new code-name he was given, 'Lyric'. While solitariness is perhaps an essential prerequisite to one who is living a secret life, nevertheless Orphan had grown in his brief operational time into a fluent poet. Under the Foreign Office career structure, he was due for a posting abroad towards the end of 1937, but such was his productivity and his belief in his usefulness to both sides that he wrote to the Personnel Department in June to say that 'I would very much rather stay where I am for as long as possible. I hope this this wish isn't unhelpful … ' In fact, his employers were keen to meet his wishes. His immediate boss praised his 'good memory and a sure grasp of detail', and added that he was, as the Soviets also appreciated, 'a quick worker … most willing and good-tempered'. He was already showing 'signs of developing sound political judgement' and a growth in confidence that would propel him to the front rank of British diplomacy and ensure that he served the NKVD as a guide and interpreter as well as an inform-ant when the future battle lines were drawn up.

But just as the flow from the newly anointed Lyric was at its peak, he was to be cut adrift, no longer praised for and nourished by spying. The whole laboriously built edifice of Soviet espionage was on the point of being pulled down as Stalin's purges of anyone he suspected might be a perceived enemy of true Bolshevism gath-ered pace in the face of potential war. Millions were arrested, put into concentration camps or executed, or simply disappeared, and a prime target for suspicion in the Great Terror was the organ of state security, the NKVD itself.* The NKVD had a staff of some 24,500 in 1936; by January 1938, a total of 1,373 of these had been arrested, 3,048 dismissed, 1,324 transferred to other departments and 153 executed via the chillingly named Association of Special Tasks. After Trotskyists, anyone who had served abroad was sus-pect, and by the twisted logic of the purges anyone who had had a hand in intelligence was likely to know too much that could be used against the state. And the more they denied it, the more guilty they were. Stalin's instruction to his interrogators was 'Give them the works until they come crawling to you on their bellies with their confessions in their teeth.' Darkness did truly seem to come at

---

* The KGB's own, probably understated estimate is nineteen million arrests in the years 1935–40, seven million of whom were either shot or died in the gulag.

noon as 'terrified to death, the Soviet man hastens to sign resolutions . . . He has become a clod,' in the words of one NKVD general who refused the call to Moscow.

Maclean's handler Maly was an early target for suspicion because of his religious background which at one time had lent him faith in something other than the system. He was fatalistic about his recall to Moscow in June 1937: 'I know that as a former priest I haven't got a chance. But I've decided to go there so that nobody can say: "That priest might have been a real spy after all."' The man of religion became a martyr to his politics. The torture broke all its victims in the end: the accused was interrogated and beaten without being given water for as long as it took for him to 'confess'; after sleeping, he almost invariably retracted and the process began again until his only wish was to be sentenced, even if that meant execution; at least he was then allowed to sleep all he liked. In the cellars of the Lubyanka, the headquarters of the secret police, Maly confessed to being a German agent and was given the *Genickschuss*, the single bullet in the back of the neck. What Maly and the NKVD did not know was that MI5 was already on his trail and had been on the point of arresting him in London. A careful watch prior to his planned arrest would have astonished the security services if they had caught Maly meeting the rising star of the Foreign Office.

The government had been concerned about the possibility of subversion and agitation since the General Strike of 1926; revolution had come closer during the short-lived naval mutiny at Invergordon in 1931. MI5 combated the 'Red Menace' through penetration of the Communist Party of Great Britain and one of their most effective secret weapons was 'Miss X', the twenty-five-year-old Mancunian daughter of a night editor of the *Daily Mail*. Miss X, Olga Gray, had been recruited by the legendary Maxwell Knight and was now working as a highly valued secretary for the Comintern and the CPGB. In 1934 she was asked to be a courier to take money and instructions to Indian Communist leaders, although this was so incompetently planned by the CPGB that she was about to arrive in the monsoon season. Maxwell Knight found himself in the peculiar position of having to make the clandestine arrangements himself to keep his agent in play as the Communists 'did not real-ise that an unaccompanied young English woman travelling to India without some very good reason stood a risk of being turned back when she arrived as a suspected prostitute'. He 'was faced with a peculiar situation whereby Miss X had to be assisted to devise a cover story which would meet the requirements necessary, without making it appear to the Party that she had received any expert advice. This was no easy task but eventually a rather thin story of a sea-trip under doctor's orders, combined with an invitation from a relative in India met the case.'

Miss X's cover still held by 1937, when Percy Glading, an officer of the Communist League against Imperialism, asked her to rent a flat in her name at CPGB expense that he might use for meet-ings. She found a place in Holland Road, Kensington. In April Glading visited the flat with two men. One was a Mr Peters, a name which she knew had to be false for a man with such an accent, but the description she gave of him is an instant giveaway: six foot four inches tall, moustached, 'shiny grey complexion' and prominent gold teeth. With the unmistakable Maly was another man, short and 'rather bumptious in manner'. Deutsch's charisma, so powerful to the Cambridge Five, had failed to win the day with Miss X. Deutsch and Maly were running a spy ring inside Woolwich Arsenal, home of Britain's weapons design and manu-facture, where Glading had worked until he had been sacked a few years earlier; he wanted to use the flat to photograph documents he received from his former colleagues in the arsenal. Deutsch and Maly often used to send the 'take' from both Maclean and Glading in the same diplomatic bag, informing Moscow Centre that 'we are sending you the films from Lirik as well as the shrap-nel samples from G.'. One day Glading was trailed to Charing Cross Station and arrested in the act of receiving a briefcase from an arsenal employee. A search of his flat uncovered a photo-graphed copy of *A Manual of Explosives* and the blueprint of an aircraft design. He was given a six-year sentence. Olga Gray, now blown as an undercover agent, was extravagantly praised by the judge for her part in the operation, yet, depressed by her experiences as a spy, she left to begin a new life in Canada. By this time, Maly had gone to meet his fate in Moscow and his terminally bad luck was a reprieve for the Cambridge spies as the only significant pre-war counter-intelligence operation came to a halt.

Before his recall, Maly had written to Moscow Centre that Lyric 'was an idealist and we must be careful not to destroy his idealism'. To the Soviet Union's great gain in the years to come, what remained firm in this period of inactivity and purge was Lyric's belief in the justice inherent in the Soviet system. Maclean's friend in later life, George Blake, the post-war spy with a strongly Calvinist conscience, explained the justification of the true ideologue for the Great Terror and other terrible crimes committed in the name of Communist ideology: they 'were not an essential part of its creed, which itself represented the noblest aims of humanity and in many respects sought to put into practice the virtues preached by Christianity'. The overtones of religious faith surely resonated with Maclean, used as he was to hearing its tenets throughout his childhood.

As an Austrian Jew with a suspect past in 'sex-pol', Deutsch was an obvious target for liquidation too. His student visa was expiring, and although he used his cinema-magnate cousin Oscar as a guarantee to get it extended, his desire to stay on in Britain was also suspicious to the Soviets, as was the fact that Oscar was president of his local synagogue. Deutsch was recalled in November 1937, almost certainly just ahead of investigation by the British security services – had he been questioned, no doubt his psychological skills would have been valuable in any interrogatory jousting. His fate remains mysterious: he was possibly purged by Stalin; possibly executed by the Nazis after he had gone back to his native Austria; possibly drowned when the transport ship *Donbass*, on which he may have been travelling from Iceland to the United States in 1942 to take up a new post in Latin America, was sunk by German aircraft.

By the end of 1937, Maclean's first links to his recruitment, the charismatic and brilliant Arnold Deutsch and the passionate ideologue Teodor Maly, had been severed. The first reports of Stalin's purges to reach the Foreign Office gave him some strong clues as to what might have happened to his handlers. He no longer had his weekly meetings with his handler and nowhere to take his bulging briefcase on Friday evenings. His life as an agent of conscience seemed over almost before it had begun and just as it seemed he would be needed more than ever.

*

At the very moment when Maclean's secret life was suspended, the evidence that should have ended it altogether was about to emerge.

Walter Germanovich Krivitsky had been born Samuel Ginsberg in 1899 but adopted his new name, derived from the Slavic word for 'crooked' or 'twisted', when he joined the Bolsheviks in 1917. An ascetic workaholic, Krivitsky was chief illegal in the Netherlands, running agents across Northern Europe in the disguise of an antiquarian art bookseller in The Hague. It was an unlikely cover for a mining engineer, soldier and career agent-runner, as 'he knew nothing about art whatsoever'. Krivitsky, wise to the fate of so many of his colleagues, chose to ignore his own instructions to return home and defected in Paris instead. He gave his cogent and still committed reasons in *The Times* in December 1937: 'I have sufficient reason to know how the [show] trials are being got up and that innocent people are being killed. By remaining abroad I hope to assist in the rehabilitation of the ... so-called spies who in reality are the most devoted fighters for the causes of the working classes.'

On his visits to the marble-floored, granite edifice of Moscow Centre, Krivitsky had heard about the starry young agent in the Foreign Office. He could have brought Maclean's potent start in the world of espionage to a halt, but Krivitsky was not seen as worthy of a thorough debriefing in those more trusting times. He went to America when war became inevitable and was not brought to Britain until 1940. The Soviets, meanwhile, were out of contact with Maclean in the absence of Maly and Deutsch, were without an NKVD *rezidentura*, or station, in London and missed a wealth of intelligence as the storm clouds continued to gather over Europe.

There was also concern in Moscow that Maclean had been turned back to the British as a double agent: they assumed that either Krivitsky had been able to identify him or that Maly's contacts, including Lyric, had been unravelled after the Woolwich Arsenal case. They wondered if Maclean's own conscience might have started to prick him in his increasing maturity when he was not in weekly or daily contact with Maly or Deutsch, that he 'might be lost to us because we have gone far beyond the time period agreed for establishing contact with him'. But as always Lyric was desperate to feed his powerful hunger for secrecy, and completely unwittingly the Centre had stumbled on another craving of his – for love. The combination would turn out to be unorthodox in the extreme and yet wildly successful as the tradecraft rulebook was rewritten.

*

A new *rezident*, Grigori Grafpen, 'Sam', did not arrive in London until April 1938 to resuscitate the network. The skills lost with Maly and Deutsch were evident in an early telegram from Grafpen: he pointed out that 'next to the Embassy there is a park [Kensington Gardens] which is convenient . . . for holding meetings with agents, as one can simply give the appearance of having gone out for a walk', not understanding that a Russian in an ill-fitting suit emerging from the Embassy to meet a tall, well-tailored English diplomat might well be noticed and questioned. Luckily for him this was never put to the test because immediately after Grafpen's arrival he was cabled with the news that a handler was being sent from New York and was to be used as the full-time liaison for Lyric. A rendez-vous, between Lyric and the young, attractive and inexperienced (in agent-running terms, if not in life) 'Norma', was fixed for 10 April at the Empire Cinema, Leicester Square. This was arranged by her calling him with a pre-agreed 'wrong number' code to enquire about 'Doctor Wilson's surgery hours'. She would be holding A. J. Cronin's *The Citadel*, he would have a copy of *Time* magazine which he would switch from one hand to another. He would ask if she had seen his friend Karl, she would say she had seen him on 7 January. Then the briefing could start.

Norma's real name was Kitty Harris. She had been born in Whitechapel, on the impoverished eastern fringes of London in 1899 to parents from Białystok. Her family emigrated to Canada, where she started work in a cigarette factory at the age of twelve, cementing her belief in the rights of exploited workers and leading to her enrolment in 1923 in the Communist Party. The cigarette-factory work, with its associations with Bizet's tragic heroine in the opera *Carmen*, along with her dark hair, flashing eyes and neat, boyish figure, was to earn her her first code-name of 'Gypsy'. After moving to Chicago Kitty fell in with (and married, bigamously on his side as he had a wife and son in Russia) Earl Browder, who became secretary of the Communist Party of the United States. She travelled with him in Russia and worked as a courier on his behalf in Shanghai, before leaving him to go to Moscow for training and on to London to get Lyric speedily back on track.

When Kitty made contact with him, Maclean leapt at the opportunity to be of use again. He wrote via her to Moscow to say 'How glad' he was 'to be in touch and working again'. He tried to lay to rest any fears that he had been turned and expressed his eagerness to get the flow of material going: 'As you will have heard, I have no reason to think that my position is not quite sound, and that the arrangements we have made for work should not be all right … I will let you have, as before, all I can, which will chiefly be the printed dispatches & telegrams and particularly interesting papers as come my way.' But this declaration of his single-minded service to Moscow also gave away the immediate personal turn his professional relationship had taken with Kitty. Their new status emerged when Maclean signed off his first letter to Moscow since coming under Kitty's control. He sent 'best greetings to Otto and Theo' and signed off with his own code-name, Lyric, which he was not supposed to know. This caused consternation. In the perceived operational need to keep every agent as isolated as possible from the workings of the wider network, it was a serious breach given the atmosphere of suspicion in the Lubyanka building that housed Moscow Centre. For anyone other than such a star agent, it would have been the end of his career in espionage, and a death sentence for Kitty if not for himself. Kitty saved them both by revealing the truth: she had told Lyric his name in their pillow talk, and what was more had told him that her own code-name was Norma. And that she loved him.

*

Norma had rented a ground-floor flat in Bayswater until Grafpen redeemed some of his own tradecraft failings by pointing out the inherent operational difficulties of that arrangement, such as that drawn curtains in daylight would attract attention or that someone standing outside could listen in to conversations, at which point she moved to an apartment upstairs. At the beginning of their work together, Maclean would leave his flat in Oakley Street in the evening twice a week. His briefcase would be crammed with documents, even though Glading's trial had led to a warning in the Foreign Office that green (secret) papers should 'as far as possible' not be taken out of the office and that 'red' (most secret) ones never should be. But nobody checked because they assumed that the edict would be heeded. Maclean would take a taxi for some distance before getting out on a street corner, walk a bit and then hail another cab which he would pay off around the corner from his destination. Kitty would photograph the documents and he would write down anything else that he had retained in his remarkable memory. One of the reasons that Moscow had decided that a woman was a suitable handler for Maclean was that they would have to meet often, so prolific was his suppy of intelligence, and a couple was a good disguise; the other, more insightful reason was that it would recharge Maclean's excitement in productivity. As Stalin's great spy-master, General Alexander Orlov, had written in his *Handbook of Counter-Intelligence and Guerrilla Warfare*, 'idealistic young women' who became agent-handlers 'acted as a powerful stimulus' for upper-class young Englishmen, deprived of female company at their private schools. But what had never been in any security service handbook was that a full-blown affair should blossom in the relationship between agent and handler.

One evening in May 1938, Maclean came for their assignment with a bunch of roses, a bottle of wine and a box with a gold locket on a chain, a bold gesture that smacked of inexperience and eagerness to love. They had dinner sent over from a local restaurant and Kitty made them a favourite dish from her Canadian childhood, pancakes with maple syrup. They listened to Glenn Miller on her wireless set as they ate. Afterwards they went to her bedroom and made love. For a trained handler this was an astonishing development. The evening ignited a passion in Maclean that was fuelled by his subliminal need for fulfilment in a furtive private life, release of the tension generated by espionage and the months without contact or praise for his work, not to mention the sexual education that his second, much older, more experienced lover could bring him. In revealing to Deutsch that he 'had an aversion to girls of his own class', he had bared himself in a way that he did to very few people in his life. In Kitty he had found a mature woman who had not been brought up in the rigidity of Sir Donald's shadow nor in proximity to the British public school system, and it changed his previously elusive confidence as he stood on the threshold of the most rewarding years of his double career.

Kitty owed her survival not only to her honesty but to Maclean's value to Moscow. Paradoxically, he had proved himself to be a true and singular agent through what could have been a catastrophic error: any double agent would have been much more careful than breezily to run the risk of giving away code-names. However, new names were in order for them both: Maclean became the much more prosaic 'Stuart', Kitty 'Ada'.

*

It was a relief for Maclean to have the escape valve of his new lover, helping to alleviate the pressure arising from his hard work and from what was happening in Europe. She at least understood his politics and he could express to her what he had to keep hidden behind his façade. His new swagger earned him the nickname of 'Fancy-Pants' Maclean to distinguish him from the exceptionally good-looking man of action Fitzroy 'Fitz-Whiskers' Maclean, then serving in the Moscow Embassy and observing the kangaroo courts of the show trials. The first Foreign Office steps taken by Fancy-Pants had been so steady that Frederick Hoyer Millar, Assistant Private Secretary to the Foreign Secretary, wrote to Sir Eric Phipps, Ambassador in Paris, suggesting that as one of the current Third Secretaries there had asked to be transferred to Moscow ('rather an odd taste') he be replaced by 'Maclean, who has done extremely well during his first two years here and is one of the mainstays of the Western Department. He is a very nice individual indeed and has plenty of brains and keenness. He is, too, nice-looking and ought, we think, to be a success in Paris from the social as well as the work point of view.' These were all the requisite qualities for the high-flyer. On being told of his new, timely and prestigious posting, to be taken up in the last week of September, Maclean was 'naturally delighted', and made the unorthodox request to Moscow that Kitty accompany him. His confidence in both roles had been greatly boosted by his doubly secret love affair.

A couple of weeks before he boarded the boat-train to Paris, Maclean went on a fishing holiday in Scotland with Robin and Mary Campbell (*née* Ormsby-Gore) and Mary's father, William, who was Secretary of State for the Colonies. As they relaxed after the day's sport, Ormsby-Gore would talk about the worsening situation in Europe, revealing the government's views and plans, without of course realising that as soon as his guest got back to London any valuable gossip would be sent straight to Moscow. At the end of that month, Sir Vernon Kell, the first head of MI5 and the longest-serving head of any government department in the twentieth century, was able to declare confidently that Soviet 'activity in England is non-existent' – just as the new star of Soviet espionage in England was to take his spy skills and his lover-handler to mainland Europe at one of the most dramatic periods in its history.

5

City of Light

Donald Maclean began his only book with the words 'Foreign policy is an emotive subject.' By the time he hurriedly left Paris just ahead of the Nazis he felt a strong emotional undertow beneath the stormy surface of world events. On his arrival in September 1938, he must have been proud to have his first overseas posting as an up-and-coming official in the capital city of Britain's foremost ally, 'the only place in which a self-respecting young man could decently make his diplomatic debut', as his diplomatic contemporary Valentine Lawford put it. He was no doubt excited by his life as a spy, in which he was already outstripping his potential and by his passionate affair with his handler, who was shortly to join him. But he must have been nervous about what the next few months would bring, wondering how he would acquit himself in both his public and his hidden lives, and how foreign policy would play out in the face of Hitler's territorial ambitions.

France's Prime Minister Edouard Daladier had warned his British counterpart that Hitler's aim was to 'secure a domination of the continent in comparison with which the ambitions of Napoleon were feeble', yet he had been pushed by Chamberlain and his voters to join the appeasement of the German and Italian dictators and opt not to form a common diplomatic front with the Russians against the Führer. In the days immediately preceding Maclean's arrival the Red Army had mobilised sixty infantry divisions, sixteen cavalry divisions, three tank corps, twenty-two tank brigades and seventeen air brigades to stand by their treaty with Czechoslovakia, yet their diplomats were stressing that the Soviet

Union would not 'lend military assistance to Czechoslovakia except in common action with France'. Ambassador Phipps, who had previously served in Germany from where he sent back 'a stream of despatches, etching Nazi leaders in acid terms', was reporting the unwillingness of the French to slide into another war with Germany. He wrote to London on the same day that Maclean was being met by the uniformed Ernest Spurgeon, head Chancery servant, at the Gare du Nord: 'All that is best in France is against war. We none of us wish for it, but they refuse to prepare; they are against it at almost any price.'

Negotiations over Czechoslovakia and the worsening situation in Spain made for a dismal European outlook. Prime Minister Neville Chamberlain's policy of appeasement (which was driven in part by the need to give Britain time to rearm, as some had been advocating for rather longer than he had) had culminated in the Munich Agreement of September 1938. Just before the Agreement was signed, Hermann Göring denounced the Czechs as 'a vile race of dwarfs without any culture': the German-speaking Czech Sudetenland had been sacrificed to the increasingly territorial and violently racist Nazi regime.

As a part of the surge of art and literature which crisis encourages, Louis MacNeice pointed out both the short-termism and the inhumanity of the Munich Agreement:

Glory to God for Munich.
And stocks go up and wrecks
Are salved and politicians' reputations
Go up like Jack-on-the-Beanstalk; only the Czechs
Go down and without fighting.

Munich had shocked those on the left; they agreed with Stalin who could see it would do nothing but 'whet the aggressor's appetite'. Maclean consoled himself and justified his espionage when he said that he believed that the information he passed on helped the Soviet government 'throw whatever weight it had against the betrayal of Czechoslovakia.' Stalin himself had not been invited to the meeting as according to Lord Halifax, now Foreign Secretary, there had not been time to issue the invitation. Within the next year Stalin would find his own accommodation with Hitler, which would shock many of the young idealists of Cambridge days, already shaken by what they knew of 'the other side of the moon, the corruption of Stalinism', enough to turn them away from Communism. This soul-searching was to have potentially catastrophic results for the Magnificent Five. The onrush of war would also bring Walter Krivitsky out of hiding to Britain to tell all he knew of the important Foreign Office spy. Paris was a short posting for Maclean, but the one in which the seeds of jeopardy were sown and the patterns of his conduct under stress emerged that were later to flourish and almost overwhelm him.

*

Maclean's office was a small room in the Chancery building, once the stables of Pauline Borghese's beautiful house in the Faubourg Saint Honoré, acquired by Wellington from Napoleon's sister and turned into the British Embassy after he had defeated her brother at Waterloo. On 30 September the new arrival leaned out of the window to watch the crowds cheering Daladier, back from Munich, as he slowly made his way towards the Elysée Palace. On the same day, Chamberlain arrived back in London to announce in a rather lower key not only 'peace with honour' but 'peace for our time' with Herr Hitler. Herr Hitler himself, a dismayed MI6 operative concluded, was 'at the beginning of a "Napoleonic era" and [the Reich's] rulers contemplate a great extension of German power'.

As he watched the ecstatic throng, Maclean must have felt that tug between decisions made in government that he would have to see through and objectives that he felt to be right for the world. It was a frustration that was to oppress him on many occasions, eventually to the point of collapse. The pusillanimity of the Munich Agreement, offering Germany expansion to the east and leaving Russia to stand alone against the tide of fascism in the final months of the Spanish Civil War, was symbolised by the flimsiness of 'the paper which bears his [Hitler's] name upon it' that Chamberlain brandished at Heston Aerodrome on his return from Germany. On a human scale, the agreement was shocking: the Czechs were not allowed into the conference room during the negotiations, yet the Sudetens were expected to 'leave only with the clothes they stood up in. Homes, furniture, animals all had to be abandoned.' Two British diplomats resigned from the service over Munich, but, much as he admired them for doing so, that was not an option for Maclean, who had his secret outlet to ease his frustration.

As often in his life, Maclean dealt with his anxiety partly by hurling himself into hard work, salving any conflict in his conscience by doing his exceptional best both for London and for Moscow. Yet with diplomacy so much in the open there was little of value to the Kremlin in his daily round. The Soviets needed to gauge the willingness, or lack of willingness, of the British and French to stand up to Hitler, and could read Munich for themselves. Maclean saw copies of virtually all the Embassy's correspondence, and his room-mate reported that he 'was always willing to take over the more boring jobs. He never frowned if I had an engagement to keep or wanted to leave early.' Missing any sort of official engagement would not have been a trial to someone who disliked formal events, was ambitiously hard-working and wanted the opportunity to gather as much material as possible.

In the brief period before Kitty arrived, Maclean passed on information to a Soviet illegal via the accepted protocols of a visual-recognition plan followed by verbal keys. As Philby found after the war had started, these could involve standing near the Thomas Cook office in the Place de la Madeleine holding a copy of the *Daily Mail*. When approached by a man carrying the same paper, the spy would ask, 'Where is the Café Henri around here?' To which the answer would come, 'It's near the Place de la République,' and the release of information could begin.

It was, at least, an operational relief to Maclean that these encounters could be consigned to the past, and a personal relief when his preferred handler arrived in Paris in December. Kitty was escorted by Grafpen, who was himself on his way back to Russia to stand trial followed by five and a half years in a forced-labour camp as reward for his service abroad. The lovers were reunited in an outdoor café in the Luxembourg Gardens. Kitty had chosen the spot because she was nervous that they might run into some of his old Cambridge chums who frequented the Latin Quarter were they to meet there. She was also clear that if he saw 'any member of our service that you knew in England, you have to avoid meeting them or talking to them … You have to tell them that you have nothing to do with us any more.' It was basic self-preservation in the atmosphere of purge and defection, particularly in the wake of her blunder in London.

Kitty soon found herself reporting to Moscow that she had nothing to deliver; although Maclean had been working hard, often all night, and still produced volumes of paper, he said he had not come across anything fresh. Diplomacy was being carried out above board. Moscow Centre, collectively anxious to feed Stalin's paranoid need for intelligence and individually anxious to save their skins, not unnaturally questioned whether their relationship might be getting in the way of good espionage. 'This combination of circumstances is not good for Stuart [Maclean]. Is this relationship justified? Does Ada [Harris] report to us about Stuart? Is she detached enough to observe him and notice changes in him that might indicate his loyalty to us?' Had the psychologically astute Deutsch still been in place he might have pointed out that the relationship could be a spur to productivity, but the Centre could not comprehend the emotional involvement of agent and handler.

Kitty's end-of-year report for 1938 gave a dark picture of Maclean's state of mind: 'While in London he could act as he liked. He had his friends and the opportunity to read a lot. Things are different in Paris. He leads a completely different social life. He must attend dinners and receptions … He hates this atmosphere.' She commented that Stuart was spending more off-duty time on the bohemian Left Bank, drinking heavily in the company of Marxist intellectuals, which at least Moscow would have been pleased about. Stuart himself sent word to Moscow that he 'was doing little' in the post-Munich gloom of late 1938 and that this upset him. He was becoming withdrawn and solitary, disengaging from the diplomatic life that served the outer, reputable man so well and provided him with the secret wherewithal to satisfy his inner desires. It would have been the NKVD's style to blame the handler ahead of the spy or the political reality, but once again Kitty's relationship with Maclean was enough to keep her in place with her sole charge. Pavel Sudoplatov, head of the 'death squads' that carried out 'special tasks' in the 1930s and known as 'the most sinister man in the Communist system', evaluated Kitty as 'a staffer with a flexible mind, capable, disciplined, and interested in the work but she lacks concentration and has no feeling for technical matters'.

Kitty had indeed proved her technical incompetence in London: she had been upbraided for sending blank reels of film on an occasion when she claimed her nerves and impatience had stopped her allowing the twenty-two-second exposure required. Luckily for her it was before her affair with Maclean became known. She did not have a flat in Paris at first so their official meetings took place in cafés or on walks at which Maclean would tell her Embassy goings-on. Their unofficial meetings took place in Kitty's bed-sitting room. When she found somewhere to rent they could meet as they did in London, and most often ended up in bed. When Kitty had photographed documents which did not need to be returned, the lovers would tear the papers into tiny pieces, put them into a large enamel bowl, sprinkle washing powder on top and add hot water; Maclean would then stir the mixture and Kitty 'would knead the mess into something that looked like porridge' until the paste could be flushed down the toilet without blocking the drain.

Although none of this was in Orlov's, or any other spymaster's, handbook, the Soviets stuck by their handler and their agent despite his being in the espionage doldrums. They both acknowledged his growing diplomatic potency and attempted to kick-start the flow of important intelligence by ensuring that Kitty was primed to brief him on where the Soviets stood on various issues. Not only would he understand what was most important to them, but he might also be able to bring some influence to bear in his daily round. This reverse diplomacy was important to a man increasingly regarded as influential, not least because the Russians felt, with some justification, that since Munich the British press had been dominated by anti-Soviet appeasers.

Kitty was right to highlight Maclean's lack of involvement in social life. The social aspect of any posting was then considered essential to diplomacy, as it is today, and more so in the Paris Embassy than most, as Hoyer Millar had emphasised in his recommendation of Maclean to Phipps. Maclean would not have been expected to entertain much himself as a bachelor Third Secretary, but he was supposed to play his part in Embassy social life. He rented 'a large, rather gloomy apartment' at 11 rue de Bellechasse, near Les Invalides. He lacked the private income of most of his fellow diplomats in the Foreign Office club, and he was sensitive to financial and class differentials. His apartment was sparsely furnished; guests sat 'on collapsing sofas of orange-crates'. He did not attempt to hide his political reading matter, and 'a book-shelf held a few of his Marxist texts, some Tauchnitz [a German literary publisher] paperbacks and the orange [sic] jackets of editions from Victor Gollancz's Left Book Club'. 'The food was primitive, the wine was French, red but definitely *ordinaire*,' as one sophisticated fellow diplomat commented. It was so uncomfortable that Lady Maclean went to stay elsewhere when she came to visit her son. In spite of Maclean not being as well off and not as stuffy as some of his contemporaries, when Patrick Reilly passed through Paris on his way back from a League of Nations council meeting in January 1939, he was surprised to be told by Maclean that the hard-up diplomat had never travelled on the Paris Metro.

*

There were only twelve on the Embassy staff altogether, and Maclean's withdrawal was noticed, as was the increasing consumption of drink used to mask his feelings. When Mary and Robin Campbell came to dinner in the rue de Bellechasse, they were surprised to find a whole bottle of claret by the elbow of each guest. On another occasion, Robert Cecil and his wife took him to see a gloomy film, *La Bête Humaine*, based on a Zola tale of murder involving the 'drunken degradation' of a wife, her abuser and her lover. They 'tried to cheer Donald up by taking him home for a night-cap; but he slouched off into the darkness, scarcely pausing to say good-night'.

Cecil, who had been intimidated by Maclean's political censoriousness at Cambridge, was 'struck by the change' in the 'assured, authoritative young man' he had known recently who now 'seemed nervous and ill at ease'. He was very 'tense ... in a chronic state of anxiety'. Cecil put this down to the strains of diplomatic life, a correct enough assessment, if not the full picture. Gone was the confidence of the previous year in London. Maclean's old friend and his political mentor since schooldays, James Klugmann, had been working in Paris for some time as head of the Rassemblement Mondial des Etudiants, but Maclean did not seek him out. When they bumped into one another on a train, 'Maclean buried himself in *The Times* and killed conversation with a few curt answers.' Whether or not Klugmann, himself one of those Deutsch had approached, knew that the man who had looked up to him so much had become a spy, it was a bitter moment. This gaucheness derived not from the requirement to distance himself from his past associations but from the profound discomfort he felt. His double life was not easy to sustain at that stage when one country was drifting towards war and the true faith of the other demanded peace. And it was in this defining power-play at the end of Maclean's first year in Paris that all the British believers had to make their choice between adherence to the creed which they had espoused over the previous decade and the move to simpler patriotism. To combine both was possible, but it took nerve-shredding courage.

*

The Nazi–Soviet Pact made the Second World War inevitable, and was arguably the lowest point of British diplomacy in the century.

In late 1938 the German Ambassador in Moscow intimated to Berlin that the Soviet Union had been more upset by France and Britain acting without it at the Munich talks than by Germany's own conduct, and tentative moves were made towards setting up trade negotiations to enable the Nazis to meet their four-year economic and rearmament plan. Towards the end of January 1939 these negotiations became public. Vernon Bartlett, a journalist on the London *News Chronicle* known to be close to the Soviet Ambassador, Ivan Maisky, wrote on the 27th of that month that 'At present, the Soviet government obviously has no intention of giving any help to Great Britain and France if the latter come into conflict with Germany and Italy.' On 30 January, for the first time in six years, Hitler offered no criticism of the Soviet Union in the speech marking his accession to power. The British were slow to realise that they had to act: in February Chamberlain became the first Prime Minister since the eve of the Revolution in 1917 to dine at the Soviet Embassy in London, but there was no hint of forming an alliance in any matters to do with international security or defence. After Germany had occupied the rest of Czechoslovakia in March, Chamberlain wrote that he had 'the most profound distrust of Russia. I have no belief whatever in her ability to maintain an effective offensive, even if she wanted to. And I distrust her motives, which seem to me to have little connection with our ideas of liberty...' This distrust shaped the events of the next few months.

In April and May, the British asked for a pledge that the Soviet Union would come to their aid and the aid of their Empire if needed, but when Moscow responded by suggesting British and French support in protecting the Soviet Union's own neighbouring states the proposal was rejected. The British, certain of their diplomatic standing, were guilty of a 'complete failure to grasp the psychology of such men as Hitler and Mussolini. These Englishmen perceive them as they would a *business man* from the City or an English *country gentleman*... Aggressors have an entirely different mentality!', as the more subtly minded Maisky observed, while carefully omitting Stalin from his list of dictators. Stalin now dismissed his pro-Western Foreign Minister, Litvinov, and replaced him with Vyacheslav Molotov, the beady-eyed chief Soviet negotiator and the man who was to see his ministry through world war and into cold war. No wonder Maclean was withdrawn as he watched his country being torn away from Russia.

He was at least useful again. All the traffic about the negotiations from the British side went through Paris en route to the Moscow Embassy. He was able to send it via his trysts with Kitty to keep Molotov one step ahead. In the last week of May Halifax told Daladier that if necessary (and it went very much against the grain for him and Chamberlain) the British would be in favour of reciprocity with Russia without French support, and on the 24th sent their terms to Paris for approval. When this document was forwarded to the Russian Foreign Ministry on the 27th, Molotov 'read it giving every sign that he was familiar in advance with its contents'. Thanks to Stuart and Ada's work he had indeed had a day's start on the news. By the end of June, there was agreement between the French, British and Soviets on a treaty under which each would help the others, and countries on the borders of the Soviet Union, specifically Poland, in the event of attack. At the same time MI6 decided not to circulate to the Foreign Office a report that they had had from an agent in Prussia code-named 'the Baron' revealing that German–Soviet talks were advancing because they could not understand how one of their own agents could have such good sources.

The Anglo-French delegation then took the radically odd step of going to Moscow by boat and train rather than by aeroplane: Admiral Sir Reginald Aylmer Ranfurly Plunkett-Ernle-Erle-Drax,* head of the military mission, told Ambassador Maisky at lunch on 4 August that they were travelling this way because a plane would be too uncomfortable for twenty of them and their luggage; they were using a freighter rather than a faster warship so as not to have to make twenty naval officers give up their cabins. Maisky couldn't believe that he was hearing 'Such tender feelings and such tactful manners!' The *City of Exeter* arrived in Leningrad on 9 August. The talks went badly from the start: the British team had not been given the authority to negotiate the necessary detail and were unprepared for Soviet demands for safe passage of their troops through

---

* Drax was the holder of the Order of the Bath, which the Russians could only translate as 'washtub', much to their own amusement.

the countries around their borders, which the Poles bitterly resisted as being tantamount to a partition of their country. When they did receive credentials to negotiate, 'they turned out to be so general and vague that it became clear to us that London and Paris had no serious intention of reaching an agreement' with Moscow.

Hitler was in close contact with Stalin at all times. He assumed that with the French and British so unwilling to go to war – as they had demonstrated the previous year at Munich – he could occupy the Free City of Danzig, gaining access to a valuable port without any trouble. Even as the Anglo-French negotiations were being prolonged, those of Hitler's Foreign Minister Joachim von Ribbentrop were accelerating: in contrast to the Anglo-French ocean voyage, he flew into Moscow on 23 August with thirty-two 'attendants', ready to sign a pact: the Germans found the airport bedecked with swastikas in welcome. Stalin had come to the real-isation that Hitler was intending to invade Poland come what may, and that although the Western allies would come to its defence, Russia would be open to attack from the German military machine and needed to buy time to rearm. Hitler understood, reportedly after watching the Soviet May Day military parade on film, that it was more critical to have Russia neutralised. It did not emerge until after the war that the two countries had secretly agreed to divide up Poland and the Baltic states from the start. Hitler ordered the attack on Poland to begin even before the signatures had been added to the pact because it was important to launch it before the mid-September rains. The Wehrmacht duly invaded on 1 September, and two days later – honouring their earlier guarantee of Polish independence – Britain and France declared war on Germany. Peace in Europe had barely lasted two decades, and the League of Nations Union that Maclean had supported so assiduously at Gresham's seemed a long time ago.

*

The effect of the Nazi–Soviet Pact, moving from a trade agreement to a high-stakes handshake that condemned France and Britain to fight alone in a matter of months, was a shattering blow to Paris and London. It was a 'bombshell' to the NKVD's agents, according to Moscow Centre, even if Maclean was able to keep a close eye on the talks and was well aware of the consequences of their failure from the British perspective. As usual, Maclean was careful to leave no record of his reaction to the devastating alliance at the time. Looking back on his life he saw it as the result of 'catastrophically irrational policies' as the leadership on both sides 'sought to exercise hegemony'. He justified the Soviet leadership's part in it as 'subjectively aimed at building socialism' but admitted that it had 'objectively stunted and twisted its development' and 'nearly destroyed' it as a result.

John Cairncross saw the pact in less abstract terms as he bitterly concluded that 'the ignorance and stupidity of the Chamberlain-dominated Allies had resulted in the most inept diplomatic negotiations since those between England and the American rebels 200 years earlier'; Cairncross 'would have broken with the KGB [sic], whatever the consequences' for his personal safety if the pact had remained in place any longer than it did. Easy to say with hindsight.

Kim Philby, for the only time in his career, wobbled: 'What's going to happen to the single-front struggle against fascism now?' he asked his new controller. Guy Burgess broke off his holiday and drove back from Antibes when he heard the news, even leaving his precious car on the dockside at Calais (not the last time he would leave a car on the dockside at a pivotal moment in his life), and called on his friend the fellow-traveller Goronwy Rees who 'denounced the treachery of the Soviet Union and said that the Russians had made war inevitable'. Burgess replied that the Soviet Union had every right to protect itself. Rees, who had just joined up, told him that he never wanted 'to have anything to do with the Comintern for the rest of my life ... Or with you, if you really are one of their agents.' Burgess self-protectively claimed that he was going to give up his secret work, which seemed to reassure his friend, yet Rees was to prove a 'ticking bomb'. The ever-melodramatic Burgess was so panicked that he would be exposed that he went so far as to propose assassinating his great friend. Moscow Centre wisely refused to countenance what at the time would have been a hot-headed move which could jeopardise their valuable British assets at the very moment when they were shut out of official diplomatic channels by the pact. Maclean could never forgive someone who had vigorously expounded the cause and then deserted it, and years later publicly denounced Rees as 'a traitor' at a moment when he himself could ill afford such talk.

Arthur Koestler, who only a few years before had described his coming to Communism as 'mental rapture' as 'the whole universe falls into pattern', had survived being imprisoned by Franco. His faith had wavered when he saw Russian interests put ahead of Spanish Republican needs and when trumped-up charges were brought against Central European comrades, but the signing of the treaty destroyed his loyalty to the cause he had been espousing so vociferously, in spite of the left being the 'better, optimistic part of humanity because it believed in social evolution'. He later commented that 'No death is so sad and final as the death of an illusion.' If Maclean was mourning his own illusion, he nonetheless had to keep the visible part of himself, the daily life of working to his government's tune, visible. He almost certainly saw the left-wing Paris paper *L'Humanité* but was too wily a diplomat to show that he agreed with its view that the pact was 'the supreme effort of Stalin to prevent the threatening imperialist war'. The finality of the pact came home to those of the left, including Arthur Koestler, as war became inevitable: 'it is hard for men to fight if they only know what they are fighting against and not what they are fighting for'.

Anthony Blunt, completing the ring of Cambridge agents who remained faithful, affected a nonchalance after his exposure in 1979 that he may not have felt at the time when he said that the pact 'was simply a tactical necessity for Russia to gain time ... to re-arm and to get stronger to resist what was clearly going to happen'. The commitment of many other prominent Communists was extinguished and the CPGB changed its leadership to present itself as an organisation working for the Comintern ideal of world peace through Communism. Extraordinarily, given the suspicious tendencies of the NKVD, there were no doubts expressed in Moscow as to the loyalty of the remaining spies in the face of the 'bombshell': this brutal distrust would follow, much to the detriment of their own intelligence gathering. The Soviets had of course bought themselves some time, but they still needed first-class material for whatever came next.

Louis MacNeice, who never actually joined the Party but for whom 'comrade became a more tender term than lover', wrote more optimistically from the darkness right at the end of his *Autumn Journal*, published in 1939:

> There will be time to audit
> The accounts later, there will be sunlight later,
> And the equation will come out at last.

Maclean's office colleague Valentine Lawford, hurriedly recalled from leave in England at the end of August, failed to see the lackadaisical British part in the Nazi–Soviet Pact and was 'appalled by German and Russian hypocrisy, duplicity and cynicism'. Maclean could not show his frustration with the progress of the negotiations and the Anglo-French hauteur that he had observed so closely. When Lawford, to lighten the atmosphere, 'declared that the only course left for decent people like us was to join the Polish or Hungarian cavalry and die fighting against hopeless odds', Maclean 'professed to agree and laughed uproariously'. Uproarious laughter is not something anyone associated with Maclean at any point in his life, and in its falsity suggests the conflict he was experiencing with his loyalties, and the anxiety he felt about his future. Meanwhile, he could continue to work as hard as ever for the Foreign Office in the hope that he would at the same time gather material that would be important to Moscow.

*

In November 1939 there was a build-up of several hundred thousand Finnish and Soviet troops on both sides of their common border, swiftly followed by Soviet incursions into a region which contained nickel and ore mines vital for the German military machine. Britain provided aircraft and, with the French, considered sending troops in response to a request from Finland; at a Cabinet meeting on 29 January 1940 it was minuted that 'the Prime Minister observed that events seemed to be leading the Allies to open hostilities with Russia'. Ambassador Maisky had commented in his diary the previous December on 'the frenzied anti-Soviet campaign in Britain' caused by the invasion; by now, 'the general curve of Anglo-Soviet relations continues its downward path'.

The British and French began to hatch a plan to land around 35,000 'volunteers' (conscripted men would be too interventionist as neither country was at war with the Soviet Union) at Narvik to seize control of the iron-ore fields, stop the Soviet invasion of Finland and gain the side benefit of bringing Norway and Sweden into the war on the side of the allies. The talks took place in Paris, which was ideal for Maclean given his access and the speed at which he could gather and transmit intelligence. They involved discussion about attacking the essential Soviet oil fields at Baku, a pet project of Churchill's for the past twenty years. On 21 April 1940, Foreign Secretary Halifax reported to the Cabinet that the French had asked, via Ambassador Phipps, for discussions about 'operations in the Caucasus'. Before any such operations could take place, but not before the Germans had seized Norway and Denmark, triggering Chamberlain's replacement by Churchill, Stalin withdrew his troops from Finland. Although it is not always possible to assess the precise impact of a spy's work, in this instance Stalin's reversal took place just as if he had knowledge of the talks and the Cabinet discussions. One of the ironies of the episode is that the retreating Russian soldiers left some half-burnt codebooks behind in their haste: in years to come, these helped to set the clock ticking on their star British agent.

*

Maclean was to come under much more immediate danger. He had survived Russian suspicions following Walter Krivitsky's defection two years earlier, but now the former NKVD general was, unknown to him, once again posing a threat. Krivitsky, dismissively described by the British security services as 'a small man, a Pole' where others saw 'an explosive inner strength' behind his 'menacing blue eyes', had operated at a high level, working in the Red Army Intelligence Department since 1919. By 1937 he was a major-general with 'responsibility for Soviet secret operations in all Western European countries'. This job description alone made Krivitsky a sure candidate for purging, even before his disloyalty in choosing to warn a fellow illegal, Ignace Reiss, of his impending assassination, following which he defected in Paris the year before Maclean's arrival there. Reiss, also known as Ignace Poretsky and, less credibly, as Walter Scott, had seen the purge writing on the wall and absconded to Switzerland where the NKVD soon found him anyway. Krivitsky had lived with his wife and child in Paris and The Hague, and in a world where there was so little suspicion of Russians living and working abroad, his sieve-like art-bookseller cover story did not matter. He was disappointed by the lack of seriousness with which he was treated by the French government when he tried to warn them about Stalin's first overtures to Hitler and sailed for New York in November 1938.

After Krivitsky's expedited release from Ellis Island he was introduced to Isaac Don Levine, an émigré from present-day Belorussia, a journalist, author of biographies of Lenin and Stalin, and publisher of letters from Soviet prisoners. Levine saw the commercial potential in the new arrival and soon they had signed up with the *Saturday Evening Post* to produce eight articles for the staggering sum of $5,000 each, to be split 50/50. The sensational serialisation ('My Flight From Stalin', 'Stalin's Hand in Spain', all parts of a book to be called *I Was Stalin's Agent*) caused outrage: the American left was appalled that he should be over-dramatising his story and betraying them by making up stories about Soviet machinations and brutality, most particularly as Krivitsky was accurately anticipating the unthinkable Nazi–Soviet Pact; the right failed to understand why a man who had held such positions was allowed to remain in their country. The Communist *New Masses* 'launched a savage campaign ... to the effect that Krivitsky was really an Austrian denizen of Paris night clubs who had never been a general in the army'. The British Foreign Office minuted in May that

Krivitsky's claims about Stalin's secret dealings with Hitler were 'twaddle', 'rigmarole' and 'directly contrary to all our other information', once again displaying an alarming lack of overt or covert insight into Soviet policy towards fascism.

On 4 September 1939, Britain's first full day of war with Germany, Levine, who believed that Soviet spies presented an immediate risk to British wartime security, went to the British Embassy on Massachusetts Avenue in Washington DC and met Victor Mallet, the chargé d'affaires. He got off on the wrong foot by saying he had been 'anti-British because of Palestine' but was now for them 'on general grounds, but still hopes that HMG will open the doors of Palestine to refugees'. Mallet replied with diplomatic understatement that Palestine 'might become rather a danger spot for refugees if the Mediterranean became a theatre of war'. They could then move on to the main point of the visit, which was the startling news that:

> he knew through Krivitsky that there were two Soviet agents working, one in the cipher room of the Foreign Office and one in what he called the 'Political Committee Cabinet Office' (?Committee of Imperial Defence). The name of the one in the Foreign Office is 'King'. He has for several years been passing everything on to Moscow for mercenary motives … [Krivitsky] does not know the name of the other man … the man was not acting for mercenary motives but through idealism … and may now be on our side owing to Stalin's treachery … The man is a Scotsman of very good family, a well-known painter and perhaps also a sculptor.

Krivitsky later said that that the 'Scotsman' 'wore a cape and dabbled in artistic circles' and commented that King's predecessor had been a spy who drank heavily and committed suicide. This fitted the description of a cipher clerk called Oldham, whose lonely, alcoholic death the security services later claimed in a propaganda move was an assassination. A brief investigation into Captain J. H. King, who did indeed work in the cipher room, soon turned up a mistress with £1,300 given to her by her lover in cash in a safe-deposit box. A confession from the crushed King (including the admission that he had passed information to his controller about the British reaction to the Nazi–Soviet Pact) preceded a trial in camera in early October on charges that 'in 1935, 1936 and 1937 [he] unlawfully did use certain information in his possession in a manner prejudicial to the safety and interests of the State'. King was sentenced to ten years' penal servitude.

King had been recruited by Maly's predecessor Hans Pieck in 1934, when he and his mistress were taken on an expensive motoring tour of Europe, which Pieck's wife described to Moscow as 'incredibly boring' and 'a real ordeal'. Encouraged by this swift success and proof of Krivitsky's truth-telling, Colonel Valentine Vivian of MI6, where he was in charge of Section V, counter-intelligence, suggested that they might now turn their attention to the 'ugly unsolved puzzle' of the other, less identifiable agent in the Foreign Office. They looked into the garbled description Krivitsky had given and realised that they would have to bring him over for interrogation if they were to get any further. Krivitsky, or 'Mr Walter Thomas', boarded a Royal Navy submarine in New York, spent the ten-day crossing reading *Gone with the Wind* and arrived in England on 19 January 1940.

At first the interviews, held at the St Ermin's Hotel in London's Victoria (where, among notable espionage events, Kim Philby had been recruited) did not go well: Krivitsky denied all knowledge of any Soviet secret activities in Britain whatsoever, and seemed unable to remember the names of any of his friends and associates in Europe. After this frustrating start, MI5 realised that this amnesia was due to understandable terror arising from his knowledge of the purges that any admission would lead either to a '"full examination" as understood by citizens of the USSR' or his whereabouts becoming known to the NKVD with assassination the consequence. He even shied away from accepting a saccharine tablet in his tea (sugar was unavailable owing to rationing), convinced it was poison.

His interviewers, led by MI5's first female officer, the brilliant Jane Archer, finally got him 'to come out of his shell' by talking about King, and impressing him with what they already knew. He began to open up, and told how, via Maly, 'Imperial Council [by which he meant the Committee of Imperial Defence] information of high Naval, Military, Air Force and political importance' from 1936 on began to arrive in Moscow; he had seen the photographs of the documents that were sent from London. There were enough pages to make a book, and Stalin's copy had the original photographs attached to it. Krivitsky had 'little definite knowledge' of the sender of the material, but:

> is certain that the source is a young man, probably under thirty, an agent of Theodore Maly, that he was recruited as a Soviet agent on purely ideological grounds, and that he took no money for the information he obtained. He was almost certainly educated at Eton and Oxford and ... is a 'young aristocrat', but agrees that he may have arrived at this conclusion because he thought it was only young men of the nobility who were educated at Eton. He believes the source to have been the secretary or the son of one of the chiefs of the Foreign Office.

This is a garbled identification of Maclean, who had not been educated at Eton and Oxford, and was not an aristocrat although he had been to public school and Cambridge, and his father was a knight, so it is excusable given the near-impenetrable social hierarchy of British life for Krivitsky to have been confused on both counts. Sir Donald had not been high up in the Foreign Office but was in the Cabinet instead, quite an easy elision to make. There was no attempt to match this later description to the one given to Mallet in Washington, and include the artistic leanings of Maclean (who indeed moved among Chelsea artists and writers) and the Scottish angle, which would have radically narrowed the list of suspects. They had stopped a clear and visible leak with the lowlier King's imprisonment, but secrets from the pre-war Committee of Imperial Defence seemed not worth much now that war was under way. It was a mistake born of lack of suspicion and rigour that was to cost the West dearly, and was a remarkably close call for the unwitting spy.

Following his debriefing, which was at least useful in providing insight into the structure, reach and power of Russian intelligence, Krivitsky went back to Canada to join his wife and son. In February 1941, he checked into the Bellevue Hotel in Washington DC, where he was found by the maid next morning, the doors locked, fully dressed, no fewer than three suicide notes in the room, a massive head wound to his temple. The bullet was never found, but the wound was presumably from the gun near his body, although the weapon was lying on the same side as the exit rather than the entry hole of the bullet, and at quite a stretch from the dead man's arm. The rooms on either side were occupied and the gun had no silencer, yet the shot in the night had not been heard by anyone. Krivitsky's lawyer, Louis Waldman, shouted murder. His client had said to him more than once, 'If ever I am found dead and it looks like an accident or a suicide, don't believe it. They are after me. They have tried before.' In spite of the doubts of the US intelligence community and most of those who knew Krivitsky, it remained a suicide on the books. Krivitsky's wife, Tonia, believed he was forced to shoot himself to keep her and their son safe. Whatever the truth of Krivitsky's death, while he was being questioned in London the oblivious Maclean was still working in Paris, still meeting and sleeping with Norma and destroying superfluous documents by making a flushable paste of them. The long arm of the NKVD was very much in evidence to protect him and ruthlessly despatch anyone who betrayed or threatened their highest-calibre spies, particularly those who had remained loyal in spite of 'Stalin's treachery' as Krivitsky saw it. Even after Krivitsky's death, his evidence continued to smoulder in the files for years, until Kim Philby decided it needed another airing.

*

For the next few years, Donald Maclean was going to be assessed by both sides on the basis of his prodigious capabilities in wartime. But only after his most important, most lasting and most puzzling relationship had begun.

6

Left Bank

One snowy evening in December 1939, Donald Maclean and Robert McAlmon were 'prowling around' the Rive Gauche. They went into the Café Flore, haunt of Sartre, de Beauvoir and other left-wing sages, artists and philosophers, where 'they saw through the steam and smoke the waif-like face and trim figure of Melinda Marling'. McAlmon made the introductions and the central human drama of Maclean's life, one of loyalty and secrecy, a circle of desertion and reconciliation, of love and solitariness, had started.

*

Maclean, as Kitty Harris had reported in December 1938, hated the stuffy artificiality of the social life associated with his posting. Every time the Ambassador came into the room, the other diplomats had to stand, and even if they had met earlier in the day they had to shake hands with each other on meeting again in a different setting. Maclean's inclination towards the more intellectual and raffish side of life, channelling Cecil the bohemian from his *Granta* 'interview' of a few years before, led him more naturally to the Left Bank with its bars, cafés and artists. He was a popular figure in the 'heterogeneous society' around Saint Germain des Prés. His taste in friends turned more naturally to Bob McAlmon than to the delightful but traditional (and Foreign Office traditional at that) Cecils. McAlmon, in his mid-forties, had escaped his South Dakota upbringing and moved to New York in 1920, where he had worked on a small poetry magazine and life-modelled for an artists' colony. Homosexual (he wrote a novel, *The Scarlet Pansy*, under a pseudonym), he had married a British shipping heiress, a lesbian, the following year, which gave him the money to move to Paris where he found work as an assistant to James Joyce, typing and retyping *Ulysses*. He formed a small publishing company, Contact Editions, specialising in works written by the expatriate community, including Ford Madox Ford, Gertrude Stein, William Carlos Williams and Nathaniel West. The previous year his memoir *Being Geniuses Together* ('the office boy's revenge', as his former employer Joyce put it), written with Kay Boyle, had been published and was a great discussion point among the denizens of the Left Bank. Although McAlmon's later years were ones of embittered disappointment, alcoholism and early death, in 1939 he represented to Maclean all that was glamorous about Parisian literary life, and sexual freedom.

Maclean enjoyed his friendship with those like McAlmon whom he did not meet in the course of his duties, but he was conventional enough to want a wife. Arnold Deutsch had identified 'the infantile need' for the 'praise and reassurance' that he did not get from his father. He needed to be admired and loved. Kitty Harris was feeding that need as well as his craving for a hidden, illicit life: it did not get much more hidden and illicit than an affair with an older woman that could not be revealed to the world because she was also his handler. In Melinda Goodlett Marling he found the person he could share his secret life with, who admired him and his intellect, who was in tune with his politics without being particularly interested in them. He single-mindedly set his cap at her.

Melinda was pale-skinned and slight with curly, dark hair. She had been born in Chicago in 1917, four years after Maclean, and was brought up with her two younger sisters, Harriet and Catherine, by their strong-willed mother after their parents separated in 1928. Her mother was also named Melinda and also the child of a broken home. Melinda the younger was used to living a fractured life, and to being with others who did the same. The close-knit Marling girls did not often see their father. Divorce was uncommon at that time and in that society (Francis Marling, who had emigrated to the US as a child, was the advertising manager for the Pure Oil Company in Chicago) and may explain why Mrs Marling took her daughters to live in Switzerland for two years from 1929 to 1931, where they were schooled at Vevey, near Lausanne. Switzerland remained a place of good memories and escape for mother and daughter, and eventually became the last European home for them both.

After her divorce had been finalised, Melinda senior married Hal Dunbar, who came from a moneyed Oklahoma family and was a vice-president of Whitaker Paper. The family lived the New England life of the comfortably off, with an apartment on New York's Park Avenue and a farm at South Egremont, Massachusetts. Melinda finished her schooling at the prestigious Spence School, and was not keen to take her education further. Her stepfather, who was funding this existence, resented the fact that she 'went to top-rate schools ... but proved to be a problem child' who abandoned her studies. From time to time she 'would have pangs of conscience at her lazy, carefree life' and set out to find a job: she took a secretarial course and worked for a while in Macy's book department, but found it hard to know what she wanted, craving travel, excitement and ultimately danger. In 1938, with a little inherited money and a favourable exchange rate, she decided to follow a well-trodden trail for smart American girls with means but not aims and enrolled at the Sorbonne to take a course in French literature and artistic appreciation. She and her sister Harriet rented a room at the Hôtel Montana, next door to the Café Flore.

Melinda was a figure of contradictions, popular wherever she went but lacking self-confidence, vague but determined at the same time, 'apparently frail and defenceless but in fact tough and self-reliant, and although she was generally tractable, she could on occasion be quite dominant'. She was small in stature, always tidily turned out and had about her a soft-voiced helplessness – her accent was often described as 'almost Southern'; she was also what her immensely supportive brother-in-law, Alan, called a 'hard little nut', perhaps inevitably after an upbringing that required such a degree of self-reliance. Mark Culme-Seymour, the rakish friend of both Donald and Melinda who hung out in the same circles as the off-duty diplomat and the student, remarked that she was 'pretty and vivacious, but rather reserved … a bit prim'. Her primness did not interfere with her habit of smoking fat Havana cigars. She too had two distinct sides to her personality, the conventional and the one that craved adventure. And that was to be her life from that December evening onwards: the Foreign Office bride, excitement of a not always welcome kind, mingled love, loyalty and loathing for her husband until betrayal became her path as well as his. Her attraction was elusive even as it was undeniable. Donald and Melinda's hidden, often contradictory depths ensured that they suited one another.

*

Melinda had rather naively, or perhaps bravely, as an early indicator of her keenness to live with risk, elected to stay in France after the outbreak of war two months earlier. Her sister Harriet, more politically astute and conventional, a steadying figure to Melinda, had followed the American Embassy advice to return home. Robert Cecil, who was soon introduced to Melinda by his colleague, said 'she found politics and economics boring'. And ideology 'did not feature in her vocabulary. It was interaction with people that brought colour into her cheeks and made her eyes shine.' Certainly the instant attraction between Melinda and Donald was not based on an intellectual union – yet they could each fill in the gaps of the other. She lacked confidence in her intellect and savoir-faire but was natural and at ease in company; he was tightly buttoned up in his divided life, suppressing any turmoil he may have felt about his commitment to espionage after the Nazi–Soviet Pact, not enjoying his official roles. Donald could bask in being the superior intellect to an attractive, admiring woman who was under-educated and slightly at sea in the milieu she had chosen, yet affectionate and popular where he was withdrawn, giving nothing of himself away. Although she had had a difficult upbringing, her psychological conditioning did not include the ingrained need for a secret life, nor would the ideological opportunity to explore Communism in any detail have appealed to her.

Her mother Melinda Dunbar believed the union was 'one-sided from the point of view of true affection'. Melinda was 'a very mixed person [who] loved Donald very much … [but] he was devoted to cultural, highbrow conversations with intellectuals, a form of entertainment to which Melinda was unable to make any form of contribution; she was guided more by impulse and emotion than reason. She would be content to leave such a discussion and retire to her room and read some magazine relating to the cinema.' She had 'practically no friends' either in the US or in Paris, so it was a meeting of two lonely souls. Melinda, like Marie in Brittany and Kitty Harris in the immediate past, could be said to be not 'of his class', the prerequisite for a relationship he had mentioned to Deutsch, if the definition were extended to women who were not British and less able to scrutinise his inscrutability and the reasons behind it.

Maclean monopolised Melinda that first evening and afterwards was rarely seen out of her company in his off-duty hours. As he had in his Brittany dalliance and in his pursuit of Kitty, he fell obsessively in love with her. But she remained unsure about her commitment: she wrote to her mother frequently throughout her life and, soon after she and Donald had met, she told Mrs Dunbar, 'I am not really in the least bit interested by him.' Maclean had by this time shed the effeminacy that his contemporaries had picked up on in London, and according to Cyril Connolly 'had grown much handsomer and his tall figure, his grave long face and noble brow … were severe and distinguished'. From this point on, there are no more comments about his girlish looks or mincing walk.

Part of Melinda's reticence may have been to do with his drinking. At that time when alcoholism was widely seen as a moral failing it is possible that the silence surrounding her father and her mother's short marriage was related to Francis Marling's drinking problem. She was certainly alert to Donald's intake: when in early 1940 she took herself to the South of France to get some distance and give herself thinking time, she wrote to him in Paris, 'If you do feel an urge to have a drinking orgy, why don't you have it at home – so at least you will be able to get safely to bed? Anyway, do try to keep young P from completely demolishing your apartment.' 'Young P' was Philip Toynbee, who had arrived in Paris for his honeymoon (such was his confidence that the German army would wait for him to have his trip), but chose to spend much of that time drinking with his old Serpentine-bathing companion. Donald 'used to join us with his delightful American wife [in fact the Macleans were still unmarried], as soon as his duties at the Embassy were over. "Us" at that time meant a haphazard group at the Café Flore consisting of the sculptor Giacometti, the ex-Dada impresario Tristan Tzara, and a whole community of minor French and English artists.' And then on to the rue de Bellechasse, leaving 'the wives' to go to bed. Toynbee's effect on her husband was a cross that Melinda would find insupportable a decade later when apartment-demolishing took on a new level of meaning.

Kitty Harris noticed on one of her visits to Maclean's flat that everything was much tidier than normal and most tellingly that there were two toothbrushes in the bathroom. It did not take her long to find a 'gossamer-thin nightdress' hanging next to the suits in the wardrobe, but she put the needs of Moscow Centre ahead of her own emotions to accept the change to a more conventional agent–handler relationship. Maclean saw the need to appease the NKVD over this turn of events and to allay any fears they might have about a shift of loyalties. He told them that on that first encounter in the Café Flore he had initially been taken with Melinda's political views: 'She's in favour of the Popular Front and doesn't mind mixing with Communists even though her parents are quite well off. There was a White Russian girl, one of her friends, who attacked the Soviet Union and Melinda went for her. We found we spoke the same language.' It was essential that such politics as she did espouse were recorded and sugar-coated because what he told Kitty next could have ended his career – if not his life. This was the first grave risk that Maclean took in his life, personally and professionally, and far from the last.

*

He had told Melinda that he was a spy. He needed a secret sharer in his life, someone to admire him, and he had appointed Melinda. She remained a silent witness, her own enigma, for as long as she needed to. He claimed he made the admission to her both to excuse his lateness for their meetings when he was handling documents and making rendezvous, and 'to make myself look better and more important than she thought'. The latter reason rings truest. Kitty immediately called a meeting with her superior, code-name 'Ford', at the Soviet Embassy. Ford's report to Moscow has the staccato disjointedness of his fear at the turn of events:

> Ada had noticed recently that Stuart had become close to some woman, though he himself did not tell Ada anything about it. Having noticed a number of changes about his behaviour and the arrangement of his room, Ada decided to ask Stuart about it straightforwardly. The latter was surprised that Ada knew about it and confessed that he had become intimately close with, loved, a young American woman. This American woman, Melinda Marling, is of liberal ideas – the daughter of well-to-do parents living in the United States without any particular interest in politics.
>
> Stuart admitted... that he had told Melinda Marling about his membership of the Communist Party and about his link with us 'in the spy business'... Ada assures us that... Stuart's action is explained by 'boyish lightmindedness' and that, as before, he works with us sincerely and with enthusiasm.

This 'boyish lightmindedness' was born of a keen desire for Melinda to be impressed by him, to open all sides of his life to her, to woo and interest her, to show passion outside the constraints of his job, to show the depth of his commitment to her as he showed her the whole man. He had found someone who thrilled to danger and could share his burden; even telling her was to take a risk in a life already fraught with risk, which he was revelling in even as it stressed him. He later explained that 'when we first met each other, she had no reason to think I was anything more than an ordinary official of the British diplomatic service. After some time she came to the conclusion that my way of life as a diplomat made our relations impossible and she left. I told her about the reason why I led such a life. Then she came back and we have been together ever since.' Even though this is stated in a document written for Russian eyes only, it is notable that he elevates his espionage work to the top spot; his diplomacy was the vehicle for changing the world through leaking. Kitty had given him sexual confidence, mentored him and praised him in espionage matters, and he had become more masculine. Now there was someone with whom he could share everything in his life. Melinda had no idea how vital her role would be in his secret world.

The rush of excitement for Melinda must have been intense as she embarked on the relationship so far from home in the tense atmosphere of wartime Paris. She understood the weight he was carrying, and that to his mind working for strong beliefs was more important than working for the government of the day. She could turn to a figure of principle and hidden depths to protect her at such a potentially deadly time. Years later, when the couple were living in very different circumstances, a letter from Melinda came to light which ended: 'You have got two lives to lead, I have only one.' It must have been a compelling relief for Maclean to share his secret life after the burden of carrying it alone (Kitty's compromised position apart) through the political dramas of the last year. He had found another place of emotional belonging, and this time one he felt could become permanent.

*

As well as Melinda coming on to the scene, things became more complicated still for Kitty. She reported in the first week of May (the week when the Germans swept across Holland and Belgium into France, having already seized Denmark and Norway in April) that she had heard from Philby via Maclean. Philby was surprised not to have had contact from the Russians for some time, and had 'some very interesting information' that he wanted to get to Moscow. But Moscow had broken with him, unsure how he was reacting to the Nazi–Soviet Pact. Philby trusted the man he had recruited at his Kilburn supper table without necessarily knowing if he had forsaken the cause, but 'didn't doubt that even if something had radically changed in his life, he would never betray me' so 'asked him to help me repair the broken liaison'. Maclean checked in with Kitty, she with Moscow, and a week later the two men met in a Paris café. Maclean told Philby everything he 'needed for a rendezvous – the time, place and password'. Moscow Centre slowly started to rebuild the links with Philby, more energetically when later in the war he showed his usefulness as he became a counter-intelligence instructor, and above all after the war when he was an invaluable agent, not least in protecting Maclean, whom he did not meet again for decades. When they did become close once more, it was a short-lived, dramatic and inevitably betrayed renewal of their friendship and comradeship.

The British Embassy was in its last stages of evacuation by early June 1940. Kitty signed off on her lover and agent of the previous two years. It was the end of a great passion as well as her most rewarding professional relationship. Her future now looked very uncertain. She kept the locket Maclean had given her until she died. They could have met again in later life but did not. She deliberately and elegiacally used his code-name from a period when he had been at his most productive, to protect him as well as her own usefulness in her final report to Moscow: 'Lirik is a good comrade and the work he does means everything to him.' His only concern is that 'his work should be appreciated', his familiar need. 'He felt that his work in France was not as important as what he did in London ... He has enormous confidence in the Soviet Union and the working class. Bearing in mind his origins and his past and the fact that he's been totally detached from Party work where he might have grown and learned, Lirik is a good and brave comrade.' When the Germans occupied Paris in June, Kitty found her way back to Moscow and later continued her staunch service to the NKVD from Los Alamos in New Mexico, home of the 'Manhattan' atomic bomb project. Her star agent now once again found himself without a handler in his successful dual career. From his arrival at the

Foreign Office in 1935 to the end of her tenure, he had supplied what was later to be gathered into forty-five boxes in Moscow, each one containing approximately 300 pages, a colossal amount of intelligence to have photographed, processed and despatched.

*

The first few months of Donald and Melinda's relationship passed in the Phoney War period of constant false air-raid warnings that were ignored, with the fashionable women of Paris 'sporting chic new gas-mask cases'. After the lightning invasion of France launched on 10 May 1940 and the bloody drama of the evacuation by the 'armada of little ships' of almost 340,000 allied soldiers from Dunkirk it was only a matter of weeks before most of the country was under German control. The advance had happened at a speed that caught everyone off guard, including Stalin, who had hoped for a couple of years of entrenched warfare to buy himself time to build up his own defences.

At this terrifying point Maclean asked Melinda to marry him. She begged him for time to think, and asked whether she could go home to mull it over as the American Embassy was now urging US citizens to leave without delay. But if she left now and decided that she did want to be with him, she might find it hard to return to Europe during wartime. Eventually she told him she could not marry him and he offered to drive her to Bordeaux and find a boat to take her home. But the speed of the German Blitzkrieg was astonishing and Paris was already being evacuated. Wives and 'lady members' of the Embassy staff had been sent home on 16 May, by which date the bonfire of documents in the Faubourg Saint Honoré gardens had already been lit. Events had overtaken Melinda's deliberations.

With German forces less than a week from Paris, and the Embassy in a state of emergency, Maclean wrote on 8 June to Victor Mallet, now back in London:

I want to marry an American girl living here. As we have burnt our circulars along with all other archives, I am not sure whether I need permission to do this. In case I do, I am writing with the Ambassador's knowledge, to ask whether I may get married ... Melinda Marling has been in France for about two years ... and was to have returned to America with her sister ... in September last, but didn't do so; I have been responsible for her staying on until now. Our intention is, in view of the situation, to get married as soon as possible, i.e. in eight days' time, and she would then probably go to a less exposed spot, possibly to America if need be, until things are better.

I am very anxious to wed at the earliest possible moment, as one can't tell what will happen in the next few months or days ...

Eventually Melinda committed herself to marriage. Another urgent reason for her decision was that she had realised that she was pregnant. Maclean's mind was understandably not on his job at this vital moment. That was noticed by the new Ambassador, Sir Ronald Campbell who commented to a senior colleague 'unfavourably on Maclean's dilatoriness and neglect of his duties during the last critical days. He thought of him, perhaps a bit harshly, as something of a weakling.'

Melinda did not need to ask permission of anyone to marry when she wrote to her mother the following day, 9 June (with additions up to 11 June):

Darling Mother
Please don't feel hurt that I haven't let you know before about my decision to marry Donald. But I honestly didn't know whether to or not. We decided very suddenly because it seemed to be the only chance as the Embassy is liable to have to leave Paris for some Godforsaken little place in the country and one is no longer allowed to travel without an impossible reason ...

I am sorry I haven't given you more details about Donald and I know you must be very worried and also probably disappointed at my marrying an Englishman. But that doesn't necessarily mean I will have to settle down in England for the rest of my life. We will probably be sent all over the world.

... I am terribly in love with Donald and am sure there will never be anyone else. He is the only man I have ever seen I would have liked to marry ...

She added that Donald was 'the soul of honour, responsible, cultured, broad-minded (and sweet) etc. Of course he has faults but somehow they don't clash with mine – except that he is stubborn and strong-willed. I needed that as I was drifting along getting nowhere.' He was indeed the 'soul of honour', a neat evasion of what she knew.

In the same letter she said that she would go straight to Bordeaux after they were married to get a boat home with little luggage. 'The rest I am leaving in Donald's flat as they will be sent to him if he has to leave France.' Not for the last time, Melinda showed little interest in or grasp of the affairs she found herself in the midst of. But again time ran out on them; she may also have decided that she wanted to be with her new husband rather than using him as a ticket home, and certainly the baby focused her mind. She broke the news obliquely (and slightly coercively) to her mother in a sudden outpouring of emotion: 'My greatest desire is to have a baby while I am at home as I am dying to have one and I couldn't bear to have it without you. Wouldn't it be wonderful, Mummy!?'

The Macleans necessarily got married ahead of Donald's planned timetable in a *mairie* in the Palais Bourbon district on 10 June, the day the Embassy left Paris (with the Ambassador's Rolls-Royce leading the convoy). Mark Culme-Seymour was the best man. Donald was neglecting his orders to help evacuate the Embassy to attend his own wedding and they joined the nightmarish 'surrealist goulash' of the columns of refugees leaving the city; Culme-Seymour made his own escape south in a large Packard with five English ladies from a refugee committee. Donald and Melinda spent their first married night in a field near Chartres, their second in their car outside Tours (which was being pounded by air raids), managing to spend a few days of their honeymoon in a village near Biarritz before being evacuated from Bordeaux on a destroyer, HMS *Berkeley*, on 23 June. Three hours later they were transferred to a British tramp steamer, the SS *Narvia*, returning from delivering coal to South America. They then had a ten-day voyage to Britain, zig-zagging to avoid U-boats and the Luftwaffe. Melinda shared the cook's cabin with three other women, Donald slept in the passageway. In the daytime they sat on deck and remembered their best Parisian meals. Finally they arrived in Milford Haven, near Sir Donald's home town of Haverfordwest in Wales, and caught a train to London. Melinda sent her mother a telegram announcing their union; Mrs Dunbar took an advertisement in the *New York Times* to share the news. The tumultuous married life of Donald and Melinda Maclean had started as it would continue, beset by difficulties and dangers, united but often not together, an enigma at times to the outside world that, like matryoshka dolls, kept hidden their deeper selves.

7

Blitz and Barbarossa

The newly-weds arrived back in Britain at the start of the German battle to knock out the Royal Air Force and pave the way for the invasion of Britain. The country was blockaded at sea and the RAF was daily fighting the Luftwaffe over the south coast and the English Channel to prevent the invasion and consequent near-certain defeat. Chamberlain's replacement as Prime Minister, Winston Churchill, made his stirring speech to the House of Commons on the evening of 18 June 1940, coining the name for the confrontation: 'I expect that the Battle of Britain is about to begin. Upon this battle depends the survival of Christian civilisation … Hitler knows that he will have to break us in this island or lose the war … Let us therefore brace ourselves to our duties, and so bear ourselves that, if the British Empire and its Commonwealth last a thousand years, men will still say, "This was their finest hour."'*

The refugees from the Battle of France had little else to stir them when they arrived, nowhere to live, no furniture, and nearly all their clothes were in occupied Paris; their car was abandoned in Bordeaux, not that it would have been of much use to them as petrol was rationed in Britain. Valentine Lawford rode on horseback over the ten miles from his parents' home to see them. Melinda's introduction to her formidable mother-in-law took place when they went to stay with her at Elm Cottage, Penn, for the first weeks of July 1940, at the height of the battle.

---

* Churchill's great friend, F. E. Smith, Lord Birkenhead, had commented long before Churchill's own finest hour that 'Winston has spent the best years of his life preparing his impromptu remarks.'

While her husband was away in Whitehall, Melinda did not find life with Lady Maclean easy. Whatever adjustments needed to be made in wartime, Gwendolen would have preferred to meet her favourite son's intended before the wedding became a fait accompli. She might even have liked the chance to meet the girl's parents. She came from a radically different, Victorian era and from a family that put great stress on things being done properly (and preferably in church). She had also had an exhausting start to the war herself after undergoing a mastectomy as well as having to care for her elderly mother in Surrey. Mrs Devitt's mind was starting to wander, and she had become convinced that her eighty-year-old maid was going to be called up into the navy and made to run up and down the ship's rigging to check it. Overall, and even allowing for Lady Maclean's essential sweetness of nature, particularly where her middle son was concerned (which might have been a problem of its own for Melinda), it soon became apparent that for the sake of Donald's work and their marriage the couple should live in London, which certainly held more excitements of the sort they had got used to in Paris. In mid-July, despite the US Ambassador Joseph Kennedy warning three weeks earlier that it was 'utterly inevitable that England will be almost completely destroyed by air raids', they moved into a room in the modern Mount Royal Hotel in Oxford Street.

*

The Foreign Office was a reserved occupation and its staff were not liable for conscription. It was in chaos with so many diplomats returning from Western Europe: promotions, leave, assignments were up in the air, and the legendarily smooth running of the service had fallen apart. The office routine was very different in wartime to how it had been when Maclean was last based in London two brief years earlier. Then there had been no reason to be in much before eleven o'clock, there was no work on Saturdays and one had two months holiday a year; lunch could be an extended affair and a tea trolley brought scones, biscuits and fruit cake in the afternoon. Now, short-staffed and in more urgent times, everything started much earlier and finished much later; Saturday mornings were working hours. There were soon to be twenty-seven departments; before the war there had been twelve.

Nearly all of Maclean's colleagues from Paris were set up in the new French Department of the Foreign Office created to cope with the arrival of General de Gaulle and the Free French. In spite of his Paris experience, Maclean was excluded, partly because of the poor report from Campbell on his untimely marriage and his failure to provide support in the evacuation to Bordeaux; it was his one career black mark. Instead he was assigned to the new General Department, mainly responsible for liaison with the Ministries of Shipping, Supply and Economic Warfare, the last broadly concerned with getting what was needed for the war and keeping it away from the Germans. Robert Cecil remembered overhearing two diplomats talking about a three-hour meeting focused on denying wolfram to the Germans without any knowledge of what wolfram (also known as tungsten, an essential ingredient of the steel used to build tanks) was, such was the level of expertise within the Foreign Office in relation to modern warfare. Apart from Maclean and a few others, the General Department was made up of visiting experts in the various specialised fields it dealt with, and Maclean's job was not particularly taxing for someone of his calibre. He was promoted to Second Secretary in October, routine for the time he had served.

Maclean's annual report that month recorded his work as being 'consistently excellent but the word "immature" recurs'. 'Immature' harks back to his start in the service, overriding the interim 'confidence'. The comment might have a number of explanations as the report did not go into detail: it might be that the word is a euphemism for being hung over in the office; his marriage and the move from France would certainly have been a distraction if it referred to lack of concentration; he might have found life in London a bit frivolous after the drama of Paris and the novelty of married life as he and Melinda escaped from the approaching German forces. He might simply have been finding the job a bit of a backwater after the excitement of the political work that had dominated his career so far, and it perhaps made him petulant beneath the dutiful surface.

Above all, he might have found it hard to engage fully with his job while he was out of contact with Moscow, a theme which was to recur, sometimes with damaging consequences. A vital part of him was not being nourished and fulfilled. For over two years now he had not only had the thrill of knowing that much of what he was seeing was clearly valuable to Moscow; there was the added drama of having been romantically involved with his controller. Now Russia was allied with the enemy which had driven him out of France, and London was grim and tense. He was cut off from his ideological centre, for all he knew for ever. Moscow Centre might well have decided that he was expendable, given the Nazi–Soviet Pact and Kitty's withdrawal, or even that the British had been subtle enough to turn him as a double agent. If they did believe he had been turned, they did not have the measure of their man. Maclean never dealt well with discomfort or with a lack of feedback to nourish his secret side, particularly after being in such close contact with Moscow Centre via Kitty. The supposition that he was of little value now, especially with British war prospects looking so bleak, induced a fundamental unease in someone so sensitive.

*

The suspicious Soviets left their London spies without a handler for six months after Maclean's return. Moscow had come to the conclusion, thanks to their perennial belief that no one who had worked abroad could be wholeheartedly committed ideologically, that their work in Britain 'was based on doubtful sources, on an agent network acquired at the time when it was controlled by enemies of the people and was therefore extremely dangerous'. It was 'recommended that all contact with the British agents should be broken'. Although this did not apply to Maclean in Paris, where Kitty Harris knew very well that he was not an enemy of her people and where his material was not in question, there was certainly a post-purge cooling at the very point when information should have been at a premium.

After Maly and Grafpen had been recalled to Moscow and respectively executed and imprisoned, the *rezidentura* in London was in chaos. Maly's quasi-religious loyalty was not taken into account and it was assumed he had compromised the Five; all but Maclean, out of the country and consistently useful, had been cut adrift. In December 1938 the short, balding, brilliant, depraved and utterly ruthless Lavrenti Beria, described by Stalin's daughter Svetlana as 'a magnificent modern specimen of the artful courtier, the embodiment of oriental perfidy, flattery and hypocrisy', had become head of the NKVD. The only remaining NKVD officer in London in 1939 was Anatoli Gorsky, official cover name Anatoli Gromov, code-name 'Henry'. Gorsky had a 'distinctly Slavic profile . . . a round, moonlike bespectacled face' with 'angry eyebrows', always wore a hat and was ignorantly unbriefed on his charges' individual personalities. He treated them instead in a grimly efficient, humourless and 'business-like manner'. Moscow Centre had so lost touch with their London network that Gorsky had to write in the summer of 1939, when Philby was about to return from the Spanish Civil War, that 'we would appreciate some orientation on him, for he is only known to us in the most general terms'.

In February 1940, while Maclean was still in Paris, contact with Philby and Burgess from Moscow Centre was suspended and Gorsky temporarily withdrawn to Moscow. By the time Maclean joined them in London after the Fall of France, his fellow Cambridge agents had been adrift for months. On top of this isolation, it was not a particularly good time to be a Communist in Britain anyway: Churchill blamed 'Soviet-inspired Communism' for the collapse of the French army and argued strongly in Cabinet that Communists, as well as fascists and aliens, 'should be put into protective or preventive internment, including the leaders'.

Gorsky returned to London as *rezident* in December 1940 and certainly made a change from Kitty. By his very lack of emotion he was to prove adept at handling the often emotional Maclean over the next few years. It was in his absences that things started to fall apart. And for all his joyless, efficient manner, it was ultimately another handler's inefficiency in a chance, brief gap in their relationship that condemned Maclean to exposure.

*

Aubrey Wolton was one of the experts in the General Department. He thought highly of Maclean's work and tried to befriend 'the rather lonely and withdrawn individual'. He went to the pub a few times with both the Macleans, but the friendship amounted to little; Wolton felt that he had 'failed to make any close contact. They both seemed so young and so lost.' They were indeed dislocated, not certain of their paths in the war-torn capital; Melinda was in a totally unexpected environment, pregnant and out of touch with her mother and sisters. But they had the excitement of each other in the heightened atmosphere of living in bombed London. Melinda declared that 'ever afterwards "love" to me was always inextricably mixed up with "bombs", it was an experience I would not have missed'. The first bombs of what became known as the Blitz fell on London on 24 August, and soon afterwards the damage to the Mount Royal Hotel meant that it had to be evacuated before more shocks weakened it to the point of collapse. Donald and Melinda moved into a furnished flat in the handsome, run-down Georgian Mecklenburgh Square, near King's Cross Station and the literary haunts of Fitzrovia.

The Blitz proper got terrifyingly under way on 7 September, as hundreds of 'bombers hemmed in by fighters, like bees around their queen, like destroyers around a battleship' arrived in the middle of an autumn afternoon. By dawn on the 8th the docks were ablaze. That night the Luftwaffe returned again and John Lehmann, who was a neighbour in Mecklenburgh Square where he ran Virginia and Leonard Woolfs' Hogarth Press, recorded in his diary the 'whistling, ripping noise' of the descending bombs. As he made his way to the shelter in the middle of the square, Lehmann 'thought part of Byron Court looked rather odd: it was only a few seconds later I realised that I was looking at a tree beyond – Byron Court had simply been blown to bits.' Only ten weeks after their escape from France, the Macleans were homeless again, very much 'so young and so lost.'

As the bombing continued, Maclean spent most nights fire-watching on the roof of the Foreign Office, brushing away and quenching the incendiary bombs before they could start to burn in earnest. Melinda decided that with her baby imminent she could not stay in London any longer. She sailed in September as part of a convoy for the safety and glamour of peacetime America. It was the first time in an eventful two years she had been home. On 22 December she had a stillborn son in New York. Melinda was 'very disturbed', not surprisingly, by this terrible event on top of all her other experiences of the previous year and, her stepfather claimed, 'fell in love' with the surgeon who delivered the baby. Whatever the truth of this (and at the time Dunbar had little good to say of any of the Marling family), the Macleans did not meet again until Melinda returned to London early the following summer. Donald was seen to 'weep like an inconsolable child' over his double loss.

In his emotional vulnerability, at a time when he might be killed any night, Maclean dropped his stoic British mask and sent an eloquent and assertive letter to Moscow that was a plea to be made useful again, to be allowed to ground himself, to be given a sense of purpose. His espionage, he insisted, 'has the same importance for me as for you – if not of even greater importance because it is my life, I live for it'. He then made it clear that he had not been turned, nailing his colours to the mast in an attempt to dispel any doubts the Centre might have, or to push away doubts he himself might have, about his post-pact single-mindedness: 'I will try as hard as I can not to do anything to endanger it [his role as a spy]. I can't say that I like my work. But I admit that it is one of the uses in our great struggle to which I am most suited and I intend to stand by it until I am relieved of it.' The strength of purpose and ideology could not hide his perpetual distaste for the actual business of spying, the subterfuge and lying at a time when his country was 'pulling together'. He never let go his Presbyterian squeamishness about wrongdoing just as he was always certain that following one's conscience was the right thing to do. The death of his unseen baby and the absence of Melinda rendered him more vulnerable to the sheer torment of spying, so that in a child-like way he wanted to feel needed and appreciated. Perhaps this is what the Foreign Office meant by his 'immaturity'.

*

Nineteen-forty-one was the pivotal year of the war: both the USA and the USSR came under attack and joined the conflict. It was also the year when the Cambridge Five were by turns essential, mistrusted, questioned and self-questioning. On 28 December 1940, shortly after his return from Moscow, Gorsky had made contact with Blunt, by now in a very good position at the heart of MI5. Blunt had had a hiccup in his early intelligence training at Minley Manor when his Cambridge Communist past came to light, but that had been forgotten by now. He had not been in touch with a Soviet controller for three and a half years. In January 1941 Blunt won back trust for them all for the moment when he passed Gorsky the debriefing reports of 'Mr Thomas', Walter Krivitsky, from the year before, no doubt hastening the defector's death in the Washington hotel a few weeks later. Had Maclean not been so emotionally forceful in pledging himself earlier, Moscow Centre might have been even more alarmed by the Krivitsky evidence, even more concerned that the British had discovered his treachery and succeeded in turning him as a double agent.

Gorsky/Henry insisted on a much more rigorous observance of tradecraft than either Otto or Norma. If a rendezvous took place in Central London, it was in a park or a café. The correct code-words were to be exchanged every time, followed by a long journey by tube to the suburbs and back to ensure they were not being followed, before any further exchange of information could be carried out. Sometimes Gorsky would meet his agents in a far-flung tube station such as Park Royal on the western outskirts of London where papers would be handed over and a location arranged, often a public lavatory, where they could be returned the following morning. The spies were equipped with tiny Minox cameras for photographing papers at home, although the skill required to focus on words with such a small device meant that this was not really a practicable option. In the course of 1941 Maclean once again hit productivity highs with an extraordinary 4,419 documents supplied; Cairncross was next with 3,449.

In the first half of the year there was plenty of material that warned of the impending German invasion of Russia and the abrupt ending of the pact that had caused some of the agents such qualms. The Weekly Political Intelligence Summary compiled by the Foreign Office had been flagging up the offensive for two months before it happened; Maclean had seen a telegram about a conversation between Hitler and Prince Paul of Yugoslavia discussing the invasion, as well as a message from Lord Halifax in Washington (where he was now Ambassador) on the same topic and an extract from a bulletin on German military plans issued in early May by the Secret Intelligence Service (SIS), as MI6 was also known. But as Stalin was only willing to listen to intelligence that suited his potent mix of narcissism and paranoia, he was unwilling to believe that any invasion of his country could come before he was ready for it.

*

During his enforced bachelorhood over the winter of 1940–1, Maclean started to show the occasional patterns of debauchery that were to become more pronounced, and more dangerous, in the years to come. Blunt and Burgess's parties in Victor Rothschild's flat in Bentinck Street, Marylebone, where they lived, were great tension-relievers during the worst of the Blitz (the flat was especially handy as it had a bomb-shelter in the basement). The gatherings were also a source of very useful high-level gossip, as Goronwy Rees recalled: 'Guy brought home a series of boys, young men, soldiers, sailors, airmen … Civil servants, politicians, visitors to London, friends and colleagues of Guy's, popped in and out of bed and then continued some absorbing discussion of political intrigue, the progress of the war and the future possibilities of peace.' As well as the occasional visit to the Bentinck Street loucheness, Maclean went sometimes as a guest to the Gargoyle Club, in Dean Street, Soho, already frequented by Guy Burgess. There was no discussion of spying or even acknowledgement of the other's recruitment when they met. The Gargoyle, with its ballroom walls made up of fragmented mirrors and its art-nouveau lift, was 'a cosmopolitan arena; an antic theatre of social, sexual and intellectual challenge'. During the war, exiled intellectuals, writers and artists, such as Arthur Koestler, George Weidenfeld, Romain Gary and Feliks Topolski, and the senior officers of the Free French, all found in it 'familiar territory' alongside the likes of Cyril Connolly, Harold Nicolson, Clive and Vanessa Bell, Nancy Cunard and Evelyn Waugh's Bright Young Things. Maclean became an habitué of its liberating hedonism; in 1950, when he joined as a member, it was to become an essential and rather public escape valve.

*

Melinda's return in May 1941 put a stop to Donald living things up and to an extent restored his evening equilibrium. She came back to England and to her exhausted husband on Pan Am's luxurious *Dixie Clipper* flying boat (which provided separate dressing-rooms for men and women and six-course meals served by white-coated waiters) via stop-overs in Bermuda and neutral Lisbon. Her family had put pressure on her to stay in America, particularly after her ordeal, but she was 'a person of stubborn loyalties', as she was to prove again and again. It was not the last time that she had to make a choice between her own family and Maclean, but there was no vacillating on her part. They needed each other. This time, toughened by her experience, and with her predilection for living with danger, she always refused to go under cover when the air-raid sirens went off, saying she would rather die in her bed than face the stench and claustrophobia of the shelters.

By the time the couple moved into a new flat in Rossmore Court, Marylebone, Hitler had unleashed Operation Barbarossa. On 22 June, four million men (and nearly 700,000 horses) of the Axis armies crossed 1,800 miles of the Russian border. Barbarossa was stunning in its scale and speed – the largest and fastest invasion in history. When Stalin had heard that the German Ambassador to Moscow was hinting at the invasion a few weeks before, on top of the warnings from both overt and covert channels for months, he said, 'Now disinformation has reached ambassadorial level!' On 10 June, the Permanent Under-Secretary to the Foreign Office, Sir Alexander Cadogan, was able to dictate to Ambassador Maisky, by now a fixture on the London scene and a shrewd observer of it, the Axis troop deployments at the Soviet frontier. This was rebuffed by Moscow as 'a clumsy propaganda manoeuvre' to get the USSR and Germany into the war. On the 21st, Maisky was warned by the British Ambassador to Moscow, Stafford Cripps, then in London, that the invasion was likely to be the next day. Maisky recorded in his diary that evening that 'an imminent attack ... seemed improbable'. With his certainty that he could set the timetable through the power of his will alone, Stalin had hoped to be given more leeway to build up his defences.

Barbarossa provided Britain with a lifeline. Much of the German war machine now headed to the east. Maclean was working for an ally (even if Churchill was careful not to use the word in his speech to the House of Commons on the evening of Barbarossa as being too dramatic a rhetorical reversal), and he could close the inner moral gap and comfort himself that he would be showing Moscow material that they should be allowed to see with their new status – information that could shorten the war. He could make good his employer's failure. Anthony Blunt felt 'a profound sense of relief' at the sudden alignment of his beliefs and the turn in the war. With Melinda at his side again and a common purpose in both his careers, Maclean must have shared that relief as his patriotism and his undimmed ideology were in harmony. After the misery of the past few years there was finally some order to his life.

*

Much of what Maclean passed to Henry during his three years in London was extremely valuable to Russia, even if not always heeded by the Kremlin. In 1943 his report of what the Poles believed about the discovery by the Wehrmacht of the bodies of Polish soldiers in Katyń contributed to the break in relations between Moscow and the Polish government-in-exile. However, the sheer quantity as well as the quality of information that went to Moscow inevitably caused suspicion. Few people could produce material on such a scale, so the Soviet logic led to the conclusion that he was being fed it, either by his employers or by the other Cambridge spies. Others, too, were proving very fertile: Blunt had gone into MI5 and between 1942 and

1945 sent 1,771 files, some of them original documents rather than photographs, from the heart of Britain's intelligence, an 'incomprehensible risk' to be so productive, according to Moscow Centre; Cairncross's intercepts of German material from his current position at the Government Code and Cypher School, the code-breaking agency at Bletchley Park, were of critical importance before the pivotal Battle of Kursk. Yet none of the Five was passing on information that would harm British interests, which therefore meant they could not be real traitors to their country: even Philby's pronounced Englishness in speech and dress made him somehow suspect. The flight to Scotland of Hitler's deputy Rudolf Hess in May 1941 was soon seen for what it was by Britain and Germany, the act of a man not quite in his right mind; Stalin, though, saw a plot between the two countries to make peace. In 1942 he wrote to Maisky, still his Ambassador in London, that 'all of us in Moscow have gained the impression that Churchill is aiming at the defeat of the USSR, in order then to come to terms with Germany ... at the expense of our country'. As late as October 1944 Stalin was raising a toast to the British intelligence services at dinner with Churchill which had 'inveigled Hess into coming to England'.

Elena Modrzhinskaya, alias 'the Blue-Eyed Gretchen', was one of the few women in Moscow Centre. Polish in origin and head of the British section, she had no feel for Britain whatsoever. But she had joined the NKVD at the height of the purges in 1937, which had enabled her to rise rapidly by double-thinking everything that came her way. By 1942 she had learned a huge amount from Anthony Blunt during the year when he worked as assistant to Guy Liddell of B Division of MI5. B Division ran the Double-Cross system whereby every German spy in Britain had been identified through code-breaking ingenuity and successfully turned.

With all the material heading east, and admiring Double-Cross as she did, there was plentiful reason in Modrzhinskaya's mind to assume that the Russians too were being played and that the Cambridge Five were working for their own side. She actually put her finger on something fairly fundamental which eluded her well-mannered British contemporaries when she asked how could such self-confessed university Communists, 'aristocrats' at that, be allowed to serve their country in such important posts? If they were sincerely working for the Soviets, 'why had not a single valuable agent in the USSR or in the Soviet Embassy in Britain been exposed'? Blunt had said that MI5 were not watching the Soviet Embassy in London; Philby that MI6 were not spying from the British Embassy in Moscow. How could this be unless there was double-dealing going on? How could the spies bring out quantities of original documents without being noticed? In fact, the British restrictions on spying on the Soviets were imposed after Barbarossa: one did not spy on one's allies in wartime even if one had the man-power. And security was nearly non-existent. Espionage common sense in Moscow Centre seemed about to undo them all.

And if Maclean was indeed a double agent, why would he be so productive when a few carefully selected intelligence items would do just as well? The answer must be that he was the only one who had not been turned, yet was being manipulated by the others, as he was passing on very little about German affairs that actually harmed British policy. A Russian surveillance team was sent to trail their prized spies, but soon got lost (luckily for them as their shabby, ill-cut Russian suits would soon have given the game away) and covered their backs by reporting that their targets, clearly trained to a higher level of tradecraft by their British masters, had shaken them off deliberately. But then some excellent intelligence-gathering reasserted a sense of trust. In May 1944 Blunt supplied a complete copy of the deception plan around D-Day two weeks before the Normandy landings took place, and followed up in July with a list of all the double agents involved in that plan. Eventually, in August that year, two years after the Soviets had started chasing their own tails, an exhaustive analysis of material from Philby in particular was checked and cross-checked against other sources, and the Five were exonerated. Maclean had used up another life.

*

Barbarossa, the very operation that gave Maclean's espionage some form of moral legitimacy, also became a factor in his future

The Maclean family on holiday in their father's North Cornwall constituency, 1925.
Left to right: Alan, Gwendolen ('Mother'), Donald (aged 12), Andy,
Ian, Nancy, Sir Donald ('Father').

Donald Maclean's parents.
Sir Donald was canvassing support in
the 1929 General Election.

Lady Violet Bonham Carter, close family
friend and daughter of Sir Donald's political
hero and leader, Asquith.

The model school-boy (back row, middle). Prefects at Gresham's School, Holt, home of the sons of the Liberal establishment and crucible for free-thinkers of the left.

James Klugmann, schoolboy friend and undergraduate mentor to Donald Maclean, whom he would later meet again in Paris just before the war.

The Cambridge Armistice Day March in 1933, which erupted into street-fighting. Maclean is in the second row, under the banner.

'The Magnificent Five' at Cambridge in the early 1930s.

Clockwise from top: Anthony Blunt, the aesthete Apostle; 'the fiery cross' John Cairncross; Donald Maclean, the talented linguist heading for the Foreign Office; the extrovert exhibitionist Guy Burgess; Kim Philby, whose occasional appearances in Maclean's life shaped its course for the next thirty years.

Above left: Arnold Deutsch, 'Otto', the charismatic, psychologically brilliant recruiter and first handler of the Cambridge Five.

Above right: Theodor Maly, the former Hungarian priest and Maclean's second handler, who met his end in Stalin's purges with dignity.

Kitty Harris, the handler who broke every rule in the spycraft book.

The staff of the British Embassy, Paris, the hub of the frantic diplomacy in the build-up to war. Maclean is the tall figure in the back row.

Anatoly Gorsky, London *rezident* when Maclean returned from France and who followed him to Washington, with the time-bomb already ticking.

Melinda Marling, whose long marriage to Maclean was a dramatic and mysterious tangle of love and loyalties.

Sir Roger Makins, Maclean's boss in Washington and during his final job in London, was the last man in the Foreign Office to see him on British soil.

Churchill and Roosevelt had few secrets from Stalin at the Yalta Conference in February 1945. Behind Churchill is his Foreign Secretary, Anthony Eden, and behind Eden the colourful figure of Sir Archibald Clerk Kerr, British Ambassador in Moscow and post-war Washington.

The British Embassy, Washington, 1947. First Secretary Maclean is sitting on Sir John Balfour's desk. His friend Nicholas Henderson is on the left.

General Walter Krivitsky of the NKVD defected in 1937 but could not escape his fate. He warned of two spies in the Foreign Office, but it took well over a decade for his testimony to be explored.

Meredith Gardner, linguist and cryptographer of genius whose Venona operation was key in the identification of communist infiltrators.

FBI Special Agent Robert Lamphere, lumberjack turned spy chaser who was astounded and frustrated by the dilatoriness of his British colleagues.

Cryptologists at work at US Army Signals Intelligence HQ at Arlington Hall, Virginia, home of the Venona operation.

unmasking through such an unlikely chain of events that without large helpings of luck and genius it might never have come about. He was undone by the most basic and essential tool of the spy's armoury – the code-book.

The ending of the Nazi–Soviet Pact naturally led to a vast increase in the coded traffic to and from Moscow. The speed of Barbarossa put the Soviet code-makers on the back foot as much as it did Stalin's military machine. The NKVD had perfected the use of the one-time pad, by which the agent sending the message (via a Soviet intelligence officer who would translate if necessary and use cover-words and names unknown to most agents) and the cipher clerk receiving it have identical pads made up of random groups of numbers. The agent would write out a message in as concise a form as possible. Most words, punctuation and many phrases had a four-number code,[*] and those that did not were spelt out using a separate 'spell table' by which the instruction 'Spell' (in code) would precede a number-by-number coded spelling of the word, followed by the instruction 'Endspell'. These were similarly broken down into four-number groups, whatever the length of the word. As a further initial disguise, the resulting four-number groups were then converted into five-number blocks by pulling numbers forward from the following groups.

With the message now in numerical form, the cipher clerk would look at his one-time pad, each page of which had sixty five-digit numerical groups known as the additive or the key. The first group of numbers on the pad would be used to indicate which page of which pad was in use. Thereafter the one-time pad would be placed over the five-number groups that needed to be sent and the two sets of numbers added together, without carrying (so if the number 9 is over the number 4, it becomes 3 on the cipher). Each number then corresponds to a letter (which did not change from pad to pad) so the message was then transformed into five-letter groups and sent. At the other end, the process was followed in reverse: letters turned

---

* Numbers themselves were encoded as words, for example '35' was written as 'three five'.

back into numbers, which would then be subtracted using the matching page of the one-time pad and then the numbers turned back into words using the code-book.

Such a system involved an extraordinary amount of manpower to produce the number of pads required given their single usage; hence the German decision to go to Enigma machines, where the cipher was produced by a primitive electromechanical computer and could therefore be broken by a superior computer made by a superior engineer, in this case Alan Turing of Bletchley Park.

With the rocketing demand for and dwindling stocks of one-time pads in the middle months of 1941, there was a crisis in the Soviet cryptography department; they simply could not produce enough to keep up. Over 8,000 pads were needed for the London *rezidentura* alone. When the US joined the war after the Japanese attack on Pearl Harbor in December 1941, the shortage got worse. The solution, introduced either by a panicky official or unilaterally by an overworked cryptography department, was to use duplicate key pages, manually inserting a sheet of carbon paper into the typewriters used to create the pads. By 1942 these duplicate pages were in tens of thousands of pads. Many of them by now were, technically, two-time pads. Even so, as the duplicate pages were shuffled into different pads, often with different page numbers, and sent around the world, only a code-breaker with huge resources and skill would be able to use this error to crack the codes.

The US Army's Signal Intelligence Service had both: in September 1939 it had a staff of nineteen; by the time of Pearl Harbor that had grown to 400, and by the end of the war it numbered 10,000. Its headquarters was at Arlington Hall, a former girls' boarding school, across the Potomac River from Washington DC. The new staff, as with Britain's Bletchley Park, were drawn from a range of disciplines – linguists and philologists, mathematicians, engineers and technicians, and brilliant English majors who revelled in solving crossword puzzles. And the service was soon to be headed by a genius.

The first breakthrough came immediately after the end of the Nazi–Soviet Pact. The Soviet Consulate in Petsamo, a warm-water port providing access to the Barents Sea in the extreme north of Finland, was overrun by Finnish troops with such speed that the NKVD/NKGB staff who had been stationed there since December 1939, during the Winter War between Finland and the Soviet Union on which Maclean had reported to Moscow, had time only to burn parts of four of their code-books, a costly piece of corner-cutting. The Finns placed great emphasis on cryptography, especially in relation to Russia, and they went to work with a vengeance. They were particularly interested in some cables they deciphered between the general staff and the military attachés in Berlin and Helsinki. Although the Finns did not crack any of the actual Soviet ciphers, they understood some of the 'general characteristics' in the cables, including standard information about weather, and polite sign-offs praising the Revolution and the Motherland. In November 1944, William 'Wild Bill' Donovan, head of the OSS (Office of Strategic Services, forerunner of the CIA), bought 1,500 pages of code and cipher material from the Finns, and the Signal Intelligence Service could get to work despite the objections about spying on one's allies raised by Secretary of State Stettinius. A trail that had a long distance to cover in the years to come and that would require a great deal of ingenuity and hard work had been started which would unravel everything, at the very point when Maclean could single-mindedly and with a clear conscience be of greatest service to the Soviets in their joint aim with Britain of defeating fascism.

*

For the Maclean family, 1943 brought the loss of Donald's eldest brother, Ian, a navigator in the RAF, shot down over Denmark while helping the resistance there on behalf of SOE, the Special Operations Executive; his younger brother, Alan, had joined the 11th Hussars on leaving Cambridge, and later crossed the Rhine in the allied advance on Berlin. Nancy was working for the Registry of MI5 in London, much visited by Anthony Blunt, first of all in HM Prison Wormwood Scrubs (it was not easy to operate in a workplace where most of the offices had no electrical sockets and had handles only on the outside of the doors), until that was bombed and the Registry had to move to Blenheim Palace in Oxfordshire.

Maclean had worked exceptionally hard in his stint at the General Department. At night he was on fire-watching duty and by early 1944 he appeared 'tired and worn'. Melinda complained that she was 'often unhappy' during their time in London, and that Donald was at times 'irritable and neglectful', and 'drank too much'. He was exhausted by his official work and out of touch with Moscow for a long period thanks to the suspicious mind of Modrzhinskaya; there was mounting mistrust of Russia in the Foreign Office as policymakers started to look at the permutations of the post war world. Melinda understood and would have made some allowances for this in the most secret part of their marriage, but her complicity could not be revealed at the time of her complaint.

In fact, Maclean's drinking was already at times far worse than Melinda later let on. He was buckling under the strain of his double life, being helped home at all hours of the night by well-meaning friends 'with his clothes badly stained and reeking of whisky'. She defended her husband with her habitual 'sweetness and under-standing' and reassured Lady Maclean that he was simply suffering from overwork, while saying privately and disingenuously to friends that 'Something's worrying Donald to death and he won't say what it is.'

Three years after Aubrey Wolton had commented on how 'lost' the couple seemed, they still had few friends, and in a confidential internal Foreign Office report of January 1944 the answers to the all-important questions 'Does he like going out and entertaining?' and 'Do he (and his ["intelligent and attractive"] wife) "represent" well?' were an ill-informed and wishful 'I think so' and 'Within reason'. The form-filler was hedging his bets in the face of a lack of knowledge of the guarded personal life of his gifted colleague.

In his working life, Maclean managed to keep his front up. In his annual report for 1943 he was described as having a 'first-rate ability and a most attractive personality', with the caveat, again, that he was 'lacking in self-assurance ... and a trifle immature'.

Comments about his immaturity remain a feature, but this time, in the wake of what he had worked on, seen and experienced in the four years since the last accusation, they are much more pointed and noteworthy. They might still refer to his guardedness, or to his slow start to the mornings after a late night out, or even to the occasional left-wing comment. Even so, his conscientiousness overcame these quibbles and unknowns and paid off handsomely in both London and Moscow. Foreign Secretary Anthony Eden singled out his 'admirably clear assessments' of any given situation and Maclean's reward was to be told in April that he was being sent to Washington as Second Secretary. The congratulatory telegrams poured in. It was some relief for Melinda to be sailing for her home country at the end of April 1944, this time not in a dangerous convoy, for a fresh start in her marriage. She was three months pregnant.

When Winston Churchill was still trying to encourage the US to join the war in 1941, he had called diplomacy in Washington 'the most important of all the functions outside this country that can be discharged by any British subject'. By 1944, weeks away from D-Day and the final stages of the war (and also weeks away from the first V-1 flying bombs landing on London), it was clear that the post-war landscape was to be set up from Washington and it was an immensely prestigious posting for Maclean. It was also one that would provide prime espionage material. Moscow Centre could not have done better if they had arranged the promotion themselves.

8

Homer

Washington, Moscow and London were the three cities that moulded the post-war world, and Donald Maclean was a notable figure in all of them. He was a senior British diplomat with unparalleled access in Washington, which in his time there was transformed from an inward-looking capital to the nerve centre of the free world, the hub of the Western allies in the rapidly burgeoning Cold War. He was so valuable to Moscow that he was given a new code-name which reflected his influence. Yet in Maclean's very first days in the States, before he had hit his considerable stride in his new posting, a tiny, seemingly insignificant mistake not of his own making became the smoking gun that doomed him.

*

The *Queen Elizabeth* docked in New York on 6 May 1944, a month before D-Day, after an uneventful and uncomfortable crossing: male and female passengers were segregated on the converted luxury liner and there were frequent evacuation drills in their convoy. Maclean's establishment credentials served him well even before he sailed. The British Ambassador in Washington, Lord Halifax, took the unusual step of writing to him to welcome him on to his staff. The fox-hunting aristocrat dubbed the 'Holy Fox' by Churchill for his political cunning, had succeeded Sir Donald as President of the Board of Education and shared his predecessor's unimpeachable austerity as well as his strong religious faith. The tall, thin, impeccably dressed Ambassador, unmistakably an English gentleman, had been Chamberlain's Foreign Secretary, one of the Munich

appeasers had been offered the premiership in 1940. After banish-
ment to Washington, Halifax had not endeared himself to
Americans. He attended a Chicago White Sox baseball game at
Comiskey Park and remarked that the game was 'a bit like cricket
except we don't question the umpire's decision so much', and left
his hot dog uneaten on his seat. The hot dog got front-page news,
next to the comment that at least King George VI had eaten his in
1939 on the first-ever visit to the United States by a reigning British
monarch. Halifax was seen as even more elitist when he took the
day off to go hunting in Pennsylvania, but he regained sympathy
when one of his sons was killed in the war and another had his legs
blown off by a Luftwaffe Stuka in December 1942.

The Ambassador and the new Second Secretary became good
friends. They played doubles tennis before breakfast on the court
behind the residence of the handsome Lutyens-designed Embassy.
Another player was George Middleton, who had arrived on the
same ship as the Macleans and saw the legation as 'the apogee of
British diplomacy'. In spite of his useless left arm, Halifax was a
keen tennis player with a very long reach. Maclean's Paris and
Cambridge colleague Robert Cecil, his career permanently
entwined with and complicated by his association with the senior
man, would eventually join them in Washington and sometimes
on the court. The best of the Foreign Office was a small world, and
Donald, although not always successful in suppressing his 'visceral
aversion' to his wife's country during his time there, was in the
vanguard of the new generation.

In the US the Macleans were free of rationing, free of bombing
and at least geographically far away from the war for the first time
in their marriage, with the possibility of living their new lives
happily together with their forthcoming baby. On their arrival in
New York they went straight to the 277 Park Avenue apartment of
Hal and Melinda Dunbar: it was the first time the Dunbars and
the Marlings had met their son-in-law of four years' standing,
and the first time they had seen their daughter and sister in the
three years since her stay during the London Blitz and the stillbirth of her first child.

Donald's mother-in-law was a formidable critic of anyone who came near her daughters and cruelly found the new arrival 'supercilious and ineffective', possibly misreading his British charm and shyness as he struggled in the face of her strong personality. On the positive side she, like many others, found him very good-looking, apart from his 'bad, decayed teeth', which were to be 'fixed' while he was in America. Mrs Dunbar was determined that this pregnancy should not go wrong, and wanted to keep a close eye on Melinda. Melinda ignored her mother's criticisms of her marriage, including her observation that her daughter was 'passionate but unsatisfied' as a wife. Not for the last time, Melinda showed her determination to protect Donald.

Maintaining this loyalty was a test for Melinda. Her first surprise occurred as the couple filled in their entry forms at the dockside in New York. She put 'British Embassy, Washington' as her address. Donald corrected her and gave that as his address only, Park Avenue as hers. He plausibly claimed that she would be very uncomfortable in the mugginess of a Washington summer during her pregnancy, and should be close to her mother after her last awful experience of childbirth. He would be thrown into the immensely hard work of the Embassy in wartime and would have little time to attend to her. But condemning her to live with the Dunbars was tough. Tensions were running high in the household (the couple were to separate the following year) and Hal Dunbar continued to treat his stepdaughter as the 'problem child' she had always been for him, in spite of her marriage to the good-looking and successful diplomat. Dunbar was so distanced from both women that he even charged them rent for living in his houses.

Money was anyway a further cause of resentment for Melinda in that Donald, presuming that she had enough of her own, did not give her any. As he had found in Paris, his colleagues tended to have private incomes and a correspondingly more carefree attitude. Maclean could stay only a few days in New York as the man he was replacing had been struck down with mumps and he was needed sooner than planned. To his brief good fortune in later life, Maclean's file in the Foreign Office never recorded his new starting date or the reason for it. Just after he got on the train to the capital for the first of his many trips. Melinda went to the family farm, Merriebrook, at South Egremont in the Berkshires, for the summer. Their son, Fergus, was born in New York by Caesarean section on 22 September.

Melinda was perhaps more forbearing of her living situation when she grasped its most compelling reason beyond what Donald had said in public. His predecessor in the Embassy Chancery was in no doubt that it would be 'unusual' for an officer of his standing to make trips to New York 'because of the high pressure of work at the time'. But it was crucial in those early days that he did visit the city and have a cast-iron excuse to do so. The war was reaching its endgame, the invasion of Europe was being planned by the British and the Americans to take place in just one month, the Red Army was on the move from the east and it was essential to Moscow Centre that their prime spy hit the ground running.

Such was the speed of his transfer, though, that Gorsky had not been able to set up his own simultaneous move to Washington, so a handler was needed in New York. Once a month Donald Maclean would come in to Pennsylvania Station, a journey of around three hours, and make his way to Grand Central to take the train to Hillsdale, New York, when heading for the Berkshires and the Dunbar farm. Between stations, or between Grand Central and Park Avenue if he was stopping in Manhattan, he would visit his new handler on a bench in Central Park or in a crowded bar. Melinda and her pregnancy were the perfect alibi.

*

Washington, its code-name 'Carthage' no doubt expressing the Russian hope that it would meet the same end as the ancient city, had swollen in wartime from being a southern town to the bustling capital of a vast nation at war. Its population in 1945 stood at a record 802,000 (it was only 602,000 in 2010). Scarcity of accommodation was an added and convenient excuse for Donald to be alone at the start of his posting: he stayed at the Hotel Lafayette for most of June (where Melinda joined him for a fortnight in the middle of the month) until he moved in with his chain-smoking colleague Michael Wright in Kalorama Road. Ambassador Halifax wrote to London asking whether the allowances for Maclean and Middleton, also married but with his wife by his side, could be raised to $200 (unfurnished) and $250 (furnished) respectively, and on that basis it certainly would have been possible for the Embassy housing office to find them a home, as it did for others. But until Melinda and the baby came to join him in January 1945, Maclean did not have a home of his own, nor did he have time to find one amid the swirl of activity. His arrival in Washington was of such importance to Moscow that an unnecessary telegram, sent to impress no less a figure than chief of NKGB foreign intelligence, Lieutenant General Pavel Fitin, and in part the result of turf wars in the New York *rezidentura*, would have irreparable consequences.

Stephen Apresyan was twenty-eight, a well-read polyglot, who had never been out of the Soviet Union before his arrival in New York at the start of the year. He was employed under the cover of the consular service. His presence was bitterly resented by his much more experienced deputy, Vladimir Pravdin (also known as Roland Abbiate), posing as the TASS news agency chief in New York. Pravdin's prevous service to the NKVD/NKGB had been as an assassin: he had liquidated Reiss/Poretsky in Switzerland, despite Krivitsky's warning to his friend. As his parents had returned to their native France when their son (who had been born in pre-revolutionary St Petersburg) was eighteen, he obviously could not be trusted to look after an agent as important as Maclean for fear of his contaminated ideology. Pravdin and Apresyan sent resentful reports about each other back to Moscow (the former hit-man saying that the more insular Apresyan was 'utterly without the knack of dealing with people'); the 'Tyre' (as New York was code-named) office was in a state of 'civil war' until the spring of 1945 when Apresyan was relocated to San Francisco, or 'Babylon' as the witty code-namers called it in honour of its free-wheeling reputation. Yet it was the more experienced Pravdin who dealt with Maclean alone before Gorsky finally came to Washington, and who soon made the tradecraft blunder, possibly distracted by the need to show off his closeness to his important subject, that was to cost Maclean, the Foreign Office and Moscow Centre so dearly.

On 25 June, Maclean made his first visit to New York since his arrival to see Melinda and establish contact with Pravdin. Three days later Pravdin sent the telegram to Fitin to reassure him that contact had been made, but 'Maclean did not hand anything over.' The agent would be able to travel regularly to New York 'where his wife is living with her mother while awaiting confinement', and arrangements were in place for him to summon help 'in case of need'. Above all else their prize asset needed protecting.

From then on the conscientious diplomat handed over copious quantities of material, mainly photographic and often by necessity, given the volume of material he would otherwise have to take out of the Embassy, from his own capacious memory. His discipline was almost extraordinary. Every paper going through the Embassy in frenetic wartime Washington was accessible to him and, as he settled in, it might have been too much to have had his new family there as a distraction. As he was to show throughout the rest of his life, he was a proud father of his sons, however neglectful a husband, and it must be assumed that he minded this absence even amid this frantic, important and satisfying work. When Maclean later looked back on his life as a spy, this period confirmed to him 'a dozen times over in all its grimness the chief assumption upon which my decision to take on underground work was based', though he acknowledged that not even he could have foreseen the path of fascism in that time.

His ability to take in and synthesise facts and opinions stood him in good stead in both his legitimate and his illegitimate work: First Secretary Roddie Barclay commented after they had worked together on the peace treaty with Italy that he had been immensely impressed with the new man's 'skill at drafting and his ability to unravel complex issues'. Even in the fragments of the telegrams that have been decoded, we can hear his own voice coming through to précis, interpret and speed the transmission of material. This was possibly unique in modern espionage, and operated to his detriment in the end.

As he came so forcefully back into play, Maclean needed a new code-name to go with his new job, and was christened, with the literary skill that Moscow Centre frequently displayed, 'Homer'. The lonely 'Orphan' of 1935 has moved through the generic 'Lyric' poet of 1940 to become a fully fledged individual with a proper name, able to take on an importance in literature that could echo down the ages as a commentary on great events. And, of course, the identity of the original Homer, who sang of war, has never been established, just as it was hoped that the new poet of war would remain anonymous.

The scope of Maclean's role was outlined in a telegram to Moscow sent on the night of 2 August. It refers to a committee 'on economic and political questions' and 'the European Advisory Commission', and states that Maclean 'is present at all the sessions'. And, best of all, that the Soviets now had access to documents 'including the secret telegraphic correspondence of Boar with Captain'. In another happy piece of code-naming, 'Boar' is Churchill, and 'Captain' is Roosevelt. The Soviet Union had access to two of the planners of the future map of the world, who were clearly mistrustful of the third.

What was of greatest importance to Stalin was the post-war division of Europe. That same telegram stated that Britain's 'vital interests lie in the North Sea' and that therefore after Germany's defeat British troops should occupy the north-west quadrant of the country, as duly happened, even though at the time 'Roosevelt did not agree with this plan.' Useful as it was to know which likely future enemy would be bordering the Soviet spoils in Germany, this telegram gives even more valuable information to Russia about attitudes towards the spheres of Communist influence that seemed possible in the near future, as it refers to Turkey, Greece and Yugoslavia. After revealing that Operation Anvil, the US and British landings on the southern coast of Europe, would now take place later that month, the telegram notes that Churchill had tried to persuade Roosevelt to stage the landings on the Adriatic rather than the Mediterranean coastline, in order to take Trieste and advance into Yugoslavia and the Balkans, through the Alps and into Austria ahead of the Red Army. It was pleasing to the Russians to see that their allies could not agree on military strategy and, even better, it was a relief that the strategy was not going to encroach on their own territorial goals. Homer also spoke out to give his succinct, personal summary of the 'aims that are being pursued' by each country: 'Britain – strengthening of her influence in the Balkans; the USA – the desire for minimum involvement in European politics ... '.

Stalin needed to have this skilled civil servant's distillation of the arguments. He was already mentally wrestling with a fear that any direct action taken by the Soviets in Yugoslavia (the Yugoslavs wanted to fight their own battle with Germany and set up their own government) would be seen by the allies as supporting their theory that he was using the war as an excuse to spread revolutionary Communism throughout the world, a line of attack which had led him to his disband the Comintern the previous year. He had had an argument with Milovan Djilas, the former Communist leader of the country, ordering him to tell his men to take the red stars off their caps so as not to alarm the British. Or, as he put it, 'the form is not important but what is gained'. Above all, Stalin's suspicion of Churchill in the matter backed up Homer's analysis of British policy when he said, 'Churchill is the kind of man who will pick your pocket for a kopeck if you don't watch him ... Roosevelt ... dips in his hand only for bigger coins.' To know the situation so immediately almost from the horse's very mouth ('Yesterday H. [Homer] learnt of a change in the plans') would give Stalin the bargaining advantage when the three leaders next met in negotiation.

*

'The budding paragon', as he was known to his senior colleagues, worked ferociously hard, often staying in the office until 10 p.m. or later, and frequently taking work home. His reputation preceded him. He was viewed as 'efficient and conscientious ... amiable to meet, imperturbably good-tempered, elegant, exceedingly self-possessed, and with rather a cynical outlook on things that betrayed no particular ideological bias', while at the same time a

fellow diplomat didn't 'altogether care for a certain cold haughti-
ness of manner which showed through at times'. Once again, the
self-possession and amiability, the conscientiousness with little
evidence of flair, the distancing edge of cynicism, show a man
keeping his thoughts to himself – the perfect Foreign Office man.
However, when not on duty, maintaining his charming front
without letting his true self show was not always easy, particularly
when he was alone, unfettered by Melinda's watchful eye. It did
not need one as well versed in foreign affairs as he was to foresee
the looming division of Europe, and his whole inner being
despised the capitalist engine of his wife's country. He increasingly quenched his discomfort with drink, which caused him to
drop his daytime self-possessed polish and sowed the seeds of the
destruction to come.

Maclean was welcome prey for the society hostesses who
assumed him to be lonely and missing his wife and son when he
first arrived. In fact, he rarely spoke of Melinda, but when pressed
would show the excellent photographs he had taken of his family;
he had become much more skilled at photography since his early
days when he had depended on Kitty Harris to do all the technical work.

The Oxford philosopher Isaiah Berlin was not a conventional
figure in the Embassy. He had been seconded from the Ministry of
Information as a specialist attaché to write a weekly newsletter to
London. He was more on the liberal side than many of his colleagues, happy to say disrespectfully that the Ambassador was 'not
of this century'. Maclean stopped by his desk early on to speak of
people whom they knew in common such as the Bonham Carters,
and to say that he was working 'with Pentagon and State Department
people. They're all so pompous. I hear you know some New Dealers.
Could you invite some?' The New Deal programmes had been
launched in response to the Great Depression and are now broadly
characterised under the headings 'Relief, Recovery and Reform', of
more appeal to the left than to the 'pompous' right-wing hawks
complained of by Maclean. Berlin arranged for him to attend a
small Georgetown dinner-party given by Katharine Graham,

proprietor of the *Washington Post*, one of the celebrated and influential hostesses who saw the Macleans as 'attractive, intelligent, liberal young people'.

Maclean, still not much one for small talk, said little early on but 'drank hard' and started to come out of his shell – to such an extent that when Berlin repeated a witticism made by the acclaimed hostess Alice Longworth, Teddy Roosevelt's daughter, Maclean 'berated him in slurred tones for being so crass as to repeat the words of the stupid and reactionary Alice'. Maclean could not but be honest in his cups, and Graham remembered him as going even further, calling Longworth 'fascist and right-wing'. He was disappointed in Berlin and foresaw the time when a choice had to be made: 'Life is a battle ... We must stick to our side through thick and thin.'

When Berlin remonstrated with him, Maclean grabbed his colleague by the lapels and had to be pulled off him. Maclean later asked Berlin to lunch to make up, which was 'amicable' until Berlin made the throwaway remark after the meal that he thought Vice-President Henry Wallace 'had a screw loose', at which point Maclean had 'another tantrum' and shouted at him that he had slighted a man 'much admired by his wife and her family'. Wallace was a strong supporter of the New Deal, 'an unreconstructed liberal reformer' and such a strong advocate of softer policies towards the Soviet Union that his bid to become the Progressive Party's presidential candidate in 1948 failed when he refused to disavow the endorsement of his candidacy by the American Communist Party. The liberal Berlin, who thought Maclean 'very very nice', nevertheless found himself 'unable to forgive him' for this drunken, public exposure of the ideological divide between them, and they did not socialise again. It was the first report of such uninhibited behaviour, but not the last to remain within the tight Washington circle and kept from the Foreign Office files.

*

Throughout the summer and autumn the information continued to flow through Maclean's hands. He was always one of the first to arrive at the Embassy in the mornings to find the overnight cables 'unbuttoned' by Wilfrid Thomas, the acting senior staff officer, so that they could be read without a code-book. Maclean's ability to absorb, summarise and redirect these was legendary: Rebecca West was told that 'in all the history of the British Embassy at Washington it was probably never so exquisitely efficient, so impeccably organised' as when he was there in the closing year of the war.

Political matters were of much greater interest to the Russians than anything the King might have to say to Halifax. Even after a debauched evening, 'which he himself would liken to an alley cat's prowl round the garbage pails', Maclean could arise and address himself to some problem assigned to him by his Ambassador and 'collect the relevant information with an inspired competence not to be surpassed by any of his colleagues'. He carried his bulging briefcase home with him, often after leaving work at 10.00 p.m., and summarised what he had not managed to photograph. At this stage he could still be comfortable that he was not so much betraying confidential information as helping shape a more equitable Europe after a war won by both those he served. Everything was running smoothly.

The British and Americans were unable to outflank Stalin in their preparations for Europe after the now inevitable defeat of the Nazi regime because so much of their thinking was revealed to him. On 5 September Pravdin passed on to Fitin the news that Churchill and Roosevelt were planning to meet in Quebec in the next few days 'to discuss matters connected with the impending occupation of Germany', information passed on to him by Homer, who had also had a hand in setting the leaders' agenda. It did not matter that Stalin had not been invited; Maclean supplied him with the full minutes of the meeting which took place two days later. The allies had discussed the British economic situation and the Lend-Lease aid programme, the Pacific War, the Morgenthau Plan to deindustrialise Germany, and Greece, where Churchill hoped to maintain the monarchy and resist Russian influence.

Greece was an issue which inspired Maclean to speak out, to guide Stalin and Molotov in a way that crossed a moral espionage line between supplying information and influencing Soviet policy, thereby betraying his government's interests. It is the first time that the stress of the divisions between the allies showed through in his espionage work. There was a chaotic vacuum in Greece after the German retreat with pro- and anti-Communist resistance forces and the Greek monarchy-in-exile determined to govern. British forces were going in to stabilise the country with the clear aim of restoring the monarchy to prevent Communist control. In a telegram sent to Moscow Centre, Maclean spoke in a directly partial voice: 'Homer hopes we will take advantage of these circumstances to disrupt the plans of the British.' In May 1944, Stalin had agreed that Romania should be primarily a Russian concern while allowing the British the same influence in Greece, to the disgust of the Greek Communists, as Maclean knew well. He desperately wanted to make his own voice heard and his own Communist ideals to be realised in the urgent reshaping of Europe. It was a hope that was bound to be dashed, and Soviet policy disregarding his advice must have been a bitter blow. This was one of the first points of self-questioning as to whether he could keep his beliefs and careers on a parallel course, a difficulty exacerbated now that the Comintern had been disbanded: Maclean understood, if he had been in any doubt through the Great Terror and the Red Army's conduct of the war, that he was working directly for Stalin.

*

Maclean's long hours did not change much in January 1945, when Melinda and baby Fergus joined him. The family moved to 2710 35th Place, a mere ten-minute walk across Observatory Circle from the Embassy. Melinda did not find the move to the busy capital or being in charge of her own household for the first time in her life easy. Donald was distracted and not very companionable when he was at home. Their house was in a peaceful and smart part of town: the previous British tenant had been David Bowes-Lyon, Queen Elizabeth's brother and a director of Cunard's shipping lines. Melinda initially hired two maids from Jamaica (one to help with the baby), but both needed to 'be sent back because they proved to be unsatisfactory'. Neither she nor Donald could bring themselves to carry out the dismissals, so Mrs Dunbar, always summoned at her daughter's times of need, came from New York to sort things out. Robert Cecil, who had had a hand in the hiring, claimed that it was the discovery by the FBI in a routine check that one of the maids was a Communist and therefore had to be deported that might explain Donald's unwillingness, skilled negotiator and diplomat that he was, to engage with the situation. The Jamaicans were replaced by Marie Morvan, whom Donald had known in Paris. There was even a 'diaper man' who came each morning to take away the previous day's nappies and bring fresh ones.

Melinda, who had escaped the less stuffy New York society life for Paris in 1938, did not take to the political and social discourse that was the currency of the city, although she did on occasion dutifully host Embassy dinners as befitted the wife of a senior member of the legation. Her stepfather, with the usual rancour he voiced about the Marling family after he had divorced Melinda's mother, described her as 'a social misfit' who 'seemed to look down upon American social life', but this sounds truer of her husband.

Throughout it all, Donald's drinking grew worse. He was becoming increasingly anti-American as the fault-lines of the post-war world split more clearly between capitalism and socialism; when drunk this became a catch-all loathing for his wife's country, standing as it did for capitalism and mortgage-holder for his country since the early years of the war. He ranted about 'his contempt … for their naïve way of thinking, their inability to converse as adults, their instinctive vulgarity … ' and offered other insults directed particularly at American women. Not only was this deeply offensive to Melinda but the risk of such talk outside the home must also have been alarming to her given his position and the people with whom he socialised.

Yet when sober he became the charming diplomat once again. His neighbours found him 'a splendid person' and 'companionable, cheerful, with perfect manners'. Robert Cecil, who had joined his old colleague in April 1945, commented that he heard nothing said against their hosts by 'the coming man'. Maclean's shipmate George Middleton painted a picture of a relaxed husband and father, in spite of perhaps having 'too few interests away from his work'. The Middletons 'shared a common interest in gardening, played tennis together, met sometimes on Sundays for a pre-lunch drink'. Away from the possibility of work of any and all kinds, on their vacations on Long Island or in Florida, the tension dissolved, and the tennis-loving, devoted family man reappeared. But he needed the release that Melinda offered, and she in turn put up with a lot from the man she loved and admired.

*

The arrival of Gorsky from London in September 1944 as *rezident* was a great relief to Maclean. Gorsky could share the hard work of copying and transporting the material to New York, from where it was still transmitted to Moscow, as well as taking over part of Melinda's role as Maclean's escape valve. Maclean continued to go to New York, although less frequently, unquestioned by his colleagues because the trips had now become habit as well as out of respect for his seniority. Gorsky too shared in the success of his agent: he was publicly promoted to Counsellor in the spring of 1945, and more quietly became a colonel and was awarded the Order of the Patriotic War. Maclean became First Secretary in April 1945.

Maclean was so well connected that often he could see a message before it got to the State Department across town. In August 1944, 'Doc' Matthews, Deputy Director of European Affairs in the State Department, was puzzled to get a call from his old British friend from Paris days asking about a memo which had not yet reached him and which he did not know existed but which had emerged from a Joint Chiefs of Staff meeting in the White House, a mere hundred feet away. He cut the conversation short to consult with Admiral Leahy, Roosevelt's White House Chief of Staff and the senior officer of the JCS, and made a note that 'Maclean did not say where it had been obtained.' Maclean had got hold of it through his membership of the Combined Civil Affairs Committee which dealt with war-related political and economic problems. This particular item would have highlighted a problem to the Russians as it dealt with a strategy for driving the Japanese out of Indochina and with the setting up after the war of political spheres of influence to be decided by a Chinese–British–American Committee. But the exigencies of the time and the impeccable reputation of Maclean meant that this conundrum was not puzzled over by the Americans. It was a puzzle that was not brought to mind again until 1951.

The stepping up of OSS counter-espionage measures caused Gorsky concern as Washington *rezident* about the risks of receiving material directly from Maclean. He urged Moscow Centre to find an American courier who would arouse less suspicion were such potential, often blameless, lapses as that involving Matthews to be investigated; at one point he even suggested Melinda. Although Gorsky did not say whether she knew about her husband's secret life or not, the implication was clear. But Maclean's ability to interpret and process information quickly in these high-volume days made him indispensable and the idea was not pursued. Pravdin gave an assessment of Homer which highlighted the very skills that made him such a success in both his official careers: he 'impressed one as a man of great initiative who does not need to be prompted in his work. He also orients himself very well to the international situation and understands what questions represent our major interests. I do not feel a desire on his part to evade working with us. Instead, he thinks that meeting too infrequently does not give him an opportunity to pass along operational information in a timely way.'

Once again in the twisted logic of Moscow Centre some saw this very assiduity as confirmation of his being a double agent after all. But for now these doubts were put to one side. The material was far too accurate and far too useful for such an accusation to be formally made at that moment. As the Grand Alliance of Britain, the US and the USSR approached its end with the imminent defeat of Germany and the formation of a new world order, Homer's espionage was about to become even more vital even as that first telegram from New York was lying encrypted in the files.

9

Iron Curtain

The Yalta Conference of February 1945 shaped post-war Europe. The geographical situation at the end of the war was now reasonably clear: the Western allies' troops had still not crossed the Rhine into Germany and were making little ground in Italy; by contrast, the Red Army had reached the banks of the Oder, with Czechoslovakia, the Baltic states, Poland and a large part of Germany already behind them. They were closing in on Berlin. When the 'Big Three', Roosevelt, Churchill and Stalin, met at the resort town on the Black Sea, Stalin not only had the upper hand in terms of territory, but held the intelligence trump cards. He was exceptionally well prepared for the conference, thanks in very large part to Donald Maclean of the British Embassy in Washington and Alger Hiss of the US State Department. But the end of the war and the new dispositions came at a cost to Maclean that would set the tone for the rest of his career as a spy and a diplomat. The risks he and the Soviets had taken during wartime would be much harder to get away with as peace brought new priorities.

*

British and American observers were denied access to news from Poland but from the government-in-exile in London they had heard tell of deportations and executions of those who opposed Communism. Stalin was so in control of the planning for the conference that, notwithstanding President Roosevelt's illness and obvious decline, he claimed that 'any change of climate would have a bad effect' on his own health. So the ailing Roosevelt and the elderly Churchill and twenty-five aeroplane-loads of officials travelled to meet the General Secretary in his own country and enjoy his remarkable hospitality.

The Crimean meeting place ensured that both delegations were comprehensively bugged in their respective grand residences. At one point Sarah Churchill, accompanying her father, mentioned that lemon juice went well with caviar; 'the next day a lemon tree loaded with fruit' had been flown from a great distance and was 'growing in the hall' of the house where the Churchills were staying. The impresario of this largesse, General Kruglov, was awarded an honorary KBE and thus became the only member of the Russian secret service to receive a knighthood. At the same time as this honour was being bestowed, a reciprocal thank-you was given secretly by the Soviet Deputy Premier Andrei Vyshinsky to one of the organisers and attendees on the US side, Alger Hiss, a star of the State Department who was to become Director of Special Political Affairs dealing with the new United Nations.

Stalin may have had the upper hand at the negotiating table through his military success, but Moscow Centre's intelligence operations gave him everything he needed to negotiate with before the conference began. On 23 and 28 January he had had full debriefings on the British and American strategies. The second briefing came a day after the NKGB had left him with a full translation of the British delegates' strategy paper, which addressed the partition of Germany (with Anthony Eden's memo of the previous December included), the formation of the United Nations and which of the USSR's republics would have a role in that, what questions the British and the Americans each thought important and which party would raise them: it included the discussion points about Poland, indeed it included everything. The briefings were a tribute to the hard work and influence of Maclean, Hiss and the rest of Fitin's intelligence network. Fitin's code-name was currently, and undeniably, 'Viktor'.

So successful were the pre-conference briefings that Stalin even had the confidence to bring to the grand opening dinner his own 'Himmler', as he put it, the 'little and fat' head of the NKVD,

Lavrenti Beria, his eyes glinting behind their thick lenses. Once he had his feet under the table, the secret policeman discussed the sex lives of fishes with the 'boozy, womanising' British Ambassador to Moscow, Sir Archibald Clark Kerr. Clark Kerr was so taken with Beria that he proposed a toast to him as 'the man who looks after our bodies' and had to be told to calm down by Churchill. Some people there had a pretty good idea of how many millions of bodies would never be heard of again thanks in part to Beria, but such was the charm and the cordiality of the whole event that the well-pampered Churchill was encouraged enough to write afterwards that 'Poor Neville Chamberlain believed he could trust Hitler. He was wrong. But I don't think I'm wrong about Stalin.' Uncle Joe, as Churchill nicknamed him, was put in such good humour by the conference that he clowned about in the photoshoot to mark its close, jovially repeating his only four phrases of English, 'You said it!'; 'So what?'; 'What the hell goes on round here?' and 'The toilet is over there.'

Poland and its governance was the subject of seven out of eight plenary sessions at the conference as the British and Americans pushed for free and open government. Stalin insisted that there must be more control to prevent the country being used as a military corridor through to Russia as it had been by Hitler and Napoleon. One of the high points of the Grand Alliance was Stalin's agreement to hold 'free and unfettered elections' in Poland, possibly within the next month, and it was left to the diplomats to see this woolly resolution through. What actually happened the following month was that the Russians, encountering more resistance in Poland than they had expected, invited the sixteen emaciated leaders of the Polish underground to come to London to discuss how relations might be improved. The sixteen duly presented themselves at Marshal Zhukov's Warsaw HQ, expecting to be flown to London, but were diverted to Moscow and never heard from again. A diplomatic storm predictably erupted. Churchill had 'never been more anxious' than he was then 'about the state of Europe', as he cabled Truman who, after only eighty-three days as Vice-President, had become President following Roosevelt's death on 12 April. Truman sent his personal emissary, Harry Hopkins (who was so close to the presidency that he was still living in the bedroom in the White House that he had slept in after a late-night session in May 1940), to negotiate in Moscow.

The embassies were lit at all hours of the day and night, encrypting, decoding, passing messages between London, Moscow, Washington and San Francisco, where the Foreign Secretary Anthony Eden was overseeing the founding of the United Nations. Maclean was at the centre of the traffic with his precision 'watchmaker's mind' and his ability to analyse complex material. He passed on Churchill's urgently worded telegrams to Truman imploring the President to be firm – 'we must not cease our effort on behalf of the Poles'. He passed on the White House's summaries of Hopkins's reports from Moscow, the emissary gloomy about getting Stalin to shift his position on the Polish leaders or the country itself. He passed on the instructions given to Sir Archie Clark Kerr from the Foreign Office via Halifax in Washington discussing 'some major differences of tactics'. The Russians had the incalculable advantage of being able to read that Sir Archie did not 'think that Molotov, despite his stubbornness, has said his last word', or that Halifax believed British intransigence over Romania would 'invite a head-on collision with the Russians'. They could drive home this advantage without any qualms that they might lose their debate. No negotiation could be easier once 'H' (for 'Homer') had transmitted the report that 'Smyrna' (the British Embassy in Moscow) had told the 'Pool' (the Washington Embassy) that the State Department had concluded that the Americans would 'pursue no course on which we should not be willing to rest our case should Molotov remain adamant'. The adamant side knew that they just needed to stand their ground to win.

The speed with which these telegrams passed through his hands meant that Maclean sometimes had whole items sent on undigested, using Gorsky as the intermediary. The urgency of the material meant that it could not go by diplomatic pouch, but had to be telegraphed in encoded cable form. As the whole Embassy was working around the clock, his hectic activity, dashing in and out of his office to take notes and photographs, would not be remarked upon. Such was his importance to Moscow that his offerings were flagged up 'Materials from H' in order to ensure priority reading on arrival. Homer himself was fulfilled and excited, working all hours in this crisis to send vital information that would shape, as he believed, a post-war Europe more in keeping with his own ideological sympathies.

*

Maclean was unlikely to be aware that under US censorship laws during wartime copies of all foreign commercial radiogram traffic sent via Western Union, RCA Global and ITT World Communications, the three commercial carriers, had to be stored for reference. Had he been so, he would have thought little of it as he would have been reassured that the one-time pads rendered the Russian codes unbreakable. The Russians had chosen this form of transmission for security reasons: short-wave radio could too easily be tapped. In August 1945, a law was passed by which these carriers had to hand over to the government their copies of 'enciphered telegrams of certain foreign targets' and the following month what was assumed to be innocent messages between diplomats at the Soviet Consulate in New York and the People's Commissariat of Foreign Affairs in Moscow were lodged with the US Signal Intelligence Service in Arlington Hall. By the end of the year over 200,000 seemingly uncrackable cables, some of them pages long, had been transcribed and stored in undecoded form.

*

Guy Liddell was a cultivated man who had been studying in Germany to become a cellist when the First World War put an end to that career and took him into the army and then to Scotland Yard after the Armistice. He had moved to MI5 in 1931 and become a Soviet expert, head of counter-espionage in B Division in 1940, where he appointed Anthony Blunt, possibly at the suggestion of his friend Guy Burgess, as his assistant. Liddell was also Philby's main contact within MI5, and was held in high regard by the MI6 man: 'He would murmur his thoughts as if groping his way towards the facts of a case, his face creased in a comfortable, innocent smile. But behind the façade of laziness, his subtle and reflective mind played over a storehouse of photographic memories.' Liddell noted in his diary, in the run-up to Yalta, that Philby came to check the Krivitsky file, ostensibly to 'satisfy himself that he was on sound ground' with regard to someone he had just taken on in the Russian section. Philby's real motives, as always, were much more self-serving: he wanted to see if Krivitsky had incriminated him and was also checking on how safe Maclean, whom he had not seen for years, might be should another look be given in the context of the emerging world order at those with previous left-wing links. What he learned from Krivitsky's debriefing he would use for altogether different ends.

With the end of the war in sight and notwithstanding Modrzhinskaya's machinations, Moscow Centre decided to reward the agents who had made the most significant contribution to victory. Fitin suggested that Philby be awarded an annual pension of £1,500; Maclean, Cairncross, Burgess and Blunt £1,200 each.* But before submitting his recommendations, Fitin asked the local *rezidentura* to contact the Five. Gorsky duly raised the subject at his next meeting with Homer. All refused the pension, on the grounds that 'it would be difficult for them to explain the existence of large sums of money', and, in Maclean's case, it would have felt like accepting money for doing a job he had no taste for but every moral obligation to perform. Burgess did apparently accept 'expenses', and after the war bought a gold, soft-topped, second-hand Rolls-Royce on the grounds that he was such a terrible driver that a 'sturdily built' car was a life-saving necessity. That was sufficiently within the former *enfant terrible*'s character (and potential means) for it not to attract undue suspicion.

*

---

* £1,200 in 1945 is roughly equivalent to £36,000 today.

Maclean had always disliked the grubbiness inherent in the physical business of spying, as he had made plain in his letter to Moscow
Centre at the time of his stillborn son and the doom-laden isolation of the Blitz. The sober, fastidious diplomat felt the shame of the
ideologue who had to break the law when his job and his conscience
fell on different sides. It was 'like being a lavatory attendant; it
stinks but someone has to do it'. For Maclean, this distaste, mixed
with his appreciation of the importance and scale of his leaks during these last exhausting, euphoric months, brought his double life
into sharp focus. The possibility that he might have to make a
choice between patriotism and ideology must have occurred to
him even as he joined the all-night celebrations on the streets of
Washington after the bombs dropped on Hiroshima and Nagasaki
had brought the Pacific War to a close in August 1945.

In many ways he was on the winning side: the Russians had triumphed at Yalta and later at Potsdam, with his intelligence playing
a crucial role in the negotiations. The Soviets now controlled
Central and Eastern Europe. A Labour government had swept to
power in Britain in July 1945 (Churchill and Eden had had to yield
their places to Attlee and Bevin in the middle of the Potsdam
Conference, so brutal is the handover of power in the British system); Communist governments looked likely to win in France and
Italy; insurgencies controlled by Moscow were threatening the
Greek and Iranian regimes. But at the level of his service to his
country on which the outer man thrived, there was the gradual,
inescapable and painful realisation that as the US entrenched its
positions on most issues, the Grand Alliance was becoming a Cold
War stand-off. Maclean feared that the United States, aided and
abetted by Britain, was on the point of launching 'a political and
military crusade against socialist states'.

In his unsettled state, Maclean now started to indulge in near-
constant off-duty drinking, acting belligerently and lashing out at
those around him and most of all at his wife's unacceptably capitalist countrymen – all the while maintaining the poise and cool
expected of the First Secretary of His Britannic Majesty's Embassy
to the United States of America. His diligence and effectiveness

were still much commented upon, but, as with the earlier side-swipes at his immaturity, less flattering notes crept in, in this case from his friend and ally Middleton, who commented that he was 'patient' and 'even-tempered', liked by his junior staff, yet 'sometimes rather sleepy and lackadaisical in manner'. Possibly this is diplomatic code for hung over, or for his withdrawal from engagement and the consequent squeamishness he would have felt from time to time about the path he was treading.

The young British diplomat came to the attention of Joseph Alsop, the influential conservative columnist on the *Herald Tribune*, a cousin of Franklin Roosevelt and one of the great hosts of Washington. A friend had told Alsop that he ought to get to know Maclean as it would only be a matter of time before 'he returned as Ambassador to Washington'. Maclean was invited to one of Alsop's celebrated dinner-parties alone, since Melinda, the tempering influence, was still away for the summer. The conversation turned to the crisis in Iranian Azerbaijan. Stalin was keeping 75,000 troops there in violation of the 1943 Teheran Agreement, ostensibly to protect Russia from Iran, but actually to command the oil fields in the region – and slide his border a couple of hundred miles east to make sure he kept them. Maclean started by attacking the young Shah, installed by the allies, before turning on American policy. He called it 'amateurish and ineffectual', strong language for a diplomat when it was also his country's policy. Alsop's good manners kept him back until Maclean launched in on James Byrnes, who had recently been appointed Secretary of State, at which point his host could restrain himself no longer: 'Jimmy Byrnes happens to be a very close friend of mine, and I find your comments grossly offensive.' But Maclean ploughed soddenly on until he was told to leave the house.

The divide between the intoxicated, angry, arrogant Maclean and the suave diplomat was becoming so marked that there was near-disbelief when this sort of behaviour was spoken of. Such a strong display of animosity towards the Secretary of State by a prominent member of a foreign legation could not go officially unremarked. But when it was reported to John D. Hickerson,

Deputy Director of the Office of European Affairs in the State Department, his reaction, recalled later, was: 'I knew Maclean and I liked him. He was intelligent and dependable ... If I had called Central Casting and said, "Send me someone to play the quintessential British diplomat," they would have sent me Maclean.' The complaint did not get back to the British Embassy, where the general attitude was expressed by Paul Gore-Booth, a close colleague who himself later came under suspicion for espionage. Maclean 'was a tall, quiet attractive man with an apparently tranquil, settled family life and a professional ability that was quite outstanding. When hard pressed, you could leave it with perfect confidence to Donald.' The recently promoted First Secretary, still only thirty-two, continued to receive the plaudits that did indeed keep him on track for the highest echelons of the service.

But the expenditure of effort against the turbulent geopolitical background was taking its toll on Maclean's mental equilibrium. He was inwardly bitter towards Whitehall and the new Labour government for kowtowing to the Americans in their anti-Soviet policy, although more circumspect about going out on that particular limb, drunk or not. He later wrote that 'British diplomacy, official and unofficial, bent itself to the task of persuading American opinion that a Communist take-over in Europe was imminent, of pushing the US government into the leadership of an anti-Soviet alliance, and of consolidating London's position as Washington's chief partner within it.' He said that 'this was the aim' of Churchill's speech at Fulton, Missouri, the following March, in which the former Prime Minister declared, 'From Stettin in the Baltic to Trieste in the Adriatic, an iron curtain has descended across the continent.' Stalin's reaction to the speech came in an interview in *Pravda* in which he compared Churchill with Hitler in his belief that 'the English-speaking nations are the only nations of full value and must rule over the remaining nations of the world'.

Maclean was worn out by the mounting tension between his twin roles, and fatigued by the falsity and pretentiousness of his colleagues. He wrote to Melinda, just before her return to Washington in early September, to report that 'I get utterly sick of the game of personalities within our own circle; everything has been said and laughed at fifty times over' by those who indulge in 'continuous tracing of people's exact social history and behaviour'. His preference, he said, was for 'the craggier characters here' (possibly meaning those who liked to drink as much as him, but certainly not any of the smooth diplomats) before admitting that he was 'rather fed up with the logic of personalities altogether'.

His efforts to keep up his front and maintain his reputation during the day while clearly longing to isolate himself at home made for an anxious time for Melinda, exacerbated by the stiff whiskies her husband would down as soon as he left the office. Melinda had been toughened over the past few years, not least by her personal trials, but she still felt intimidated by Donald's superior intelligence and had the burden of being the only person who knew of his secret life and bitterness. She said she 'could criticise America; there's lots to criticise. But I do so with love and affection; Donald did so with hatred.' Keen to establish a stable base for herself and the children, she spent a lot of time with her sisters and her mother. Lady Maclean came to visit the family shortly after the end of the war, escaping the gloom and rationing in Britain that persisted well into the next decade (Melinda would never live in a Britain without rationing), and her visit coincided with one of Mrs Dunbar's. According to fellow diplomat Robert Cecil, 'There was not much cordiality to the encounter between Mrs Dunbar in her silk dress and high heels and Lady Maclean in tweed coat and skirt and sensible walking-shoes.' A further division between the formidable grandmothers was perhaps created by one favouring a dry Martini and the other a Scotch and soda, symbolising a core difference for the English grandmother, widow of a pillar of rectitude, who admitted she 'does not find herself in sympathy with Mrs Dunbar, who has been twice divorced'. Donald felt that 'part of [his mother-in-law's] charm' was 'her readiness with the drink', but when she was 'high, which she becomes very quickly, she becomes very tiresome indeed', turning into 'a remorseless and conscienceless talker'. George Middleton described the joint visit as 'at times both painful and comic'.

Melinda felt so insecure in this unpredictable environment that her shyness became almost overwhelming. If her husband invited a couple of mutual friends over for dinner he would not tell her in advance for fear that she would ask for the evening to be put off because she was so uncertain of how he might behave. The new atmosphere of mistrust, at work, at home and on the larger stage abroad, was soon to threaten their personal stability – and Maclean's professional standing.

10

Distant Thunder

The dramas in the second, pivotal, act of Donald Maclean's life took place mostly offstage. For the first time in his career as a spy, there were serious threats of discovery, yet the most dangerous of all worked quietly in the background, unknown to him until years after it was too late. At the same time, the British establishment and security services received their first clear warnings that some of those in whom they had placed their trust might have put their ideology ahead of the Official Secrets Act, yet they did not institute retrospective background checks.

The atmosphere got chillier and chillier between the West and the Soviet Union, but Maclean's access to both sides enabled him to play a part in preventing what could have been a bloody escalation of bad feelings into hostilities. And his most outstanding peacetime service to the Soviet Union was still in the future. Although the urgency of the war was now past, the post-war period had less clear rules and alliances, and more uncertain outcomes.

*

The first threat to Maclean's charmed existence came from a country he would never visit. It would have been a disaster for him if Moscow Centre, the late Arnold Deutsch in particular, had not taken such care in building their top British network. The Cambridge Five, by now penetrating ever further into the vital and secretive branches of their government, had never come closer to exposure.

On 4 September 1945, Konstantin Volkov, the Soviet Vice-Consul in Istanbul, walked into the British Consulate with his wife and asked for a meeting with Chantry Page, his opposite number. Zoya Volkov was in 'a deplorably nervous state' and Volkov himself 'far from rock steady'. Page had had a letter from Volkov the previous month but had dismissed it as a prank, or maybe he had forgotten it as he was prone to memory lapses after being caught in a bomb blast in the city's Pera Palace Hotel a few years before. He did not speak Russian, so he brought in a colleague to interpret. Volkov turned out to be the deputy chief of the NKGB in Turkey and prior to that had worked for years on the British desk at Moscow Centre. John Leigh Reed, the Russian-speaking First Secretary at the Embassy, sent a top-secret memo to London on the same day stating that Volkov had said 'he had some information of great importance to give me. For the last two and a half years the Soviets had been able to read all the telegrams between the Foreign Office and the British Embassy in Moscow.' Moreover, the Russians had 'two agents inside the Foreign Office ... and seven inside the British Intelligence Service [including one fulfilling the function of head of a section of British counter-espionage in London] passing them information of great importance'. In Volkov's flat in Moscow there was apparently a suitcase containing the names of 314 Soviet agents in Turkey, 250 in Britain, and 'a great deal of other information connected with Soviet activities' which the putative defector would be grateful if the British could arrange to collect.

Volkov wasn't prepared to divulge the names of the two Foreign Office agents unless the British were 'interested' in the information he had to give, and begged that the note of this meeting go in handwritten form and not by telegraph, as the Russians had broken so many British ciphers. He would be in touch again in a few days. Volkov was not a defector who had fallen out of love with the system, as Krivitsky had been, but a frightened man who had had a blazing row with his Ambassador and wanted asylum and £50,000 for his information.* If he did not hear from Page within twenty-one days, he would assume the deal was off and take his business elsewhere.

---

* Around £1.5 million ($2.5 million dollars) today; $200,000 is the rough equivalent of £50,000 in 1945.

The British did not believe that their ciphers had been broken but respected Volkov's demand that the papers go via the diplomatic bag, which meant that it was some days before they reached 'C', the boss of MI6, Sir Stewart Menzies. Menzies decided that the best person to assess the matter was his head of Soviet counter-intelligence, Kim Philby. Philby saw at once that the two agents inside the Foreign Office must refer to Maclean and Burgess and that the 'head of a section of counter-espionage in London' was none other than himself. He 'told the Chief that I thought we were on to something of the greatest importance' and that he would report back in the morning. His secretary was not to disturb him as he pondered the situation in his office, which gave him time to alert his handler, Boris Krötenschield, 'Krechin'. Philby was in the unique situation of being asked to investigate something that would bring down the network he had built up, and there could be only one desired outcome. His persuasive sangfroid made him just the man for the job – he merely needed to be told to take it on.

However, Philby was greeted the following day with the news that C had met Sir Douglas Roberts, head of Security Middle East, the previous evening in White's Club and had decided to put Roberts on the case instead. Luckily for Philby, Roberts was known to hate flying to the extent that it was in his contract that he would not have to do so. He planned to return to his base in Cairo by sea before travelling on to Turkey. This was the ideal pretext for Philby to suggest he go himself to save time on Volkov's looming deadline. He could get there soon enough and could see through his scheduled meetings in London first.

When Philby did finally leave, the weather played into his hands: a storm over Malta forced his plane to land in Tunis, and then by the time he got to Cairo it was too late to catch the flight on to Istanbul. He eventually reached the city on 26 September, five days after the Turkish Consulate in Moscow had given visas to two 'diplomatic couriers', in fact Moscow Centre assassins, to travel to Istanbul. Since Philby had arrived on a Friday afternoon, the Ambassador had already left to sail his yacht on the Black Sea for the weekend and could not be contacted. Philby went to the British

Consulate on the Monday to meet Reed and Page. They rang to speak to the Soviet Vice-Consul, and after some clickings and unexplained transfers, a voice on the other end said that Volkov had left for Moscow. He and his wife had indeed gone home, heavily sedated and carried to a waiting aircraft on stretchers, en route to their inevitable fate. Philby wrote a report on what he thought might have happened to alert the Russians: perhaps the couple had been seen to act nervously. 'Another theory – that the Russians had been tipped off about Volkov's approach to the British – had no solid evidence to support it. It was not worth including,' he coolly wrote. Such dismissiveness had the desired effect of making the Volkov episode disappear from official view. It had indeed been 'a very narrow squeak indeed' for him and for Maclean.

*

Maclean was in perfect ignorance of all that went on in Istanbul, fortunately for his increasingly fragile temperament. He did get to hear about the next moment of danger. The day after the unfortunate Volkov had presented himself at the British Consulate, a twenty-six-year-old cipher clerk working for the GRU (Soviet military intelligence) in Ottawa put 109 documents inside his shirt and left the Soviet Embassy, sucking in his stomach and 'hoping that as the evening was so warm … a sloppy-looking shirt wouldn't arouse undue interest'. Igor Gouzenko then took a streetcar downtown and into the Ottawa *Journal* building. Just before he knocked on the editor's office door he realised in a panic that an important newspaper like the *Journal* would surely have NKGB moles on the staff, and promptly ran out. At home, his wife (who had earlier told him he looked pregnant with his contraband, and was herself heavily pregnant) told him to calm down and try again – but by this time the editor had gone home for the night. Gouzenko incoherently offered the documents to a man with a green eyeshade, who could not read Russian and said he thought it really sounded like a matter for the Royal Canadian Mounted Police.

A Mountie on the street pointed out that, as it was midnight, whatever it was he was trying to say could just as well wait until morning. After a sleepless night, Gouzenko tried the *Journal* again, which showed no interest, and the Ministry of Justice, whose staff thought he wanted to take out Canadian citizenship rather than asylum effective immediately. In desperation he and his wife followed the Ministry's advice and went to the Crown Attorney's office to enquire about naturalisation, which would give them the protection of Canadian citizenship; they wept when they were told that it would take months. They had no recourse except to go back to their flat. By the time they got there, the Soviets had realised that both he and the papers were missing (the cause of all this was that Gouzenko had been summoned back to Moscow to explain why he had left classified documents unlocked one night, and they were keeping an eye on his paperwork security) and had arrived to break down the door to his flat. Under Soviet rules, the family should not have had a flat of their own so that junior operatives could keep an eye on each other, but Gouzenko's boss's wife could not bear the crying of the baby when they had cohabited, so that rule had gone by the board. The Gouzenkos clambered over the balcony with their terrified two-year-old son and into the next-door apartment, where a Royal Canadian Air Force sergeant lived. The Russians were soon beating on his door. The police arrived to find the Gouzenko flat being ransacked by NKVD *rezident* Pavlov and the matter went back to the Ministry of Justice and to Prime Minister Mackenzie King. Gouzenko had at last found sanctuary after one of the most challenging defections of the century.*

When the papers that had been inside Gouzenko's shirt were translated, they revealed the existence of a comprehensive infiltration of Parliament, Royal Canadian Air Force intelligence, the Department of Supplies and Munitions, and allied atomic research

---

* The NKVD and their successor agencies spent the next thirty-seven years searching for Gouzenko to punish him. When a Progressive Conservative MP, Thomas Cossitt, asked a question in the Canadian House of Commons about Gouzenko's pension, they assumed the defector was a constituent of his, tried and failed to 'befriend' Cossitt, and then until the MP's death in 1982 dug into his private life to try to find material for blackmail.

laboratories. Among the code-words Gouzenko passed on were 'neighbours' for the NKGB, 'roof' for a front to conceal espionage operations and 'shoemaker' for a forger of false passports. In the course of twenty-four hours, Prime Minister King was awakened to the new reality of espionage and went from being prepared to hand the man back to the Russians (who were now claiming he was on the run because he had stolen money from them) to shock and despair at what had been perpetrated. On the night of 7 September, he wrote in his diary that 'it is all very terrible and frightening' and that it could 'mean a complete break-up of the relations we have depended upon to keep the peace. There is no saying what terrible lengths this whole thing might go to ... I can see that from now until the end of my days, it will be this problem more than any other that, in all probability, I shall be most closely concerned with.' The FBI Director J. Edgar Hoover sent two agents to Ottawa on the Monday to question Gouzenko. On Wednesday the 12th Hoover reported to the White House that Gouzenko's spoils showed that a British physicist, Dr Alan Nunn May, who had been working at the Chalk River establishment (the Canadian equivalent of the US Manhattan Project) in Ontario since January 1943, had been leaking atomic secrets to Russia. The news that any atomic information had leaked only a month after the highly classified Nagasaki and Hiroshima bombs had ended the Second World War was momentous.

Nunn May was a brilliant scientist, but an unassuming man, with the perfect cover appearance of 'rather a mousy little chap like a suburban bank clerk'. He had not only been at Cambridge at the same time as Maclean but at the same small college, Trinity Hall. Nunn May had been no more noticeably left-wing than anyone else at the university but he was less public about it than Maclean. After he left Cambridge he had been in close contact with Communists, but that never emerged as a possible issue. Following the award of his PhD in 1936, Nunn May went to continue his studies in Leningrad and on his return joined the editorial board of the *Scientific Worker*, from where he 'continued his unobtrusive, persistent support of the left'. He came to the notice of the security services only once, in 1938, when he attended a 'Communist Party fraction meeting' at the British Association of Scientific Workers conference in London. Like many scientists, he believed that scientific knowledge should be freely shared around the world – particularly to allies in time of war. Seconded to Tube Alloys, as the British atomic research programme was originally code-named, and without any background checks whatsoever, Nunn May travelled to the safety of Canada in 1942 with his fellow scientists to continue the work there; he passed to the Russians scientific material and samples of uranium (in return for a faintly insulting $200 inside a Haig whisky bottle). He was now back at King's College, London, working on his research, unaware that he had been fingered by Gouzenko.

The news of the defection was fed back to London via the Washington Embassy. Although Maclean had not been a particular friend, personal or political, of Nunn May (who did not feature in the CUSS) even as a fellow left-wing student in a small college, and had had no contact with him since, who knew what else Gouzenko might know and be saying, or what links might be made by a suspicious mind in London to more vociferous Cambridge Communists? If Maclean was chilled by the news, Philby was highly 'agitated' as Krechin reported, coming as it did at the same time as the Volkov bombshell.

The natural interrogator for Gouzenko in London would have been Jane Archer, who had done such a superb job in opening up Krivitsky in 1940. If better use had been made of her reports, she could have ended the careers of both Maclean and Philby, as Philby knew from recently checking the file. The difference this time was that Philby had become her boss after she had moved from MI5 to MI6, and understood how skilled she was. So in order to neutralise her Archer's next job was to analyse intercepted radio activity in Eastern Europe while Philby got word to Moscow that it was imperative that Nunn May's London rendezvous with his controller, the first of which was due to take place the following month, be aborted. The scientist's security tail did not see him, as they had hoped they would following Gouzenko's testimony, walking up and down outside the British Museum, a rolled-up copy of *The Times* under his arm. MI5 were thwarted in their determination to catch the traitor red-handed, the only sure way to a decent legal case should he deny everything since Gouzenko's evidence could not be admitted in court for reasons of national security, not to say of national embarrassment. But Nunn May had no stomach for a fight and gave a relieved partial confession: he had been approached in Canada by a Soviet agent and had given him a report on atomic research and two samples of Uranium-235 'because he thought it was in the general interest that the Russians be kept in the picture' as allies. Influential voices supportive of this view were thin on the ground, but Joseph E. Davies, former US Ambassador to the Soviet Union and an outspoken admirer of Stalin's, wrote in the *New York Times* in February 1946 that Russia 'in self-defense has every moral right to seek atomic-bomb secrets through military espionage if excluded from such information by her former fighting allies'.

In May 1946, the first of the atom spies was handed down a ten-year sentence. The Attorney-General Sir Hartley Shawcross, who had been Britain's Chief Prosecutor at the Nuremberg war crimes tribunal, prosecuted this 'somewhat squalid case'. The trial lasted only a day, 'a rehearsal in an empty theatre' with the judge's summing-up accusing Nunn May of 'crass conceit ... wickedness ... and degradation'. After his conviction, Nunn May said, in his mild-mannered way, that 'the whole affair was extremely painful to me and I only embarked upon it because I felt this was a contribution I could make to the safety of mankind'. When the news reached Los Alamos, fellow scientist and spy-at-large Klaus Fuchs commented that he didn't believe Nunn May knew much of importance anyway.

The exposure of Nunn May shook the British security services, and awakened them to the need to look at their own more closely. John Curry, who had spoken for many of his MI5 colleagues when he said he had felt 'an acute sense of shame' after Munich, argued for increased counter-espionage resources: 'We are now in a position vis-à-vis Russia similar to that [which] we had vis-à-vis Germany in 1939/1940 in the sense that we have little positive knowledge of the basic structure of the organisation which we have to counter.' His plea fell largely on deaf ears in the war-exhausted departments of Whitehall. A stretched MI5 never looked into other prominent left-wing contemporaries or possible indoctrination in formative university years. Although the investigators realised that Nunn May must have been working for the Soviets in London before he went to Canada, because it emerged that the Soviet Military Attaché in Canada had been 'instructed to approach him and give him a password', the link between early Communism and later espionage had not been made.

The Washington Embassy was the forwarding office for the traffic between Ottawa and London, so Maclean had an uneasy if informed view of the proceedings, though he was ignorant of Philby's role in them. His first recruiter, the man he had barely seen since, was taking up the protective role that would be his for the next few years, for self-interested reasons as much as any. When Philby eventually became aware of the secrets Maclean had been conveying, he could see all the more clearly the importance of this protection to both source and recipients. They 'dealt with political problems of some complexity, and on more than one occasion Homer was spoken of with respect' by the normally callous Moscow Centre. The stakes were getting higher.

*

The next alarm came from closer to home in more than one sense. Elizabeth Bentley, an American, was variously described as a 'svelte and striking blonde' and a 'Nutmeg Mata Hari'. Her code-name was 'Helen'; given the inventive Russian humour in nomenclature, maybe the model was Helen of Troy, whose sexuality was the most notable feature in her life choices, as it was for Bentley. Bentley's family had come over on the *Mayflower* and she herself was an alumna of Vassar, Columbia University and the University of Florence, where she had abandoned her membership of the Gruppo Universitario Fascista and moved to the other side of the political spectrum after an affair with her anti-fascist faculty adviser. She joined the Communist Party of America in 1935, and started to give information to the Party after getting a job in the Italian Library of Information, which was in effect the Italian fascists' outlet in the US. In 1938 she met and became the lover of Jacob Golos, a Russian-American Jew two decades older who was also one of the key Soviet controllers in the US, running dozens of agents in New York and Washington, including Kitty Harris's ex-husband, Earl Browder, the former head of the American Communist Party. In her memoir *Out of Bondage*, Bentley described her seduction in poetic terms, when 'time and space seemed to stand still' until she floated 'away into an ecstasy that seemed to have no beginning and no end'. Golos rather lowered the high-flown tone by saying, 'You and I have no right, under Communist discipline, to feel the way we do about each other.' Bentley described Golos meeting American spies on street corners; she often answered the telephone to them herself to arrange their rendezvous with her lover.

In 1940, the same year that Golos's planning for the assassination of Trotsky in Mexico bore fruit, he was forced to register as an emissary of the Soviet government under the Foreign Agents Registration Act in order to take up his cover job with the United States Shipping and Service Corporation, a Comintern front organisation. This registration would have endangered his agents, so he needed a courier to act as go-between. His mistress moved her work to the same company. She was given the inept code-name of 'Wise Girl', and became the key courier, often bringing back forty rolls of microfilm a fortnight in her knitting bag. After Barbarossa, Golos became increasingly anti-American and grew to dislike the NKVD operatives he was working with; he even talked about leaving the country to fight alongside his son in the Soviet army, while his masters showered him with medals to keep him in place. Any hint of espionage activities would have brought the FBI into the heart of their network. But his struggles came to an end when, after lunching with Bentley at the London Terrace restaurant in New York in November 1943, he suffered a fatal heart attack.

Bentley was now in the position of knowing more (and caring more – she used to buy agents Christmas gifts, a practice that was very much not in the manuals) about the US networks than

Moscow, and this, coupled with her increased drinking, led her to a conflict with her new controller, Itzhak Akhmerov, who noted that 'she doesn't have any interests beyond her work, and that she loves our country more than anything else ... ' Her emotional restlessness meant Gorsky was sent to meet her to instil some balance, one of his special skills. The involvement of Maclean's controller, essential to his stability and sense of self-worth, could well have brought the diplomat's career to an end.

The meeting between Henry and Wise Girl was, predictably, a fiasco. Bentley turned up drunk and informed Gorsky that he reminded her of Golos and that she was feeling 'the lack of a male friend to satisfy her natural needs'. Gorsky cabled Moscow urgently that it was imperative to find her a husband. Early in 1945 she announced that she had a new lover, Peter Heller, whose description as a lawyer, former government investigator and Russian-speaker rang deafening bells in Moscow even if Bentley herself appeared not to notice her predicament They considered taking her to the Soviet Union, or even liquidating her, but the day after her last, friendly meeting with Gorsky (at which she told him she had given up Heller anyway after discovering that he had a wife and children) she walked into the FBI offices in New York and informed them of the real work of the United States Service and Shipping Corporation and its offshoot, Global Tourist. On 20 November 1945, Philby broke the bad news to Moscow that Hoover had consulted William Stephenson, head of the British Security Co-ordination in New York, and told him the investigation had 'revealed that Golos's agents penetrated into government circles ... It succeeded in spotting 30 Soviet agents at present, whose names the FBI [have] not given Stephenson.' One of these later turned out to be Alger (though Bentley thought he was called Eugene) Hiss, the star of the State Department.

The effect of the Bentley news on top of Volkov, Gouzenko and Nunn May was panic in Moscow Centre about the possible exposure of Maclean when he was performing so well. Gorsky might have been photographed at his last meeting with Bentley, and was now being followed. Fitin recalled Akhmerov and Pravdin, and

Gorsky was called back on 'vacation leave', while a 26 November cable made clear that meetings with and material from Homer should be stopped, and new passwords and 'conditions of a future meeting' put in place. It was a bad moment for the Kremlin to risk an intelligence gap, but Fitin was determined to take a longer-term view and 'deactivated' his 'minor agents' while ensuring Maclean was 'safeguarded from failure'.

Meanwhile, there was much discussion about how to assassinate Bentley, and one of Gorsky's last memos before he left the US ran through and dismissed various options: shooting would be too noisy, a car accident too risky and a fake suicide tricky as the victim is 'a strong, tall, healthy woman and X [Joseph Katz, the assassin who was to carry out the deed] has not been feeling too well lately'. As the years passed, and Bentley gave evidence to various committees, including the House Un-American Activities Committee on several occasions, there were other plans to remove her from the scene, but Cold War necessities changed and she died of natural causes in 1983 having done well out of her memoirs and on the lecture circuit. On his return from Russia, Gorsky spared Maclean the details of his narrow escape, but it was a forcible underlining of the new perils and the sharpening of security wits.

*

Unaware of and therefore unshaken by these developments, and protected by Philby and Gorsky, Maclean emerged from the war as a diplomat entrusted with some big secrets and important work. When his former landlord, Michael Wright, was posted elsewhere, Maclean was soon appointed acting head of Chancery. As an American diplomat neighbour put it, 'there was virtually nothing in the way of transactions in an Embassy that both the Ambassador and the head of the Chancery were not aware of with the exception of particular matters that, for example, the King of England might have the Ambassador look into'. His duties involved overseeing all cable traffic and Embassy security, even renovation of the cable room. William Clark, the Embassy Press Secretary, was summoned by him for a security briefing. Clark 'had not been so excited since, a dozen years earlier, my housemaster had given me (similarly belatedly) my obligatory talk on sex'. Maclean must have enjoyed the irony when he asked Clark to sign the Official Secrets Act's brief declaration, and then censoriously told him:

> Of course you should talk to good journalists. It's not them we're after, it's people who might make use of the information. For instance [as he disconnected the telephone on his desk] I always disconnect the phone when talking to businessmen, because of course our phones are tapped by the US government, and we don't want them to get all our trade plans. And ... don't ever tell secrets to the French, they leak like sieves.

One of the important tasks Maclean was entrusted with was to handle the negotiations for British bases in the Atlantic and Pacific that were to be leased to America as part of the massive war debts Britain had incurred. He and Melinda (five months pregnant again and happy to spend time on the beach) went to Bermuda in February 1946 for a week where he was the lead negotiator on the subject which was to preoccupy him for the next three months. His deftness in the negotiations opposite Hickerson of the State Department (who had chosen not to make anything of Joe Alsop's complaint the previous year) was notable, although one puzzle went unsolved. How could the Russian press on 20 May publish a totally accurate list of every base under negotiation? They claimed to have received the information from the British press, but only the merest outline had been handed out. When he realised in the years to come how the Russians had got there first, the ebullient and optimistic Hickerson said with sadness of his former friend: 'He hurt us in more ways than one. After that, I found myself involuntarily being more suspicious about foreign diplomats, sometimes even my own colleagues.'

*

At the same time that these arrests, defections and discoveries of the winter of 1945–6 were rumbling in the background of Maclean's worlds, the man who would make the difference was signing up at Arlington Hall.

By late 1943 the first five groups of the numbers encoded using one-time pads from 10,000 of the messages lodged with the cable companies had been transferred on to punch cards. These messages were about trade to and from Russia, and when sorted by an IBM computing machine it was discovered that there were seven pairs of matching messages – the odds against that being somewhere in the region of 1,000 million to one. The Arlington cryptographers also had the plain-language cargo manifests produced in the US for many of the ships leaving for Russia carrying supplies being sent under Lend-Lease. By comparing these manifests with the Russian messages they were able to spot some patterns: there were only so many variations possible in cargo and sailing details, with cross-checks against tide tables and shipping schedules always possible as back-up. For words which did not have codes assigned to them the 'Spell' code before the word in question (which was then spelt out in letters), and the 'Endspell' code after it, had been used, so the repeats of the Spell/Endspell formula were valuable in introducing repetition into the telegrams. Once the code-breakers had begun to identify some of the words (such as times of arrival), they could then begin to strip away one layer of coding and spot where the duplicate one-time pads had come into play. It was into this tiny chink in the daunting mass of encryption that Meredith Gardner stepped early in 1946.

Gardner was gangling, shy and reserved, with a long face and intelligent eyes. He was born eight months before Maclean, in Okolona, Mississippi, and was an exceptional linguist. He was fluent (and often self-taught) in French, German (Old and Middle High), Greek, Italian, Latin, Lithuanian, Spanish and Old Church Slavonic, as well as Sanskrit (which very few in the West could even begin to read); at the time of Pearl Harbor he was Professor of German at the University of Akron, Ohio. Once the US entered the war he was quickly recruited by the US Signal Intelligence Service to work on breaking German codes. He astonished his colleagues by mastering Japanese in three months and took over decoding that traffic as well. Now that the war was over, the critical work was in Russian decryption, so Gardner quickly learned the language and joined those pulled off the Japanese desk to start studying the old cables at Arlington Hall. It was not expected that anything of importance would be discovered from them: Colonel Carter Clarke of the US Army's Special Branch had set up the separate operation in February 1943 to look at diplomatic cables to see if the Soviets, as was rumoured, were negotiating their own peace with Berlin. The surprise factor of the Nazi–Soviet Pact still rankled at that tricky stage of the war. But when the telegrams proved so much harder to crack than had at first been hoped, the best approach was to look for clues to the current codes in the past.

Using the trade-messages breakthrough, as well as Gouzenko's first-hand knowledge of the workings of the Ottawa cipher room, Gardner and his team were now able to start examining NKVD/NKGB as well as trade telegrams. It was painfully slow work, with often as little as 1 per cent of each telegram decipherable. Yet by the middle of 1946 they had cracked enough groups and text to realise, shockingly, that many of the cables reeked of espionage. On 20 December 1946, the breakthrough came when Gardner was able to read part of a message from 1944 that contained a list of names of leading scientists working on the Manhattan Project, the atomic-bomb programme in Los Alamos – or 'Enormoz', as the Russians had code-named this most secret of all wartime ventures.

By August 1947, at the time of Gardner's first report in what became code-named the 'Venona' operation,* he had found a number of agents all referred to by their code-names. One, 'Liberal', appeared in six separate messages, but the only way he was eventually identified was by one of the more prosaic insights that often only real genius is capable of: later messages made plain that the Soviet clerk had spelt out the name of Liberal's wife in single letters, but in three groups, the first being 'Spell' and the letter 'E' and the last 'L' before 'Endspell'; in the middle was a much used code for a three-letter word. Gardner 'had never come across a three letter

_____

* 'Venona', fittingly, has no definition in the dictionary.

meaning in the spell code … Then I said: ah, but they anticipate sending a lot of English text, and the most common word in the English language is "the".' The name was therefore 'Ethel', which led to Ethel Rosenberg. Liberal was Julius Rosenberg. They were both sent to the electric chair in 1953, much to Gardner's distress as he was confident that 'those people at least believed in what they were doing'.* Before Venona was to home in on Homer, there were many more people who also 'believed in what they were doing' that it would ensnare.

However, for now, the operation was highly classified: not even the Director of the FBI knew of its existence, let alone America's British allies. The progress through the mass of material was slow and unproductive – 1944 was the year when most of the duplicate pads were being used and 49 per cent of the Moscow Centre messages were eventually decoded; but for 1945, when Maclean was seeing extraordinarily valuable material, a mere 1.5 per cent was cracked.† The odds against Maclean being caught were long once he had survived the evidence given by Krivitsky and Volkov and suffered no fall-out from Gouzenko and Bentley. Had he even known of Arlington Hall's work, he might well have felt safe from discovery.

*

Maclean's fingerprints were to be found on one of the earliest flashpoints of the post-war era. The Turkish Straits – the Bosphorus, the Sea of Marmara and the Dardanelles – link Russia's land mass and Europe's, providing the sea path from the Black Sea to the Mediterranean, straddled inconveniently by Turkey and fought over since the Trojan Wars. The waterways had been a major topic at the Potsdam Conference where Truman observed after another fruitless debate that 'Stalin wants the Black Sea Straits for Russia, as have all the Tsars before him.' The British and Americans wanted

---

* The Rosenbergs were the only American or British spies executed during the Cold War.

† Less than 2 per cent of the 1942 traffic was readable and only 15 per cent of 1943 telegrams.

different outcomes themselves: the British were most concerned to protect the route to the Suez Canal through to the Indian Ocean and their dwindling Empire; Truman had said at Potsdam that he believed waterways should be international to prevent wars. Stalin did not have anything like the measure of President Truman's resolve yet and, crucially, he needed to test the West's underlying willingness to go to war over the Straits in order to strategise future politics. So Homer, the chief British negotiator once more, with direct access to all that was going on in Washington and Ankara as well as in London, was ideally placed to help.

On 21 October 1945 the State Department's Loy W. Henderson sent Maclean the American proposals for government of the Straits by an international commission, in the spirit of the post-war founding of the United Nations. They were despatched on the tacit understanding that they were for British Embassy eyes only. Two days later an article appeared in the *New York Times*, datelined London, in which the journalist reported learning 'on excellent authority' that the British and American governments were collaborating on a proposal for the Straits under which they could, with Turkish support, confront the Soviets. The following day, Molotov must have enjoyed himself in his meeting with the American Ambassador in Moscow as he 'pretended to throw a fit about this double-cross' and demanded an explanation for the anti-Soviet collusion. The allies professed themselves completely baffled by the leak, the repercussions of which escalated through the week as Stalin sent three Red Army divisions to Romania and Bulgaria to watch over Turkey's borders, and the Turks sent troops to their borders with Bulgaria and Georgia. The first great game of Cold War bluff was under way, with the Russians, thanks to Homer, able to see both hands.

A rattled Secretary of State Byrnes gave a press conference on 30 October in which he was economical with the truth when he said 'it was a mistake to suppose that the US government and His Majesty's Government had put forward a joint proposal' and lied outright when he went on to deny that there had been 'joint consultations with the British'. He then immediately called a shaken

Halifax to accuse his team of giving Molotov a golden opportunity; the apologetic British Ambassador took the time-honoured line of promising a full investigation into the leak.

On the very same day that this high-level frost was developing, Maclean was summoned to the State Department to a meeting with George Allen of the Near East Bureau. Allen reiterated that the leak was 'very unfortunate' and had occurred only because of 'the British request to see our proposals in advance'. Maclean brazenly declared that it 'could not have occurred in the Foreign Office' as it was British 'policy to not give the Russians any basis for feeling that they are being confronted by a united Anglo-American position'. He followed this with a dismissive non sequitur which passed unnoticed by Allen when he said that if the leak had indeed come from the Foreign Office, which of course he had just said it did not, 'strong disciplinary action would be taken'.

With this out of the way, Allen went on to tell Maclean that State had conceded 'Principle 3', dealing with naval access by non-Soviet and Turkish ships to the Straits in the event of war and on which the two allies had differed, and had now adopted the British position. From the Russian point of view, Principle 3 enabled the British and Americans to have standing navies in the area. On Saturday 3 November, with tensions running high as more Soviet troops were deployed from Czechoslovakia to the borders, the US Ambassador to Turkey Edwin C. Wilson was told to present the new proposals to the Russian Ambassador Sergei Vinogradov. It looked as if the next world war was going to start just months after the close of the last on the visible boundary between Europe and Asia.

When Wilson went to see Vinogradov, he expected a very brief meeting, as would be normal: Vinogradov would pass the documents back to the Kremlin, which would look at anything emanating from the West from every paranoid angle before issuing the inevitably blocking or bullying instructions back up the line. It was therefore astonishing when Vinogradov took only 'moments' to look at the document and then gave 'forthright opinions on several of the proposals, and spoke at length about the stationing of foreign warships, which was anathema to the USSR'. Before a stunned Wilson could answer, Vinogradov dismissed the document out of hand, sneering at the Turks' weakness and their war record with 'bitterness and hostility'. Wilson was appalled and immediately wrote to Secretary of State Byrnes expressing his intense embarrassment and anger at the betrayal of trust. The leak was damaging to the British and very destructive to their relationship with the Americans, leaving Foreign Secretary Bevin feeling obliged to say to Halifax that 'I do not propose to make any communications to the Turkish Government.' His Turkish counterpart remarked that 'the effect of the American proposals [for an international commission] would be to turn the Black Sea into a Soviet naval base'. The American proposals were by now the only ones left on the table, and were unworkable in the face of such a reception.

Halifax, Foreign Secretary before the war had diminished so much of his country's power, deeply regretted the leaks, which 'will certainly increase American reluctance to share their intimate thoughts with us'. He did nothing to follow up on his promise to hold an inquiry. After all, he had told Byrnes 'we would investigate the matter, but not that we would tell him the result'. Had the first part of that promise been followed through, particularly in the light of subsequent investigations into leaks, it would have been unthinkable that the outstanding Donald Maclean would have been suspected. Ironically, by passing on the material that ensured the provocative American plan was the only one on the table, Maclean had in all likelihood unwittingly prevented a lurch towards armed conflict, and enabled Russia to win the latest round in the centuries-old struggle over the Straits.

His outstanding post-war work was about to yield Moscow an even bigger prize.

11

Access All Areas

Alan Nunn May's brief courtroom appearance did not attract much public attention. At the time the British people were far more concerned with the trials and executions of wartime traitors such as William Joyce, who had broadcast from Germany as Lord Haw-Haw. Besides, Russia was the ally that had reached Berlin first. But as the memories receded of the German war and that awful, sneering voice broadcasting each evening on the radio, the realisation of the indiscriminate destructive force of the atom bomb, which had ended the Second World War by obliterating Hiroshima and Nagasaki in August 1945, began to take over. 'The Bomb' would power the dreams, both waking and sleeping, the politics and the protests, of generations. It defined the Cold War. It became the most discussed diplomatic topic of the ensuing years, its cataclysmic potential of critical significance in the foreground and background of all the discussions about how the modern world should look. And, in what was to be a defining part of his life, Donald Maclean was at the heart of those discussions.

*

Britain lacked the resources to develop its own bomb. Roosevelt and Churchill had signed the Quebec Agreement in 1943 under which there should be 'complete interchange of information and ideas on all sections of the Project' among the members of a top-secret Combined Policy Committee. The Hyde Park Agreement (named after Roosevelt's home) of 1944 declared that the bomb should be kept in 'the utmost secrecy', and 'full collaboration' for its 'military and commercial development ... should continue after the war'. So secret* was the agreement that Vice-President Truman had less knowledge of it than Stalin when he assumed the presidency. When at Potsdam Truman 'casually mentioned ... that we had a new weapon of unusual destructive force ... the Russian Premier showed no special interest. All he said was he was glad to hear it and hoped we would make "good use of it against the Japanese".' That night Stalin ordered his own scientists to get a move on with making the Soviet bomb.

After 'good use' of the bomb had been made, Truman was blunt about the US position: 'The atomic bomb is too dangerous to be loose in a lawless world. That is why Great Britain, Canada, and the United States, who have the secret of its production, do not intend to reveal the secret until means have been found to control the bomb so as to protect ourselves and the rest of the world from the danger of total destruction.' Although the secrets were shared (and more widely shared yet by Klaus Fuchs, Nunn May and others) the essential ingredient – uranium – was still controlled by the two Anglo powers. As the world stock of uranium came from the Congo, this was reasonably uncontroversial during the war: the Belgian government-in-exile was based in London and the British could lead the negotiations for the mineral, a stock of which was sitting in a Staten Island warehouse. Under the Quebec Agreement, the British had surrendered their half-share of the uranium 'on the basis of need' during the war, a clear recognition that the only bombs that were going to be produced in that period would be under the auspices of the Manhattan Project. In peace, they had expected that the shares would go back to being equal, and were horrified to learn that, in keeping with the new balance

---

* The Hyde Park Agreement itself was a victim of wartime secrecy and of Roosevelt's habit of running his diplomacy on a very personal basis: one copy of it fell behind some books in the library of his Hyde Park home and was not discovered for nine years; another was misfiled by an American clerk (who thought 'Tube Alloys' probably meant the file had something to do with torpedoes and submarines) and came to light only in 1957.

of power in the world and the size of their war debt to the US, the Americans were insisting upon a reallocation of uranium 'on an actual use basis', meaning that almost the entire world's stock would go to America.

Maclean had been sharing information about uranium since he was based in the General Department in London in the early days of the war, and he was well up to speed on its usage and importance. He had been cited in Moscow as the source of 'a most secret report of the Government Committee on the development of uranium atomic energy to produce explosive material which was submitted on 24th September 1941 to the War Cabinet'. He was able to disclose that General Leslie Groves and his Manhattan Project scientists were planning to use 600 tons of uranium a year, which could only mean acceleration rather than a slowdown in output. Groves himself had been in no doubt when he joined the project in September 1942 from whom the real secrets needed keeping: 'There was never, apart from about two weeks from the time I took charge of this Project, any illusion on my part but that Russia was our enemy. I didn't go along with the attitude of the country as a whole that Russia was a gallant ally. I always had suspicions and the Project was conducted on that basis.'*

The lines between the three allies that determined the shape of the Cold War with respect to its most terrible weapon were thus already in place before Maclean arrived in Washington. The commanding figure of Sir Roger Makins, as charming as he was tall, who brought his infectiously booming laugh to the Embassy staff in January 1945 as Economic Minister, was the link between the Ambassador and the British missions in Washington created to co-ordinate the supply of products and services (including the all-important Treasury and Food missions) to war-deprived Britain. 'But my most important task was under cover, for I was the Embassy official at the operating level who dealt with atomic energy.'

---

* Groves is widely credited as an inspiration for the swivel-eyed, bomb-crazed General Jack D. Ripper in Stanley Kubrick's *Doctor Strangelove*.

Makins's significant role in the last years of Maclean's Foreign Office career began in early 1947. The Combined Policy Committee (CPC) had been set up in 1943 by Churchill and Roosevelt to coordinate Anglo-American atomic energy research and policy. Makins, who was appointed Joint Secretary of the committee, had no hesitation when he recruited as his deputy the Embassy's 'faultlessly efficient and hard-working' First Secretary. Maclean was entrusted with these vital global matters on the grounds that he was 'meticulous in security matters'. The importance of his seat is easily shown by a list of some of those present at his first meeting, when he stood in for Makins on 3 February 1947: Secretary of State Byrnes; Under-Secretary of State Acheson; Secretary of War Patterson; Director of the Office of Scientific Research and Development Vannevar Bush; the British and Canadian Ambassadors; Field Marshal Lord Wilson.

The Soviets may have been delighted with this dazzling access, but even as Maclean fed back the extraordinary information, it only increased his unease. The Americans were taking the lead and hardening their stance ever more determinedly in the Cold War, hosting and dominating the United Nations, and lessening what had been full atomic co-operation with Britain. They had set up the US Atomic Energy Commission (AEC), in which Britain had no role, in 1946. Maclean's patriotism and his moral centre, the twin pillars of his life, were simultaneously affronted. His 'distaste for the Americans' was to play out more often, now both professionally and within his own circle. But for the immediate and critical future the meticulous outer man was to continue to serve Moscow Centre well.

*

The British response to increasing American atomic hegemony was to open the Atomic Energy Research Establishment at Harwell, where the Soviets were adequately represented for scientific information through the person of the German-born Klaus Fuchs, head of the Theoretical Physics Division. Fuchs had been leader of a group of Communist students at Kiel University and a prominent member of the KPD, the German Communist Party, until the Reichstag fire in 1933 made plain the future of left-wing opposition to the Nazis. He fled to England. His strong left-wing views hardened when he was interned in a Canadian camp as an enemy alien at the start of the war, but his ideals and principles were not investigated prior to his Harwell appointment. In the mass of paperwork brought back by allied intelligence officers from the ruins of Nazi Germany was Fuchs's Gestapo file, which stated that he was a Communist and instructed that 'he was to be arrested as and when' the Gestapo caught up with him.

Fuchs and Maclean did spend a few days in each other's company. In November 1947 both men attended a conference held in Washington to discuss which wartime secrets could now be declassified, mostly an ironic waste of time given what had already been leaked by at least two of the delegates. Strangely, the two spies found themselves on opposite sides of the declassification debate: Maclean was delighted that the British 'managed to get declassified a lot of borderline documents', and that he was able to interpret American intransigence as 'useful clues as to the productive areas to pursue' (in both his roles, presumably); Fuchs was much more conservative, and often the lone vote for secrecy among the eight scientists. Maybe this was rather naive cover, or he could simply afford to play it this way as it would ultimately make no difference. He never named Maclean among his contacts. Once again, the care Moscow Centre took to separate their agents proved essential. When they failed to do so, the results could be catastrophic.

At the Washington conference, one of the main topics was how long it would take the Russians to build their own bomb – estimates were between five and ten years, based more on hope and expectation than on science. Thanks to Maclean and his seat on the CPC, the Russians did not have to get involved in this sort of guesswork when assessing American strength. The number of bombs, and therefore the extent of the stockpile, could be measured by the detailed reports they were getting on the world supplies of uranium and thorium, the essential ingredients. Through the latter half of 1947 and 1948 the British and Canadians were brought back into the political fold at least because good relations with Commonwealth countries and Belgium were vital in the extraction and transport of the minerals. Once again, Maclean's indispensability gained him unparalleled access to the right information. His knowledge that the Americans were buying 2,547 tons of uranium in 1947–8, for example, enabled the Russians to calculate that around fifty bombs would be made in 1948.

*

In the same month as the Washington conference, November 1947, Maclean's trustworthiness (and a degree of luck) got him the espionage golden ticket. He was given a permanent pass to the AEC's headquarters, a pass 'which was of a character that did not require him to be accompanied while in the building'. Members of the US Cabinet and Congress were not allowed in unescorted. Even J. Edgar Hoover, Director of the FBI, was unhappy at being required to have an escort. Admiral Lewis Strauss, head of the Commission, was told after Maclean had left Washington that 'from the records maintained by the guards at the building entrances … this particular alien was a frequent visitor in the evenings after usual work hours', even though at the time 'high Army and Navy officials were required to have escorts in going through the building'. Strauss had no suspicions about Maclean, whom he had met 'several times in agreeable circumstances'; he simply objected on principle to anyone, especially a non-American, having such access. As well he might do in the light of Britain's financial war debts to the US and its poor security as revealed by Nunn May's treachery.

When the FBI looked into the pass in the 1950s, all those whom they spoke to, with one exception, commented that Maclean seemed an 'able, stable and capable person'. The exception was Joseph Volpe, General Counsel to the Commission in Maclean's time, who found him to be of a 'nervous temperament', which he put down to the Briton being 'a hard worker' with 'heavy responsibilities'. The FBI weakly concluded that Maclean had been given his pass because the Combined Policy Committee met in the building. The late workers trusted and enjoyed seeing the tall, familiar figure in his pinstriped suit as he walked the hallways, and did not question what he was doing there at a time when his fellow diplomats were plunged into the evening round of cocktail parties. His farewell lunch from the atomic community at the Hay Adams Hotel the following year was a most 'comradely' occasion, and such a significant one that Roger Makins delayed his own departure for London to attend it. What Maclean found out informally as he prowled the building was passed on to Moscow via New York along with the formal proceedings of the AEC itself. What was in his mind on these solitary wanderings in one of the world's most sensitive buildings is open to conjecture, though no doubt the planned scale of potential destruction deeply troubled the man who had been working for peace, or so he rationalised it, since his schooldays.

The most dramatic and critical piece of information from Maclean's privileged position was that the Americans were far less advanced in their work than might have been expected and than Cold War brinkmanship would allow them to admit. 'Pincher', a war plan drawn up in mid-1946, assumed fifty bombs a year later; by April 1948, only a dozen were available and no more than twenty-seven B-29 bombers had been modified to deliver those bombs, and these out of range of the Soviet Union, being based only in Britain and the Cairo–Suez region. When the Chairman of the AEC reported back from his visit to inspect the nuclear arsenal at Los Alamos in April 1947, 'the shock was apparent on Truman's face'. With so much of America's weaponry destroyed or mothballed, and no appetite for a peacetime draft to increase the size of the services, US military strategy was tenuous without these weapons, and its rhetoric hollow.

To complicate matters further, the British assessment in March 1946 was that 'the USSR will not have atomic weapons before the early 1950s and ... that the numbers of atomic weapons ... will not be significant until about 1955–60'. These estimates were based on projecting the speed of research and development of the Western allies on to the Soviets, assuming they too were working from scratch in spite of what Nunn May and others may have told them. The Americans were astonished when they analysed rainwater samples from contaminated clouds coming from Asiatic Russia which confirmed that the Russians had exploded a bomb on 29 August 1949. This was just days after Venona had identified an agent 'within the British Mission to the Manhattan Project' who had leaked complicated scientific information about the gaseous diffusion process. Once they had triangulated this with his Gestapo file, Klaus Fuchs was arrested.

*

Maclean had a clear idea of his standing when his posting was up in October 1947. He wrote to London to ask whether there were plans to move him or whether he should make new housing arrangements, as 'we are still happy here and have no particular desire to move. If I go, some other arrangement will have to be made about the special work which I do for Roger Makins.' Amid the other matters he was handling so deftly, it is hard not to read some sort of threat into the mention of his 'special work', as well as a statement of its importance in his mind, since it served his Soviet masters so well. In the end, the importance of the 'special work' and the excellence of Maclean's performance in the crucial Embassy meant London did not hesitate to extend his effective tenure. The family moved to 3326 P Street, in Georgetown, the classiest area of town, where two retired admirals lived on either side. Once again, Maclean made a good impression on his neighbours: Mrs Owings, two doors down, said the family were 'fine people' and that Donald was very 'fond of his children'; she added that when he came to visit her he refused a second glass of sherry, which presumably was a comment on her sherry. He could quite often be absent-minded and 'would leave his automobile with the door open allowing dogs and cats to climb into the car and sleep there'. The cohabitation of dogs and cats is puzzling, as is the fact that this clearly happened on more than one occasion; it is possible that absent-mindedness is an innocent synonym for coming home intoxicated, or that Mrs Owings had had more than one glass of her own sherry.

The sense of fulfilment that his spying gave him could not make up for the widening divide within him, and that divide manifested itself from time to time in the Embassy as well as outside it when he was not charming the neighbours. Staying on in Washington suited both his British ambitions and his espionage soul, yet the outbursts about the place he had 'no particular desire' to leave continued. When Lady Balfour, wife of the new senior Minister Sir John, said what a relief it was to be among friendly people who would 'talk and smile on trains, even if you're a complete stranger' after their previous posting, Moscow, she received 'a very hard stare' from Maclean. He seemed to her to be making a great effort 'to suppress some cutting reference to my naïveté and ignorance. The cross look ... betrayed how strongly he felt.' He was barely keeping his mental turmoil under control.

On one occasion his temper had a direct impact on a fellow diplomat's career. Peter Solly-Flood was Second Secretary in the Embassy. He was politically right-wing, had served in the Polish underground with distinction and most of his Washington friends were 'in émigré circles'. In many ways he was much less the stereotypical official than Maclean. Maclean may have been jealous of Solly-Flood, the man who did not have to keep his true beliefs hidden and yet could continue to serve his country; he may have been threatened by the openness of his junior colleague. And his tension spilled over into rage (which was again kept from his superiors) when Solly-Flood 'fell in love' with Melinda's sister Harriet. Solly-Flood's advances were rebuffed, according to the Marlings' over-dramatising Aunt Eleanor because Harriet discovered he 'liked wild parties and ... "sex orgies" at the Egyptian Embassy'. His 'extremely unbalanced character', in Foreign Office terms, tipped over into even heavier drinking at which point Solly-Flood 'became unstable'. Solly-Flood was sent back to London where the Foreign Office put him in the hands of Dr Wilson of Harley Street, the psychiatrist who took on their 'problem' cases and who was to struggle to get to know Maclean. Whether or not his dismissal took place on Maclean's direct orders or merely through his influence, Solly-Flood's exit from Washington led to poison-pen letters about Maclean (he is an 'awful swine') and 'remorse' from Maclean at treating a frequent visitor in such a way: 'he much regretted his sudden attitude of hatred'.

Maclean's hair-trigger temper also exploded on an occasion when Christianity came up in the course of a casual conversation. He exclaimed, 'Jesus was a shit – cause of all our troubles!' Behind that remark were the family prayers of his childhood and Sir Donald's strong conscience, as if Maclean had to efface his background to justify his own morality and actions. The anguish of the double life, the importance of the papers he was seeing, the amount he was drinking, were all causing him to turn on his colleagues, friends, family and forebears. Yet no official complaints were made and he remained in place as Stalin's most important spy during the rest of his time in Washington.

*

The new Ambassador arrived in May 1946, also from Moscow. Sir Archibald Clark Kerr, newly ennobled as Lord Inverchapel,* was the Australian-born Scotsman who had toasted Beria so surprisingly at Yalta and was in Rebecca West's eyes 'one of the most bizarre human beings ever to rise to the rank of ambassador, which is saying a very great deal indeed'. Inverchapel was involved in a discussion about baseball (seemingly a journalistic test of aptitude for the job) on his arrival in North America, but this time passed it, unlike his predecessor: he announced that he was looking forward to watching some baseball as cricket was 'the dullest game ever invented' and he would rather watch spillikins. His press secretary had to return some time later to a puzzled press corps to explain that spillikins was a 'bar-room game akin to skittles'. Although Maclean's Scots blood was probably not stirred much when at official dinners Inverchapel had kilted bagpipers playing in the dining-room, he leapt at the chance to impress his new boss. Walter Bell, Inverchapel's

---

* On being raised to the peerage, Inverchapel added two naked male figures as supporters to his family coat of arms, one holding a pen, the other a discus, reflecting two of his interests. He chose as his motto the Latin 'Concussus Surgo', meaning 'Having been shaken, I rise'. *Burke's Peerage* found the figures (possibly in conjunction with the motto) too suggestive, and added underpants to the supporters in their 1950 edition.

special assistant, noted that 'Donald was obsessed with his work. No trouble was too much for him. When Philip Jordan, the Embassy press attaché who became quite a friend, arranged special background briefings for foreign correspondents, Maclean invariably enjoyed the business of parrying tough questions and giving as far as possible the reasons behind new policy decisions.' This work rate would also allow Maclean to become indispensable, as he had on the CPC, and gave him the Embassy equivalent of an unescorted pass, a licence to know exactly what was going on. He soon became as close to the new Ambassador as he had been to Halifax, and Inverchapel declared him 'a sweetie'.

Inverchapel had brought with him a valet, a dwarf named Yevgeny Yost, a parting gift from Stalin, or, as he called him in a jokey comment that fell predictably flat, 'a Russian slave given to me by Stalin'. Maclean was not the only one who looked with concern (some would say disdain) on 'this incongruous little body servant from the steppes, who followed his master like a shadow and dressed up as a poor itinerant Cossack' and 'insisted on poking his nose into every corner of the building, including the Registry'. Apart from the security concerns aroused by bringing a Russian into the heart of Washington diplomacy, Maclean might even have wondered in his more paranoid and drunken moments whether Yost was a Soviet plant to keep an eye on him. Yost himself took the same line as Lady Balfour on one occasion when Maclean asked him how he liked life in the US compared to the USSR. Yost (who was a Volga German of a type not much liked in Russia anyway) gave reasons why he much preferred America and 'Maclean's face dropped and he quickly left the room.' Maclean then led a campaign to get rid of Yost, and it was with some relief to all that the dwarf left with the Inverchapels on their first leave in July 1947 to retrain as a chauffeur and farm worker on their Scottish estate. There he was a source of equal bemusement, but without the added danger of reports to his homeland, or of criticising the country that the First Secretary had yet to visit but held in such high regard nonetheless.

*

Tension inevitably spilled over into Maclean's home life. Melinda could not but continue to feel uncomfortable in her own country as her husband voiced his 'distaste' for its citizens' values. The false situation that his other life put her in meant that she still could not entertain as a First Secretary's wife was expected to and was to be seen standing at the edge of diplomatic parties, often silently holding hands with her tall, unmistakably British husband. Shades of Donald's mother standing with him on the fringes of London dances when he was first down from Cambridge. She was certainly shy on formal occasions, but there might also have been a justifiable desire to stop her husband knocking back too many drinks and starting an argument about the moral standing of America. She disliked drawing attention to herself. On one occasion she ordered from a New York dressmaker a 'dazzling new creation' that she thought 'perfect' for wearing to a White House ball. But when the day came she left it hanging up and wore one of her sisters' more modest dresses instead. Throughout their marriage Melinda was bored by politics and had seemingly been happiest living the bohemian life in Paris, but by now she appeared to have lost all taste for joining in on the social circuit, no doubt made tired and anxious by the strain of keeping up appearances as her husband became more unpredictable.

Nicholas Henderson, later Ambassador to France and the US, remembers Maclean coming to the house he shared with another Embassy staffer after work of an evening, without Melinda, and 'keeping late hours' until he became 'dissipated'. Motherhood was a preoccupation for Melinda: Donald, the second Maclean son, known in the family as 'Beany', was born in New York by Caesarean section like his brother Fergus, in July 1946, at the beginning of the long American summer break. Beyond such family distractions, it is plausible that she simply refused to play her part in the diplomatic life because she knew too much about the other side of her husband, and the true reasons for the relief he sought in drink.

Melinda told her friend and fellow Embassy wife Kathleen Cecil that Donald's drunken forays 'brought out the homosexual streak' in him. This is the first hint of homosexuality since Burgess's boast that he had slept with Maclean at Cambridge and Toynbee's urge to kiss him when they first met. There is no evidence that Maclean took part in the more lurid wartime goings-on in Victor Rothschild's Bentinck Street flat, nor, even as Guy Burgess continued his countless and well-publicised affairs, did anyone else come forward to say that they had been involved with the buttoned-up diplomat who paradoxically might have found it hard to risk his official career to take part in this illegal act. His need for a secret life was being more than fulfilled by his espionage. Perhaps Melinda made this comment from puzzlement or anguish from lack of a sex life, or perhaps she used it to deflect attention from the real betrayal Donald was perpetrating against Britain.

Melinda still spent long periods in New York, and all summer out of steamy Washington. The farm in the Berkshires was no longer available owing to her mother's divorce from Dunbar, so the family rented houses on Long Island or Cape Cod. Much of the time she would be alone with her two boys, as in 1947 when they hired a young English nanny, Phyllis Smith: Donald met Smith from the boat in New York, treated her to the air-conditioned movies, visited the Empire State Building and put her up in the female-only Martha Washington Hotel. The next day they took the train to Harwich Port on the Cape and went to the Macleans' simple rented house in the woods, Tree Pines. Donald flew back to Washington without even spending the night with his family. Smith rarely saw Melinda or her favourite sister Harriet, who was staying there (and liked to walk around the house naked, much to the teenage girl's discomfort) as they were off socialising with other vacationers.

Although their French maid, Renée, was frequently in tears when she had to clear up the mess made by his all-male drinking parties in a summer Washington largely empty of families, Maclean wrote to his wife during one of these separations to say, 'I scarcely get drunk at all, although you are not here to remind me of the morrow's sorrows. I think it must be that we drink so much whiskey every day anyway that it don't signify to have a few extra; also it disappears in sweat.' This collusive nudge at Melinda is simultaneous confession and denial.

*

As the wartime and diplomatic population of Washington thinned out after 1945, and the tall, distinctive figure of Donald Maclean became better known, Moscow Centre decided that he should be briefed on what to look for and extract by Anatoli Yakovlev, a nuclear expert working undercover as a Vice-Consul in the Soviet New York Consulate. Gorsky (by now code-named 'Al') remained his main handler. But his six-hour round train trip to see Yakovlev when his family was in Washington now left him exposed. Robert Cecil asked Maclean to lunch at the Wardman Park Hotel, so that they 'might talk undisturbed'. As they walked there through Rock Creek Park, Maclean was 'strangely silent', and when Cecil said, 'It's about going to New York that I want to talk to you,' 'the tension was palpable'. What he wanted to discuss was whether the acting head of Chancery would grant him leave to go to New York to hear weekly lectures by the exiled Russian mystic-philosopher P. D. Ouspensky. Cecil later realised that Maclean's fear was that he might start to interrogate him over their hotel lunch. Although the two men had known each other since they were undergraduates, and Cecil was his junior, a trigger to Maclean's ever-alert nervous system might have been that Cecil had served for two years before his arrival in America as personal assistant to the head of SIS, 'C'. At the time, Cecil was surprised that, once he had given his explanation, Maclean was short with him, asking if it was really important that he went and telling him to make up the time on Saturday afternoons.

Worse was to come. After Gorsky had left in the aftermath of Elizabeth Bentley's testimony, there was a handling crisis, a breakdown in the critical link between Moscow and their spies, in Washington. Moscow Centre did not know who had been compromised and who had not, although they were confident they had taken the necessary steps to protect Homer. It was important that he was handled in the capital again, not least because of the amount of material he was producing. Boris Krotov, who had been the *rezident* in London for the last three years, took over in December 1947. The frequency with which Maclean needed debriefing became apparent the following June, when the highly trained Krotov detected that he was under surveillance from the more flat-footed FBI while on his way to a meeting with his mole; he broke off contact. The station then told Maclean to leave all his material in dead letter drops such as in hollow trees or under stones, mostly at designated points in Washington's Rock Creek Park, which he found unsatisfactory as his ability to synopsise and remember large quantities of material meant the personal contact was essential. If he was caught separated from his material, it would also be much harder to give a plausible explanation for why it was stashed away in the park. After years of painstaking, even intimate, care taken with Maclean by the Russians, this first disruption between spy and handler could have had a disastrous effect on someone who had shown signs of fragility. A compromise was reached: Maclean and Krotov would meet every third week, but in the intervening weeks the system of dead letter drops would hold. This compromise was to see Maclean through his last great productive period.

*

The political stakes were rising throughout 1947 and 1948. In January 1947, the austere figure of General George C. Marshall[*] replaced Byrnes as Secretary of State. In March, it was revealed to Congress that $400 million would be sent in aid to Greece and Turkey as part of the global commitment to the struggle against Communism, a bitter blow to Maclean. At the end of April, Marshall returned from a meeting with Stalin about the future of Germany at which he had realised that the General Secretary was hoping that all the Eastern European economies would continue their post-war collapse, allowing Communism to flourish. At the Harvard Commencement ceremony on 5 June 1947, where he was

---

[*] When Marshall's staunch ally and benefactor President Truman asked if he might call him George, he got the reply, 'No, General Marshall will do.'

being given an honorary degree alongside T. S. Eliot and Robert Oppenheimer, father of the atom bomb, Marshall made a speech of a mere seven minutes in which he announced the European Recovery Program, or Marshall Plan as it soon became known, by which massive investment in Europe would allow those countries, particularly divided Germany, to get their economies moving – and keep Communism in its place. Rarely has such a game-changing announcement been made in such an unreported setting. The British knew nothing of this in advance, but Bevin, the Foreign Secretary, was galvanised by it, calling it 'a life-line to sinking men'. The Marshall Plan would reinvigorate post-war Europe.

Stalin saw the plan as America trying to subjugate Europe to its own political ends. He wanted to plunder Germany's resources as repayment for its wartime destruction and to keep as weak as possible the country that was the bulwark between his empire and the West. The Marshall Plan included Europe's eastern countries and indeed the Soviet Union, where some, Molotov included, argued that they should accept the American dollars. They would be their only source of hard currency.

Stalin did not need his army of bankers and experts to see that to give America entrée into the finances of the Soviet Union or its allies would be the death of Communism, but he nevertheless allowed Molotov to go to the Paris conference of foreign ministers to discuss the plan. On 30 June Molotov received a cable passed on by Maclean detailing a meeting between US under-secretary Will Clayton and British ministers which made it clear that the Anglophone allies were intent on building up Germany to be the industrial powerhouse of Europe again. Molotov, forewarned by Maclean, accused the British and Americans of dividing Europe, gathered up his papers and swept out of the conference.

In January 1948 Bevin cabled Marshall with the proposal that because 'the Soviet Government has formed a solid political and economic block', Western Europe must do the same. The ageing and eccentric Inverchapel's reply that Bevin's plan 'has filled the hearts of the senior officials at the State Department with joy' was curiously inappropriate to the tension of the times. In February the

Harvard-educated, half-American Czech Foreign Minister Jan Masaryk, a non-Communist who had been asking Marshall to help his country, was found dead on the ground outside his office having fallen from a high window; the official verdict was suicide, although the size of the window, which was marked with his excrement, his mismatched pyjamas and the bruising on the soles of his feet told a different story. The Communists now held undisputed sway in the country. In March, Truman gave Marshall permission to discuss a Northern European and US military alliance; the talks would be kept secret from the rest of the administration. Maclean drafted a note of congratulations that must have stuck in his craw, expressing British delight that 'we and you mean business and are prepared to see [the alliance] through, and not stop at exhortation'.

Maclean was in charge of the British side of these talks with the State Department about the alliance. The Foreign Office considered them possibly 'the most secret ever held in Washington'. They included discussions about how troops would be commanded and what the nuclear options were in a partnership. A meeting between the British, Canadians and Americans in March was so sensitive that it was held in a steel-lined room at the Pentagon rather than anywhere the press, or Congress, might get wind of it. No notes were allowed to be taken, and the delegates were not even allowed to break to leave the building for lunch. Robert Cecil, the junior member of the British delegation, hoped that Maclean would write up the minutes with his celebrated Foreign Office mind but 'no doubt he was preoccupied in making his own summary for a recipient to whom it would be a good deal less welcome than it was in Whitehall' and he refused. Maclean drafted a cable for Inverchapel urging London to limit severely the distribution of the minutes, while in his own handwritten notes was the comment that 'if the Soviets know where the holdline is drawn, they will move on what is protected like any predatory animal'. The savagery of that image is so out of keeping with his normal restrained style that it gives a clue to the fractured anger beneath, even as he passed the holdline on to the Soviets. From this meeting and six more over the next eleven days Moscow Centre would have a day-by-day account of the formation of the North Atlantic Treaty Organisation, or NATO, the military alliance that cemented the European battle-lines through 'negotiating mutual security arrangements to meet the danger of Soviet expansion' for the decades to come and which continues to be debated to this day.

*

Maclean was there to provide the inside information on the hardening of the European situation through the formation of NATO and technological advances. The allies pursued their policy of building up Germany as a buffer to the Communist bloc, as it was now starting to be called: the Americans printed a new currency, the Deutschmark, in their own mint for the western half of Germany, calculating that this would kick-start the economy. The Russians responded with the Ostmark as their replacement currency for the east and, on 24 June 1948, shut down the road, rail and canal links, as well as the power supplies, to the western sectors of a divided Berlin. Even as Truman announced four days later that the US was sending sixty 'atomic capable' B-29 bombers to bases in England and Germany, Stalin knew from Maclean's earlier intelligence that they had only half the bombs and three assembly teams to arm these planes. Maclean was also able to help defuse the situation further by telling Moscow Centre that an order had gone out from US General Lucius Clay that the transport aircraft carrying out the heroic Berlin Airlift, with daily supplies being flown down a narrow corridor to Tempelhof Airport until the siege was lifted (327 days laer), would not be accompanied by fighters. Although allied courage and flying skills made the Berlin Airlift an overwhelming propaganda victory for the West, Maclean's intelligence may once again, as with the Turkish Straits crisis a couple of years earlier, have helped avert a conflict that could easily have seen shots being fired and a subsequent escalation. But he would have to watch the conclusion of the Berlin Blockade from his next posting.

*

Maclean had been in Washington longer than any other diplomat in recent times apart from the former Foreign Secretary Lord Halifax, whose wartime service could not have been interrupted. He now had to agree to transfer and promotion. However distasteful the US might be in the early days of the House Un-American Activities Committee, presaging the McCarthy era of Communist witch-hunts, it remained at the very heart of events. He had once again proved himself conscientious in his work and just discreet enough in his behaviour and outbursts in the world beyond the office. When it was time to leave, it was proposed that he go to Baghdad as Counsellor, the next rank above First Secretary. But the personnel advice was that such a move would be 'discouraging' to John Brewis, the head of Chancery there, as he was three years older than Maclean, as well as 'to other members' of the delegation who thought highly of Brewis. It was decided to offer Maclean Counsellor in Cairo instead, justifying this on the grounds that it 'would be a better post from the point of view of his young family'. Egypt was a politically tricky place at a highly sensitive time, and one of the five Grade A embassies, alongside Washington and Paris, where he had already served, and Moscow and Beijing, which would have been of obvious interest to him. Cairo and this 'accelerated promotion', as Foreign Office parlance had it, which skipped another First Secretary role, was a clear stepping-stone to an ambassadorship next time.

At thirty-five Donald Maclean became the youngest Counsellor in the Foreign Service, five years younger than Sir Roger Makins was when he had attained the rank; Makins went on to become Ambassador in Washington and Permanent Secretary to the Treasury. The outgoing First Secretary must have felt profoundly mixed emotions at this point – relief that such a momentously geopolitically and personally divisive period had come to an end, alongside the sense that his work for both sides might never be as important nor as risky again; anger at the cementing of his employer's opinions against his ideological allies; a sense of achievement knowing how well he had performed and influenced events on both sides of his fence; and, above all, exhaustion laced with apprehension about what was to come in his espionage life. His old Paris friend Valentine Lawford met him for tea and strawberries at the Palm Court in the Plaza Hotel, New York, where the Macleans were staying before they boarded the *Queen Mary* back to England at the end of August 1948. For Donald, it was his last visit to the city after four years and countless trips to see his family and his handlers. Lawford commented that 'Donald looked a bit strange, sort of puffed-up and beaten down simultaneously ... But both he and Melinda were very nice to me, and we laughed at some of the good old jokes.'

*

The Maclean residence on P Street would now become the home of Albert Parker, Custodian of the Alien Property Office of the Department of Justice. Parker's daughter Charlotte found an unsigned letter that had been dropped on the doorstep as the Macleans moved out. The letter started 'Dearest Melinda' and was in 'handwriting that was very difficult to read' (Maclean's hand was very clear, even allowing for the difference in British and American styles, so the letter was in all probability written while he was drunk) and 'said something to the effect that "I am going away, take care of yourself"'. It sounded very 'grim ... like he was either going away on a very long trip, or was contemplating suicide'. This remnant is a puzzling and poignant counterpoint to the four years of high drama and swirling emotion, perhaps even a practice departure for the solitary man who had roamed the night-time halls of the AEC in turmoil as he felt the increasing tug between his lives: his conscience and concern for his family and world peace against his informed, nuanced understanding of global politics. It was a gnawing tension that was threatening to overwhelm him.

12

Chaos on the Nile

Cairo was the last, and briefest, of Donald Maclean's overseas postings. His time there was characterised by chaos and damage, his marriage seemingly in a terminal state, the accelerating collapse of a man tormented by his fears and his tangled conscience. Ever louder in the background, the Venona clock was ticking that would prove his treason. But it was also the time when those around him showed themselves in their true colours. Astonishingly, his Cairo assignment did not see the end of either his career in the Foreign Office or his role as a top spy working for Moscow Centre. As he sweated at his desk after a late-night bender, he must have felt that his life was simultaneously playing at double speed and slowing down to protect him in its most tense, dramatic period.

*

Sometimes Maclean's efforts at discretion collapsed completely when he was drunk. It was remarkable that this was not taken up as an issue by his superiors. At the atomic community's farewell party in the Hay Adams, where champagne, whiskey, bourbon and dry martinis flowed, Edmund Gullion, the suave, Kentucky-born assistant to Under-Secretary of State Dean Acheson and another rising figure in the diplomatic world (he was to become 'John F. Kennedy's favourite diplomat'), congratulated his friend, contemporary and colleague on his important new posting. He was put out to hear the 'unprofessional' way that a man of Maclean's 'calibre and attainment' stated that Cairo was not the right place for him: 'He made disparaging remarks about the country, its people, British policy in the region, and about diplomatic life in general.'

For all the discomfort he felt about Anglo-American policy in the early Cold War and his understanding that his time was up after his elongated stint, Maclean was undeniably piqued at having to leave Washington, where he could see everything and cherished, most of the time, by Moscow Centre. Actually, Cairo was a vital and absorbing place to be sent to, the hinge via the Suez Canal of what remained of the British Empire. Britain was a major power in the region, with troops in both Palestine and the Canal Zone. Egypt was one of the few countries that had a department to itself in the Foreign Office, and the Embassy was larger than that in Paris. In the previous year Indian independence had made little difference to the Suez Canal as the essential route to the Middle East for British trade and for defending the interests of the Empire. Not surprisingly, British troops in the Canal Zone were resented for their colonial presence, although among Cairo society the British, who had cleared the Italians and the Germans out of the country in the previous few years, were still sought after. But for someone who was increasingly to go against the grain of the policies he was asked to propagate, who needed secret support, whose marriage was complicated, it was always going to be challenging.

Maclean had written from Washington to ask for travel arrangements to Cairo to be made for the family for September 1948. He imagined that 'it would be fairly tough going at times, and we are girding ourselves accordingly' (although he was looking forward to 'counting the number of night-gowned servants we may be able to acquire!'). The importance of the posting was fully brought home to him in London during his fortnight's briefing by George Clutton, head of the Egyptian Department, and Bernard Burrows of the Eastern Department, which dealt with Palestine. Guy Liddell, Deputy Director General of MI5, had started the annual round-up of world trouble-spots in his diary that year with the comment that 'Palestine is in a shocking state.' Palestine had been administered under British mandate since the First World War, but critically the state of Israel had been created in May 1948, prompting immediate attacks by the Arab states. Israel survived thanks to Arab disunity, contraband arms and aeroplanes from Eastern Europe and elsewhere, and an all-volunteer air force. This, and the way the USSR appointed an ambassador to Tel Aviv just ahead of the Americans, revealed the Soviets' desire to use the new state, Egypt's neighbour and now enemy, as their centre of influence in the Near East, just as much as it demonstrated their anti-Arab approach. Britain meanwhile was more concerned to bolster its interests in Egypt and the Arab world as a whole. In the Macleans' first week back from the US the Swedish diplomat Folke Bernadotte, who had negotiated the release of 31,000 prisoners from German concentration camps during the war, was assassinated by the Zionist Stern Gang in Jerusalem. A month after the family had arrived in Cairo the police stopped four men in a jeep loaded with a sub-machine gun, eight revolvers, 2,700 rounds of ammunition, forty-eight hand grenades, two bombs and maps of the American and British embassies. There was absorbing work to be had for the new arrival, albeit of less interest to the Kremlin than he was used to.

As well as being brought up to date on the situation that they would find in Cairo, the Macleans spent their leave catching up on his family and their friends after their long absence in the US. For Melinda, it was the first introduction to some of Donald's British colleagues and acquaintances. A dinner-party given by Burrows led to their first meeting with Geoffrey Hoare of the *News Chronicle*, who became a very close Cairo friend, and Hoare's fearless journalist wife-to-be Clare Hollingworth, notable as the first reporter to spot German tanks massing on the Polish border in 1939. Melinda, 'this delicate-complexioned, soft-voiced little American girl', made a deep impression on Hoare, not least in downplaying her reasonably well-travelled sophistication to come across as 'rather out of her depth' in the gathering of Near Eastern hands. 'She was thrilled at the thought of going to Cairo' as she listened to Hoare's description of the city; she was almost certainly thankful as well to leave America, to have the chance of a fresh start in a country where neither she nor Donald would have any prior claims of nationality or friendships and where she might reasonably hope his work would make him less tense. Hoare 'found her utterly charming ... possessing the fragility, and defencelessness, that made nearly all men feel they wanted to protect her'. It is hard not to detect the ingénue in Melinda in this account, a role she had cultivated throughout the first half of her marriage, as well as Hoare's attachment to her which made him such a faithful chronicler of her life in the next few years. At the same party, Donald showed no 'marked enthusiasm' for his new appointment, surprisingly undiplomatic in front of Burrows, but they 'seemed a harmonious couple' to Hoare and Hollingworth.

Cyril Connolly went to a dinner the Macleans themselves gave and recognised how much his friend had matured during his time in America. Nothing now could stop him emerging as 'Sir Donald', the top diplomat 'On His Majesty's Service': 'He had become a good host; his charm was based not on vanity but on sincerity, and he would discuss foreign affairs as a student, not an expert.' Connolly felt particularly warm towards his host because, 'incidentally', Maclean enjoyed *Horizon*, the CIA-funded new magazine Connolly edited, which was 'a blue rag' to the more transparently left-wing Burgess. Although Burgess was working at the time for Hector McNeil, a Foreign Office minister who shared his love of smoking, drinking and the seedier sides of London life (in the minister's case topless night-clubs in particular), and was passing on material about Palestine to Moscow Centre, the two agents did not meet.

Philip Jordan, the Press Attaché from Washington and now Prime Minister Attlee's Press Secretary also entertained the couple in this hectic two weeks. He had asked Malcom Muggeridge and his wife Kitty, the niece of the Fabians Beatrice and Sidney Webb, to dinner in his Covent Garden flat. Muggeridge, who had been very left-wing in his youth and had written from Moscow for the *Manchester Guardian*, had become increasingly anti-Communist and worked for MI6 during the war. His diary records a discussion about war with Russia, which Jordan with his high-level access feared might well happen: 'there was no question of appeasement. [Jordan] expected that the Americans would act, but not for some months, since they won't be sufficiently armed ... It really does begin to seem as though the inconceivable must happen, and that an atomic war with Russia is almost a certainty.' The person in whose honour the dinner was being given, who knew the true state of American nuclear preparedness, and who would have been pleased to have quietly listened to a conversation to pass on to Moscow, is noticeably absent from the recorded discussion. He was certainly aware of Muggeridge's MI6 connections. The only mention Muggeridge makes of the withdrawn Macleans apart from noting their presence is the somewhat dismissive remark that Melinda, no doubt exhibiting her usual shyness and unwillingness to draw attention to herself, was 'rather pretty, well off'.

*

Maclean ranked third in the massive Cairo Embassy, ahead of the knighted chief of the British Middle East Office. As head of Chancery, running an embassy's offices and in effect the Ambassador's chief of staff, he saw everything and decided what was sent on to London, to the extent that when the Ambassador, Sir Ronald Campbell (a different Sir Ronald to the Ambassador to Paris under whom Maclean had served), reported on a meeting with King Farouk it went over Maclean's signature. Campbell was 'gentle and prone to regard American diplomats as amateurs', and was very well disposed towards Maclean, with whom he had worked in Paris. Jefferson Caffrey, his US counterpart, was anything but amateur, a tough career diplomat who served mediocre white wine at dinner with a pitcher of very dry martini at his own elbow. Maclean, with his time in Washington under his belt as well as his tendency to look askance at the pulling of American weight in the Cold War in general and its financial and military support for Israel in particular, was under no illusions about the shift in the region. He was serving on a potential fault-line of the Cold War in a place where British imperial interests were at their most unattractive to him, keeping a corrupt regime in place to suit commercial and defence requirements.

One of Maclean's favourite books was the diary of the 'poet, lover, orientalist, adventurer, champion of the underdog' and anti-imperial polemicist Wilfrid Scawen Blunt. Like Maclean, Blunt was 'obliged' by his rank, as he wrote on 6 December 1888, 'to be very careful how [he] meddled with politics, even in conversation' as he was 'under a certain obligation to avoid any kind of publicity in sympathy with the Nationalist cause'. Blunt was, however, free to publish his *Atrocities of Justice under British Rule in Egypt* in 1906, the year before his cousin Anthony was born. Maclean's posting in the middle of the century required much greater circumspection and would always be a tough test of his character.

*

Thanks to Maclean's seniority and to the history of British indirect rule which dated back to the end of the previous century, the family was allotted a handsome three-storey house built for British servants of the Egyptian government on the Sharia Ibn Zanki in the European suburb of Gezireh, a retreat from the noise and squalor of Cairo. The house, with its shutters closed against the heat and its garden a colourful blaze of jacaranda, flame trees, mimosa and bougainvillea, was maintained by the Ministry of Works and furnished with beautiful oriental rugs and curtains. One of the features of the drawing-room was a mother-of-pearl chess table with ivory pieces. Maclean's increased salary and the low cost of labour meant that he and Melinda employed four Egyptian and Sudanese servants and an English nanny for Fergus and Beany, now aged four and two, 'all-American boys who delighted in being cheeky to their parents'.

In his marriage, Donald was no longer playing either the protective or the controlling roles that he had been for the previous decade of their relationship. For the first time, Melinda was free of the burden of keeping house, being attentive to her mother and sisters or being constrained by her countrymen. Donald was also not as over-worked and strained as he had been, and did not, in the early days, require her vigilance. He would go each evening after work to swim and play tennis at the Gezireh Sporting Club, founded by the British fifty years earlier and admitting only the most elite Egyptians as members. She was free to go out to Groppi's, the coffee house where many of the smart women of Cairo would meet to discuss the party of the night before. Her time in Paris, 'the spiritual home of Middle East cosmopolitans' and smart fashion sense, meant she was treated with respect outside the diplomatic community. She was able to relax away from wartime London and the serious social scrutiny of official Washington, and with her husband's rank and the help they had could at last play the role of the diplomatic hostess.

Even so, the hidebound British could be painful. Many of the servants of the Raj had moved to Cairo after Indian independence in 1947, bringing with them their cocktail-fuelled love of entertaining; as Melinda was younger and more attractive than most of them, their snobbery, combined with jealousy, came oozing out as they sneered behind her back at her 'American housekeeping'. Donald's sister Nancy, who was working for MI5 (she was to appreciate the bitter irony of that when her American husband Bob Oetking lost his State Department job for no reason other than his marriage) and living in Cairo, asked her servant Mohammed to buy 'stop-gap glasses, cutlery and plates ... from Woolworth's to be used [by Donald and Melinda] until their own stuff arrived', but when she went to dinner with them was astonished to see 'heavy linen table cloth and napkins, glittering crystal glasses, silver place settings, plates with gold trim'; several of the guests were similarly surprised to see their own property in use. The Maclean servants had put word out that Nancy's 'stop-gap' place settings were not good enough and the servants of the invitees had brought the necessary goods round earlier in the day.

Sir Ronald Campbell, a bachelor with the elegance and charm of a David Niven, took a great shine to Melinda and started to use her as a hostess for his engagements, a further boost to the 'new self-confidence to replace her shyness and diffidence'. When the dashing young Prince Philip, two years married to the heir to the throne, Princess Elizabeth, came to stay with the Ambassador in March 1949, she gave a 'young people's evening' with dinner for fourteen and then party games, including 'Murder' around the house. Geoffrey Hoare, who had been away on assignment in Beirut for a few months, commented on how Melinda had emerged from her shell. She wrote to her sister Harriet that 'I have become more extroverted and enjoy gayer and simpler people.' Cairo had a flourishing social scene among its top echelons, and attractive and important diplomats would always be asked to the 'endless round of Cairo parties'. On the rare occasions they were not at a party they and the Hoares would often play bridge 'with a rather intense efficiency', befitting the man of control that Maclean with his 'watchmaker's mind' could still be in his early days there.

But he was never completely at ease. He had always preferred the company of those with what Philby described as 'independent minds', artists and writers, intellectuals rather than socialites. Even though he went to the parties, the high life just exacerbated the falseness of his situation in the quasi-imperial nature of Britain's relations with Egypt.

Cairo was the most populous city in Africa and it was the first time that Maclean had witnessed such poverty and slum-living at close hand, his resulting distress intensified by his comfortable billet and the high life surrounding those with whom they socialised. The 'covenanting conscience' that defined his childhood and informed his beliefs was being tested. Support for the regime of King Farouk and the old policy of non-interference, letting the hostile Egyptian factions play themselves out against each other, did nothing to improve the conditions in which most of the country lived. Maclean was outspoken in private about his disagreement with British policy and said that 'we should accept our responsibilities' as a previous colonial power and try to persuade the rulers of Egypt to adopt the reforms which, in his opinion, were the only way to 'save the country from Communism'. In the context of the time, this was more a sensible policy view, the expert saying what he believed was right, rather than any sort of bluff on Maclean's part: revolution in Egypt might have dire consequences in the region, and the peaceful amelioration of the lot of the people was his real aim.

His distaste for the inequalities at times emerged more publicly, as they had done in Washington. The Ambassador's nephew, Colin Campbell, came to stay with his uncle over the first Christmas that the Macleans were there and after a Sunday lunch at his uncle's residence walked out with Donald, whom he found charming, 'funny and friendly', on to the balcony outside the drawing-room. They looked across at a line of 'shabby Nissen huts' on the other side of the road, the married quarters of the junior members of the Soviet Embassy. Campbell made a 'naïve' remark about how they must be envious of the smarter British accommodation, and was taken aback by 'the look of disapproval and even contempt' given to him by his previously warm and generous fellow guest. The resentment felt towards the British by all but the elite of Cairo whose protection they seemed to be working for had aggravated Maclean's own class views to the point where his mask was starting to slip. He 'inveighed' against 'the rich' to the Embassy Naval Attaché, Captain H. P. Henderson, and remarked how 'he had become disgusted with the way the upper classes in Paris had rushed screaming from their capital in 1940', which in the light of the Wehrmacht's behaviour towards those who resisted conquest is a particularly unforgiving choice of words.

Maclean often grew withdrawn in the midst of Melinda's new-found gaiety; he could be 'a little remote' in the home and 'slightly condescending, slightly mocking' about Melinda's lack of knowledge of 'social and political problems'. He took refuge from his own unease in putting her down. She was starting to take the rap for his moral and political disquiet.

*

The discomfort Maclean felt about Cairo developed not only because he felt he would be out of the intricate centre of Cold War diplomacy, but also because he saw that Moscow was behind in recognising the importance of the Arab world. His urge to pursue the greatest good in foreign policy terms for the greatest number was always present, whichever side he was working for. In spite of what he might be able to tell them thanks to his position in Cairo, he would be of much less use to the Soviets, which could be disastrous for his equilibrium and self-esteem. Yuri Modin, a Leningrad Naval Academy graduate and member of the London *rezidentura*, warned his counterparts in Egypt that 'a vitally important agent was on the way, that he should be treated with the greatest care and that everything should be done to maintain excellent relations with him'. But the Cairo *rezidentura* 'reacted somewhat oddly to this message' and perhaps the unnamed *rezident* 'never even read it'. After fifteen years of tact and closeness, even intimacy, that had made the relationships with Deutsch, Maly, Harris and Gorsky vital sources of stability through unsettling as well as powerfully motivating times, the ineptitude with which he was handled in Cairo was degrading, anxiety-inducing and dangerously neglectful for all concerned. If Moscow Centre had been aware of the dangerous balancing act Maclean had been performing recently, they would not have been so heedless of him. They were on the verge of jeopardising their brilliant agent, and possibly their entire high-level British network.

*

This seeming indifference took place against an intense military and political backdrop as the Arab–Israeli War continued with undiminished ferocity – a time therefore when Moscow might have received valuable information from Homer. Israel attacked Egyptian forces on 22 December 1948, and Egyptian aircraft and ships bombed and shelled Tel Aviv and Jerusalem. On 7 January 1949 four British reconnaissance Spitfires flying over Israel were shot down by Israeli ground fire which had mistaken them for Egyptian attackers; the Israelis then attempted to conceal their part in this, and the US Special Representative to Israel sent a message to Washington that 'all political officers and service attachés of Mission are of opinion that British actions are destroying the chances of peace.' In the ensuing negotiations it seemed as if the Egyptian demands for a corridor linking Transjordan or Gaza with Egypt might well bring about a war with the British on the Egyptian side and the Americans on the Israeli.

Attention in late 1948 and early 1949 became focused on the possibility that the region would play a part in any confrontation with Russia as a new front in the Cold War. The Pentagon's planning for a projected nuclear war included a scenario for 133 atom bombs to hit seventy Soviet cities, with a loss of 2.7 million lives. All parties knew that Armageddon would not be on this scale, as the Americans had only about fifty bombs, but even so the bases in Egypt's Canal Zone were vital for military access to the Middle East. Maclean entered negotiations with the Egyptian government to renew the alliance and extend the leases for the bases to include America.

At the same time he was asked to set up the evacuation plans for British personnel in the region. As both the British and American ambassadors had been targeted for assassination and anti-British feeling was running high, this was not simply playing war games. All this was testing to work on even for a man of British sangfroid, and was much more so for Maclean. Without an outlet enabling him to inform and impress others regularly and receive due appreciation in return, it was troubling and isolating for him. Washington's aim to become the dominant power in the region and to lessen British influence fuelled his anti-Americanism. He wrote to Michael Wright, now back in London, that, 'Judging from the brashness and take-charge attitude of the US mission, America is ready to assume the dominant economic and military position in the Middle East.' This dent to his patriotism could not play well at a time when he felt isolated from his ideological allies.

The 'insensitive handling' of Maclean over this high-level information meant that rendezvous were proposed in the Arab quarter of Cairo where the tall, blond diplomat, elegantly dressed in his immaculate tropical suit, would be 'as about as inconspicuous in the souk as a swan among geese', as the London *rezident* was able to discern. When Maclean managed against some opposition to get the venues changed to restaurants and bars where he would not look like a 'skulking informer', the documents he handed over 'were accepted without comment' and he was given no feedback about the usefulness of his material or about 'what the Centre expected of him'. The name of his Cairo contact was not recorded by Modin: a sign of the different times and and lower regard in which the posting was held compared to the days of Deutsch, Maly and Gorsky. Deutsch's identification of the 'infantile need for praise and reassurance' and 'a yearning to belong' held true, if not truer, in the changed world fifteen years later where fascism was no longer a threat. In Maclean's case, such praise and reassurance were essential prerequisites, the plainest recognition of the human factor underlying successful agent-running. These needs were, indeed, increased by another of the characteristics noted by the master-recruiter, the 'inherent class resentfulness' which Maclean was so aware of in starkly class-ridden Cairo. Added to the loneliness he was feeling in his marriage as Melinda blossomed in her new life, the result was a significant blow to his self-esteem. At one stage he was even suggesting that Melinda should hand over the documents herself to save him from the danger and humiliation. She could meet the *rezident*'s wife in the hairdresser, for example. This belittling notion appears to have been ignored in spirit as much as in fact by Moscow Centre.

*

The news coming from America only ratcheted up Maclean's anxiety. The anti-Communist House Un-American Activities Committee had been hearing from Elizabeth Bentley and the journalist Whittaker Chambers, a sallow-faced man who had decided his own life was in danger and renounced Communism in 1938 after hearing about the purges in the USSR. Chambers had produced five rolls of microfilm hidden in a hollowed-out pumpkin on his family farm as evidence of his good faith in turning in his fellow former agents. One of these was blank, two others contained not very essential information from the Navy Department about fire extinguishers and life rafts, but two contained memos from US embassies to Washington still encoded, so the supplier had presumably passed on the diplomatic codes as well. Typewriter experts proved that the State Department secrets had come from Maclean's high-flying contact and acquaintance Alger Hiss. Hiss, with whom Maclean had had meetings in 1946 to discuss Soviet troop numbers, was accused of being a spy by Whittaker Chambers in front of the House Un-American Activities Committee in early August 1948. He followed the terrible precedent of Oscar Wilde fifty years earlier and took the step of issuing a writ against Chambers for libel. Hiss was indicted in December on two counts of perjury. After the first trial had produced a deadlocked jury, another was held and, in spite of the impressive character witnesses Hiss's lawyers called on his behalf, he was convicted in January 1950 and sentenced to five years' imprisonment. He spent the next thirty years protesting his innocence, increasingly peevishly towards the end of his life. Although it is unlikely that Maclean knew about Hiss's activities, or even how much of their combined intelligence had been useful at Yalta, it was a stark reminder of the heightened danger to him in the febrile and suspicious post-war period.

If Maclean had had knowledge of Venona working in the background, he would have found it impossible to continue. One of the few Soviet agents still active in the US after Bentley's evidence and Gorsky's recall was William Weisband, who was working on cipher analysis in the Army Security Agency (formerly the Signal Intelligence Service). The 'very gregarious and very nosy' 'Zhora', the son of Russian immigrants to the US, had sent, in the blunt words of Moscow Centre, material 'concerning the work of Americans on deciphering Soviet ciphers, intercepting and analysing open radio-correspondence of Soviet institutions'. Weisband's Russian heritage was not brought to anyone's attention when he peered over Meredith Gardner's shoulder in 1946 at a decrypted telegram from the New York residency to Moscow. He had other clumsy tendencies: as remarked by leading cryptanalyst Cecil Phillips, 'he cultivated people who had access to sensitive information. He used to sit near the boss's secretary, who typed anything of any importance.' Little wonder the Russians refused his request for a camera to carry out his own photography for fear he would be caught in the act.

Venona was so secret and so infiltrated that Moscow Centre knew about it some years before it was divulged to the President and the CIA. A mass of evidence about Soviet wartime espionage was emerging. Thirty-year-old FBI Special Agent Robert Lamphere, broad-shouldered and open-faced, as suited his former profession as a lumberjack in his native Idaho, arrived at Arlington Hall with a brief to use the decoded documents to unravel Soviet activities in America. Lamphere had been transferred to the Soviet Espionage Squad from the criminal beat in New York in 1945, unwillingly as his new assignment was called 'Siberia time' because for each agent or controller identified, another would come in to take his place. But the more Lamphere read of the cases and more particularly of what life under Communism was like, including Arthur Koestler's 1940 novel *Darkness at Noon*, whose protagonist Rubashov is imprisoned in the purges by 'Number One' in the system he had helped to create, the more passionate he became in his desire to pull its roots out of American soil. One converted ideologue was chasing the others. He went to Arlington Hall 'every two to three weeks' and began to get behind Meredith Gardner's reserve and modesty to the point where theirs became the critical Arlington working relationship between the code-breakers and law enforcement. And just as Maclean arrived in Cairo, Gardner and his team started work on the New York–Moscow cable traffic of 1944, and soon turned up classified information of which they could decrypt very little. But what they did get was a telegram from New York sent on 2 August 1944 about the planning meetings for Operation Anvil, the proposed allied invasion of the Mediterranean coast, at which 'Homer is present at all the sessions'.

They had the code-name of a traitor.

*

The first real clue to Homer's identity came to light in January 1949 as the rest of the series – about 'Captain' and 'Boar' meeting in Quebec, about post-war planning for Germany and entire despatches from the frantic period of March 1945 about the future of Poland – began to emerge. The breakthrough came when it was realised that in a sloppy piece of tradecraft and a near-miraculous piece of luck an over-literal Russian cipher clerk in New York had passed on a telegram in March 1945 complete with its internal Foreign Office serial number. There could be little doubt that it originated in the British Embassy. This tiny detail, an 'appalling blunder' as Moscow Centre said when they learned of it, changed everything as the spotlight swung on to America's closest ally.

Not only was the clock ticking that much faster with respect to Maclean's fate. The FBI investigation highlighted the tensions in the intelligence relationship between Britain and America. Lamphere had the healthy scepticism of the rougher FBI about dealing with the smooth, clubbable MI6 operatives, 'a bunch of skilful horse traders with whom you trafficked at your peril'. In particular, he didn't trust the 'clever, witty and charming' Peter Dwyer, MI6's man in Washington and 'one of the most skilful horse traders', who would exchange a few crumbs of British intelligence for a great deal from America, which was obviously frustrating since the two organisations were dealing with a common enemy.

But in late 1948 Assistant Director Mickey Ladd overruled Lamphere and decided to tell Dwyer and his MI5 opposite number Dick Thistlethwaite that material had been uncovered which the Brits would be interested in. Dwyer demanded that Lamphere give them access to all that the FBI had uncovered, not just the material where there was a British interest. In the ensuing row, Lamphere threatened to withhold as much information as he could within the barest niceties of co-operation, but eventually he told the two 'startled' men about the spy in the British Embassy in 1944 and 1945. Further, he made it clear to Thistlethwaite (known as 'Thistle' in MI5) that if he let on to the CIA what he was doing, MI5 would be 'persona non grata' in Washington. However, in a 'classic flanking maneuver' the highly strategic British in fact put their own man directly in touch with Arlington Hall through military rather than intelligence protocols in order to have access to more of the telegrams. The consequences of this in-house secrecy, and that between 'the Cousins', as John le Carré later called the services on either side of the Atlantic, were to reverberate for decades after the discoveries and defections of the next few years, in fiction as well as in life.

*

In Cairo Maclean did not have even the first glimmer that a spy had been unearthed in Washington, but 1949 nevertheless became the year in which his mask could no longer be kept in place. The social life, described by their friend Isis Fahmy, the first Coptic female journalist in Egypt, as 'a strenuous pastime, with parties one after another in quick succession', became monotonous: in the words of Madame de La Fayette referring to the court of Louis XIV, 'Always the same pleasures, always the same hours and always the same people.' Work finished at eight o'clock and dinners often did not begin until around 11 p.m., leaving plenty of time for drinking at home or in the clubs (or possibly to meet a contact in bars) beforehand. Maclean tended to work through the siesta hours of noon until 4 p.m., both because of the amount on his official plate and often because his secret work of photographing and copying could not be done in his much busier household, now frequently full of guests, and with his growing boys and extensive staff. Lady Maclean, who visited her favourite son as she had in his other two postings, had no doubt that his Cairo troubles were due to a combination of his being 'compelled to live a life of social gaiety which he would find absolutely alien to his character' and 'his size and fine mentality', which demanded 'more sleep than most'.

Fahmy reported that often Melinda did not know where her charming husband was in the evenings. Sometimes he was likely to be at the house of the hedonistic Princess Faiza, one of Farouk's four sisters, who 'liked her friends to organise parties and dances for her on an almost daily basis'. On 'more than one occasion' the Embassy Military Attaché was rung by the Princess and asked to take away 'a friend of his', Maclean, who might be sleeping on her doorstep or fighting with her servants. Maclean would be helped into an Embassy car or poured into a taxi to be sent home, where he would pass out on his bed.

Maclean was struggling through drink to withdraw from his unfulfilled existence, while daily witnessing the miserable poverty that a system of gross inequality could bring about. His spiritual isolation was made even harder by Melinda's separate life; she would say to Kim Philby in a very different time and place that her marriage had in effect ended in 1948.

Even when Maclean had to take time off work to cope with his monumental hangovers, it was kept from his Ambassador, Sir Ronnie Campbell; any unexpected absences were attributed to 'a bad cold'. But the cracks were beginning to show in public now: at one dinner-party Maclean found himself seated next to the wife of the Dutch Ambassador, whom he horrified (and he must have rattled himself if he remembered the remark the next day) by saying, 'If Alger Hiss felt as he did about communism, he was quite right to betray his country.' This at a time when Hiss was in the daily news and when the reach of Soviet espionage in the West was beginning to be understood thanks to the revelations pouring out of the House Un-American Activities Committee.

Once again, the loyalty Maclean inspired through his charming daytime inscrutability, reinforced by the codes of the close-knit club of the Foreign Office, conspired to keep his decline within boundaries, undetected by Campbell or London. The Embassy security officer was Major 'Sammy' Sansom, a moustached and squarely built man who had come up through the non-commissioned ranks of the army and revelled in being the 'most hated man in the embassy'. He was unremittingly tough on any potential breaches of security such as love affairs between secretaries and what he saw as 'local gigolos', and managed to have several of the former sent home for their dalliances. He was pleased when the new head of Chancery 'showed a keen interest and understanding of my little set-up' and took an especial interest in 'the procedure for the safety of secret documents'. The pugnacious Sansom approved of his boss's security-mindedness and asked Maclean whether they should do spot checks on a junior staffer who, although 'fashionably dressed', used to leave the Embassy with 'an unfashionably large handbag'. The Counsellor got quite heated and insisted that there 'will be no snap checks while I'm Head of Chancery'. Maclean soon came to his notice in a different context. His boss used to stoke himself up with whisky at home before going to cocktail parties with Melinda; afterwards he would wander off in search of solitude, hiding from whatever demons were chasing him, and more than once he had been found in the early hours of the morning, shoeless, in a stupor and blackout on a bench in the insalubrious Esbekieh Gardens, the last place the Egyptian police would expect to find a member of the British *corps diplomatique*.

After he had left one royal party, Maclean climbed over the wall of the Gezireh Sporting Club to sleep in a flowerbed; he was found next morning wandering through the rush-hour traffic, shoes in hand, his linen suit in an indescribable state. The police were obliged to report this to Sansom, who thought Maclean 'a brilliant chap but highly unreliable'. Sansom found himself in a bind: the prescribed route for dealing with such matters was via the head of Chancery, but that was Maclean himself; he could have gone straight to Ambassador Campbell in these exceptional circumstances but both Macleans were so popular with His Excellency that he doubted that he would get a hearing there. Melinda even said to Sansom when he raised this behaviour with her that 'everybody knew … that when Donald goes on a drunk he just smashes the place up'. Instead Sansom passed the matter legitimately upwards to George Carey Foster, head of Foreign Office security back in London, suggesting that a transfer might be considered for Maclean, who could represent a security risk.

Sansom's clearly and carefully worded reports were rebutted. The head of personnel in London, George Middleton, Maclean's Washington tennis partner, asked Campbell about Maclean's behaviour and was sharply put in his place by the Ambassador, who disliked hearing 'tittle-tattle about an able officer like Maclean'. The Foreign Office sent inspectors to look at the Embassy in general in June, and they seemed to pay particular attention to Maclean, but he was clearly on his best behaviour and lived up to every perception London had had of him since he joined the service. The inspectors reported that he gave 'an impression of great confidence' and although quiet in manner 'appeared to have very sound judgement in all staff matters which he handled with great tact'. They thought his administrative side was not quite up to speed, 'possibly because of pressure of other work'.

*

Lees Mayall was two years younger than Maclean and ranked just below him as First Secretary in the Cairo Embassy. Shortly before his arrival there Mayall had married Mary Ormsby-Gore, whom Maclean had courted while swotting for the Foreign Office exams at Scoones, but she had instead chosen his friend Robin Campbell (son of the Paris Sir Ronald) as her first husband. The Mayalls were well known to the Maclean family and 'Lees was a dear,' according to Nancy. Melinda seems to have been less warm to them, possibly sensing an historical threat to her husband's fading affections: Mary found her 'very difficult' and felt that she pulled Donald's senior rank unnecessarily and rudely, insisting on occasion that she herself went through a door first at formal events, for example. Even if this animosity from Melinda was the jealousy of a close friend of her husband from his former life, Mayall's reaction was much more strongly put: he described her to his colleagues only a year later as 'a cold American bitch'. Towards the end of his life, Maclean still spoke of Mayall as having his 'permanent affection'.

Mayall in turn was 'extremely fond' of Donald, whom he found 'amusing, highly intelligent and an excellent talker'. He was 'good in the office' (although 'hopeless' on the administrative side and always fighting shy of 'unpleasantness' in his dealings with staff) even if 'his judgement about things outside the office and about the world in general was absolutely infantile'. The echoes of the early reports of Maclean's immaturity resurfaced, in this context perhaps as part of his 'burning hatred [for the disparity] between riches and poverty in Egypt' about which he was 'woolly' and 'had no practical solutions', also complained of by Mayall. The only real global solution, Communism, he felt, was not one that could be voiced, nor indeed did Maclean see it as the specific answer to Egypt's woes.

The Mayalls and Harriet Marling were witnesses to the first, public, crack in the Macleans' marriage, the agonising start to the next act of what was beginning to look like a tragedy. In late June 1949 Donald and Melinda, whose sister was staying with them, decided to have a picnic party. They booked two feluccas to sail their party of eight up the Nile, 'supping and wining in the moonlight', to the grand house of a British businessman, Eric Tyrrell-Martin, fifteen miles upstream at Helouan. The boat party would join forces with Tyrrell-Martin's dinner guests for port and coffee and after-dinner chat and games before returning to the city by road. This plan, simple enough, went badly wrong from the very start. They were meant to meet their feluccas at 7 p.m. but arrived an hour late to find that only one boat was waiting. The vessel was slowed by its double cargo, and to add to that there was barely a breeze on the Nile, so they tacked laboriously against the current without any moonlight to provide visibility. There was at least plenty of food and a huge amount to drink on board – Donald had seen to that. He himself was drinking a mixture of whisky and zebib, an Egyptian version of arak, a disastrously potent combination. After some hours of this progress they came ashore to see where they were, and Donald's frustration with the spoiled adventure spilled over. He blamed Melinda for the whole shambles, and to the horrified embarrassment of the party grabbed her around the neck and made as if to throttle her. Lees Mayall and the others pulled him off her and told him to calm down. He skulked alone at one end of the boat for the rest of the journey; she maintained a bright façade which could not disguise her own mortification.

By the time they had arrived at what they reckoned was their destination in the very small hours of the following morning their host was falling-down drunk. The able-bodied men, Mayall, an American businessman, John Brinton, and a colonel in the military administration of Cyrenaica, went ashore. They became aware of some 'white-robed *fellaheen*' flitting through the palm trees behind them. The colonel grabbed one of them and held him in a 'commando grip' until the prisoner had guided them to the house at Helouan, where he was released and tipped handsomely. Nobody answered the bell, and a sudden spotlight coming on above their heads gave Brinton, not at his most sober either, such a start that he fell over and knocked himself bloodily unconscious on the stone step. The door was finally opened by Tyrrell-Martin, furious that they had not turned up earlier when his guests were waiting for them; he had eventually sent their cars back to Cairo. Grudgingly he allowed them to carry the concussed Brinton upstairs to a bedroom and gave them some towels to staunch his blood, but refused to help them beyond that.

The colonel and Mayall had to take charge of the outing. They decided to go to the nearest village on foot to see if they could find cars. They got back to the boat and announced the plan. The others needed no persuasion to get off the cramped, rancorous felucca and were taken ashore, where they were joined by a *ghaffir*, an armed guard employed to patrol the river bank. Donald was having a heated argument with the *rais*, the boat's skipper, about his payment for the trip as he came onshore: the *rais* was claiming he had not been paid enough for such a prolonged journey, with Maclean berating him for sending only one boat and not knowing where to disembark. The *ghaffir* turned out to be the *rais*'s cousin and joined in the debate which carried on until Maclean seized the *ghaffir*'s rifle from him and started to beat him with it. All the Egyptians present (more *fellaheen* had joined them to see this fascinating night-time spectacle) started up in 'an ugly excited murmur'; Mayall feared that a diplomatic incident might ensue and the ever-practical colonel urged him to knock out his superior, which would have left two broken skulls among the four men of the party.

Mayall decided that he could not actually knock out cold an 'unsuspecting' man he 'had grown to like very much' and instead thought a more humane plan of action might be to tackle him around the neck and floor him, then sit on his head until British Foreign Office reason could reign again. But he had not had much practice with tackling blind-drunk men: Maclean's sixteen stone collapsed on top of him as he went in for the heave, there was a crack like a rifle shot and the First Secretary was lying on the bank in agony with a double fracture in his ankle and a spiral fracture in the tibia of his left leg. The rest of the appalled party repaired to Tyrrell-Martin's house and bedded down as best they could on sofas and armchairs while Maclean bullied the Egyptian servant into opening the locked drinks cabinet so that he could take a bottle of gin to Mayall as anaesthetic. He sat by him, 'maudlin and contrite' and rambling his remorse until first light, when 'a ramshackle taxi' arrived. Maclean, still plastered, at first refused to get into it, claiming that the driver was 'an abortionist', but Mayall was heaved in to be given 'a rough ride' back to the city in silence. The expedition finally ended just before lunch the day after it had set off, the shocked and silent eightsome looking like the exhausted survivors of a short war. Nobody knew what to say to Melinda.

There was no report of the Helouan incident made to London, nor did Major Sansom comment on it. Inevitably Campbell got to hear of his First Secretary's hospital stay, but not of its direct cause. It was put down to an accident. Even if he had been told the full story, Campbell knew that there were rumours about his relationship with his manservant, a very camp man called Charlie, which 'predisposed him to ignore all stories about the private lives of his staff'. Campbell 'hated any form of gossip, and would only have dealt with proven fact', so if the injured First Secretary chose not to tell him the full circumstances of his accident there was nothing to report. Mayall himself, on his return to work for the last weeks of his tour of duty before he was posted back to Whitehall in his callipers, played the whole incident down. His next job was in the Far Eastern Department alongside Guy Burgess, whom he disliked intensely.

Once again, the diligent and credible Maclean had escaped notice and censure. Campbell never sent 'an adequate report' about any aspect of his behaviour in Cairo, partly to prevent Melinda, who was so useful to him as his diplomatic hostess, being taken away. Even years later, when Lees Mayall was happy to tell MI5 that at Cambridge his erstwhile colleague had been a Marxist, drank too much and 'consistently gave vent to very left-wing opinions', he did not mention the tussle and its sorry consequences. The

Macleans went on a month's planned leave to Italy two days later, and must have had some very tense, remorseful conversations once they were alone.

*

Almost as a companion piece to the official blind eye being turned to the debacle on the Nile, the FBI were astonished at the lack of excitement shown by 'the British bulldogs' about the Homer bone they had been thrown in the form of the leaked telegrams from 1945. In March 1950 the Washington Embassy admitted to the Foreign Office in London that the total number of staff it employed was 'of the order of 6000 and the majority was Canadian'; that the circulation of telegrams was 'depressingly wide'; even 'the typing of the names alone would fully occupy a secretary for some time', to say nothing of the vetting which also ran the danger of reinforcing 'the American attitude towards the Dominions in security matters' if they were to get to know the 'real story.' It seemed as if the British were keener not to admit their shortcomings than to unearth someone whom they knew had had access to the correspondence between Churchill and Roosevelt. It was a myopia born out of disbelief, or too much belief in their own people. One bright idea for narrowing the field a bit came from Sir Robert Mackenzie, the more psychologically astute head of security in the Embassy. He suggested an investigation into those junior members of staff who had had 'nervous breakdowns', but only those in the cipher room during the war, and no senior employee showing troubling signs later. This turned up Mrs Mary Brown, a 'permanent nervous wreck', and Miss Hewitt, who claimed to be related to Harry Hopkins of the White House, obviously a sign of delusion for someone so lowly, but no real suspects.

Lamphere knew that if the US authorities had been told about an American spy 'in an office of comparative size and importance' they would at the very least have obtained within a couple of days a list of all personnel who might have had access to the information, 'matching names and dates against transfer and vacation lists and entry-and-exit lists'.

In London, Liddell of MI5 pointed out quite casually that the telegrams were 'so obscure in the missing groups that it is very hard to get at the facts', which was true, but does not take into account the reality that the telegrams were important and had reached Moscow. He too refused to countenance the possibility that any leak could come from someone high up in the Embassy. In the memorandum to the Foreign Secretary which first disclosed the leak to the British government at the start of February 1949, Sir Orme Sargent seemed anxious only about the current relations between the two security services, not about the possible source or about what else might be going on within the British services at a time when there was plentiful evidence of infiltration of the US secret world: 'Provided we tell the Americans that this case has shocked us and has provided us with an excuse for overhauling our security arrangements, it seems unlikely that they will use it as an excuse for withholding top secret information from us.' In the absence of real emotion in the mandarin class, saying they were 'shocked' was the next best thing because they could forget the past and assumed that as it was the past the Americans would forget it too. They meant that there was no urgent need to look further despite the cumulative evidence of Soviet penetration of the British Embassy, the State Department and the Manhattan Project, and the revelation of the early Soviet bomb.

In May, some months after he had been told of the severity of the security lapse, and paying no attention at all to the wider implications of Moscow being able to read transmissions from Washington, Liddell was wondering rather aimlessly in his diary: 'It is still not clear exactly how the leakage from the British Embassy occurred, but there is at least a possibility that the documents were obtained through Alexander Halpern's secretary.' Halpern's secretary Trudi Rient was Czech-born and had been married to an Indian; they had both lived in Moscow before the war, when her husband had disappeared, presumed liquidated in the purges. She had worked in the US Embassy in Moscow before coming to Washington, where Cedric Belfrage, known to have Communist sympathies and later acknowledged to be a spy, had left his wife to live with her for a time. The small matter of the disappearance of her husband at Soviet hands aside, Rient was a good candidate to be the leaker, until it was established that she could not have possibly have seen most of the telegrams.

The confidence with which Liddell made his pronouncement is surprising when one considers that her boss, Alexander Halpern, head of the Minorities Section at the Embassy, had been born in Russia and was now a member of the London Bar who 'always retained business relationships with the Soviet Union'; he was known to have been a target for Soviet recruitment but 'there was no positive evidence in 1944 that he had ever been recruited'. He had since worked for SIS which put him even further from scrutiny, as Philby found, and should have meant he was a good picker of secretaries. Halpern was on a list of eight names compiled in July 1949 of those 'known to have communist views at the time', but there was no investigation of him as thorough or as early as that of his erstwhile secretary. The others on the list did not have access to the relevant material. Maclean, of course, did not come into the category of having had 'communist views' in spite of his outspokenness a mere fifteen years earlier.

When Dick White, head of MI5's B Division for counterespionage, visited George Carey Foster, head of security in the Foreign Office, to tell him of the spy, Carey Foster at once said, 'It's inconceivable that any senior member could be a traitor.' As with Krivitsky's information a decade earlier, the authorities could countenance investigating secretaries and cipher clerks, but could not imagine that anyone with the same privileged upbringing as they had had could hold any values other than their own. Anyone who did not share those values would have been weeded out during the rigorous selection process and interview. Never mind that, as Kim Philby could plainly see, 'there could be no real doubt that we were dealing with a man of stature' rather than 'the petty agent emptying waste-paper baskets' judging by the importance of the wartime events described in the fragments. It seems probable that, even if the story about Helouan had got back to Whitehall through official channels rather than just through the sight of Mayall limping around his new job, the same blind eye of mandarin and class prejudice would have been turned on it in order not to upset the status quo.

But just as the rudderless, fragmented Maclean did not seem ready to accept and deal with the consequences of his drinking, nor did the Embassy or Foreign Office. His first spell in Cairo had closed with the terrible image of the brawl on the river bank at the same time that the FBI was handing over evidence of his wartime spying to their British allies. Yet even as Gardner and Lamphere did their work in Arlington Hall and Maclean's inner furies gnawed at him, luck, toughness, tradition and loyalty rallied around him and Melinda.

13

Collapse

Away from the increasing stresses and evasions of Cairo, Donald Maclean was once again the relaxed family man on holiday in Italy, playing tennis, drinking in moderation and enjoying the company of his wife and sons. The family returned to Egypt in July 1949, the Helouan trip and his drunken attack on Melinda seemingly forgiven, although with Melinda understandably harbouring grave concerns about the effect that the stress in his life was having on his drinking. The family spent most of the rest of the Egyptian summer in Alexandria, where the Embassy decamped to escape the unbearable heat and dust of Cairo. It was soon after they had returned to the capital in September that both the global and the personal combined into an agonising and squalid spiral downwards to the lowest point of his life, a vortex of shame and fear.

Maclean was already feeling isolated as a result of Moscow Centre's neglect compared to the heady espionage days of Washington, while Melinda's increasing self-confidence and enjoyment of her own life was proving very hard for him in a marriage where he had been used to relying on his intelligence, reputation and charm to be the dominant figure in their relationship. Moreover, she was receiving 'pressing attention' from a wealthy princeling of King Farouk's house, Prince Daoud, which led to an increasingly independent and high-flying social life much encouraged by her sister Harriet as an outlet from the mounting difficulty of being married to Donald.

The realisation in early September that the Russians had carried out their first nuclear test five days earlier, years ahead of expectation, caused consternation in the West, following closely as it did the defeat of Chiang Kai-shek's Nationalists by Mao Tse-tung's Communists in China. War crept a little closer. Maclean's time on the AEC in the early nuclear days must have been in his mind as he worked on the evacuation plans, drafting a top-secret telegram to the Foreign Office on 27 August headed 'Evacuation in case of war'. But it was not until later in the autumn that he could have had an inkling of the circlings of Venona and the potential exposure of his secret life.

*

In early October, Peter Dwyer introduced his successor as MI6 representative in Washington to Robert Lamphere. The FBI man had previously been told by Dwyer that he would be meeting an extremely bright and senior operative, who would probably be head of the service one day. In the context of what Venona had just uncovered, spies in Los Alamos and now in the British Embassy, it was vital to have such a good mind on the case. Lamphere was accordingly surprised to be shaking hands with a 'seedy' figure with 'loose-fitting and shabby clothes'. It was his first introduction to Kim Philby. Philby, who was renowned for his charisma, managed to make their meetings so painfully boring that it was a relief when he suggested they became monthly and with another FBI colleague present, rather than weekly and one to one, as they had been with Dwyer. Meredith Gardner too was not that impressed, and was similarly grateful to find that he did not have to see the offhand and unlikeable new MI6 man. Dwyer had been very help-ful in Gardner's decryption work, often filling the gaps in the telegrams, but the same could not be said of his successor. When Philby was in Arlington Hall, Gardner noticed that as he and Dwyer were discussing their progress, 'Philby was looking on with rapt attention but he never said a word, never a word. And that was the last I saw of him. Philby was supposed to continue these visits, but helping me was the last thing he wanted to do.' Although shortly before Philby's arrival the MI5 investigation was despair-ingly aware that 'at least 150 people had access to [the telegrams]' and 'this number is likely to be increased as enquiries proceed', it certainly would not do to help winnow the list too vigorously.

Philby had leapt at the proposed move from Istanbul to Washington as he was 'beginning to suspect' that the American intelligence organisations were 'already of greater importance' than the British ones. He didn't even bother checking to see if his Soviet 'colleagues' approved. He was briefed in London by the 'formidable' Maurice Oldfield and given 'a communication of the gravest importance'. The communication was that the Anglo-American investigation of Soviet activity in the US had yielded the 'strong suggestion' that there was leakage from the Washington Embassy and from Los Alamos during the war. 'A swift check in the relevant Foreign Office list left me in little doubt of the identity of the source from the British Embassy.' The news from Arlington Hall came in some respects as 'a relief' to Philby when he saw that he was not implicated, but it also caused him some anxiety as it clarified what his Soviet contact in his last posting had been asking him for some time – what were the British doing about a case involving the British Embassy in Washington which they had heard about from William Weisband? It was another instance of Philby's recurring good fortune that six telegrams with material from 'Stanley', as he was then code-named, sent in 1945 were not decrypted until some years later. Back in London his 'Russian friend' confirmed that he had indeed 'stumbled into the heart of a problem' with regard to his new job. It was one he and Moscow Centre had to solve ahead of his own country if the Cambridge Five were to remain at liberty. It would take all his considerable guile. And he would rely on Homer keeping himself together until the time was right.

*

In mid-September Lamphere was shown a newly deciphered message from 1944 which had clearly come from one of the scientists working on the Manhattan Project in Los Alamos: 'Rest arrived in the Country [America] in September as a member of the Island [Britain] mission on Enormoz ... The whole operation amounts to the working out of the process for the separation of isotopes of Enormoz.' A message from the following November indicated that 'Rest' had transferred to 'Camp No. 2', Los Alamos, to work on 'Balloon', the atom bomb. Fuchs was easily identified but, as had been the case with Nunn May, the evidence that caught him could never be brought to court as it was too highly classified. Nor could it be revealed to those being investigated for fear of Moscow Centre keeping abreast of the decryption efforts and triggering a spate of damaging defections. They were, of course, up to speed anyway through Philby. Although Fuchs had been back in Britain since 1946 and was working at the Atomic Research Establishment at Harwell and supplying material to the Soviets, he would either have to confess or be caught red-handed for a conviction to be achieved.

William (always known as 'Jim') Skardon was the man. A former Metropolitan Police officer, most often wreathed in pipe smoke like Sherlock Holmes, Skardon was now MI5's skilled interrogator. He got his results by being a 'nice, unpretentious and even cosy man'. Lamphere, when he came to meet Skardon, took to the ex-copper immediately, mostly because he was not, as were all the Brits he had met so far, 'from the upper crust of British society, but rather was a friendly, low-key fellow ... complete with dishevelled appearance and an intellect that was sometimes hidden until the moment came to use it to point to incongruities in a subject's story'. Skardon (who despite his crucial role in the espionage investigations was never given any sort of promotion to senior officer before his retirement in 1961) came up with a brilliant plan. Fuchs's father was about to accept a post at the University of Leipzig in East Germany; Skardon started to talk to Fuchs about the possible blackmail he would lay himself open to. As he began to gain Fuchs's confidence, he let slip that the authorities knew about possible espionage activities in the United States during the war. After a period of denial, in January 1950 Fuchs laid down his burden with relief and confessed to Skardon that he had given the Russians 'all the information in his possession about British and American research in connection with the atomic bomb'. Fuchs was so soothed by

Skardon's manner and politeness that he thought he might be allowed to continue at Harwell, or work in academia (and indeed he was allowed to remain in place for a while in the hope of catching more spies around him), but in March he was sentenced to a fourteen-year sentence after pleading guilty to violation of the Official Secrets Act, the only charge that could be brought without revealing his actual security breaches and the intelligence operations behind the arrest. On his release after nine years Fuchs finished his working life as a highly respected scientist and academician in East Germany. Afterwards Skardon used to refer to Fuchs as 'Dear Old Klaus'.

*

In his confession Fuchs summarised the way he had managed to combine his professional and conscience-driven lives: 'I used my Marxist philosophy to establish in my mind two separate compartments: one in which I allowed myself to make friendships, to help people and to be in all personal ways the kind of man I wanted to be, and the kind of man ... I had been before with my friends in or near the Communist Party ... I knew the other compartment would step in if I approached the danger point' of 'disclosing myself'. After the war, after the Russians had tested the bomb Fuchs had helped them to build, he came to realise that he 'would also have to stand up and say to them that there are things which they are doing wrongly' and felt unable to hand over all he knew. Since the Nazi–Soviet Pact, spies of sensitivity and conscience had been aware of living with what Fuchs called 'controlled schizophrenia' but with the Russians as wartime allies control could be maintained. For Maclean, the non-scientist with his true feelings buried deep, this 'schizophrenia' was less easy to control; his 'compartments' were overflowing into each other and were plainly visible when his defences were down, such as when he was drinking. As the hunt for traitors was intensifying, so, for Maclean, was the tension of serving one system and yearning for and abetting another.

Fuchs's conviction would not have given succour to anyone living a double life as attacks on Soviet Communism were stepped up in the West at the beginning of the new decade. President Truman announced that now the Russians had the atom bomb the Americans would raise the stakes by building a hydrogen bomb. The Communist agent Judith Coplon, snared by Venona, was tried for the second time in the US and found guilty of passing government documents to Moscow; Alger Hiss's second trial ended in his conviction for perjury (as we have seen) after he had denied that he had ever been involved in espionage. Most publicly of all, Senator Joseph McCarthy made his explosive statement in West Wheeling, Virginia, on 9 February 1950, that he had in his possession a list of 205 Communists in the US State Department. The McCarthy era, with its attendant bigotry and witch-hunts, had begun.

Maclean must have wondered if the exposure of Nunn May and then Fuchs would lead to an investigation of those who might have been at the 1947 declassification conference, or whether the spooks would go further and deeper, to those who had been on the left at Cambridge in the mid-1930s and now had access to secrets. After the Atomic Energy Commission had reacted to the uncovering of Fuchs in stark terms, by saying he 'alone has influenced the safety of more people and accomplished greater damage than any other spy not only in the history of the United States but in the history of nations', there might have been questions raised about other 'aliens' who had had passes to the AEC in the new atmosphere of mistrust. The rhetorical stakes were being upped alongside the political.

*

The FBI investigation into the wartime British Embassy leaks, in a move which Philby did nothing to discourage, began looking at the technical and support staff rather than the senior diplomats, for the reason that 'since almost every American has relatives abroad . . . the loyalties of those people are divided between America and their historic homeland'. Accordingly they did not bother scrutinising Anglo-Saxons, senior or not, or even those with German antecedents (as wartime enemies of the Soviet Union) but concentrated on those with more dubious origins, even generations back. They would question the friends and neighbours of anyone with Eastern

European or now Soviet bloc origins, and Mickey Ladd of the FBI would answer Philby's twice- or thrice-weekly calls to ask 'if they had found anyone with a Russian uncle or a Ukrainian aunt' with the succinct 'A big zero.' Although it was barking up the wrong trees, the FBI was at least showing energy and a sense of direction lacking in the British investigation.

*

The cracks in Maclean's bearing were now beginning to show in the office as drink took an even stronger hold. With his two lives pulling more and more in opposing directions, his levels of fear and discomfort ramped up his alcohol intake. There were more absences for 'bad colds' in the sweltering climate than there had been before, although when at work he remained, as the Press Secretary, James Murray, commented, 'tirelessly conscientious. He demanded first class work, you could never let a shoddy telegram go by him.' But Murray added, 'Why he would go off and drink too much, I never knew.' Another perspicacious colleague noted with admiration his ability to stand up to the immense workload 'while having the obvious appearance of one who was completely loaded'. In the gossipy aftermath of the Helouan debacle, the unwisdom of failing to control his daytime drinking or of still being drunk from the night before showed that he was beyond being able to prevent it. At one dinner-party given by the Assistant Military Attaché, Maclean 'steadily insulted a Mr Duncan of the British Community ... for no good reason', refused to leave the table and shouted for more brandy. When his host protested Maclean 'knocked him to the ground'. The Military Attaché took the desperate Melinda home but did not report the incident 'for reasons I would prefer not to put in writing' – reticence possibly inspired by Ambassador Campbell's dislike of 'tittle-tattle', or by gallantry in the face of Melinda's pleas.

In November 1949, the finger of suspicion might well have come around to point to Maclean again. Philby, who had checked up on the Walter Krivitsky file during his time in London, decided to make absolutely sure that he was not implicated by the defector's vague mention of an agent during the Spanish Civil War, who was 'amongst the friends' of the Scotsman 'of good family' and had been ordered to assassinate Franco while working as a journalist in Spain. He also wanted to be certain the evidence pointed squarely at Maclean (whom he had not seen or spoken to since he asked him for help in Paris in 1940) so that he could plan his future actions. From the Scottish name to the important father, it was clear that anyone suspicious of the diplomat could use the testimonies as strong circumstantial evidence to start digging deeper. Philby's devious mind calculated that he could serve a treble purpose here: by bringing the Krivitsky evidence to the table he would be seen to be actively on the Homer case, so could have no vested interest in suppressing the investigation; he could deflect attention away from the reference to the British agent in Spain which could conceivably draw him in; and in playing his key part in the search he would ensure his own inclusion in every conversation about it should he need to warn his recruit or Moscow Centre. The master-spy had worked out all the odds.

Philby's top-secret memorandum to the head of security in the Washington Embassy, Sir Robert Mackenzie, omitted Krivitsky's details about 'artistic circles' and cape-wearing, just as it naturally omitted any mention of Spain, and dealt in the vaguest of terms with the facts, the person being of 'good family' and 'young' and 'ideological'. Before he came to his conclusion which would cover him in the event of mishap he admitted: 'The description would, of course, fit a very large number of persons in the Foreign Service; and it is a far cry from Krivitsky's statements in London in 1939 to the leakage from the Embassy in Washington in 1945. But in case this disquieting possibility is overlooked, I thought it advisable to draw it to your attention.'

In Whitehall, Carey Foster offered his opinion a month later that 'there is absolutely no evidence to connect the Washington case with the "Imperial Council" story contained in Krivetsky's [sic] interrogation report'. But it did prompt a look at which members of staff were in London in the late 1930s and then in Washington in 1945. Carey Foster settled on a list of six names on this basis:

Balfour, Makins, Robert Hadow, Wright, Gore-Booth and Maclean. As a roll-call of the coming men in the Foreign Office, that could scarcely be bettered. In the end, the lack of 'evidence' and the refusal to believe that any of these high-ups could even be considered as a traitor when there were so many junior staff to explore meant that this list did not get looked at again for some time, and the links between the six men and their subsequent Washington responsibilities not examined at all. Philby's stratagem of bringing evidence that could expose Maclean and then soft-pedalling his presentation of that evidence was brilliant: his due diligence deflected attention away from himself just as it effectively buried the evidence for now.

The risky irony of the Krivitsky reminder is that, if it had been rigorously followed up and Maclean identified, then it could have kept the other Cambridge recruits hidden from the investigators – if Maclean's nerve held under interrogation by Skardon. Such an outcome might even have been in the subtle sinews of Philby's mind: if they were going to catch Maclean anyway, which surely they would do at some point, his confession might not implicate the others. Philby claimed to be amazed that, even though Krivitsky and Volkov had both said the Foreign Office had been penetrated at a high level, 'the FBI were still sending us reams about the Embassy charladies, and the enquiry into our menial personnel was spinning itself out endlessly'.

*

In the autumn of 1949, Maclean becomes more silent, there are fewer sightings at parties, less comment on his work. Helouan was a signal to him that his two working lives, and alcoholism, the three now indissolubly linked, were an unbearable combination, and in December he tried to throw in the towel. The schizophrenic life he had not signed up for was out of control, he had had enough and he wanted out.

He wrote a short letter to Moscow Centre and handed it over to his handler. The letter declared that he 'had always wanted to work in Russia' as 'the best place for him to carry on his struggle against American and Western imperialism'. It was, in other words, a thinly veiled request for him to be exfiltrated to Moscow to follow his guiding conscience, a place where he could hold his head high, do his work and be a whole, united man rather than languish in Wormwood Scrubs with the scientist spies. He had not taken this decision alone, and may even have been guided by Melinda, who could not bear the humiliation being heaped upon her and was standing by him come what may. Perhaps there was a chance of a sober, happy marriage with a husband who was not being torn apart. Donald said that Melinda too was 'perfectly prepared to go'.

The spy whose every word had been fallen upon in Moscow Centre a couple of years earlier, who was able to add his own gloss to the policy documents he would send on as being helpful to the Kremlin, was ignored. Unlike the Western countries in the wake of Krivitsky, Gouzenko and others, the Russians did not have a template for defectors. Perhaps they did not appreciate the danger to the other members of the network if Maclean was apprehended. Perhaps they thought he was trailing his coat to become a double agent for the British, hence the reports back from their Cairo *rezident* that he 'was making an ass of himself ... week after week, the tales of Maclean's increasingly unpleasant behaviour filtered through'. They might have thought he was not worth the candle at this stage, particularly because in their neglect they seemed not to appreciate the importance of what he could send them from Cairo. But most likely they simply failed to hear and deal with the *cri de coeur* from their agent now that the psychologically minded handlers had all gone. Whatever the reason, true to the treatment Maclean had received thus far from Moscow during his Cairo posting, this surrender and appeal, which would have saved all sides many problems in the ensuing eighteen months and beyond, were ignored. Yuri Modin of the London *rezidentura* said later that he was 'quite sure nobody looked at' the letter, but in the deep paranoia of the times in Moscow even if they had they might well have revisited their fears that Maclean had been turned.

Ignored at his moment of gravest crisis in Moscow's service, Maclean followed up this desperate plea with another appeal in April 1950. At this point his first letter was read as well, but while the Centre was considering its position on the request, a prominent figure from Maclean's pre-war life reappeared and his final, messy, tragic exit from overseas service was under way.

*

Melinda had expressed her disapproval of Philip Toynbee almost as soon as she met him in Paris before their marriage. Recently he too had been showing signs of coming unstuck: he had undergone a bitter parting from his wife and in the aftermath ramped up his own drinking; but his Communism had moved into the background and was soon to be replaced by a fervent Christian belief. Arnold Toynbee, Philip's father and a socially committed economic historian, asked David Astor, the great liberal owner and editor of the *Observer*, if he would take his son on at his newspaper. Astor commissioned a series of articles from Philip about the Middle East, and the correspondent started to make arrangements to go to Cairo where he would naturally stay with his old friend Donald Maclean. They had not met much while Maclean was posted abroad, although while on leave in 1946 Maclean had spent a few days with the Toynbees on the Isle of Wight, where he had shocked his old friend by taking a Marxist view of T. S. Eliot's *Four Quartets* and described them as 'decadent and effete'.

The political trouble started when Toynbee applied for his visa. As the *Observer* was banned in Egypt for its pro-Zionist stance it did not have an official correspondent in the region. Instead, it relied on Clare Hollingworth, the Macleans' close Cairo friend and bridge partner, to file pieces for them. When she heard about his looming arrival Hollingworth got in touch with the Information Department in the Embassy to complain that Toynbee's Communist past would make things difficult 'among the Arabs here'. She was soothed on being told that he was staying with her friend the head of Chancery, who would explain how things were done in Egypt and keep him from writing anything that would cause trouble. Fadel Bey of the Egyptian Ministry of Information made it clear to the Embassy that any hostile pieces in the *Observer* would result in Hollingworth, the 'real' correspondent, being expelled.

To cover his back, Maclean wrote to William 'Rids' Ridsdale, head of the Foreign Office News Department, to say that he knew Toynbee had been expelled from Rugby School because of his Communism, and had then been a 'leading Communist' at Oxford, but he pointed out that Toynbee had given up Communism at the beginning of the Finnish war and was absolutely not a security risk. He had been asked 'some time ago' if he would put Toynbee up and had agreed 'and thought no more of it'. He was happy to 'put him off altogether' if that was the advice from Whitehall, which no doubt would have pleased Melinda, but it seems likely that this was merely the diplomat speaking.

By the time Rids replied some days later, the Egyptian paper *Akhbar Al-Yom* had reported on the arrival of 'Mr Philip Toniby [*sic*]' to stay with 'Mr Ronald Maclean [*sic*]' of the Embassy. Rids said that he had had a word with the diplomatic correspondent of the paper, who had confirmed that Toynbee had indeed been a Communist in his youth but under 'the inoculation theory' was 'quite convinced that Toynbee is now very definitely anti-Communist'. In confidence, and with no irony intended, Rids was happy to tell Maclean that Toynbee's visit was 'therapeutic' as the journalist had recently separated and was 'inclined to go round the bend, and was sporadically drinking much too heavily – a state of affairs particularly bad in the case of one who is of a brilliant but slightly erratic, if not unbalanced, temperament'. This careful character analysis led Rids to the conclusion that it might be better if Toynbee stayed in a hotel. Maclean replied that the visit would not only keep Toynbee on the journalistic straight and narrow but might 'help' him with his 'drinking difficulty', so it would be fine to have him to stay after all. Inevitably, with two such seasoned dipsomaniacs brought together with their separate woes, the drinking difficulties stood a greater chance of multiplication than of division. Maclean may even have been looking forward to having a partner in the bottle.

Toynbee had arrived 'in a state of extreme depression' after the 'violent and painful changes' in his life, but 'my spirits rose at once when I saw the delightfully reassuring figure of Donald advancing to meet me at the airport, dressed in the golden-white of an antique tropical suit'. 'Philippo', as Maclean affectionately called his old friend, was launched into the diplomatic whirl, which he hated as much as Maclean and which undoubtedly contributed to their bonding isolation as the month wore on: 'I went to a party at the Embassy ... for the press. DM was there at first to offer some protection, but when he left I found myself sweating, untidy, confused and somehow *small*, in the middle of these brisk, high-powered men and women.' He went on to dinner with some of them, but found them 'ODIOUS, racist and xenophobic, a terrible end-of-Empire gathering'. The British Military Attaché was less enraptured at meeting Toynbee, who was 'always dirty, always drunk, very argumentative and always at least an hour late for everything'.

Two weeks later, Maclean was spinning out of control, in misery as his second plea to be taken to Russia went unheard. He spiralled down from 'extreme gentleness and politeness ... [with] the occasional berserk and murderous outbursts when, so to speak, the pot of suppressed anger has been filled' to going into a 'two-day trough together' of drinking with his friend while Melinda was off for a week's tourism with her sister Harriet. His alcoholism was now unfettered and unhidden as his demons had emerged, an age away from the June evening of fourteen years earlier when the two young men had got cheerfully drunk together at a white-tie ball in London before taking their dawn swim.

They went to another party. Toynbee 'was back in bed by midnight but Donald rushed out again to disaster after disaster, ending by hitting Eddy [Gathorne-Hardy, a very old friend of them both and a colleague of Maclean's] and throwing glass after glass against the wall. In the morning I came down at half-past eight ... to find him snoring and a pool of water all around him.' Young Donald, Beany, called out gleefully to his nanny that 'Daddy's wet the bed.' Toynbee 'sobered him with talk and took him all the way to his room at the Embassy. Somehow, once there, he managed to heave on his armour … I admired it.' It was that morning that Toynbee gave names to the two sides of Maclean: 'Sir Donald', when he was in On His Majesty's Service mode, the brilliant, unflappable diplomat; and 'Gordon', after his favourite brand of gin, whose label had on it a scarlet boar's head, long-tusked and mouth gaping.

Toynbee did not see Maclean that evening but was awoken by him at 2.00 a.m. and made to talk over whisky until 5.30 a.m. Maclean's 'pot of anger' turned into rage at Melinda, an easy target to bring into view rather than investigate the true causes of his anguish. 'Donald told me he wished … for the death of his wife. He was in a queer and terrifying condition – still very funny, very lackadaisical (tho' voluble), yet the genuine depths were there behind his words and his face.' The two 'clung together' and decided to form a new Communist Party just for themselves, but Maclean 'tried to expel me so he *should* be alone'. Toynbee had 'been inoculated against the disease of Communism' and 'understood that [its] doctrine was no good thing for people with any true intellectual or democratic ideas'. He believed that Maclean had come to the same realisation since the war and through his work, so he read this isolating loneliness and psychic pain as being all about Melinda. He tried to comfort Maclean in 'his glorious and passionate ambivalence' about his wife, whom he 'really does love and hate … almost equally'. Or perhaps his dissatisfaction with both Communism and Melinda, the two fixed points in his life, was merely the reflection of a man filled with self-loathing, one who could not stand the strain of his torn allegiances.

The morning after such outpourings, Maclean had not 'the least idea of what it was or where it came from'. In the manner of alcoholics trying to rationalise their hopeless condition the pair would 'ruminate together … about what it could be that drove us both to drink and him to violence as well'. Toynbee's own rationale, that he thought his own drinking was triggered by his shyness, he saw later as an 'absurd and unconvincing excuse', but at least it was an attempt to grasp what was going on, unlike his friend's 'charming' and elegantly evasive 'Oh, do you? I'm shy because I get drunk.' From his appearance in *Granta* as an 'Undergraduate in the

Witness Box' through his interview for the Foreign Office to now, Maclean was always the master of the deft deflection. The longing to escape his demons was leading him to the destruction of every anchor in his life. The 'armour' Toynbee had seen only a few days earlier as Maclean went to work could not conceal the surging self-destruction.

The final scenes of this terrible drama were played out immediately following the Marling sisters' return. Melinda's agony is written between the lines of Toynbee's diary for 4 May: 'an evening of Rabelaisian exhibitionism ... wilder and wilder attempts to shock [Melinda and Harriet]. Failure. They retired in good order long before we did. Donald began to get aggressive.' This time Donald went on alone; even his drunken friend was frightened or unable to stay by his side, and Maclean 'disappeared' into the night with another guest, not reappearing until the following Saturday lunchtime. Melinda was waiting to see him and plead with him in her bedroom. On Monday morning, recorded Toynbee, 'Donald came down with those terrible, tell-tale bleary eyes and told me that he had gone wild again last night, publicly insulted Harriet, hit Melinda ... "I am really getting near to the point where I shall have to be shut up."' A hospital or mental institution might be preferable to this life. He was desperate but could neither conquer nor surrender to the hold alcohol had over him quite yet.

The next day was the end of that last Egyptian binge. The Macleans, Harriet and Toynbee went to a cocktail party and were due to go on to an evening party. Melinda, who was pregnant again,[*] making her husband's behaviour towards her all the more shocking, felt tired and went home after the first party. Toynbee had somewhere else to go, so Donald and Harriet went to the evening party. By midnight, Donald had gone far beyond the point where any companion could have a good time, so Harriet went home too. Donald lurched back at about two o'clock in the morning and an hour later woke Toynbee and 'urged' him to come out again. 'Not much persuasion was needed, and soon we had tiptoed

---

[*] She was later to miscarry the baby.

out of the house, past Melinda's door and embarked on a destructive orgy which had surpassed everything that had gone before.'

*

Following their all-night debauch the two men spent most of that day in the sun on the balcony at John Wardle-Smith's house, Wardle-Smith being Lees Mayall's replacement in the Embassy. They steadily worked their way through a coma-inducing six bottles of gin (Gordon's, naturally) according to Toynbee's diary. Wardle-Smith, who seems to have shared the Embassy view that there was no point in drawing Ambassador Campbell's attention to these bouts, claimed that he had thought the best thing was to give them 'so much alcohol that they would pass out' before wisely taking himself off to the office. The next stage of the day is understandably a little vague, but Toynbee claimed that he and Maclean decided to move on, 'girl-hounding'. More likely that they were simply looking for more to drink, booze-hounding. They went downstairs to a flat in the same block shared by Sheila Engert of the State Department, who was spending a year teaching at Cairo University, and Jacqueline Brannerman, a secretary in the US Embassy. Engert knew Maclean slightly (and had heard plenty of gossip about the 'much more liberal' Toynbee), and had taken the room in the flat previously occupied by Geraldine Williams, Film Officer at the British Embassy and one of the 'closest associates of Maclean and his wife'. When Maclean and Toynbee did not find Williams, or anything to drink, they apparently left quietly and decided to go next door, to the flat lived in by Eunice Taylor, secretary to US Ambassador Caffrey, and Ellen Speers, wife of an executive with the Arabian-American Oil Company. They pushed past the 'astonished *suffragi*' into the empty flat and began their 'long miasma of destruction'.

As Maclean and Toynbee were the only witnesses to their berserk behaviour and were awash in gin, not surprisingly there is little detail of what went on. Sheila Engert reported that when they found the flat dry, they 'emptied drawers, upset furniture' and threw dishes into the bathtub before the pair left. Melinda told Geoffrey Hoare that 'a lot of the girls' clothes were pushed down the lavatory'. Toynbee through his own haze had 'a clear view only of a single episode ... Donald raises a large mirror above his head and crashes it into the bath, when to my amazement and delight, alas, the bath breaks in two and the mirror remains intact.' Alcoholic remorse kicked in immediately but only briefly: 'We wept in each other's arms, confessed we'd much rather be dead – we ended up a stepladder on the balcony in some vague hope we might fall.' They returned to Wardle-Smith's flat and passed out on his bed, Maclean still holding a leg of mutton which he had been 'gnawing'.

In the early evening, Melinda found out where they were after some frantic telephoning around his known associates, and she and Harriet 'half carried, half dragged a completely sodden Donald down the stairs and into their car'. Harriet then returned and with the *suffragi*'s help, carted Toynbee back too. He was promptly 'banished as the serpent in Eden' – the cavalier way he could write that in his diary suggesting the lack of seriousness with which he took the entire incident and the lack of understanding of what it might have done to his friend's marriage and career. The following day he wrote to his friend Lady Julia Mount from the Metropolitan Hotel, declaring that 'after three weeks snuggery, I am out on my ear and no mistake about it. Poor Donald has indulged in a wild crescendo of drunken, self-destructive, plain destructive episodes – and his wife has made me responsible. Actually, I've done my honest best to control him, but, as you can imagine, not with much to show for it.' Just over a year later, when Melinda was describing her life with Donald she did not attach any blame to Toynbee but simply characterised his stay as one 'of a few weeks immediately before Donald went amok'.

The morning after his rampage, Donald had a conversation 'shivering and retching and groaning in front of the Marling sisters'. Melinda took it upon herself, pale but resolute, to go to see Campbell, making the most of his affectionate reliance on her, rather than encourage her remorse-filled husband to do the deed. She told Campbell that Donald was very ill, undergoing a nervous breakdown, and must be sent to London to see his doctor. Campbell agreed, and despatched an understated telegram to London: 'Maclean has applied to me for leave of absence to return to the United Kingdom for a few weeks. He is suffering from strain and obviously in need of a break at home which has made him rather over-wrought. I gather he has not had more than a short period in the United Kingdom for several years. I have reached the conclusion that the sooner he goes the better for his health and state of mind.' No mention of drunkenness or the flat incident (about which Campbell had probably been told little or nothing) officially got back to London. When the American Embassy lodged the inevitable complaint, Campbell pleaded to his flinty opposite number, Ambassador Caffrey, for his understanding in keeping the business quiet on the grounds that Maclean had chosen to have treatment. Caffrey, who found Maclean 'a heavy drinker and somewhat offensive', agreed not to take it up with the State Department and the Foreign Office. Maclean wrote a contrite letter to the women whose apartment he had destroyed, promising to pay for the damage, and the sisters visited that evening to explain his breakdown and his return to London.

*

The immediate reaction from Maclean's Cairo colleagues was both supportive of their man and wilfully blind to Melinda's constancy during his descent into alcoholism. Edwin Chapman-Andrews, Minister in the Embassy and friend and neighbour of the Macleans, also made no mention of the final events when he wrote a long and confidential letter the following day to head of personnel, George Middleton, Maclean's long-standing service friend. Middleton would have needed no persuading that Maclean 'is a very good man, fundamentally, and well worth making the effort for', and probably would not have been surprised to hear that 'he was inclined to hit it up a bit and had gone in with rather a fast set keen on sitting up late at night or all night and assing about a bit', although Chapman-Andrews 'had no idea' how far this 'assing about' had gone. Maclean's night-life in Cairo sounded like undergraduate high jinks.

The near-inability to attach blame to their colleague led to a diplomatically veiled attack on both Britain's closest ally and the person who had loyally supported and protected her husband (and his colleagues) for the previous eighteen months. At first Chapman-Andrews did not even name Melinda, whom Middleton knew perfectly well from Washington. He wrote in syntax so tortured that it is clear he found it hard to build his case:

> As you know, Donald has an American wife ... She is a vivacious and no doubt attractive person and the whole build-up of her character is so definitely American and can never become anything else that I think there has been some maladjustment almost inevitable in the case of an American woman of this sort married to a man who has to represent some other country (in this case Great Britain!) in a third country.

The US diplomatic corps was characterised as a crew of rather idle topers: 'Anyway, Melinda has associated a good deal with Americans here and members of the American Embassy staff and *some* of the latter (at all events), having not much else to do perhaps through the day, are inclined occasionally to hit it up with a bit of hard drinking through the night. And this is where Donald was inclined to fall down.' '*Some* ... perhaps ... a bit' – the qualifiers cannot abnegate the responsibility for the British man who 'has the cares of Head of Chancery on his shoulders' while his wife took 'to Cairo social life rather as a duck to water whereas Donald ... took to it less gladly and, no doubt, in order to launch himself with more gusto, started to hit it up and the whole thing became a vicious circle'.

Chapman-Andrews was nevertheless right when he noted that this 'vicious circle' had damaged Maclean's self-esteem. He recommended rest and convalescence and suggested that a London position might be the answer 'where his wife would at least have a chance to become a little anglicised'. In spite of the terrible burden of having an American wife who has apparently driven him into this pit, 'the amazing thing', to Chapman-Andrews, was that

Maclean's work 'has been so good considering what he must have been suffering'. The potential damage to Britain's standing abroad, and indeed the possibility that Maclean might have become a victim of blackmail, did not occur to him. They were protecting the colleague they liked and admired, not leaving anything on his file that would prevent his climb to the top of the ladder, compassionately standing by their own. And with no idea of what was coming out of Arlington Hall.

*

Early on the morning of Thursday 11 May 1950, the day after this letter had been sent, Geoffrey Hoare drove to Farouk airfield on his way back to England. He had spent the previous ten weeks on assignment in Pakistan and knew nothing about what had been going on. At the airport he found Donald, 'a rather strained and unhappy Melinda', Harriet and Chapman-Andrews. Unable to admit to a close friend the scale of his defeat, Donald told him that he was on his way to London 'on private business for a few days'. They sat opposite each other on the journey, chatting 'desultorily' from time to time, shared a meal in Rome and arrived in London that evening. Hoare 'noticed nothing wrong with him in any way except possibly he was rather more silent than usual'. It was a remarkable feat of self-control for Maclean, who must still have been queasy from the binge of two nights earlier. It was also a sad indictment of how he could not confide in a sympathetic ear at a desperate moment.

The trip was the last time Hoare was to see his Cairo friend, and the last time Maclean was to arrive home in England.

14

Reconciliation

As the Foreign Office had no knowledge of any of the disastrous excesses of Maclean's last weeks and days in Cairo, and believed that he was 'suffering from strain and obviously in need of a break at home', they welcomed him back with every show of solicitous concern.

For as long as Homer was unidentified and his importance unrecognised, the unknown potential for yet more damage to international relations, morale, reputation and, that vital ingredient of British life, *amour propre* was still threatening. As the investigation took its serpentine, credulous course, the danger to Maclean's liberty, marriage and health grew ever greater.

*

Maclean went straight from the airport to his mother's flat in Kensington. Lady Maclean was puzzled by his reappearance, announced by telegram only the day before, but was reassured that he was going to get treatment for his nervous condition. That night they went to the cinema to see Vittorio De Sica's *The Bicycle Thieves*, which was soothing in its normality.

The next day Maclean had a lunch appointment with his old Washington pre-breakfast tennis partner George Middleton. Middleton was surprised that Maclean did not want to come into the office or meet him at his club. In spite of his position he had no idea of the reasons for Maclean's return, or of his sense of shame and hence his desire to avoid anywhere he might be recognised. They settled on 'a small and rather obscure restaurant'. Middleton wrote immediately after their lunch that his guest was 'clearly in a nervous state' but looking physically well. Maclean was able to mask his anxiety pretty effectively as he had with Hoare. Middleton was later to say that 'Even in the light of subsequent events I cannot recall any danger signals in his general behaviour and conduct as they were known to me.'

Maclean described his symptoms without any acknowledge-ment (maybe without any real knowledge) of the part that alcohol might be playing in his current state: Middleton reported that 'He said "there was something wrong with his head"; his mental pro-cesses were erratic and he was not always in control of himself. Specifically, he had attacks of ungovernable rage which frightened him and he realised that he was in need of medical help ... In his present mood he was anxious to see a psychiatrist. He feared that if he delayed treatment the mood might change and it would be too late to effect a rapid cure.' No mention of specifics, no mention of the effect on his family, but possibly the hope for a fresh start where he might not have to be a spy any more and run the risk of feeling as worthless to Moscow as he had during the recent period of cas-ual neglect.

He might now be in a position to re-establish himself back in England, and back in the Foreign Office, after six years of continu-ous service abroad and fourteen and a half years of high-stakes espionage. He could belong to one side only. He must have hoped to some degree that he had been discharged by Moscow: he had not heard from them after his plea for release and may have assumed that in their eyes he was blown after Cairo and could now be left alone. Perhaps his need for a single life rather than two was taking precedence over his ideological ambitions. Middleton was antici-pating a 'long spell of treatment if he is to get back to normal and avoid the danger of a relapse, so we shall probably have to count him out for Cairo'.

The letter he wrote to Melinda, 'Darling Lin', that same after-noon from his mother's flat ('I am tucked away in the womb very comfortably') is hopeful, remorseful, sincere, lonely and self-laceratingly loving.

I am so grateful to you my sweet for taking all you have had to put up with without hating me. I am still rather lost, but cling to the idea that you do want me to be cured and come back. I am leery of making promises of being a better husband since past ones have all been broken; but perhaps if some technician will strengthen my gasket and enlarge my heart I could make a promise which would stick … I think very much of you my darling, miss you badly and love you. Don't feel sad about me as I will come back a better person and we can be happy together again I am sure.

He is 'overwhelmed with sadness' at leaving the boys, and will never forget Harriet's 'sweetness' to him. It was a reminder of what they had shared so far in their eleven years together: the stillbirth, the miscarriages, the dislocations, the duplicity, the desperate rage, his desire, as expressed in the letter left behind in P Street, to disappear, all bound up in his struggle with alcoholism. At this crucial moment, he realised that he could not bear the thought of carrying on without the wife who had shared the tumult and suffered for it, his only emotional prop. The letter gave no hint that he felt himself to be on the brink of exposure or defection, unaware as he was that the wheels of the Venona and the secret services were in motion.

The 'score' as told to Middleton did not seem to include alcoholism and flat-wreckage. An appointment had been made for him through the Treasury Medical Adviser, Dr Chiesman, to see Dr Henry Wilson, a psychiatrist used 'when employees' psyches missed a beat', as Peter Solly-Flood's had been deemed to do when he had made his drunken advances to Harriet Marling in Washington. 'Missing a beat' reads like a civil service euphemism for a drink problem. That his case was being handled with care and urgency was evident when his first appointment was set up for 9.00 the following day, a Saturday. The kindly, frankly speaking Wilson, who had rooms in Harley Street, was one of the leading authorities in his field, had been 'adviser to the Royal Navy in the war' and was much consulted by neurologists and specialists. He himself specialised in 'psychiatric emergencies'. Even before they met, Maclean was hedging about putting himself in Wilson's care: 'I see no point in resisting George's offer to start me on this path anyhow; but also if it looks like being what I need, I shall get an analysis for nothing; but I promise to be expensive and go to Erna or elsewhere if it doesn't look good.' 'Erna' was Dr Erna Rosenbaum, a pyschoanalyst in Wimpole Street whom Melinda already knew. Either Donald was resisting the pull of the official man, with the fear of what Wilson might feed back to the office, or, more likely as a man in touch with the intellectual currents of his times, he genuinely felt that the real cure for what he was suffering from might be in analysis.

In his letter, Maclean told Melinda how much he hated leaving her with all the responsibility for house, family and servants; he also said to Middleton that he was worried about going on sick leave as that would presumably entail losing his overseas allowances. Middleton was as reassuring as he could be in saying that Maclean would get 'the most favourable treatment' possible, but that the first thing was to get Wilson's opinion. That came fast, on the Monday morning, and recommended investigation of a 'cerebral dysrhythmia' (an irregularity in the rhythm of the brain waves) as the 'attacks are so episodic and they are associated with a degree of such frightening aggression'. Wilson, ignorant of Cairo debacles, 'found it very difficult to believe' that the patient he had just seen 'has got on as well as he has in the Foreign Office', thinking that for a 'man in his position he was somewhat slow and retarded'. For which we might read that he was in shock, guarded about what he wanted to divulge, and possibly still stupefied by his last bender and subsequent detoxification.

Wilson touches on alcoholism in what followed in his report, but even a man of medicine at that time had little understanding of the disease, and he failed to remark on Maclean's denial of responsibility. Maclean's father, he noted, had 'rather strong temperance ideas'. His mother was 'that type of strong personality you often do get as the parent of episodic drinkers'. Maclean himself said he had been 'liable to be very demanding if he was frustrated and he was inclined to blame all of his present troubles on this and difficulties with his wife'. Maclean's colleague and friend Nicholas Henderson was puzzled by what Maclean said to him about Melinda in this period, that 'his attitude towards his wife was not conducive to ideal married life', yet when he had seen the family together in Washington they appeared to be close. Maclean knew that this report would have influence in the Foreign Office, and that it was safe to blame his mother and Melinda, to whom he was so solicitous on paper. Lady Maclean was similarly 'inferentially critical' of Melinda for keeping news of herself and the children from her favourite son for 'weeks on end', and 'explained her rather curious behaviour' by saying that she was 'perhaps typical of American wives'.

Melinda, unaware of the slanders being blithely disseminated about her, was in close touch with her husband at the beginning of their separation, receiving daily letters from him. He wrote to her after his examination by Dr Wilson to say that he did not want to go into the Maudsley psychiatric hospital for the recommended tests. 'Fear plays a leading part in my resistance, but I also much doubt there is any point in it.' That 'fear' may well have been the fear of what to tell any psychiatrist, particularly one appointed by the employers he had been betraying throughout his working life; or fear of a further collapse. A year later his colleagues took a more dramatic view, suggesting that he had chosen an 'unqualified psycho-analist [sic]' because if he were to 'undergo proper medical psychiatric treatment' he would be 'frightened about what he might say under some such truth drug as "pentothal"'.

Toynbee had made the case to Maclean for being psychoanalysed, and his mother-in-law, the New Yorker, was also keen on the discipline. Lady Maclean, indomitably British, was not countenancing any such treatment and sent her son to see the family GP, Dr Herbert Moore, in Wandsworth. Maclean told Moore that 'he preferred treatment by a psychoanalyst of his own choice' rather than following Wilson's advice. Moore felt such treatment was 'unorthodox' and too long drawn out for it to be of any use to the Foreign Office in getting their man back on the rails and ended his letter bleakly: 'Personally I think a solution is going to be difficult to find as the whole family (4 sons & 1 daughter) are definitely unbalanced & there is a marked alcoholic tendency which is surprising with such a family background.' It is ambiguous, and a breach of patient confidentiality for a family doctor to write to the Foreign Office in these terms, whether by 'family background' Moore was focusing on Sir Donald's temperance or his knighthood or Lady Maclean's very conventional nature, or none of those things. The 'alcoholic tendency' had been plainly stated for the first time, but was not discussed any further by the medical team.

The 'unorthodox' route meant that Maclean put himself in the hands of Dr Erna Rosenbaum as he had planned to do from the start. The German-born Rosenbaum was an analyst of some standing, 'of considerable charm and intelligence', and was married to a British psychoanalyst. She was one of the founders of the Society of Analytical Psychology and, before she arrived in London as a refugee from the Nazis, had been interned during the war as an enemy alien. She was a trusted colleague and pupil of Jung, and the dream material from her own analysis became the basis for his *Psychology and Religion*. But even these qualifications and Rosenbaum's Upper Wimpole Street address failed to convince Chiesman who did not believe 'analysis is really desirable'. He thought pursuing the physical options (and rest) were the only real possibilities. Furthermore, Dr Rosenbaum was 'not qualified in England', a cause for concern not so much for security reasons as because Chiesman 'feared she might be a quack'. Middleton and Carey Foster later said that, because of Dr Rosenbaum's Eastern European background, they sent her details to MI5 but the message came back 'Nothing Recorded Against'. MI5, with little more understanding than the Foreign Office, wrote in 1951 that their investigations had shown Rosenbaum to be 'highly regarded by fellow psychotherapists', although they understood that the profession 'consists of sheep and goats and as we do not know to which class Dr Rosenbaum belongs this does not help very much'. Even before this background check could be carried out Middleton had agreed to Maclean's chosen treatment, although he found it 'unfortunate'.

In Maclean's first week in England a small, anonymous and accurate piece found its way into the *Daily Express*: 'Men Wreck Girl's Flat', where the wreckers of the Cairo apartment were identified only as 'a member of a European embassy and a journalist friend'. This was the first the Foreign Office knew about the episode, and Maclean 'admitted' to Middleton that the story was true. But since his apologies had been accepted and the police were not involved, it had merely served to 'bring home the seriousness of his condition'. In the light of this discovery, he would agree to ask Dr Rosenbaum to allow him to have a physical check-up as well and the results were to be forwarded to the office, on the grounds that Drs Chiesman, Wilson and Moore had all mentioned alcoholism as a part of his 'trouble'. The physical tests on his brain came back negative from the Maida Vale Hospital for Nervous Diseases, and he dropped from the medical scrutiny of the Foreign Office other than in the context of when he might be able to report for work.

*

When Harriet Marling 'roundly ticked off' Toynbee for leaking the incident to the papers, his response in his diary was that Maclean would have 'profoundly and brilliantly' understood why he had blabbed. 'It was no use concealing it. After all, we broke up that room in order that it shouldn't be concealed.' This is either the braggadocio of a man in crisis and caught in the wrong, or an acknowledgement that at some point during their late-night conversations Maclean, violently ambivalent about his marriage and wanting to set up a new Communist Party just for himself, had said he had to leave Cairo to deal with his nightmares. Given that in his sober moments he would have been able to request leave without risking nearly everything, it is likely to be the former.

The newspaper report (which had also run in the leading Arabic newspapers) should have brought a degree of public shame and consternation to the Cairo Embassy. Sir Ronald Campbell wrote to his successor-elect, Sir Ralph Stevenson, ten days after Maclean had left:

You may have heard that Donald Maclean has had something
of a breakdown. He may not have spoken to you himself, but
he has, I am sure, spoken to Middleton and perhaps others.
This is to say that when I expressed my opinion of his capacity
etc., I had no idea of there being any possibility of this kind,
but I still adhere to my high opinion of him, and feel sure that
if he can get out of his present difficulty (and it would be
worth while encouraging him in every way) you would find
him a very useful member of your staff.

It might be seen as diplomatically unwise to consider sending
someone back to a post which they had left so spectacularly and
now more or less publicly.

Maclean's Cairo calamities were in fact the subject of a great deal
of gossip in his own circle, which did not overlap with his work
much. It was garbled and exaggerated like all gossip but in essence
true: Janetta Kee told Frances Partridge in June 1950, when Nicholas
Henderson had just brought Maclean to tea at Ham Spray, the
Partridges' house and one of the last Bloomsbury bastions, 'that
[Maclean] had been a member of the Embassy at Cairo, but had
just been sent home because he tried to murder his wife ... and
another friend got his leg broken going to her rescue. It happened
because he got fearfully drunk with Philip Toynbee.' Partridge had
been struck by Maclean's good looks, friendliness and smiling
charm so was very surprised to hear this. In a personal letter to
Middleton, Chapman-Andrews wrote that the incident 'was the
subject of a certain amount of gossip and speculation here', but
blithely and learnedly concluded that it would pass, 'for Cairo is a
snakepit of gossip and Cairo society, like the Ephesians of old, is
always seeking after some new thing'. However, Middleton
acknowledged that it might be 'best for the Service as well as best
for Donald' if he did not 'appear again in Cairo' despite Sir Ronald's
strange commendation. The events in Jacqueline Brannerman's flat
were already becoming the stuff of exaggerated story-telling:
Sansom, in charge of security at the Embassy, was soon menda-
ciously recounting how he had been sent to the flat by Melinda,

who had apparently not seen her husband for days, and found him 'horribly drunk and completely naked. He stared at me for a moment and then mouthed an obscenity and aimed an unsteady fist between my eyes.'

For Toynbee to receive a mere 'ticking off' from Harriet seems mild in the context of the anxiety and shame her sister was feeling. Practically and immediately, Melinda was left to run the house and family in Cairo without knowing whether Donald would be returning, or whether she should pack up and go to England to be with him. But in spite of the Embassy's tact and generosity over the allowances, the uncertainty was understandably too much for Melinda. Mrs Dunbar arrived on 1 June and helped solve one pressing dilemma, whether the family should go at the beginning of July to the house they had rented in Alexandria, where everyone not on leave elsewhere decamped in summer, in the hope that Donald would be back by then to join them. But as his letters gave no indication of how long his treatment was likely to last, they decided not to run the risk, cancelled the house, went to the US Embassy to secure visas, put their car on a boat and sailed for Spain on the 18th. Mrs Dunbar settled all the outstanding bills. She also noted that in their master's absence, the 'usually excellent' servants in the Sharia Ibn Zanki house were 'slack, dirty and slightly insolent', as if they knew that Donald was 'never coming back'. It was now the end of Melinda's life as a diplomatic wife abroad, the end of two years in which she had grown in confidence and self-possession to become a polished hostess and able to cope with the increasing and embarrassing nightmare that her husband had become.

*

The double-bind of Maclean's situation, which he had been in for all his professional life, was that if he could admit to every betrayal of a moral code that he had had hammered into him in his childhood, then Dr Rosenbaum could set him on the path to a cure for his alcoholism and the pain it was covering up, as well as enable him to cease the devastating evasions to all those who had placed their trust in him. But if he could do that he would be saving Jim

Skardon a lot of time in due course and would be spending the next decade behind bars, his reputation in tatters. As Dr Rosenbaum's teacher Carl Jung had written: 'Clinical diagnoses are important, since they give the doctor a certain orientation; but they do not help the patient. The crucial thing is the story. For it alone shows the human background and the human suffering, and only at that point can the doctor's therapy begin to operate.' Jung's emphasis on balance and harmony, integrating opposites, would be an impossible treatment for one who needed to keep his opposites separate, and not allow the honesty in telling the story which would begin the healing he so badly needed.

Whatever he was getting from his sessions with Dr Rosenbaum (and he cryptically said to Lees Mayall that he was 'fighting her hard'), Maclean did not seem to recover much over the course of that summer, in spite of his reassurance to Middleton on 14 June that he was much better and would return to work in August: that meeting itself was prompted by Chiesman telling Middleton that Maclean had failed to keep his last two appointments. When he did turn up the following week, Chiesman reported that 'he bears no evidence of suffering from any physical disease. His blood pressure is rather low which confirms the impression that he is suffering from nervous exhaustion.' On hearing the news that a return to work was planned, the Treasury doctor said that 'Maclean is playing fast and loose with us … I would not advise you to allow [him] to return to duty on the opinion of a lay analyst.' By mid-August, he was certain that Maclean was 'by no means normal'. Maclean's brother Alan was alarmed to see 'his most unbalanced condition' and noted that 'he seemed to have taken a dislike to people generally'. But in July Alan left to assume his appointment working for Sir Gladwyn Jebb as part of the British mission to the United Nations. It was the last time for thirty years that he would see the elder brother who had played soldiers with him when they were boys as they convalesced from flu. Maclean's anticipated sick leave of three months was extended, although without any sign that the alcoholism was being acknowledged and addressed.

From early June onwards, there had been only intermittent contact with Melinda, with little mention of his health. He picked up his old London behaviour quickly and seemed to give her less thought, and almost none to the Foreign Office. Cyril Connolly saw that Maclean would often be unable to go through with his psychoanalytic sessions, hovering on the Rosenbaum doorstep for a while, hopping from foot to foot, before slipping away around the corner. The damage he was continuing to inflict in his personal life and the consequent pain which that caused him, even at a distance from his family, led to heavy drinking. He took up many of the old haunts and friends of his pre-war bachelor days in London. The Gargoyle Club was then in its last years, but still maintained its louche 'theatre of social, sexual and intellectual challenge', its mix of writers, artists, intellectuals and scions of Bloomsbury with the more classless post-war social scene, and it admitted both sexes. It was very different from the Pall Mall clubs where Foreign Office mandarins spent their lunchtimes and evenings, the Reform, the Travellers and Brooks's. Among the Gargoyle's members were Lawrence Durrell, A. J. Ayer, Philip Toynbee, Victor Rothschild, Rosamond Lehmann, Frederick Ashton, Arthur Koestler and, inevitably, Guy Burgess. Maclean joined in July, presumably something that Dr Chiesman did not know about or Middleton would have had another stern note to leave on the file. He was proposed for membership by his best man Mark Culme-Seymour.

Although the Gargoyle was to become one of the more notable places where Maclean could let his inhibitions fall away later in his year in London, in the summer of his return his guard was up when in the company of the close friends of his youth. His erstwhile flame Laura Grimond, daughter of his father's (and his) old ally Lady Violet Bonham Carter, had lunch with him but got nowhere: 'There was nothing wrong with his memory, nor with his grasp of the international situation. He made light of his own troubles too, even suggesting that he might soon be going back to rejoin the Embassy staff in Cairo.' With other friends, less associated with the upright side of his upbringing (and at less formal times of day), his alcoholic demons were irrepressible. He went to stay at Stokke Manor in Wiltshire with Lady Mary Campbell, whom he had also known before the war and who was now married to Robin Campbell, his fellow swotter for the Foreign Office exams in 1935. She could see what a desperate, sodden state he was in when she picked him up from Hungerford station and took him to a friend's garden to relax, piling up cushions under a beech tree. Maclean, in a fit of *delirium tremens*, kept jumping up and 'fighting the overhanging branches, shouting, "They're after me!" "Who are?" "The Russians!"' The paranoia, even terror, about what retribution he might face, as Maly and others had encountered on their arrival in the USSR, now that he was no longer useful in passing on secrets, could not be suppressed; or perhaps it was on some level a wish to be discovered, to be released from his hell. After a while, Lady Mary thought that 'the thistle-bashing on the farm was doing him a tremendous amount of good', even if she had never seen a 'worse case of the DTs.'

The Campbells had known Maclean long enough not to be surprised by his left leanings, of course, and Lady Mary certainly thought that this psychotic episode was merely 'a symptom of his clinical condition' and did not make any connection with the fears of 'the Russians' expressed during it. But when in more sober and contemplative mood Maclean talked to his old friends about 'Communism in the same way that a potential Catholic aware that he lacked the gift of faith might discuss religion', and spoke of his longing 'for a leap of faith that would convince him that Communism was right'. The man raised by a strictly religious father who had kept a tight hold on his own faith after his dark night of the soul was now openly questioning his beliefs in the same way, if more lucidly now, as he had in his drunken rantings to Toynbee in Cairo. There was no contact with any handler during his sick leave, so once again he was not rooted by 'praise and reassurance', to use Deutsch's now long-ago words, from Moscow. He no longer had the daily support of Melinda or the approbation of his Embassy colleagues.

He had gone from being a spectacle of dissolution in Cairo to a solitary and aimless convalescent in London. The doubts about his usefulness, the very basis of his self-esteem, were overwhelming him again.

*

World events took a decisive turn on 25 June when the North Korean People's Army, armed with Russian weapons and T-34 tanks, invaded its southern neighbour, long seen by America as a crucial bulwark against the spread of Communism in Asia. The Soviet delegate to the UN Security Council walked out and a resolution was passed by the other members, with the exception of India and Egypt, which abstained, demanding that Kim Il Sung's forces should withdraw. The Korean War, the first armed conflict against Communism, the first major armed test of the United Nations, had begun. Britain, all but bankrupted by the war and dependent on American loans to keep afloat, despatched its Far East fleet to support the United States, and extended National Service to keep troop numbers up. When Maclean later wrote his book about British foreign policy, by then undivided in his ideological loyalties, he was scathing about the American interventions in Asia. With Fuchs's confession and Hiss's conviction earlier in 1950, and McCarthyism rampant in Washington, he had good reason to question his faith and fear for his liberty.

In July a brilliant physicist, Bruno Pontecorvo, Italian-born but now a British national and senior principal scientific officer at Harwell since the start of 1949 (before that he had been in Canada, working alongside Nunn May), went on holiday in Finland with his Swedish-born wife and their three children. He was due to return to attend a conference in September but had continued on to the USSR. The previous March the Security Service had received information from Sweden indicating that both he and his wife were Communists. On being questioned, Pontecorvo had denied the report but said that some of his family back in Italy were 'Communist sympathisers'. This was not followed up. If it had been to any degree, it would quickly have become known that Bruno's brother Gilberto Pontecorvo was playing 'a conspicuous part in the party's service as a politician and a journalist'; that his brother-in-law was 'an open Communist who worked ... on the Party's staff'; and that his cousin Emilio Sereni was 'one of the best-known Communists in Italy', a member of the Italian Chamber of Deputies. When Pontecorvo had been screened for naturalisation, Sereni held two ministerial posts and was in the public eye. The physicist himself had left Italy in 1936 to escape the Fascist regime. His MI5 vetting file had read 'No Trace Against'.

At the very point Pontecorvo's defection was uncovered, Sir Percy Sillitoe, Director General of MI5 since 1946, was in Washington trying to re-establish relations and rebuild confidence with Hoover and the FBI regarding nuclear security in Britain following the Fuchs case; keeping the 'Cousins' in the dark had already led to an 'explosion'. Sillitoe was briefed for his meetings by Kim Philby.

*

Maclean's Cambridge friend and fellow spy Guy Burgess was going about his own alcoholic journey. Since Maclean had last been based in England Burgess had done a brief stint in the News Department, handy for seeing all Foreign Office communications in good time; then he worked for the minister Hector McNeil, before a brief spell in the Information Research Department followed by the Far Eastern Department, a useful position for Moscow Centre in the build-up to the Korean War. In 1949 he had gone on leave to Gibraltar and Tangier, boozing and brawling on an epic scale, 'insisting on visiting the local representatives of MI6 and on discussing their characters, habits, opinions and professional inadequacies with anyone who chose to listen to him in any bar in which he happened to be drinking'. In Tangier, Burgess was to be found at the Café de Paris at noon each day, where he would recite 'Little boys are cheap today, cheaper than yesterday,' to the assembled company. The local gay community, a number of whom were British, were outraged when to cap this he began to make approaches to their local favourites. Burgess returned to London in February 1950. The arrest of Fuchs the week before was a reminder to him that the previous September he had forgotten to pass on to Modin a warning given to him by Philby that Venona was on to a scientist code-named Charles (that is, Fuchs), which might have given Moscow Centre time to exfiltrate him.

During Maclean's last week in Cairo, it had been decided that Burgess (a few days before he was cleared by a disciplinary panel for his many indiscretions) should be posted to Washington as a second secretary. This would be 'a last chance to make good' as Carey Foster told Sir Robert Mackenzie, head of security in the Washington Embassy. Mackenzie wondered what Carey Foster could possibly mean when he said that they had better take care of Burgess 'as he was capable of worse things' than he had perpetrated before. 'Surely he can't mean goats?'

Burgess arrived in Washington in early August and, much to Aileen Philby's horror and outrage, moved in with his old friend Kim Philby as a lodger. Goronwy Rees summed up what she might expect: 'cigarette ends stuffed down the backs of sofas, the scorched eiderdowns, the iron-willed determination to have garlic in every dish, including porridge and Christmas pudding, the endless drinking, the terrible trail of havoc'. Philby found himself in a dilemma as to whether he should tell the loquacious Burgess about Venona and the possibility that Maclean would be identified. He 'made two lone motor trips to points outside Washington' to meet his handler and was instructed that Burgess's 'special knowledge of the problem' might prove useful. By now 'some dozen reports' referring to 'Material G',* which Philby knew to be material from Maclean sent via New York, had now come in, so a solution to 'the problem' might be needed sooner rather than later. 'G' himself was out of contact and in a parlous state. The fate of the three Cambridge spies, mirroring their recruitment, was now irrevocably entwined.

*

Maclean sank further through the summer. Nicholas Henderson, who had served with him in Washington, asked him down to his

---

* There is no letter 'H' in the Russian alphabet, so 'Homer' transcribes as 'Gomer', hence 'Material G'. This led to later confusion within the Foreign Office.

parents' cottage when he was on leave for the weekend where he was 'struck by his feebleness'. Henderson did not keep much alcohol in the house so 'Maclean was unable to drink a great deal, but drank all that was provided'. Also staying was Robert Kee, then of *Picture Post*, and his wife Janetta, who together were co-founders of the left-wing publisher MacGibbon and Kee. At the time the Kees were experiencing 'awful personal troubles' and going through a divorce, and when back in London Maclean would go round to Janetta's 'house in the morning and stay there all day drinking, frequently getting violently drunk'. As Philip Toynbee lived in the same Bayswater house when he was in London, the association in Maclean's mind with his partner might well have triggered even greater bouts. Henderson reported Maclean's self-absorption 'in trying to find someone to be left-wing with' and in rejecting Kee, who was in a desperate state and had attempted suicide. When Maclean was told of this, his response was, 'I wish I had known, because I am sure my Analyst could have helped him as she helped me.' As Kee had already told Henderson that 'when Maclean was drunk it was very frightening' and that he 'would threaten people in the street and knock them out', something nobody else mentioned in their keenness to dissect the man, it seems this desire to help someone else in pain by referring them to Dr Rosenbaum was buried fairly deep or his remark was edged with sarcasm.

In August Maclean stayed in a friend's house in Oxford and wrote that he was living 'on a diet of sedatives and pints of bitter', which presumably provided a little more nourishment than gin or whisky. His handwriting was by now sliding down the page and getting harder to read. 'There are two men in a car waiting outside. They've been there for four hours. Are they after me?' He then checked his paranoia to wonder if he was not imagining the men anyway. Certainly MI5 were months away from taking any interest in him, and the Russians appeared not to care. Connolly was horrified when he saw the formerly suave diplomat at this time: 'His appearance was frightening: he had lost his serenity, his hands would tremble, his face was usually a vivid yellow and he looked as if he had spent the night sitting up in a tunnel.' Maclean still tried to keep up his social front, 'as detached and amiable as ever' although 'it was clear that he was miserable … In conversation a kind of shutter would fall as if he had returned to some basic and incommunicable anxiety.'

By now, through his own isolating choice, Maclean had moved out of his mother's flat and was living in the Mascot Hotel, off Baker Street. Sometimes he did not make it back to spend the night there. Lees Mayall 'would often return to find [Maclean] in his drawing-room, having climbed over the back wall because he did not like coming in through front doors'. Mayall would no more let his codes of honour and friendship tell Middleton this than he had told him about the broken-leg incident in Helouan the previous year. Connolly recorded that 'One evening a man leaving a night-club got into an empty taxi and found [Maclean] asleep on the rug. When awakened he became very angry and said he had hired it for the evening as his bedroom.' He became known as 'the Lurcher' as his tall frame swayed pathetically from Soho bar to Soho bar. Yet none of the reports of his depraved behaviour appears to have made it back to his Foreign Office superiors. His close-knit circle of colleagues in the Foreign Office remained solicitous for his recovery from his 'nervous condition'.

*

By the end of September he appeared to have reached the end. He wrote a letter to Melinda in which 'he seemed desperately discouraged about himself and said he did not see why she should ever return to him'. He didn't feel that he could be a good husband or father, and the family would be better off without him. He had conspicuously not joined them in Spain, nor offered to do so, nor had he suggested that he and Melinda should be alone together, leaving the children with his mother-in-law. Melinda had just as conspicuously not suggested that he join her, nor had she come back to England to see him. But his despairing message, though it was unclear whether it presaged defection, desertion or even suicide, changed her mind. She ended her Spanish sojourn, parked her mother and boys in Paris and went to London.

Over the next two weeks Melinda had 'the most momentous' conversations of her life – with Lady Maclean, with Middleton, with Erna Rosenbaum and above all with Donald himself as she struggled to find a resolution. She was in no doubt that she loved her husband, but found that after the experience of a decade of married life with a 'split personality like Donald's, love was an insufficient foundation for happiness'. That 'split' might refer both to the sides of him divided between country and conscience and to the duality of the loving, sober Dr Jekyll who wrote on his first night in England and the drunken, destructive, near-murderous Mr Hyde. Or maybe by now those divisions were too intricately bound up with each other to be separately investigated. If so, that must have made these momentous conversations with all but her husband feel very false to her. She wrote to her sister Harriet in New York, acknowledging that 'we have both, alas, developed in different directions. I have become more extroverted and enjoy gayer and simpler people, but Donald will have none of that at all.'

While Melinda was obviously considering leaving Donald, Middleton put the Foreign Office position to her in very plain terms. She was necessary to him, and to his continuing employment. The office had 'a strictly pragmatic attitude towards matrimony ... The happiness of couples is a secondary consideration; but keeping them out of the divorce courts and so avoiding publicity is primary.' Also, as Melinda had found in Cairo, a diplomatic wife could serve as an unpaid hostess and housekeeper, oiling the wheels of diplomacy for nothing. Middleton had heard from Dr Rosenbaum that, if Donald and Melinda could be brought back together, he would stand a chance of full recovery and would be able to resume his career. The 'lay analyst' had pinpointed his dependence on his wife, the need for the secret sharer with whom he could begin his recovery. Melinda might even have become an extension of him in Donald's psyche, the one who was always there and whom he could hate when he could not live with himself and felt he was not being helped by her. The Foreign Office view was that they very much wanted an employee with a 'penetrating mind, sound judgement and quiet industry' to come back, particularly at a time when hostilities in Korea involved British personnel and had the potential to escalate into a global war with Communism. Lady Maclean also showed her daughter-in-law unheralded warmth in her efforts to persuade her to resume her married life, playing on the love both she and Donald felt towards their boys.

Donald himself, in his haze of self-doubt, realised that whatever the ambivalence of his feelings towards his wife, she was a safety line to his sanity and career, possibly even to his liberty. He must have yearned for normality, for an end to the fears that led to yet more binges. After her two weeks in London, Melinda returned to Paris to fetch her boys, from where she wrote to Harriet again: 'Donald had very grave doubts at first about our ability to be happy together but we decided to try it again. To me it was the only decision to take on account of the children, and I think Donald has already benefited tremendously. He realises many things which he has never allowed himself to think before … If we are frank and above all don't repress our feelings perhaps we will work something out.' The bond between them, born out of an inner loneliness and dislocation, what Deutsch had spotted in Donald when he codenamed him 'Orphan', remained fragile but true.

Under pressure from her husband, loving him, fearful that he would destroy himself, nudged by the upright Foreign Office who were uneasy about ending Maclean's sick leave if he lacked a strong family base, not wanting to undermine the happiness of her boys, Melinda could rationalise her decision to live with Donald in England again. She ended her letter to Harriet, 'He is going back to the F.O. on November 1st – poor lamb!' And that gave his delicate ego the strength he needed to move past his despair, pull on his armour and resume his old working life again. Against her doctor's orders after the stillbirth and miscarriages, and to the surprise of those who had known them offstage in their darkest time, she was soon pregnant again.

Their unusual marriage was about to enter its next extraordinary phase.

*

For the second time in the two years of his spiralling decline Melinda raised the issue of whether Maclean's homosexual proclivities were a further destabilising factor for him. She felt that Dr Rosenbaum had made Donald 'definitely better', but she was still 'baffled about the homosexual side which comes out when he is drunk and I think slight hostility in general to women.'

In his youth, Maclean had expressed an attraction to Jasper Ridley at his first meeting with Toynbee (at which Toynbee himself had wanted to kiss his new friend), but since then, unlike Burgess or Blunt, he had not shown any sign or left any trace of homosexuality since Burgess's boast of a one-night stand at Cambridge. When a few months earlier Maclean was in his drunken frenzy with Toynbee, wanting to tear down his life and to murder Melinda, he does not mention any leanings to his private chronicler. Geoffrey Hoare, to whom Melinda spoke from the heart, makes no independent mention of it. Melinda said to Kathleen Cecil that she assumed Donald had been off on a 'homosexual spree' immediately after his defection, at a moment when she had to cover any of her own complicity in his absence. Nor did any of the others who knew him as well as anyone could – Henderson, Connolly, the Bonham Carters, Robert Cecil, his siblings, his handlers – comment on it. Perhaps Melinda, the only person using the word homosexual, was doing so again to set up a smokescreen for Donald's treacherous work at the same time as rationalising his sporadic and mortifying rejection of her.

Lees Mayall, who had no cause to associate himself with Maclean later, said that he 'knew [Maclean] was a homosexual largely because when drunk he was more apt to throw his arms around men than women'. Yet it was widely acknowledged that 'no other member of the Service ... mentioned homosexual tendencies'. Nor did MI5 in their thoroughgoing investigation of Maclean's life. The sensationalising stories that came out when he could no longer defend himself, and at a time when he was always going to be associated with his widely acknowledged homosexual partner-in-flight, built up a rich sex-life with Arab boys in Cairo and the coloured night-club doorman at the Moonglow Club in Soho 'who repulsed his advances'. It is as if the betrayed establishment needed to build a further case of gross immorality and illegality to help lessen the shock of discovering that one so trusted could have been a spy all along. Maclean's old friend from Cambridge Tony Blake said that he had 'no knowledge or belief' that he was 'inclined to … perversion', and that was at a point when Blake had nothing to lose and plenty to gain by distancing himself. When the Macleans were once again the gossip of artistic society, Eddy Sackville-West, a lover of trouble as well as many men, claimed to Frances Partridge that he had been to bed with Maclean, but if that is true it is a far cry from stories of constant rent boys and doormen. Maclean's devoted but always truthful brother Alan said 'positively no' when asked the question. Anthony Blunt in his unpublished memoirs never mentioned Maclean's sexuality while being frank about his own. And Burgess, who got great satisfaction from 'blazoning' his conquests, never raised the subject after Cambridge.

*

On 29 September, Maclean saw Middleton 'and reported that he was feeling very much better' and that 'his own doctor thought he could count on being fit for duty by November 1'. Middleton agreed with Maclean's request that he be given a home posting, which he was due anyway after six years of diligent work in Washington and Cairo. He was delighted that his friend, whom he had thought was by now although 'not exactly malingering … probably just running away from realities', was deemed able to return by Rosenbaum and therefore Chiesman. All sides were well aware that after six months' sick leave, Maclean would have gone on to half-pay if he stayed out of the office, which would have made his life impossible, so it was, once again, a kindness to a valued servant to re-employ him without digging deeper. The head of the American Department had had to go on leave himself to undergo an operation, so Middleton decided, in consultation with Michael Wright, Maclean's colleague in Paris and Washington, that this would be an appropriate place for him, 'on a more or less temporary basis', whatever that meant. Wright was the Assistant

Under-Secretary with responsibility for the Department and thought highly of Maclean, 'rather shy and nervous, but with a vast capacity for work, a willingness to take responsibility and possessing one of the clearest brains of any officer'.

Middleton was under the impression from Sir Ronald Campbell that the 'breakdown' in Cairo was the result of 'prolonged over-work coupled with his rather nervous, highly strung disposition', and that the drinking dated only 'from the arrival of Philip Toynbee in Cairo'. The destruction of the flat, although now known in London, seems to have been the subject of as little gossip, just as the reports from doctors were not widely discussed before the new appointment was made. Middleton and Wright cleared the new job with Sir Roger Makins, then acting head of the office and another colleague with a very good opinion of Maclean from Washington and their secret work together on the AEC. They decided not to put it before the Promotions Board since that body had already discussed Maclean 'informally' and there was not likely to be 'argument' about it.

What the post actually entailed was very different from how it was presented after its most notorious occupant had vacated it. The Foreign Office claimed that it dealt principally with Latin American affairs. 'Korean questions' were handled by the Far East Department and atomic matters by the Permanent Under-Secretary. Technically, that may have been the ideal, but when the questions involved the Korean War rather than trade or other matters, the British or American atom bomb, the head of the American Department was very much in the loop. As Sir William Strang, who had been Permanent Under-Secretary since 1949, was to write in his authoritative book *The Foreign Office*, published in 1955, 'the duties of the American department [are to] advise the Secretary of State as to the policy to be followed in regard to the political, economic and other relations between this country and ... all countries in North, Central and South America'. With the Korean War boiling up, there could be no better place in London for a keen foreign policy specialist to be placed. When Yuri Modin of the London *rezidentura* heard about Maclean's new job, he could only explain it to himself 'in terms of a somewhat warped British sense of humour', just as he did in respect of Burgess's move to Washington at the same time.

*

The Macleans, together again as a family, threw themselves into house-hunting. It was thought best to be outside London and away from its myriad bars tempting Donald to stop for refreshment between work and home. Lees Mayall was certainly relieved that after the 'trouble' Maclean had caused him 'during his period of convalescence' this move meant that 'he began rather to fade out of his life', although Maclean's appointments diary shows that the two men lunched regularly in the early months of 1951. As a home posting meant Maclean was no longer eligible for a foreign allowance, living outside London was also the most economical choice. They settled on a handsome but faintly run-down and rambling (certainly by Melinda's American standards of modern comfort) three-storey Victorian house, Beaconshaw. Down a gravel drive, with useful outbuildings and standing in over an acre of garden, it was located on the North Downs at the Kent–Surrey border in the ancient village of Tatsfield, near Westerham, about an hour from London. They paid £7,000 for it, raising part of the mortgage through Mrs Dunbar, and hired Sylvia Shrubb to come in from the village every day to help out. It was the first house they had owned in their peripatetic marriage, and was destined to be the last. They moved into Beaconshaw on 18 December 1950, in time for the newly reunited and expanding family to celebrate the only Christmas they would spend there.

Maclean had turned a corner that winter, the desperate alcoholic tremors of the summer had subsided, his career was back on track with his file unblemished, his wife and sons were back with him and Melinda was in the early stages of pregnancy. He wrote to his brother Alan about his relief at being back in the Foreign Office, the work he loved, that it was 'cosy to be part of a grinding, familiar old machine'. For a man who had remained hidden for so much of his life, he particularly cherished 'how much more anonymous' and less emotionally demanding it was to be in London than serving in an Embassy. He might have felt his spying days were now behind him as he had had no contact with Moscow Centre for so long.

Above all, as he contemplated his fresh start in Whitehall, he still had no knowledge of the suddenly more urgent progress of Venona and the search for 'G'.

15

Curzon

'From my discussions with my friends at meetings outside Washington, two main points emerged. First, it was essential to rescue Maclean before the net closed in on him ... Second, it was desirable that Maclean should stay in his post as long as possible.' Kim Philby's near-paradoxical instructions from Moscow Centre, his 'friends' at their meetings in out-of-town diners, were clear: Maclean needed to be exfiltrated before he blew the entire ring, but also kept in place for the time being to exploit the intelligence potential of his new post. With Maclean as head of the American Department, Philby as station chief in Washington, and Burgess in the Washington Embassy, the Russians had the British–American establishment in their pockets – yet they also had a puzzle. They knew from Philby that Homer had not been identified, but during Maclean's descent in the past year there must be a very high chance that he had been turned. If so, their man in Washington surely would know – unless he too was involved in a fiendish double-cross. Against that, Maclean had been committed enough to ask to live in Moscow, and was in a prime job to help them. Unknowingly, he was trapped in the wilderness of mirrors in which a spy must live, possible victim of both ruse and counter-ruse. At the start of 1951, the Russians had reached a positively British compromise: they would 'leave him alone' but find a way to exfiltrate him should they need to. The reports from Cairo, on top of whatever emotional volatility they disapproved of in the relationship with Kitty Harris, might well have kept them at arm's length for now as regards any fresh espionage.

*

Maclean himself knew nothing of the developments in Arlington Hall and Whitehall, but there had been little that would have alarmed him during most of his convalescent leave. As Lamphere had noted, MI5 and MI6 did not in 1949 seem very perturbed by the wartime spy. With a large cipher section in the Washington Embassy and 'from half-a-dozen to a dozen "unofficial" spares' of the vital telegrams 'run off and kept on shelves in the Distribution Room' in a cupboard which did not even have a lock until 'some time' in 1945, they were looking in the proverbial haystack. Apart from glancing at the two unfortunates thought to have had 'nervous breakdowns' and those with Russian relatives referred to by Philby, their renewed assumption that the mole could not be a 'senior man' left them no closer to their goal.

In March 1950 a despairing situation report was written in the Foreign Office which admitted that 'the standard of security and control of classified papers was very bad' and that so far 'at least 150 people had access' to the telegrams known to have been sent to Moscow, a number 'likely to be increased as enquiries proceed'. As Maclean went back to work in the Foreign Office the investigators had a long shortlist of names with very little to go on: one suspect since 1949 was Samuel Barron, known to have had pre-war 'Communist connections' and to have been approached as an agent in 1934, result unknown to the Security Services. Barron had been in the cipher room in Washington and was still on the list in 1951 but with no 'reasonable' evidence that could be found to interrogate him. Another name was Gavin Ranken, a decade older than Maclean, on the list because he had been stationed in Rome in the 1920s where there had been a leak, and where he had coincidentally bought 'an expensive car'. Ranken's spendthrift habits continued in Washington, where he had bought 'an expensive house' in 1946. Again, there was nothing to pin on him from the material or even any circumstantial evidence that he had direct access to or had ever seen the stolen telegrams.

At this stage, the name of Donald Maclean was not included on the list of suspects, so improbable was it that such a diligent servant should be a traitor.

*

In 1949, five telegrams had been partially decoded dating back to March 1945 laying out Churchill's and Roosevelt's ideas for post-war Eastern Europe. Four of them were about the make-up of Poland, the fifth concentrating on Romania. In August 1950, as Maclean was spending his desperately confused summer in England, a telegram from 1944 was cracked open by Gardner and his team which contained information on 'at least three subjects' of much greater interest: 'the source of the information on the last of these subjects is referred to in the Russian telegram by the letter G' – 'G', as it turned out, for 'Gomer'. 'Agent G' was a development from 'Material G' because 'G' was now definitely a spy with a code-name that began with that letter, as opposed to the more amorphous 'Material G'. This latest decrypt included correspondence between the Prime Minister and the President about the invasion of Europe by either Operation Overlord (which became the D-Day landings) or Operation Anvil (the proposed landings in southern France), as well as about the German occupation zones they hoped to per-suade the Soviets to adopt. The importance of the material that had at some point passed through the Washington Embassy to Moscow (and critically not been circulated to any American departments) meant the hunt took on a different hue. This was top-secret intelli-gence of the most highly classified order, prompting a momentous change in the tone and pace of the investigation.

*

Meanwhile, Maclean, oblivious, took up his new position to open a fresh chapter in his life. The American Department was based in the magnificence of the old India Office, no longer needed for its original purpose since India had achieved independence three years earlier. Even the Third Room, where the lowly Third Secretaries sat, 'was a cavernous barn ... with windows so high that they could have occupied another storey'. Around this vast space ran a minstrels' gallery, from which one of the members of the department used to play his violin. At four o'clock each day the nine-strong department would down tools to take tea, their boss standing in front of the coal fire at one end. Maclean's two deputies (one of them Robert Cecil, his colleague from Paris and Washington) had another subdivision of this large outer office, while he himself had a private room. The tea ritual apart, Maclean was withdrawn from his staff, and notably never asked any of them out for a meal or a drink. John Cairncross, who was then working in the foreign currency control section of the Treasury after a useful (in espionage terms) spell at the Ministry of Supply, without any knowledge of his common bond with Maclean, set up a dinner meeting with an American contact which 'was not a success' as the diplomat appeared 'sleepy, almost drugged'. Part of the danger of a dinner invitation was that Maclean might be too drunk to hide his boredom.

After the wartime bustle the Foreign Office had reverted to many of its old ways and never abandoned others such as the elderly frock-coated messengers who carried files done up with red ribbon, a bureaucratic detail 'inherited from the Mogul Empire'. A handbook of diplomatic etiquette written with his quill pen by Marcus Cheke, the Vice-Marshal of the Diplomatic Corps, was just being produced and was full of helpful instructions for what to say at funerals and what not to say at dinner-parties – mentioning birth control at the latter was a grave faux pas. The incoming Foreign Secretary and former trade union leader Ernest Bevin had it withdrawn soon enough, after pointing at it 'with his stubby finger' and saying, 'Either 'ee or I must go.' Women of diplomatic rank, of which there were only four or five in the whole service, two of them in Maclean's department, had to leave their jobs if they married; and they were not allowed to serve in South America as it was feared 'they would swiftly suffer "a fate worse than death" at the hands of some passionate Latino, and become unreliable'.

Margaret Anstee was one of these two female Third Secretaries, at the start of a career that took her from an Essex village school to

Under-Secretary-General of the United Nations. She remembered Maclean on his arrival as 'serene, unfussed and calmly in control of everything'. She and the rest of the department were told that he 'had had a nervous breakdown … and his marriage had collapsed. We would all have to be sensitive to his state of mind.' When the news emerged about Melinda's pregnancy, they assumed everything had been 'patched up'. Margaret Anstee was a Labour Party supporter, outspoken about social justice, but assumed from what her boss said at the daily tea parties that he was a 'pale pink liberal' of whom she was well to the left. Maclean was back in the swing of being a model diplomat and was once again the darling of the typing pool, where he had been christened 'Fancy-Pants' Maclean before the war. His charm and good manners contrasted strongly with the recently departed Burgess. He always stood up when Daphne Carroll came into the room to take dictation and 'spoke at a proper speed'. He was 'very popular' all round. 'Sir Donald' seemed calmly back on track.

*

Once Burgess had gone to America, Anthony Blunt and John Cairncross were the only two active members of the Cambridge Five in London. Both had been temporarily dropped for fear they had been compromised when Gouzenko defected, which also coincided with Blunt's departure from MI5 at the end of the war to resume his career as an art historian. He became Director of the Courtauld Institute as well as Surveyor of the King's Pictures, in which role he both charmed (by his personality) and puzzled (by his intellect) the royal family. With Maclean a risky proposition, Burgess out of the country and Cairncross seeing nothing of interest to Moscow Centre from the Treasury, Blunt was the only one in touch with Modin in the London *rezidentura*, passing on titbits gleaned through his friendship with Guy Liddell, Deputy Director General of MI5. To the distaste of the aesthetically aloof Blunt, their meetings took place in Modin's chosen venue in the west London suburb of Ruislip, with its dull ranks of semi-detached houses.

That left Maclean the lone spy in a prime position of influence and access in London at a politically crucial time for the war in Korea. President Truman stated in a press conference on 30 November that the US would take 'whatever steps are necessary to meet the military situation' there. On being asked if those steps might include using the atomic bomb, he replied, 'That includes every weapon we have,' adding 'There has always been active consideration of [the atom bomb's] use.' Britain was already anxious about America escalating any confrontation with Communist China in a world where McCarthyism and a lessening of focus on divided Europe were already sending out loud signals. The rhetoric being ramped up to nuclear levels was terrifying. Prime Minister Attlee concluded a debate in the House of Commons that evening with the announcement that he intended to fly to Washington to hold a meeting with Truman four days later. Maclean had a copy of the hurriedly written forty-page briefing document for the Prime Minister's visit to Washington, New York and Ottawa which included Attlee's plan to persuade the President to avoid violating China's Manchurian frontier and risking Soviet intervention. He kept it in his safe for the rest of his time in the job.

After years in which he had been almost exposed, had been driven close to suicide and had suffered a massive breakdown, Maclean still saw everything of classified value, despite the government's claim that the American Department dealt 'principally with Latin American affairs'. Everything passing through the Foreign Office to do with the Korean War came across his desk, and he made doubly sure of that when he approached the Distribution Selectors, as they were known, in the Communications Department on 25 January 1951 to check that he was 'getting all the telegrams he should on the Korean question'. He saw documents commenting on NATO dispositions, mobilisation plans and bases. He saw classified material detailing how overextended Britain was, with its garrison in the Middle East 'cut to the bone'. He saw a cable sent from Ambassador Franks in Washington with the highest confidentiality of all. Once the Washington meetings had established that the Truman administration were not in fact considering using the atom bomb, their strategic thrust was, in essence, led by the British desire to keep the war in Korea local, not involving China, which despite the attacks it had launched the US persisted in seeing as the pawn of Russia. In fact, Stalin had initially offered support and weapons to China but on the very same day, 8 October 1950, he had sent a message to Beijing via Molotov stating that 'We do not agree with the decision to send in your troops, and we will not supply you with military equipment.' Feelings ran so high between the Western allies that at one point the Chairman of the Joint Chiefs of Staff, General Omar Bradley, 'inquired sarcastically whether a Chinese attack on [the British colony of] Hong Kong would mean war, when it was not considered war for the Chinese to attack American troops in Korea'.

Stalin was of the view, shared by much of the rest of the world, that 'a Third World War was imminent' and did not need high-level British espionage back-up for this opinion. Maclean, out of contact with Moscow Centre since his desperate and solitary departure from Cairo, seemed calmer, able to voice his own political certainties now that he was relieved of the need to over-correct in order to compensate for his espionage, more confident with his peers in the diplomatic corps. But he was nonetheless anxious about the war, the first major conflict between his ideological and his patriotic homes, and dissatisfied with the British status quo and American drift further to the right. When Maclean had lunch with Nicholas Henderson in December, Henderson was 'struck by the fact that he seemed to take the side of the [Communist] North Koreans in a way that made argument impossible'. In the same month Maclean explained to Cyril Connolly over lunch at the Travellers Club that both sides had forgotten that the North Koreans were 'people' and were exploiting the war for the sake of their own 'prestige'. The relief he derived from airing his true beliefs began to unmoor him from his professional diplomatic impartiality; if Moscow Centre had been in touch with him, they might have been able to steer him through careful handling back to his old state, but they might also have regarded his lapses in the office as justification for cutting him off. Henderson had been 'very upset when he saw [Maclean's] Minute ... on the Korean War and American policy'. He wrote a 'counter Minute' and Maclean was only 'half-friendly' when he said that Henderson 'had no right to say what he had about his Minute'. Maclean also put his own 'alarmist' views on the minutes of a meeting about Korea, saying that American aggression 'was pushing the world into a pointless war', an opinion that was open to any newspaper reader.

*

The net began to close in on Maclean during his first week back at work. Geoffrey Paterson, sent to Washington on behalf of MI5, passed on to London Lamphere's suggestion that the 1944 leaks from New York (the Russian handler had said in June 1944 that they were meeting in 'Tyre') and the extraordinarily damaging 1945 ones about Yalta and post-war Europe from Washington could have come from the same source. They now knew that Gorsky (working under his cover-name of Gromov) 'took over certain commitments in Washington DC' as 'Chief MGB Resident at the Soviet Embassy', so 'it is not unreasonable to suppose that G worked at first to New York and later to [Gorsky]'. In other words, that the supplier of 'Material G' from New York was probably the same person as 'Agent G' in Washington. This supposition led to some sharper detective work, which was once again handicapped by prejudice.

By 8 December there was a list of 'Certain' criteria: that 'G' had been a member of the Embassy staff in 1944; that his work had 'included personal telegraphic correspondence between Churchill and Roosevelt'; that the spy had had access to papers about the allocation of occupation zones in Germany; that he had personally deciphered a telegram from Churchill to Roosevelt; and that he had had access to a highly classified War Cabinet Memorandum about uranium after its internal circulation. The list of those supposed to see the last were Michael Wright, Sir Ronald Campbell, Lord Halifax and Maclean, but 'G' had to have had it afterwards as none of those men could be suspect. Two other 'Probable' and 'Possible' criteria raised in this top-secret note, that the mole still had access in March 1945 and had a wife who lived with him in Washington at the time, do not seem actually to have been applied to the candidates. The sifting would continue into 1951, just as Maclean began to feel more settled in his new role.

If any link had been made at this stage to the Krivitsky evidence put back into play by Philby, or to the recent behaviour of one of the four men (realistically one of two because Halifax and Campbell were genuinely above suspicion in even the most fevered imaginations), much time would have been saved. Eighteen months earlier, Arthur Martin of MI5 had suggested that Michael Wright be security-cleared by the Foreign Office in respect of the investigation before Carey Foster apprised him of the leaks, but Carey Foster prevailed when 'he said he did not think this was necessary'. On the other hand, a committed and able member of MI6 who dealt daily in secrecy, Dwyer, had to be vetted before 'indoctrination'. The assumption was that anyone who had served ably in the foreign service was a pillar of patriotic moral rectitude, whereas MI5 and MI6, used as they were to looking into other people's secrets, could not be trusted. History has shown that the second assumption was not always wrong either.

It was decided that the person to ask about who might have been leaking from the Embassy was Wilfrid Thomas, a sensible choice in the circumstances given that he had been head of the cipher room (which was directly accessible by about fifty cipher officers, distributors and typists, as well as by the diplomats) 'unbuttoning' the telegrams in the war. Thomas was now British Consul in New York. This would be a tricky conversation as Thomas was by dint of his former position a prime suspect himself, so Carey Foster suggested to Bobbie Mackenzie that he might take the experienced Philby to New York with him to assist. On the other hand, that might alarm Thomas, so 'on the whole' maybe Mackenzie and Philby's opposite number in MI5, Paterson, should accompany Mackenzie. We can only speculate whether Thomas might have been a more useful red herring for Philby to exploit and thereby baffle his own side, keeping Maclean in place a while longer as his orders from Moscow Centre had instructed him to do. Philby could see by now that his recruit's days were drastically numbered, and he urgently needed to find a way to fulfil the second, 'rescue' part of his orders.

*

While these moves were being made across the Atlantic, the Maclean family once again seemed harmonious. Melinda described the 1950 Christmas holiday and the weeks that followed it as 'amongst the happiest in [her] married life'. Fergus and Beany were not only starting at a new school but were running through the childhood illnesses of mumps and chickenpox; the house was too big and very shabby; she was pregnant. But her furniture had arrived from Cairo, her mother had left Europe in November and family life had started again. Most of all in those first few months of their reconciliation, Donald was behaving like a model husband and father, leaving on the early train after bringing her a cup of tea and, above all, eschewing the cocktail-party round and the post-work sessions in the pub to come home most days at around 7.30. Weekends were spent clearing their large garden, sometimes with friends offering to help.

Until the Cold War got under way in earnest and his drinking increased in concert with the global situation, Maclean had been able to live with himself, both his moral and his patriotic sides praised and satisfied. But now he seemed only to find this peace, as on that Christmas holiday, when he was with his family, able to behave like a senior civil servant at leisure in tending to them and his garden. He appeared relieved to be out of the spying game, was ignorant of the advances being made in Washington regarding his own case, and yet was well aware of the exposures of Communists and the rabid witch-hunts of the McCarthy era. As the world slid more towards ideological conflict, right against left, once again he had a ringside seat, but this time without the usefulness of an outlet in Moscow Centre, feeling he had a purpose. His alcoholism was also largely untreated. As the rhetoric was ratcheted up he had to remain the polished diplomat, but he found it harder and harder to restrain his drinking in the early months of 1951 and soon descended into his final spiral.

*

In early January, the very first mention of drunken behaviour appeared on Maclean's file in a handwritten memo from Robin Hooper, who had succeeded Middleton as head of personnel. Patience Pain, who worked in the office and was thus a 'reliable source', had heard something from a cousin, Humphrey Slater, who had been a Communist and had written a novel entitled *The Conspirator*. True to the trajectory of many converts, Slater was now 'violently anti-communist'. He was an artist, as were many others at a party Maclean had attended, including Rodrigo Moynihan and Robert Buhler. Melinda was not present but Philip Toynbee was. Toynbee had recently returned from the Middle East, accompanied by his new fiancée Sally, and the tightly bound men took up with each other again. 'A lot of drink flowed' at the party and 'there was obviously a lot of rather silly alcoholic argument'. Maclean, 'stung to fury' by something derogatory Slater had said about Communism or North Korea, said, 'Of course, you know I'm a Party member – have been for years!' Whether or not this was intended to get a rise out of Slater, it was not only pointlessly dangerous but also a completely unnecessary lie, given that he was not and never had been a member of the CPGB. From his Foreign Office interview on, Maclean had got away with charming evasions to allay suspicion about his true beliefs, but this was a bad moment to fall back into the late-night habits of his Cairo days and unwittingly incriminate himself.

Slater, who disliked Maclean, told his cousin Patience Pain about this exchange. Even as the Foreign Office and security services were struggling to come up with any plausible identities for Homer, the official line that ended the head of personnel's minute was 'Obviously, this is not to be taken seriously, but it is evidence that D is still hitting it up and that he is apt to be irresponsible in his cups.' There is at least acknowledgement of the dangers of Maclean behaving badly 'in his cups', but even with the wreckage of the Cairo flat known through the press clipping from the *Daily Express*, there was no indication that the head of the American Department was considered in any sense a liability to the office. It was 'not to be taken seriously'. Small as his declaration might seem in the scale of Maclean's drunken indiscretions, and as indirectly as it had come to innocent official attention, Patience Pain's almost accidental evidence was soon to assume importance as the hazy situation gained focus.

*

As in Cairo, Maclean could 'put on his armour' and was very much his urbane self in the office. It was when he was away from there, and away from his warm new home environment, and drank, that he was increasingly getting into trouble. In spite of his attempts at recovery over the previous year, Melinda seems to have resigned herself to his absences and hangovers; at least this time he was neither strangling her nor causing criminal damage and official embarrassment. He was more often a good husband, father and homeowner. Maybe she even appreciated his need to have the release of binge-drinking to manage his stress levels, which she could understand.

Goronwy Rees had disavowed Communism at the time of the Nazi–Soviet Pact, had worked in MI6 and had made his post-war career as a journalist and an academic while maintaining his close friendship with Guy Burgess. It was nonetheless an intense relief when his friend went to Washington as 'one was no longer liable to be rung up late at night and asked whether he might come round for a drink, or to have him for lunch and find him still with you at breakfast'. Early in 1951 Rees was in the Gargoyle Club, that 'favourite resort of intellectuals', when Maclean, whom he had not seen for fifteen years and had had no 'reason even to think of', 'lurched over' to his table and 'said in an extremely aggressive and menacing voice, "I know all about you. You used to be one of us, but you ratted"'. Then, clutching the edge of the table, he collapsed to his knees, 'his large white face suspended like a moon at about the level of my chest, and from this absurd position he proceeded to direct an incoherent stream of abuse at me' until 'he rose unsteadily to his feet and stumbled away'. Rees's mind spun for a few days before he concluded that Maclean had retained his 'communist beliefs, and with time had gradually become more outspoken about them, for the very reason that it was no longer so necessary to conceal them' to a former fellow-traveller. But Maclean was giving voice to those beliefs because they had no other outlet, now that it was safe to reveal them to Rees. When he was unleashed by drink, he posed a danger to himself and proved a spectacle to others. He was once again coming off the rails at speed.

Both Fuchs and Nunn May had experienced relief on confessing to Jim Skardon. Maclean hated the murky business of espionage, put concisely when he likened it to cleaning lavatories as a necessary job, and was on that level pleased not to be in the game. His idealism was intact even as it failed to be supported. His resort to drink meant that he was capable of blurting out the truth without understanding the importance and impact of what he was saying. Perhaps he was still craving removal from his world of capitalist imperialism where all but a handful had 'ratted'. Perhaps he just did not know where to turn.

He had told Janetta Kee that Dr Rosenbaum 'had said that his occasional violence was caused by the fact that he did not ever give vent to his feelings or passions on the surface, and something had to be released ... by means of alcohol, and took a violent form'. When he did try to let go of his secrets he often could not be heard because of his daytime, lifelong and totally convincing mask. At a party in Chelsea, he shouted at his old friend and best man Mark Culme-Seymour, 'What would you do if I told you I was a Communist agent?' Culme-Seymour, understandably, had no answer to this and, as he stammered, Maclean carried on.

'Well, wouldn't you report me?'
'I don't know. Who to?'
'Well, I am. Go on, report me.'

This was followed by 'a diatribe' against the State Department and its handling of the Korean War.

The next day the shaken Culme-Seymour went to see Cyril Connolly to discuss the incident, as he of all people surely knew Maclean well enough to be confident that what had been said could not be true. He and Connolly decided that it was 'a loyalty test with a high alcoholic content', rather than a plea to stop living the lie. Philip Toynbee, no doubt remembering the nights before the final Cairo debauch, later claimed that 'when intoxicated Donald would be most anxious to make extremely dramatic statements. His only intention would be to surprise and shock the person to whom he was talking.' In fact, these episodes all offered glimpses into the inner man and were just as true as those that Toynbee had experienced when Maclean was rambling to him from his armchair as dawn broke over Cairo.

The Gargoyle Club was also the scene for the agonising test of Maclean's friendship with Toynbee, his closest with any man, with any person with the exception of Melinda. In mid-March, Toynbee had written an article in the *Observer* under the headline 'Alger Hiss and his Friends' in response to the US Supreme Court's rejection of Hiss's appeal. Toynbee reminded his readers that Alistair Cooke had taken the line in his book on the Hiss–Chambers case the previous year that 'the tragedy of Alger Hiss lay in the fact that the conduct of the thirties was being unfairly judged in the radically changed climate of the late forties. Hiss was condemned for having been a Communist when a whole generation of good and reasonable people believed that this was a proper thing to be.' The puzzle was why Chambers had ruined his own career (he had been editor of *Time* magazine) and was now a 'recluse' because of his actions in denouncing Hiss, whom he believed to be a Communist still giving away secrets when the charges were levelled against him. To Toynbee, who in his own words had 'bitterly rejected Communism' and was now turning to the religious spirituality that became his new morality, this denunciation at the cost of Chambers's own career was a 'strange confusion of the liberal spirit, which so much prefers the appearance of Alger Hiss's integrity and respectability to the reality of Whittaker Chambers's change of heart'. One can hear the echo of biblical repentance in that last phrase.

A few days after the article had been published, Maclean was once again in the Gargoyle Club having missed his usual commuter train to Oxted (the station nearest to Westerham) and no doubt having made some excuse to Melinda, when he spotted Toynbee there. 'According to Donald, [Chambers] was a double-faced exhibitionist too revolting to be defended by anyone,' let alone by one of his greatest friends. Nearly incapacitated by booze as well as holding his pint glass, he took a swing at Toynbee and sent him reeling into the band. 'I am the English Hiss,' Maclean muttered as he turned away from his loyal friend. It was the penultimate time the two men, the youthfully idealistic and boisterous Serpentine swimmers of 1936, the crazed flat-wreckers of 1950, would ever meet.

*

To Nicholas Henderson Maclean was 'extremely likeable ... kind and considerate', and was one of the few fellow Foreign Office employees he saw outside the office. Just after Maclean had started work again, and before the move to Beaconshaw, the two of them went to a pub together and Maclean said to Henderson that he felt 'racked' knowing that 'his weakness for drink was having a bad effect on him'; he added that when drunk he 'reacted against all authority ... and liked people who were rebels'. He blamed his father, 'for whom he did not seem to have much admiration', and Sir Donald's teetotalism for his drinking. Young Donald knew all about his father's tireless and effective work to further social good, about his great and undivided public service, and his admiration for him now openly crossed the thin line into shame at some of his own actions. Through his own religion of Communism, as expressed to the Campbells a few months earlier, which guided his conscience and which had helped bring him to this desperate point, Donald Maclean was, in fact, probably closer to Sir Donald in spirit and integrity than he could admit.

At the beginning of April the Hendersons gave a dinner-party, attended by the Labour minister Lord Pakenham (later Lord Longford). Melinda, her dislike of these formal occasions as strong as ever, over seven months pregnant and with her hands full with the two boys, did not come. Pakenham was a staunch Catholic and humanitarian, 'violently anti-communist' on account of his religion and liberal beliefs. Maclean got himself into a futile row with Pakenham over 'some Foreign Office business about sending a Catholic to America' which ended with the diplomat behaving as undiplomatically as he possibly could, saying, 'this government is just as bad as any other British Government – suppressing coloured people', before storming off to the Gargoyle. One of his fellow guests put her finger on a profounder observation than she knew when she said, 'he looks like a Tory and talks like a Communist'. Maclean rang Henderson the next day to apologise, simply saying 'it happens'. Henderson, who lunched or dined with Maclean on at least five occasions in the first four months of 1951, later translated the incident as Maclean showing 'marked sympathy for North Korea'. He rightly regarded the evening as a 'disaster'.

That apology to Henderson, shrugging off his aberrant behaviour, would not have lasted through many more incidents, inside or outside the tolerant Gargoyle. But that same month Meredith Gardner had his breakthrough, the Brits on the case in Washington finally started to put the pieces of the puzzle together and the pronouncements about Maclean being a Communist and a spy became all too believable.

*

At the same time as Maclean was lurching about the Gargoyle Club, Sir Robert Mackenzie, head of security at the British Embassy, wrote from Washington on 3 April to say that he, Paterson of MI5 and Philby of MI6 were now all firmly of the view that 'Material G' and 'Agent G' definitely referred to the same person, and related to 'Gomer'. The earlier meetings had taken place in New York and Embassy travel records had been requested to see who had regularly travelled there. Most importantly, they had realised that as Homer 'gave his views on matters of policy' and was clearly 'an ardent Communist' he was likely not to be working for monetary reward so much as for ideological ends. The fact that the handler had so respectfully passed on Homer's views on some of the situations led Mackenzie to deduce that 'the Russians attached considerable value to the agent's views and … he was therefore a man in a responsible position'. The security services, hampered by Philby and the prejudices and fears of the Foreign Office about Homer's unlikely seniority, had failed to see this.

Mackenzie took the lead. Now that he had had this break-through, he realised the importance of the Krivitsky information put into his path by Philby and he began to go over the evidence of more than a decade earlier. He looked at who was in Washington from the beginning of 1944, when he mistakenly believed the first telegrams had been sent, until March 1945, who had been in London from 1935 until 1937, and who was a regular member of the service, not one of the hundreds of staff taken on during the war. This gave him two candidates on all counts, Paul Gore-Booth and Michael Wright. A third possibility was Donald Maclean, but according to the records he had not arrived in Washington until the summer of 1944. The next step was to look at who had been a recent recruit in 1935–7 and who had been at Eton and Oxford. Wright was out. Gore-Booth scored on both counts. Maclean, of course, did not go to Eton and Oxford, a further strike against him. So Gore-Booth was the man.

From here, Mackenzie was quickly able to bolster his case. 'G' is the first letter of the code-name and of the suspect's real name, and 'Gomer' close enough to being an anagram of 'Gore'. As Carey Foster, to whom this top-secret sleuthing was addressed, knew, 'Secret Services often use some form of alliteration or make some punning allusion to an agent's habits or country when christening him.' Gore-Booth had been a classical scholar at Eton and Oxford, as 'was brought home' to Mackenzie (himself an hereditary baronet and Old Etonian) at an old boys' dinner in Washington on the Fourth of June (Eton's day of celebration) 'when he drafted a telegram of greetings to the head of the governing body, the Provost, in Latin without a moment's hesitation'.* If Mackenzie had known it,

---

* The upright and patrician Gore-Booth also had some ability in French. He saw Maclean only once after their simultaneous service in Washington, in late 1950, when he was struck, as he recorded in his memoirs *With Great Truth and Respect*, by his 'aspect of *dégringolade*', meaning 'falling to pieces'.

he would probably have added that Paul Gore-Booth's aunt was the Irish republican and socialist revolutionary Constance Markievicz, muse of W. B. Yeats (which would have satisfied the bohemianism alluded to by Krivitsky) and Minister for Labour in the Sinn Féin government of 1919, as more conclusive evidence of espionage potential than his classical proficiency. For now, a simple mistake over the date of his arrival and a healthy dose of upper-class insider knowledge had earned the real Homer a brief reprieve.

In London, Carey Foster found Mackenzie's analysis 'most interesting and useful', although he was 'disturbed' that the 'new evidence' had only just come to light – a possible dig at the security services. He could not resist going back to his own shortlist of diplomatic stars from 1949 of Balfour, Makins, Hadow, Wright, Gore-Booth and Maclean, which when put together with Krivitsky came down to 'Balfour, possibly Makins, and Gore-Booth'. Maclean did not make the final cut because of 'the more detailed information supplied by Krivitsky'. This is not specified but might well refer to schooling. Excluding Makins and Balfour on the grounds of age gave the same result that Mackenzie had reached: Gore-Booth – but only if Krivitsky's spy of the 1930s was the same as 'G' of the 1940s, for which they had no evidence. Carey Foster was still not keen to have 'a senior man' as a spy of such magnitude and asked that 'junior members of Chancery' should be looked at while the wartime travel records were obtained.

Lamphere, meanwhile, was badgering the British about their progress and had asked about the Krivitsky evidence. Following the unpleasant matter of Nunn May and Fuchs there was a tense relationship between the FBI and the British over security matters. Paterson had hoped that Gore-Booth would soon be posted back to Britain (he was currently serving in Washington himself, which hobbled his masters a bit) before the FBI, having 'jumped to premature conclusions', demanded interrogation. There is condescension (mixed with alarm) in the attempt to regain a little of the security high ground as well as a justifiable desire to avoid feeding the febrile atmosphere of 'Senator McCarthy and anti-administration politicians'.

Now that he had a theory ahead of his security service colleagues and the less gentlemanly FBI, Mackenzie was determined to make it stick. He offered Philby 'short odds' that Gore-Booth was the spy. After all, 'as for ideals, Gore-Both was a Christian Scientist and a teetotaller', so what more evidence could Philby want? Philby, inwardly delighted that they were at the wrong end of the spectrum if they believed Christian Science and abstention were the marks of Homer, wanted to buy all the time he could. He knew that if this was handled the wrong way and Maclean was rumbled before he could be safely smuggled behind the Iron Curtain, his own cover could be blown and the Cambridge Five would go down like dominoes. He agreeably went along with Mackenzie.

It became important to make sure that the pieces that did not fit the puzzle were dovetailed in. Mackenzie noticed that Gore-Booth had been transferred to Vienna in April 1936, while Krivitsky had spoken of seeing documents from the source now known as Homer as late as 1937. That could be glossed over: they might have been sent from Vienna rather than London, however unlikely it might be that the Embassy in land-locked, post-*Anschluss* Austria would need to see the Committee of Imperial Defence minutes. Another possibility was that 'the prints seen by Krivitsky [who had told them he saw photographs of the minutes] were old ones' that had only recently made their way to Gore-Booth, or perhaps ones that he had failed to send earlier and had taken with him. The 1944 Embassy travel records were missing anyway, so any omissions for Gore-Booth's trips to New York did not need accounting for. That Gore-Booth had not initialled certain files that were known from Venona to have been passed on to Moscow was 'entirely possible': if the most sensitive, including the correspondence between Churchill and Roosevelt, had been read in Washington in one sitting, Gore-Booth would only have initialled the top file. It took another few weeks before Paterson gently wondered 'whether we might be attaching too much significance to initials on telegrams' in cases of espionage at this level. There was no mention of Maclean putting his mark on the telegrams in question, as he could take them from the registry any time he wanted.

Paterson joined in the hunt for Gore-Booth evidence on 11 April, while stressing that it had to be kept between him, Carey Foster, Philby and Mackenzie. 'It would be alarming if H[is] E[xcellency] were to hear any unhappy rumours of our suspicions via the FBI, A[ttorney] G[eneral], State Department and [Secretary of State] Mr Acheson,' and to let on to the FBI in particular 'would be asking for trouble and any hope of handling the matter quietly and discreetly would be blown sky-high'. The real reason was perhaps to do not so much with fear of early exposure as with saving face, because 'it was highly undesirable that they should again be able to claim, as with the Fuchs case, that they had been responsible for uncovering a British agent of the Soviet intelligence system'.

*

Despite Mackenzie's claim that they backed his Gore-Booth theory, MI5 got properly back on track and were definitely getting warmer at the beginning of April, when Paterson forwarded to London an accurate but unsigned top-secret memorandum. Literary criticism and date-checking (late in the day, perhaps) came into play when it was pointed out that 'in style and content' there were similarities between the partial decrypts of 2/3 August 1944 and of 7 September, so 'G' and 'Gomer' could now definitely be assumed to be one and the same. In spite of the 'fragmentary information' and many 'ifs and buts', a pattern seemed to be emerging of four- or five-weekly meetings in New York, and the material being handed over on a Sunday. These weekend visits both strengthened the case for the agent being stationed in Washington, and made the travel papers a tree that at least need no longer be barked up as records were not kept for out-of-hours travelling.

The telegrams were sent to Moscow four days after the New York meetings with the agent but no classified material was sent following the first meeting on 25 June. This might be because the spy had been 'absent from his post in the period immediately preceding' or, 'alternatively', because this was the first contact between agent and handler and nothing was handed over. In Philby's view, which was of course bolstered by knowledge of the truth which gave him other puzzles to grapple with, the security services were acting with a great deal more intelligence and psychological nous than the Foreign Office in looking for the 'odd man out', the loner who hated the diplomatic round, rather than the 'depressingly conformist' names on the rest of the list, those who could make an accomplished toast in Latin to warrant the name of 'Homer'.

While these late-exploding and accurate bombshells were being sent to London, Philby's extraordinary run of luck seemed to be holding up. The British Ambassador informed the State Department in mid-April that Guy Burgess was being recalled to London. Goats were not involved, but the final straw after so much sloppy work and drunkenly offensive behaviour was a trip to Charleston, South Carolina, at the end of February. Burgess was going to give a lecture at The Citadel, a military college, on 'Britain: Partner for Peace', defending Britain's recognition of Communist China. He was stopped for speeding twice on the way there, but got himself off by claiming diplomatic immunity. The third time the young black homosexual he was travelling with, James Turck, was driving and the patrolman did not accept that a diplomat's chauffeur could have immunity, nor indeed could the diplomat himself when Turck let slip it was the third violation of the day. The Governor of Virginia complained to Franks, who had had enough. Handily enough for Moscow Centre and Philby, he ordered Burgess's return to London. Burgess dined with Philby on his last night in the US in a New York Chinese restaurant where each booth had piped music loud enough to drown out their voices. Burgess was given a 'step-by-step' briefing on how he was to conduct himself when he got back to England, how to warn Maclean that he was going to be rumbled any day now, and how to set up an escape plan. Philby's last words in the West to his friend and fellow spy, 'spoken only half-jocularly were "Don't you go, too."'

Burgess sailed on 1 May from New York, where he had stayed at 123 East 55th Street in the apartment of Donald Maclean's unsuspecting younger brother, Alan. The Maclean brothers' employment by His Majesty's Government now had only a few weeks to run.

The innocent younger man was to have his life changed irrevocably by the ideology of the older.

*

George Carey Foster and his colleagues started to dig deeper, no doubt encouraged by Paterson's work in Washington. They finally 'examined' the personal files of the seven Chancery officers who had been in their sights at various times. Hooper's handwritten memorandum of the rant at Humphrey Slater had come to light, including Maclean's lie that he was a Communist Party member of long standing, and this time it was deemed perhaps to 'have direct security significance'. If they had had a mole in the Gargoyle Club they would even have had their confession. Maclean's name was back on the list and a more focused comparison with the life and times of Gore-Booth could be carried out. At a meeting of White, James Robertson and Martin for the Security Service and Patrick Reilly and Carey Foster for the Foreign Office on the 17th (a Saturday when the office would be quieter), it was agreed that the political sympathies of both men should be looked into, as well as their movements in 1944 and 1945.

When the pair were compared objectively by MI5 to Krivitsky's evidence, Maclean had three more ticks in his column than Gore-Booth: he could have seen the Imperial Defence Committee minutes in 1937, by which time Gore-Booth was in Vienna; he had access to material in London about defence measures in the same year; under 'Was young aristocrat?' he got 'His father was an MP and Knight', where the socially superior Gore-Booth (his grandfather was a baronet who owned estates in Ireland covering thirty-nine square miles) got 'No obvious reason for such a description'. Three days later Carey Foster had spoken to Roderick Barclay, Maclean's predecessor as head of Chancery, and established that Melinda did live in New York when they arrived, and that Maclean had started work in June, not July as planned, because Barclay had been struck down with mumps and had to leave early. So Maclean, after all, had been in place for the first telegram at the end of that month. The scales had tipped to his side. Gore-Booth, who went on to become head of the Foreign Office and a member of the House of Lords, knew none of this. He was in the clear and free to pursue the career that could have been his co-suspect's.

As the case was starting to look bad for their trusted friend and colleague, Carey Foster 'stressed that, without exception, everyone who now knew of our suspicions was incredulous that Maclean could be the guilty party and had made numerous counter sugges-tions'. Carey Foster was therefore 'anxious' that those who had come under suspicion 'in the past', including Ranken and Barron, be investigated again, as well as Miss Randall, in her role as head of the Green Registry through which the telegrams had passed.

In spite of this last plea, the evidence against the head of the American Department was sufficient for a tap to be put on his home telephone and a tail to be put on him that day. Taps were also put on Lady Maclean's telephone and, perhaps in the belief that Maclean would be telling all his secrets to his psychoanalyst (who would be bound by her oath not to reveal them), on Erna Rosenbaum's. A censoriously accurate description of their target was circulated to the watchers: 'big build; broad-shouldered; good looking; clean shaven; very slightly florid face . . . I am told he drinks quite a bit and the general effect is to make his appearance a little more slovenly than it would be otherwise.' For a man who had had code-names assigned to him by Moscow for fifteen years, it now became necessary to give him one from his own side – and 'Curzon' was chosen. Although almost certainly chosen because the head-quarters of MI5, Leconfield House, was in Curzon Street, the irony of the name of that zealously devoted public servant the Marquess Curzon, late Foreign Secretary and Viceroy of India, who had died when his new namesake was eleven, might not have been lost on the mandarins, who would have taken comfort from such a famil-iar and patriotic figure being chosen to stand for a man they were loath to believe a traitor.

On 23 April, the day the taps came into action, it was decided by the Foreign Office and MI5 to inform MI6 of their 'strong suspi-cions', 'owing to the fact that Philby himself is already in the picture'. Michael Wright was visited in Oslo and confirmed that

Melinda had lived in New York in 1944 while Mrs Gore-Booth had been at her husband's side in Washington. Wright could not resist getting in a couple of digs about Melinda's 'lower-middle-class family' and her lack of intellect.

As the *Queen Mary* transported a sodden Guy Burgess and his secret instructions to Southampton, another high-level meeting was held in the Foreign Office on 4 May. The heads of MI5 and the Foreign Office agreed that the FBI should be told about the suspicions but would be asked to keep them quiet until they had had a chance to interrogate their suspect, within a fortnight 'at most'. Maclean was now alone in the spotlight of suspicion. A failure to follow through on their decision within the fortnight would do lasting damage to their reputation and have further reverberating international repercussions. But they were confident all would be well.

*

The final evidence against Donald Maclean was contained in the very first telegram clumsily sent by Pravdin on 28 June 1944 after the two men had first made contact. The fact that this contained no espionage material meant that it might have been simply commenting on the first meeting between Homer and Pravdin, as MI5 had already wondered might be the case. The decoded fragment read:

> Your No. 2712. SERGEI's [Pravdin] meeting with HOMER took place on 25 June. HOMER did not hand anything over. The next meeting will take place on 30 July in TYRE [New York]. It has been made possible for HOMER to summon SERGEI in case of need. SIDON's [London] original instructions have been altered [thirty-four groups unrecoverable] travel to TYRE where his wife is living with her mother while awaiting confinement …

The devastating lack of tradecraft in the personal detail about Melinda's pregnancy and living arrangements was the smoking gun that led to the appalled Foreign Office's ultimate acceptance that Donald Maclean, the man many of them expected to run the show in due course, the star they had hitched themselves to and protected, had to be Homer. The quiet genius of Meredith Gardner and his team and their years of work had uncovered the very detail that meant Homer could be only one person. When he realised a few weeks later what had happened to his decrypts, Gardner 'thought, "Just think of that! I made them do it!" I didn't really feel self-important but I was impinging on the real world more than when I was just a scholar and studying philology.' Sir William Strang, Deputy Under-Secretary at the Foreign Office, went 'quite white' on being told the news – 'I just can't believe it.'

*

There would have to be a confession, as with Fuchs and Nunn May, or evidence was needed that would not compromise Venona, too classified to be revealed in court, if Maclean was to be brought to book. Meanwhile, the head of the American Department went about his duties immaculately, took part in the tea parties in the old India Office and most nights caught the 6.19 from Victoria to Oxted and drove from the station in his 'large American pale green car', still with its Egyptian licence plates, to his new home and newly cleared garden, his heavily pregnant wife and their two sons, who were now losing their American accents. The most senior spy ever detected inside the British government was still allowed to go about his business, his colleagues and the security services paralysed with indecision about how to bring in him and deeply embarrassed about how to deal with their closest allies, who had uncovered him in the first place.

For Maclean himself, the solution to the dilemma he did not know he was in was steaming across the Atlantic in the unlikely guise of Guy Burgess.

16

Endgame

For a man who had been in crisis, at his nadir eighteen months earlier begging to be taken to Russia, it was a profound irony that life seemed to have settled into an agreeable normality before the first, secret meeting that started what had been a desired union of his lives. Some mornings Melinda would come up on the train to London with him, and they would part at Victoria, she taking a bus with Fergus to see Lady Maclean in Kensington ('Give my love to Mother!' he would shout as they parted at Sloane Square), he making his way to his desk at around 10.00. The couple lunched at Schmidt's with a third person, unknown to those watching him, in Charlotte Street on 26 April. Schmidt's, with its cheap meals of Hungarian goulash, Würst, braised pork knuckle and red cabbage, served by elderly and famously surly German and Austrian waiters, was so much a favourite haunt of his that Maclean was to choose it for his last meal in London. With Melinda the talk was of the impending birth, friends in Egypt and their companion's matrimonial prospects. Donald was 'drinking quite heavily', but as usual was back at work by 3.15.

On the last Saturday of the month, when the office shut at lunchtime, Donald was joined at Victoria Station by his brother Andy, visiting from New Zealand. They returned to London on Monday morning after Andy had seen the new house and his nephews, and been put to work in the garden. The following week was for old friends, lunch with Toynbee at the Travellers Club, drinks with Nicholas Henderson, Mark Culme-Seymour coming down to Kent for the night. If he was going home alone, Maclean would always stop for a quick whisky and soda at the Red Lion in Whitehall, or drink at the Fountain in Wilton Road, on his way to Victoria.

There had been no recent outbursts about being a Communist or being betrayed by his friends. From the start of the year his lunches (and the occasional dinner) had been in the respectable establishment surroundings of the Garrick Club, Army and Navy Club or the Travellers. As well as 'Nicko' Henderson and Culme-Seymour, Lees Mayall and Toynbee lunched with him. He saw some of his intellectual circle, including Cyril Connolly, the composer Constant Lambert and the philosopher Freddie Ayer. George Carey Foster, still head of security at the Foreign Office, lunched with Maclean on 1 May, but did not record whether this was an uncomfortable occasion for either man: the watchers simply noted that nothing was said by Maclean 'which would be of value' to MI5. Once again, the accomplished 'Sir Donald' seemed to be carrying the day against dissolute 'Gordon'. His last appointment with Erna Rosenbaum had been in the middle of February; given his patchy attendance record when he needed the therapist's professional help most, this failure to see her again might reveal nothing more than that a few months into this 'happiest period' Melinda and he felt he could maintain his stability. They were looking forward to the birth of the baby – with the attendant anxiety about the birth itself, given their past experiences – the boys were happy at school, work was interesting. Donald Maclean had no idea of the catastrophic discoveries and calculations closing in on him from Venona, MI5 and Moscow Centre as he went around this innocent daily round.

*

The atmosphere changed in early May. On the first weekend of the month, Lady Maclean found the family 'in a state of complete devotion one to the other', with Donald playing games with his boys and generally being an 'unquarrelsome sort of person'. He was more downcast and anxious the following weekend when Harriet Marling Sheers and her new husband Jay, a documentary producer, came to stay. Harriet had been with Donald and Melinda at many of their critical moments and was the confidante of both of them in most matters. The Sheers arrived in the evening, expecting to see a harmonious picture in the new home and a warm greeting for Jay, whom the Macleans had only met at the January wedding in Paris. Harriet was struck by the 'great change' in her brother-in-law from his nadir in Cairo. He was no longer drinking to destructive oblivion, but instead 'was tense, strained, and ... desperately worried.' She and Jay, the stranger to whom it is often possible to show more of oneself than to someone closer, had 'an extraordinary conversation' with him in which 'he openly supported Communism' (Harriet had never heard him make more than a 'passing reference' to his beliefs) and 'although he did not say so in so many words, suggested he was a Communist'.

Although Harriet did not take this particularly seriously at the time, as Donald was given to posturing and teasing with her, his conversation with Jay Sheers in the pub, loosened once again by alcohol, took on a very different tone: 'he railed bitterly at his life and his job; he mocked himself as a sheep amongst hordes of other sheep going off to London every day ... he was sick of it all and longed desperately to be "cut adrift"'. He may have suspected his nemesis was getting closer – maybe he was not seeing certain files he knew about, maybe there was an awkwardness from his superiors, or he heard the underwater echo of the tapped telephone, but if so, he did could not know from which direction. He could unbuckle his desire to start again to Jay, someone not connected with his job, not of his own country or gossipy social circle but of his family and personal world, in a way that he could not otherwise do. By the next day 'he seemed his normal self again and his outburst of the previous night was forgotten'. He kept the mask in place in the office but could not when he was caught off guard, as he was when a fellow Foreign Office commuter and Washington acquaintance, Fred Everson, caught sight of him. Everson was 'struck by Donald's shabby dress and moroseness ... He walked, untalkative, with his hands thrust deep into his tweed coat pockets and his shoulders hunched.' Away from his family and that connection, he seemed defeated, exhausted by the worlds which he had strived to straddle for so long.

*

For the first couple of days of the following week Harriet stayed down in the country with Melinda, while her husband came up to London with Donald on the train on Monday morning, just as the *Queen Mary* was docking at Southampton. There Anthony Blunt met Guy Burgess. The two former lovers had kept in touch since they had met at Cambridge, just as Burgess had gone against good tradecraft in staying with Philby in America. They went straight to Blunt's exquisitely furnished flat in Portman Square near Marble Arch for an urgent exchange of news. The next day, Blunt met 'Peter', as Modin was known to him, in Ruislip, 'deeply worried': 'Peter, there's serious trouble. Guy Burgess has just arrived back in London. Homer's about to be arrested. MI5 … have a lead which points straight to Maclean. It's only a matter of days now, perhaps hours.'

Blunt stressed, as if it needed emphasising, the implications of Maclean's arrest. There would be panic for the rest of them if the depth of penetration and betrayal in the past fifteen years, the most internationally turbulent in modern history, were to be revealed. There was heightened concern about what had reached Blunt's ears, slightly belatedly, regarding Maclean's collapse: 'Donald's now in such a state that … he'll break down the moment they question him.' The surveillance, which Philby had told Burgess about, meant they would have to be extremely careful. Modin needed a couple of days to get instructions from Moscow. When they came, they could not have been clearer: 'We agree to your organizing Maclean's defection. We will receive him here … if he wishes to go through with it.' Burgess, still officially a Foreign Office employee pending whatever action was planned for his latest misdemeanours, had a meeting with Modin and Modin's superior, the London *rezident* Nikolai Korovin. He was ordered to put Maclean fully in the picture and to convince him to defect.

*

Things were not as clear-cut for MI5. They needed more than 'days' or 'hours' to work out how to handle the Homer case. They needed weeks and wanted longer. Apart from the lack of evidence to bring about an arrest, in the absence of which Maclean might well 'do a Pontecorvo' (they were counting on the impending birth to prevent that), they had the potentially explosive issue of how to handle the embarrassment of breaking the news to the FBI. They were still tying themselves in knots about whether to inform the Americans about the suspected traitor's identity. Lamphere had told Paterson that 'the Bureau wants action'. Paterson prevaricated by saying that Alexander Halpern 'could of course have been shown some of the signals on his frequent visits to the Embassy and he may have known Pravdin. But the rest of it does not fit in.' Finally, on 5 May it was agreed that GCHQ, the government communications centre, should tell Arlington Hall about their working out of the Tyre pregnancy message and that their suspicions were now centred on Maclean, who would be interrogated within 'a fortnight at the most'. But in another embarrassed volte-face, just before the fortnight was up they were suddenly less confident about how things would play in Washington and decided that 'the FBI should only be informed after Maclean has been interrogated'.

There were now two clocks ticking behind Maclean, his own country's and Moscow Centre's, to both of whom he had given such extraordinary service. But in Britain's case diplomatic shame was overcoming justice and Moscow Centre were moving to a more urgent beat.

*

The 'watchers', as MI5's surveillance unit A4 was known, consisted of twenty men and three women, mostly former Special Branch officers, even though the 'ideal watcher' should look 'as unlike a policeman as possible'. They were selected for their good eyesight and sharp hearing. They had to be of average height so as not to stand out by being either conspicuously tall or conspicuously short, and the men were dressed in raincoats and trilby hats; a clever double-bluff, perhaps, to disguise the spy-spotters as spies themselves. They communicated with each other by hand signals from street corners, but they plainly stood out to one of Maclean's lifelong wariness even as they ramped up his anxiety.

Confronted by this turn of events, the Soviet London *rezidentura* remained calm. A4 had been watching their Embassy on the edge of Kensington Gardens for years, and they in turn had watched rather more analytically back. The Soviet counter-surveillance had noted that the watchers did not follow Maclean in the evenings or at weekends, which helped immeasurably with escape planning: anyone in a raincoat and trilby standing on a street corner in the village of Tatsfield, with its population of a thousand souls, would be far too noticeable. 'At Victoria, MI5's men saw the train out of the station, then headed home like good little functionaries,' as Modin tartly observed. Rebecca West, with her usual glorious acerbity, remarked that saying a house could not be watched was 'a remark which could never be worth making, except by a house agent attempting to sell a castle in the Yorkshire moors to an exceptionally trusting foreign criminal'.

Another A4 error was not to tailor their men's average height to their above-average prey. One Under-Secretary, who was in the know, was surprised one spring afternoon to see Maclean 'following a diagonal course at great speed' across St James's Park while 'another man, with much shorter legs' was practically running to move 'at the same speed and a fixed distance'. Patrick Reilly, Assistant Under-Secretary at the Foreign Office and not in on the identity or even existence of Homer, saw Maclean at the Duke of York Steps on his way back from lunch one day. Maclean was 'walking very fast and looked badly in disarray. The man following him could be fairly easily identified.' The Steps were on the route between Whitehall and Pall Mall, home of the gentlemen's clubs habitually visited by Maclean – the Travellers, the Royal Automobile Club and the Reform. On 15 May, the clumsy watchers spotted Maclean and Burgess emerging from the last two of these.

*

By comparison with MI5's uncertainty and in contrast to their dilatoriness of the year before, Moscow Centre was now working efficiently towards its goal. Filip Kislitsyn had been a Soviet cipher clerk in London from 1945 to 1948, and among his duties was handling material coming from Guy Burgess. After Maclean sent up his cries for help from Cairo and even more urgently when Philby reported that the net was closing in on Homer, Kislitsyn attended a meeting in Moscow Centre alongside Colonel Raina, Chief of the First Directorate (dealing with Anglo-American affairs) and his successor in that post, head of the Second Department Pavel Gromushkin,* and Gorsky, who felt a special interest in rounding off his work with his 'topline agent'. It was Maclean's faithful and gifted handler's last act in their partnership before he was 'dismissed from his post because it had been discovered that he had hidden some discreditable facts about his relatives'. Kislitsyn reported that 'the perils of the proposed plan [for exfiltration] caused much misgiving and many plans were put forward and rejected'. To create forged British passports would take too long as they would have to make paper with the 'right fibre content', but they calculated that if the pair could somehow reach continental Europe without showing their passports, the rest could be managed.

*

Maclean knew that his Cambridge contemporary had been living with Philby in Washington, that his career was in the balance in Whitehall; he must have been aware of the possible significance for his own future when Burgess made contact. Burgess had paid one visit to the Foreign Office already, on 9 May, where it was suggested to him that he should consider resigning after the 'last chance' fiasco of Washington, and he did not dare show his face again in any official capacity during the acutely sensitive mission he had

---

* Gromushkin was poorly educated and 'spoke in the vernacular'. A favourite KGB joke about him was that when he gave an award to 'some girl' on International Women's Day, instead of saying 'Give her a big hand' as he meant to do, he said, 'It's not enough just saying it – congratulate her with your hands!'

been entrusted with by Philby. Since then he had been to an
Apostles dinner at Cambridge and had had further meetings 'with
his Russian contact about Donald's escape'. Burgess was often to be
found at the Reform Club from the morning onwards, 'without
having shaved and dressed like a tramp' (although always with his
talismanic Old Etonian tie, as if to ward off any suspicions that he
might be a traitor), voicing his 'hatred for the Americans with great
vigour', as Virginia Woolf's nephew, Quentin Bell, was unfortunate enough to hear. When Burgess got his instructions from
Moscow Centre, transmitted through Modin and Blunt, he rang
Maclean on the 14th to say they should meet for lunch at the Reform
Club the next day.

The call unsettled Maclean, and brought the worst of his old
behaviour back. After a blameless couple of weeks of catching his
commuter train each evening he rang Melinda from the office,
something he had not done all month, just before he set off for the
Reform, to say that he would be late back as he was planning to have
a drink with Isabel Lambert on the way home. Melinda sent
Lambert her love. Maclean found Burgess waiting for him in the
club's majestic and gloomy lobby, and they sat over a couple of
drinks for twenty-five minutes before moving along the street to the
RAC where the dining-room was less full, possibly less full in particular of people who might want to come up to the two men to chat.
On the way over, Maclean said, 'I'm in frightful trouble, I'm being
followed by the dicks,' pointing out 'two men jingling their coins in
a policeman-like manner'. Over the next hour and a half Burgess
delivered the news he had come to give – MI5 were on to him.

Maclean showed no surprise, even found it welcome to share the
psychological pressure that his constant London tail was putting
him under: 'They've been watching me for some time … I'm expecting a summons any day now.' When Burgess went further and said
that Moscow Centre and Philby agreed with him that the only
course of action was for Maclean to 'run', he 'sagged visibly'. After a
long pause, he said he hadn't the strength for the 'coming confrontation', he would 'confess everything'; he knew himself well enough
that he could not 'soldier on for months, denying everything'. But

he couldn't bear to abandon Melinda and the new baby, the commitment that MI5 were counting upon. He would stay. The decency of the husband, repaying his wife's loyalty that had got him more or less back on track in the last couple of years, perhaps some echo of the Honour System of his old school that claimed it was better to turn oneself in than be caught in a lie, and perhaps above all the possible relief of laying down his secrets now that they were no longer as urgent – the relief that led to Nunn May and Fuchs deciding to confess rather than have the pressure of watchers and suspicion – all militated against his going. The two men parted at 3.00, Maclean to go back to work, Burgess to report back to the London *rezident*. That evening, within an hour of the report reaching them, Moscow Centre telegraphed back to say, 'Homer *must* agree to defect.'

The day then took on a familiar turn. Maclean stopped at his own club, the Travellers, for one more drink on his way back to his office, where he diligently got through his in-tray, the routine possibly the best distraction for a whirling head. At 6.00 he telephoned Melinda again. Having not rung her from the office in the weeks that his telephone had been tapped, the fact that he had now done so twice in one day is an indication of his unsettled state. He reminded her that he would be late home as he was now meeting Isabel Lambert for a drink at the philosopher Freddie Ayer's house in White Horse Street, Mayfair before they went on alone. Ayer, who had been an MI6 agent in the war and was currently teaching philosophy at London University, was very much the highly intelligent, open-minded and free-thinking bohemian (he was married four times to three women) that Maclean, trapped by his job in the conventions of diplomatic circles, had been seeking out from his first days in the Foreign Office. Lambert's husband was the composer Constant Lambert, a brilliant alcoholic (he was to die later that year from complications brought on by his drinking), who was currently rehearsing pieces to be performed at Covent Garden and the Royal Festival Hall. Isabel was 'fascinating ... a tall, dark, elegant woman ... who combined working as a painter with assiduous bohemianism' and who had briefly been in the same Parisian Left

Bank set as Melinda and Donald just before the war. She and Maclean left Ayer's house and went to the nearest pub at 8.00, leaving again at 9.00, plainly having trouble walking, the watchers noted, and went on to Isabel's local, the York and Albany pub on the edge of Regent's Park, until just before closing.

Lambert then went home while Maclean continued on his last bender on British soil. Another taxi took him to the Gargoyle, from where he incoherently rang the anxious Melinda after 11.00, and then he took another taxi to Cyril Connolly's Regent's Park house after midnight. He hammered on the door, probably hoping for Philip Toynbee to answer as he and Robert Kee had a flat in the same building, and Connolly, 'sober-drunk' himself after a dinner-party, saw him for the first time 'in this legendary condition'. 'He began to wander round the room, blinking at the guests as he divided the humble sheep from the well-adjusted goats, and then went out to lie down to sleep in the hall, stretched out on the stone floor under his overcoat like some figure from a shelter sketch-book.' Connolly 'put him to bed and gave him an Alka-Seltzer breakfast. Hardly a word was spoken.' Maclean's lack of aggression, so often a feature of his inebriation at time of stress, is noteworthy on this binge: maybe he really had come to accept what was going to happen next. Maybe he had lurched in with the confused intention of some sort of farewell to Toynbee, or to confess what was about to happen to his oldest companion, finally sharing the last and greatest secret with him. The exfiltration itself, already practically and psychologically fraught, would be more complicated and stressful yet.

*

On that same Tuesday the 15th, a top-secret meeting was convened in Whitehall. Bobbie Mackenzie had come from Washington, Dick White, Robertson and Martin were there from the Security Service, Carey Foster from the Foreign Office. The main item on the agenda was to discuss the American side of things after a Washington gathering six days earlier attended by Makins, Paterson, Mackenzie and, of course, Kim Philby. Philby had followed up by sending a letter to Burgess metaphorically urging him to get a move on: Burgess's car was still languishing in the Embassy car park and Philby told him that 'if he did not act at once, it would be too late', his car would be sent 'to the scrap-heap'. The Whitehall panjandrums vacillated some more but eventually backed the Washington station's conclusion that it would be 'unwise' to tell the FBI about their well-founded conjectures regarding Homer's identity until they had interrogated Maclean, ostensibly for fear of 'leakage'. This was a decision that would come back to haunt them.

Although it was not stated as a part of their discussion, the more diplomatically sensitive minds would also have been aware of 'the strong wave of anti-British feeling', as the US Ambassador to Britain characterised the atmosphere in Washington to Foreign Secretary Morrison after Britain's heel-dragging in its support for the Korean War. The Fuchs revelation was too serious and too recent for the British to want to bring up further top-level spies for a while. The meeting attendees thought they had 'three to four weeks' in which to dissemble to the FBI, although accepting that it was risky and that there were many questions 'which could be answered only by a lie'. They decided their best hope was to spend the next two weeks seeking evidence that could be used against Maclean in the absence of a confession, given that Venona remained too secret. They would inform Arlington Hall on 28 May, and finally the FBI on 7 June that they were going to interrogate their man on the following day. This was a handy breathing space for Philby, but no wonder he was keen to set a brisker pace to get Maclean out of the country. He ended his letter to Burgess pointing out that Washington was 'very hot' that summer.*

The painstaking efforts to back up what the authorities already knew continued: on the 18th Barty Bouverie, 'late of SOE' and now of the London South American Bank, told Guy Liddell that Melinda had lived in New York and that he thought she had been

---

* This letter was found (and pocketed) in Burgess's flat by Anthony Blunt when he was sent by MI5 to have a look around a few weeks later to save them the rigmarole and possible publicity involved in obtaining a search warrant.

Donald and Melinda in the garden of their home in Cairo, 1949.

Philip Toynbee, Maclean's close friend, drinking companion and chronicler of his worst excesses.

Melinda's sister, Harriet Marling (far right), was a witness to the end of Donald and Melinda's diplomatic life abroad in Cairo.

Beaconshaw, the first and last house the Macleans owned in Britain.

The high-flying diplomat in his trademark bow tie and pinstripes.

The Maclean family, 1950. *Left to right*: Donald, Fergus, Melinda, Donald.

Moscow Centre, the ultimate destination of Maclean's espionage.

Above: The Foreign Office, symbol of British power and importance, found it impossible to believe it could harbour a high-level traitor.

Yuri Modin, handler and liaison between the spies in London in 1951.

THE NEW T.S. "FALAISE"
SOUTHAMPTON. ST. MALO AND CHANNEL ISLANDS SERVICES
SOUTHERN RAILWAY

The *Falaise*, the ship on which passports were not needed, even when it put in to St Malo.

Wanted posters of the 'Missing Diplomats' were distributed throughout Europe. Here being scrutinised on the border of Germany and Czechoslovakia.

Melinda Maclean, holding her daughter Melinda, arriving back in London with her sons and mother after their escape from the press in the south of France, September 1951.

Below: Donald's brother Alan and their mother seeing Melinda and the children off on their way to Paris, June 1952.

Below: Jim Skardon, the deft and genial confessor for traitors.

Melinda and the boys in their last European home, Geneva, 1953.

Below: Vladimir Petrov, Melbourne 1954. The defector gave the first clues about Maclean's mysterious exit three years after the event.

Below: Melinda in 1953, the photograph used to apply for Swiss residence.

Above: The end of an uneasy thirty-year friendship: the funeral of Guy Burgess in 1963. Melinda and Donald stand together in the foreground.

Right: The final betrayal: Melinda and Kim Philby in Moscow.

Donald Maclean's coffin being carried out of IMEMO, Moscow, in 1983 after he was honoured for his work there.

The gravestone of Sir Donald Maclean and his son, loyal servants to their causes. Penn, Buckinghamshire.

pregnant in the summer of 1944. Bouverie reversed the normal denigration of diplomatic wives in general and Melinda in particular by saying that it would be better to ask Esther Wright for her recollections of their Washington lodger rather than her husband Michael as she 'was much brighter than he was'. Wright had, of course, already confirmed the Macleans' living arrangements in 1944. Given the lack of impetus with the Krivitsky investigation, Liddell had been verging on the disingenuous when he said to Bouverie that they had been looking for the spy 'since the beginning of the war'.

*

After his drunken outing on the 15th, Maclean found it in himself to act normally for the rest of that week, having a drink in a pub before boarding his train, making arrangements with decorators to do some work at Beaconshaw starting on his birthday, the 25th, lunching with the now heavily pregnant Melinda at Scott's fish restaurant in Mayfair. Scott's was far beyond Schmidt's in price, service and quality: maybe this visit was in recognition that this might be their last restaurant meal together. Culme-Seymour and BBC producer Laurence Gilliam were the following day's companions. He had a drink with Nicko Henderson on the 16th and talked about his plans for leave around the time of the baby's birth; his parting comment was that Nicko 'must come down for a night' after the birth, as he could be helpful with the gardening. The routine of renewing his season ticket, leaving his trousers at the dry-cleaners on his last Saturday at work and lunching with his best man and not going on drinking binges and letting on about his turmoil was impressive. His future was now out of his hands and he could live calmly in the moment. Throughout that last week he was at home by 8.15, playing the attentive father to his boys.

*

Despite what she had to say in a few days' time when Jim Skardon called on her, and despite her advanced pregnancy, it is now clear that Melinda knew what her husband needed to do and had given it her blessing, maybe even stating that she would stand by him come what may, as she had since he first told her he was an agent in Paris before the war. She must have realised that Donald could not withstand much interrogation without confessing everything, that (in Modin's words) 'he would fold very rapidly', and the events of the evening of the 15th had reinforced that likelihood. Although she would be left pitied, even censured, and alone in a country in which she had spent barely a tenth of her life, it might be better that Donald should be free to live a new life in Moscow than spend the next decade behind bars. Maclean's outward calm in the face of what he was now being asked to do was greatly bolstered by Melinda's support. Just as she had given him the comparative strength to go back to work the previous autumn, now she helped him move towards something far bigger.

In the course of that week the Security Service had got more jittery about what they could do to nail their man. They produced a paper called 'Assessment of the Evidence against Donald Duart Maclean', which broadly concluded that there was not enough of it. Ideally, they would watch him for two to three months to obtain 'the necessary background for interrogation', or hope that he would lead them to associates they could pin something upon, but even if he was still spying that would not guarantee them what they needed. Perhaps he could be removed from the Foreign Office under the 'existing machinery of a Civil Service Purge' (any echo of Stalin's purges which had removed Maly, Krivitsky and many others from the espionage game would have been completely unintentional). But on reflection it might be best to stick to the timeline agreed at the beginning of the week, as this did at least enable the service to appear to have collaborated fully with the FBI, 'lessening the recriminations' and reducing 'to a reasonable minimum the possibility that the FBI might independently identify Maclean'. That was their main fear. Paterson was now meeting Lamphere in Washington almost daily, and the FBI agent was growing 'rather frustrated' at the lack of 'action' which he thought would still be against other candidates, including

Halpern. Even the name of Gore-Booth had been withheld from him as a likely 'Agent G'.

*

The wires between Moscow and London had been humming since the RAC lunch, the MGB showing much more decisiveness than their British counterparts. Moscow Centre were pragmatic and ruthless in response to the fear that Maclean might crack up and tell all, or that the irrepressible Burgess would spoil things. They knew they 'had not one but two burnt-out agents on our hands' and they saw that Burgess would have to go with Maclean. By now Burgess was also under watch (code-named 'Berkeley') as he had cropped up on the telephone intercepts before the men's lunch the previous week. If he were to go too, it might solve two problems for Moscow, even if it need not be pointed out that he was on a one-way ticket. Above all, it might protect Philby, with his unquantifiable value in Washington and MI6.

Maclean and Burgess next met a week after their lunch, on Tuesday 22 May, for an evening drink at the Grosvenor Hotel, near Victoria. Burgess, true to form, arrived forty minutes late. Maclean left a quarter of an hour later for his train. A quarter of an hour was all it needed for Burgess to pass on his simple message: Maclean had to go and go soon, and Burgess would accompany him some of the way.

The next problem was how to get the two out, given that it was a safe bet that the airports and ports would be watched. Given that there was not time for false papers of sufficient quality, Moscow Centre toyed with 'that classic spy-novel device, a submarine appearing at a discreet rendezvous somewhere along the coast', but time was too short, and starting the Third World War off Beachy Head a risky possibility. Blunt, the coolest head on the case outside Washington, warned Modin that Burgess too was now on the point of cracking up, and, walking through Regent's Park, suggested a solution. There were cruise ships that left the Channel ports on a Friday night, put in for brief stops for meals and shopping in France and the Channel Islands before returning on Sunday evening. As they were deemed not really ever to leave Britain, passport checks were 'virtually non-existent', the French authorities showing 'unique restraint'. Given that the passengers were largely made up of adulterous 'businessmen and civil servants' with their mistresses, not at all a shocking carry-on to a Frenchman, discretion was fairly well guaranteed. And on Fridays the watchers would start taking their own well-earned weekend rest. Modin visited an Oxford Street travel agent and saw that the *Falaise*, 'the cliff' in translation, would be sailing that Friday. In three days.

*

The following day, Wednesday the 23rd, the pair met again, this time for lunch at the Queen's Head pub in Sloane Square. For two confirmed lunchers, this was to be another very brief encounter, and a charged giving of orders. They arrived separately at 1.30, and Burgess left again at 2.05. He rejoined Maclean for a few more minutes before they parted again. Maclean then went into Peter Jones department store, ostensibly to ask about chandeliers for Beaconshaw, but possibly only hoping to shake off the irritating 'dicks'. A surveillance report, perhaps exceeding the watchers' brief to stick to what they saw rather than interpreting, characterised the difference between the two men:

Guy Burgess seems to have something on his mind and is, in fact, obviously deeply worried. He will order a large gin … and will then pace the bar for a few seconds, pour the neat spirit down his throat and walk out, or order another and repeat the performance.

In the open he frequently shows indecision with, apparently, his mind in turmoil.

With Curzon there is an air almost of conspiracy between the two. It is quite impossible even in a bar to hear a word of what they are saying. It would seem likely that Burgess has unburdened himself to Curzon as the latter does not display any normal emotion when they are together.

Maclean was by now the calmer, the man who had asked to go to Russia over a year earlier, accepting and even looking forward to his new, unified life. Burgess was more in shock at their orders.

*

Thursday 24 May was a warm and sunny day, the first in an otherwise chilly month. Maclean arrived at Victoria and worked as normal in the morning. Meanwhile, in Sir William Strang's grand office in another part of the building a meeting took place between him (the Permanent Under-Secretary of State), Deputy Under-Secretary Sir Roger Makins, Assistant Under-Secretary Patrick Reilly, the head of security George Carey Foster, MI5 Director General Sir Percy Sillitoe and Sillitoe's deputy and successor Dick White. They were still very cautious about condemning such a trusted colleague. Sillitoe acknowledged that MI5 had gathered no further evidence against Maclean beyond the fact that secret information had been passed to the Russians in 1944 and 1945 and that the 'agent concerned appeared to have a wife resident in New York in 1944'. He was clear that 'the danger of attaching too much importance to coincidences was very real', although Maclean was 'the most likely suspect' and on those grounds an interview could take place.

Makins pointed out that from the political point of view 'this was the worst possible moment for anything to occur which would aggravate anti-British feeling in America' and if this leaked it 'would cause a sensation in the USA'. Sillitoe reminded the meeting that they would be going against intelligence-sharing protocols as well as perpetrating 'a breach of faith' if this was kept back, and claimed that he had sufficient influence with Hoover to get him to keep it quiet.

A new timetable of events was drawn up which included telling Arlington Hall and the FBI of the British work on the fragment which had led to their suspicion in the first week of June; a telegram swiftly followed by a visit from Sillitoe to Hoover on 12/13 June, and interrogation started between 18 and 25 June, a month hence. The last was an acknowledgement that Melinda was expected to have her baby on or about the 17th and this would enable them to search the house if necessary in her absence in the nursing home. Sir Roger Makins, who had shared the high-level atomic work with Maclean, confirmed that some papers had been kept from Maclean but by no means all of interest to him as 'nothing further could be done about this without arousing suspicion'. Robert Cecil, the deputy chief of the American Department, later said that boxes containing the more classified documents 'requiring special keys' were being withheld. (In the end, Maclean knew perfectly well from all sides that he was being watched.) Finally, it was agreed that Prime Minister Attlee and Foreign Secretary Morrison should be informed of the case the following morning, Friday the 25th, and the ball could start rolling on this extended programme.

As this meeting which was meant to decide his future was coming to its close, Maclean made the five-minute walk to the Reform Club for his lunch date with Anthony Blake. Tony Blake had been the third person on the holiday at Saint Jacut in 1934, alongside Cumming-Bruce, by now a senior lawyer. Blake was the only one of the three not to have had a holiday fling with an older French woman. He had seen little of Maclean recently as his old Cambridge friend had been in America and Egypt, but they had made this date when Blake heard that Maclean was back in the country. At lunch, Maclean talked of his 'personal plans in the immediate future in such a way as to give no suggestion that he was thinking of running away'. He was planning on going to France for his summer holiday and invited Blake to visit them in Tatsfield some time. Once again, Maclean's calmness, maybe numbness now that a decision had been made and it was out of his hands after the chaotic stress of recent times, is remarkable. Burgess was also in the Reform Club that day and the pair were confident enough to be seen to leave together at 3.00 at which point Burgess passed on the next day's schedule. After putting in an afternoon in his office, Maclean had a swift drink in the Windsor Castle pub by Victoria Station before catching the 6.48 home for his last night in England.

*

Friday the 25th was Donald Maclean's thirty-eighth birthday and it
had a low-key start. The boys had both come down with measles,
Melinda was exhausted and full of dread. Donald himself was cast
down but feeling the adrenalin surge of the day ahead. He arrived
at work at 10.00 and straight away rang his mother to see if she
would lunch with him that day: she was having lunch with a friend
and declined. If she had been able to see her favourite son on that
day, she was sure he would have 'made her privy to his troubles' and
an appeal from her would have prevented him from 'going off'. She
was never to see him again.

Maclean's next call was to his oldest and closest friends, Mary
and Robin Campbell, who had taken him in the previous summer
and whose friendship went back to his time in London just after
Cambridge, studying at Scoones and standing on the edge of debutante dances. Mary said she would come and pick him up at
lunchtime and they would celebrate the occasion. The only appointment in his diary was a reception in Belgrave Square that evening
for the Argentinian National Day, but he was never going to make
that as he had his birthday supper that evening. He also had to prepare to meet his new brother-in-law Bob Oetking, who worked for
the State Department, and see his sister Nancy, who were en route
from Beirut to London via Marseilles and Dover. Earlier in the
week he had arranged to take the Saturday morning off so that he
could be in Dover to collect them.

Just after his arrival in the office, his next-door neighbour, the
Assistant Labour Adviser Frederick Mason, came in with a telegram from the Dominican Republic with the news that a trade
unionist in that country had disappeared, presumed kidnapped.
Maclean 'spared it a languid glance'. Even on a normal day, this
would not be something to excite the most passionate diplomatist.
At midday he greeted Mary Campbell in the courtyard with the
brim of his black hat turned up, a sure sign that he was in good
spirits according to the code they had drawn up the previous year:
if the brim was down, her friend 'was feeling shaky and had to be
treated with kid gloves'. His habitual bow-tie was unusually jaunty
as well. Over their half-bottle of champagne and dozen oysters at

Wheeler's oyster bar in Soho, Donald was 'completely himself'. They discussed the imminent baby, to be named Melinda if it was a girl. Donald was planning to stay with the Campbells at Stokke Manor while his wife Melinda was in hospital.

As they left Wheeler's to make their way to Schmidt's where Robin was joining them for their grumpily served lunch, they bumped into Cyril Connolly, who had last seen Maclean ten days before to give him an Alka Seltzer breakfast. Connolly introduced himself to 'Sir Donald Maclean' to 'efface' that last meeting and to make the point that the 'calm and genial' Maclean was the man he was seeing now. Humphrey Slater was lunching with Connolly and saw him chatting with Maclean and the Campbells, but 'kept out of it as he did not wish to get involved with Maclean again' after the unpleasantness at the party earlier in the year the disclosure of which had been such an unwitting factor in Maclean's exposure. For his part, Connolly was pleased to hear from the Campbells later that afternoon that his friend was 'mellow and confidential' and that he did not need to visit his psychoanalyst so often. Maclean was at ease – it would not be possible to fool a critic as acute as Connolly – and seemed determined to put his closest friends at their ease too on this, their last meeting.

Maclean insisted on paying for lunch, birthday or not. Even though Schmidt's was very inexpensive and he would have little need of more British currency himself, he went to the Travellers on his way back to the office to cash a cheque for £10. While he was in the club, rather than waiting to get back he telephoned Geoffrey Jackson in the department and asked, rather incoherently as Jackson thought, if he would 'hold the fort' the next day, followed by some 'garbled explanation' about meeting his sister at the docks. His nerves were starting to get to him after he had said farewell, for all he knew for ever, to his dearest friends, his eccentrically favoured restaurant and his club, all of them part of the establishment which would shortly know of his betrayal. The man following him noted that he was 'steady on his feet' and back through the Foreign Office doors for the last time by 3.00.

His last official visitor was Señor Leguizamon, the Argentine Minister-Counsellor. Maclean took careful notes about Anglo-Argentinian trade negotiations to leave in his out-tray and wrote a letter to Sir Nevile Butler, Ambassador in Rio de Janeiro. Making sure that his absence would not come as a surprise to any of his colleagues, he put his head around John Curle's door to say he wouldn't be in in the morning. When Third Secretary Margaret Anstee brought him the last papers of the day he said, 'Can you manage on your own tomorrow? I can't come in. Something has cropped up.' The new recruit was 'flattered' by this trust and made a quip about there being no revolutions looming in the Americas to cope with.

Sir Roger Makins, his colleague at the AEC whose proceedings had been so comprehensively leaked to Moscow and the man who had made him head of the American Department, was the last person from the Foreign Office to see Maclean in London. They met by chance in the courtyard. Maclean was carrying a parcel under his arm and said that he was on his way home, reminding Makins that he would not be in in the morning as he had his sister staying with him. Makins, thinking he meant Harriet, Melinda's sister, whom he had met frequently in Washington, sent his regards to the sister-in-law and, as his 'main concern at that point was not to give the slightest hint that anything was amiss', left it at that. He did realise the potential importance of Maclean's absence the next day, however, and went back into the office to see if Carey Foster was still there, but the office was empty. After a 'pause for reflection', Makins, who was running late for his social engagements, 'concluded that as Maclean was under surveillance by the Security Service, his movements were being monitored and that therefore there was no need to start a hare by raising an alarm'. Nobody in the Foreign Office had been told about the watchers knocking off when Maclean boarded his train home. The watchers' last sighting of him was recorded as 'after a drink, he boarded the 6.10 p.m. train'.

That also means that once he was on that train to Oxted, the only witnesses to what happened over the next twenty-four hours were the highly unreliable Burgess and Melinda, who still had her husband's best interests at heart after all they had been through, and was now about to be tested as never before.

*

Guy Burgess had spent much of the day packing and telephoning. He bought the tickets for the *Falaise* on that evening's sailing from the Continental Booking Office in Victoria for himself and Bernard Miller (a medical student he had met on the *Queen Mary* coming back from New York at the beginning of the month), hired a cream Austin A40 saloon from a garage in Crawford Street, Marylebone, had lunch at the Reform as usual, where he ostentatiously looked at road maps of the north of England and discussed routes with a club servant, and purchased some dapper new clothes at Gieves in Old Bond Street. Returning to his flat, he packed his tweed suit, dinner jacket, shoes, socks and his one-volume collected edition of Jane Austen and, like Maclean, left London for the last time around 6.00. He also had with him 'a couple of old green Penguins', the Agatha Christie novels *The Murder of Roger Ackroyd* and *The Mysterious Affair at Styles*, handy because light reading might be useful in the days to come, as well as for when he needed a temporary pseudonym.

*

Melinda's is the only account of the rest of the evening, as she related it to Jim Skardon in the weeks that followed. She told him Donald had called her from his office that morning (later she said she thought he had rung the day before his birthday) to tell her that he would be bringing a friend of his, Roger Styles, home to dinner. But this call, we now know, was not registered by the Beaconshaw tap nor by Donald's office telephone intercept, so in fact he must have told her in person earlier in the week. She had never met Styles before but described him as about thirty-five, black-haired, medium build. Donald got home at 7.00, Styles arrived half an hour later and the two men 'wandered about in the garden for a bit' before sitting down at around 8.00. Dinner was 'perfectly normal ... three civilised people talking casually and amicably'. The meal itself was 'a special ham' she had spent the day preparing. She wasn't quite sure what Styles's 'means of livelihood' was but decided that he was 'in the publishing line' as 'his talk was mainly about books'. The men abruptly announced after dinner that 'they would be going off to see somebody, and might be away the night' which left her 'pretty incensed' as the boys both had measles, her sister-in-law was due to arrive with her husband the following day (in their own car, contrary to what Donald had told the Foreign Office about going to pick them up at Dover as his reason for taking the morning off) and she was uncomfortably pregnant. But Donald said it 'couldn't be put off' and went upstairs to pack the double-handled rawhide Gladstone bag he had bought in a market in Cairo with his pyjamas and 'night accessories'. She apparently 'thought his conduct pretty outrageous' given her condition but could not prevent him and Styles getting into Styles's 'new-looking, tan-coloured saloon car' and driving off at 10.00. She stayed up reading for a while in case Donald returned home but when it became apparent he had indeed gone for the night she went to bed. It will never be known whether they had a more passionate farewell than she claimed or what the tenor of their conversations had been in the previous days.

Melinda was certainly not worried enough to make any calls on the Saturday morning and maintained radio silence. 'Mrs Grist and her young women', minding the telephone intercepts in MI5's headquarters at Leconfield House, picked up nothing until 8.00 in the evening when Nancy Oetking, *née* Maclean, rang to say they were at Ashford on their journey from Dover and would arrive at about 9.30. Had Donald been telling the truth about their arrival time, he could have gone to work that morning and still have had plenty of time to meet them. In Nancy's mistaken recollection (as the telephone intercepts prove) they arrived at 6.00. Melinda told them as soon as they were in the house that Donald had rung to say he would be back late and they were not to delay dinner for him. As only three places had been laid the Oetkings accepted this, but do not appear to have enquired where their host was. At nine minutes past ten o'clock Lady Maclean telephoned to discuss arrangements for the next day with her daughter: Donald had suggested that

Nancy and Bob should rest in the morning after their journey, lunch at Beaconshaw and then go on to her afterwards. Nancy might want to check that with Donald while she was on the line. After a brief chat with Bob, Nancy came back and told her mother that she had confirmed with Melinda rather than her brother that they would lunch at Tatsfield.

There was no mention of Donald, who by this time had missed the train from Saint Malo to Paris, changed some money in a hotel and had his hair-raising taxi ride to Rennes to pick up the train at 1.18. He and Burgess were just having a largely liquid supper in a café in Paris before they got into their berths to Bern. They were well on their way, thanks to Melinda's care on the telephone as she had probably deduced that the taps were in place. Mrs Grist and her team reported 'there was nothing ... on the 26th to indicate Maclean was not at Tatsfield'.

*

Nancy realised that Donald was not simply on a bender the next morning when she found Melinda in the bathroom helping the boys to wash. Before Nancy could say a word of greeting, Melinda looked up at her: 'Your brother has disappeared.' Nancy had not seen much of Donald over the past few years and was 'taken aback' by Melinda's phrasing: 'What do you mean, my brother has disappeared? He's your HUSBAND, isn't he?' In the weight of the moment, Melinda could offer no answer and 'suggested we make ourselves some breakfast then get on our way to London as soon as possible'.

Bob and Nancy went alone to London and broke the news to her mother that Donald had disappeared and they had no news. Lady Maclean 'wasn't all that surprised that something was wrong' and said she could 'kick herself' for not accepting her son's urgent lunch invitation. Later that evening Nancy spoke to someone called 'Di' on the telephone and mentioned 'Donald and Linda' still being at Tatsfield. Either family loyalty and the need to protect her mother from Donald's drinking sprees were trumping her wartime MI6 training or Melinda had spun a story that would make Nancy believe Donald would be back by then: a bender would be plausible, one that would end before he had to go to the office the next day.

By Monday morning Melinda could afford to sound 'very upset' when her mother-in-law rang at 8.17 to say she was sorry to hear that Donald had not returned and had he come back the previous evening? Lady Maclean asked if 'everything was all right'. She feared another breakdown or marital rift, but was reassured by Melinda. This news was immediately reported to the Foreign Office, where Carey Foster confirmed to MI5 that Curzon had not come in, but 'thought there was no cause for alarm, since he had in fact asked for a day off'. When Carey Foster checked with Sir Roger Makins, the senior man, still believing that the watchers had Maclean permanently in their sights, said he thought he might have given him the Monday off as well. This was British *sang* at its most *froid*, given what they knew about Curzon. Although Melinda was to tell Geoffrey Hoare that she had rung the office on the Monday morning, Mrs Grist's record shows that in fact she did not do so until Tuesday 29 May at 10.58, over eighty hours since the *Falaise* had weighed anchor at Southampton and her husband, Britain's hardworking and brilliant servant, had had his last sight of his sleeping country as he moved on to his new life. The watchers had waited in vain at Victoria for the previous two mornings. Their last report dramatically signed off, 'Thereafter the great search started.'

17

Establishment

On the evening of 6 June 1951, eleven days after Maclean's last day in England, the front page of the London *Daily Express* was about to be put to bed with a lead story that was already gripping the nation: Alan Poole, a nineteen-year-old Royal Corps of Signals soldier had shot a policeman dead with a Sten gun and was now defying a siege of 200 armed officers at his home in the naval town of Chatham, Kent.

That same evening the paper's French bureau chief, a stocky, powerfully built, well-connected journalist of the old school, Larry Solon, was dining alone in the Restaurant de la Forêt, on the outskirts of Paris, when he was summoned to the telephone. Puzzled that anyone should know where he was, Solon was told by a man with a German accent 'Don't go round asking questions about missing persons,' and instructed to stop his 'Interpol nonsense'. Solon had visited the international police organisation's HQ the day before, desultorily following up a tip-off from the crime reporter of *France-Soir* that the French police had been asked to keep an eye open for two unnamed diplomats 'on a spree'. Solon's Interpol contact had told him that the whole affair was a matter for the British government as it was a 'political escape' and Interpol could not get involved unless it was a civil crime such as a kidnapping.

The realisation that 'this was no routine story of some Foreign Office employees lost on a binge' meant that Solon left his dinner half-eaten and hailed a taxi to take him to another favourite watering hole, a bistro near Montmartre. He was sure to find there his mole who specialised in smuggling stories, a former police officer who 'had lost his job because of his taste for cognac'. Solon hoped that he would not be too far gone and could be helpful enough to earn his next bottle. Once Solon had established that there were any number of ways that two men without papers could be spirited out of the country undetected, he moved on to meet a police contact he called 'Vincent' in the bar of the Scribe Hotel. Vincent said that in this instance what he knew was 'too hot' to pass on: 'there's going to be a hell of a blow-up'. He blamed the British for 'stupidly waiting a week before telling us about it', but let slip that there was 'not a chance' the diplomats were still in the country; 'the Stalinos had that one organised like the Monte Carlo rally'. This was enough for Solon to make a final call to a contact in the British Embassy who simply said, 'So it's out.'

Solon was ready to file the biggest story of his career, about 'two British Government employees' who had left 'with the intention of getting to Moscow ... to serve their idealistic purposes', possibly taking vital papers with them – a story that would bump the Chatham siege from the front page of his newspaper.

*

That night, Philip Jordan, the friendly Embassy Press Attaché from Washington days and now Prime Minister Attlee's press officer in Downing Street, was dining with the Muggeridges when he was called to the telephone. He came back, 'his face ashen', and excused himself as there were 'things he had to attend to'. He had been told for the first time about the next day's newspaper, and the disappearance of his friend. Kitty Muggeridge said that he looked 'so tragically ill it seemed that the bottom had dropped right out of his world'. The following morning she heard that Jordan had died of a heart attack in the night. When Kitty's husband Malcolm and others wrote a letter to the Prime Minister suggesting that his widow might be granted a pension they were met with a flat refusal. His association with the traitor, however ignorant he was of Maclean's wrongdoings, had made any special pleading bound to fail.

*

The Foreign Office realised that there was no point in keeping quiet any longer, their men had gone and they might was well get it over with. They put out a press release naming Maclean and Burgess, reporting them as missing and reassuring the taxpayer that 'Owing to their being absent without leave, both have been suspended with effect from June 1.'

*

Maclean's deputy, Robert Cecil, was coming back from a week's leave in France on Tuesday 29 May, and was surprised to have his passport checked on the road to Orly airport. The next day the staff greeted him with relief, 'Thank God you've turned up anyway.' He, too, was excluded from the real reason his friend and boss from Paris, Washington and now London might not have come in. When he heard Burgess had disappeared as well he only semi-facetiously assumed that 'the pair had gone off on a drunken spree, had perhaps accosted a burly French sailor and been dumped unceremoniously in the Seine.'

Maclean's other departmental colleagues found out what had happened from the *Daily Express* and the subsequent press release, in the same way as the rest of the world. Third Secretary Margaret Anstee assumed that Melinda was having her baby early when he did not appear the week after he had told her to keep an eye on things on Saturday 26 May. His office was orderly, his in- and out-trays containing 'exactly the kind of papers you would expect when someone had left on a Friday evening with the confident expectation of returning: not too much ... but not too little either'. Even on Wednesday the 30th when 'every cupboard and drawer' was being 'ransacked' under the 'watchful eye of the head of security' and they his colleagues were joking that 'Donald has done a Pontecorvo' the penny did not drop. It was 'totally unthinkable that a member of His Majesty's Foreign Service would ever betray his country', a concept that changed for ever with the double defection. Anstee and her colleagues in the Third Room were never spoken to or questioned about what Maclean had done or said in his brief time as their chief. There was no point.

*

Chaos and consternation had reigned in the top echelons of Whitehall for the previous ten days, and, in as much as the tightly buttoned denizens of those heights showed emotion, panic. They had been playing a desperate and unconvincing game of catch-up, trying to keep what had happened quiet. They knew it could not succeed. They alerted British ports to be on the look-out on the 29th, the Tuesday after the flight, and the day that Melinda reported her husband's absence. By that evening they knew about the *Falaise* and contacted 'Mr Reilly's friends' representative' in Paris, also known as the MI6 head of station, to enlist their help. On the 30th, while Maclean's office in the American Department was being turned over, Dick White flew to Paris (after an embarrassing delay when he arrived at Heathrow to find that his passport had expired) and French and French North African ports were put on the *qui vive*.

That same day, five days after the disappearance, all the Western European embassies except Madrid were notified and advised to invite the local security outfits to help them; however, the British Legation in Switzerland was cautioned not to alert 'internal police authorities' in that country 'in the interests of secrecy', as if anything could be kept from Moscow Centre's informers. If MI6 had moved faster and involved the Swiss police, the most famous defectors of the decade might have spent the next years of their lives in a British prison.

On 2 June a telegram went out saying that if the diplomats, missing for a week by now, were seen, their passports were to be impounded, and over the next few days mugshots were sent to the embassies. On the 6th, the day before the news broke, 'Mr Reilly's friends' in the South American embassies and in those of Mexico, Turkey, Greece, the Lebanon and Egypt were all informed of the disappearance. 'All posts except those behind the Iron Curtain, which had not so far been asked to obtain the help of the local security authorities to identify the men should they show up, were asked to do so' on 14 June, exactly a week after they had read all about the story in the newspapers and three weeks since the flight. The defection was discussed in Cabinet on the 8th, and on the 11th a short statement was made to the House of Commons confirming what had been splashed across the nation's breakfast tables for four days. Colonel George Wigg (who was later to lead the anti-establishment charge in Parliament that led to John Profumo's downfall) asked the Foreign Secretary if he would 'institute inquiries into the suggestion made in a Sunday newspaper that there is widespread sexual perversion in the Foreign Office'. Herbert Morrison deftly replied that 'I can only say that perhaps I have not been long enough at the Foreign Office to express an opinion.'

*

Once the decision had been taken not to tell the Americans about the earlier identification of Maclean, it would have been most politic to let them in on the defection right away, as soon as MI5 realised what had happened, days before the *Express* broke the story. With that opportunity gone, it might have been prudent and polite to have included them in these round robins to British embassies and high commissions from the start. But establishment embarrassment, shame tinged with arrogance, prevailed. The wire-service machines in the State Department were so full of the news on 7 June that they ran out of paper. Secretary of State Acheson was so furious at being given piecemeal the bulletins that his country's closest ally, with the two countries' troops fighting alongside each other for the second time in a decade, had kept from him for weeks that he ordered the press office not to waste time running up to his office with the tear sheets as they came in. Instead, a secretary in the press office read the material over the internal telephone to Acheson's secretary who took them in to her seething boss once she had typed them up. Some of the items, such as that '15,000 Secret Service men, master detectives, diplomatic personnel and policemen are combing Western Europe, peering in to cafés, hotels, airports and bordellos' in 'the largest manhunt in history' made for sensational, if even more enraging, reading that morning. When the mortally embarrassed British government later downplayed Maclean's knowledge in turn, Acheson was right on the mark when, recalling Maclean's time in Washington, he exclaimed, 'My God, he knew everything!'

That same afternoon Acheson appeared before the Senate inquiry into the dismissal of General MacArthur from the command of the UN forces in Korea. On being asked what reports he had had 'on the recent episode involving apparently Britons high in the foreign service' he could only answer that he had 'heard that on the radio this morning', after which he had 'had inquiry made at the British Embassy about it but they knew no more than the radio report'. Public political humiliation was heaped on top of the rage.

Philby had been shocked when he heard at the end of May that Burgess had gone as well as Maclean: exactly what he had told his friend not to do in the Chinese restaurant on their last night in New York. His 'consternation was no pretence', as it had been seconds before when Paterson told him that Maclean had successfully got away. Later that day Philby put his camera, copying equipment and other espionage accoutrements into the boot of his car and drove to the woods at Great Falls, where he had often been to fish the Potomac with James Jesus Angleton, one of the founders of the CIA and soon to become its head of counter-intelligence. There Philby, aware that he would soon have to lie as never before, buried the tools of his secret craft.

The FBI's Robert Lamphere was told of the men's absence on 31 May in such a manner that he assumed they were 'taking French leave' and continued pursuing the other angles about Homer's identity which his British friends had not dissuaded him from doing. It was now two and a half years since he had come across Homer, and Maclean's name was not ringing any bells. Mackenzie, security chief at the Embassy, admitted to his masters that 'We can probably only maintain this casual interest for a few days,' but they attempted to do so until the *Express* and US newspapers broke the story on the 7th. Only then did Philby and Geoff Paterson shamefacedly go to see Lamphere in his office in the FBI building, where, as the laconic agent recounted, 'to say the least, it was a rather uncomfortable meeting'. Lamphere was not alone when his thoughts went straight to where Philby's loyalties lay: 'I'm not saying much. They're not saying much. I know one thing for sure: I've been lied to for a long time by MI5 ... I'm thinking, "Maclean has fled. Burgess, who had been in Philby's house, has fled with him. Surely Philby tipped off Maclean.'"

Elsewhere in FBI headquarters an urgent teletype went from J. Edgar Hoover's office that spelt Maclean's name every way except the correct one asking that his New York address, non-existent as he had never lived in the city, from 1943 to 1945 be supplied. Such was the total lack of knowledge in the US law enforcement and espionage hierarchy of the spy they had been co-operatively and painstakingly helping to identify over the past three years. Sir Percy Sillitoe's office were already looking into flights and discussing where the MI5 Director General might stay on his second trip to Washington in a month to talk to Hoover about spies within the British ranks.

In keeping their own mortification under control by putting a brave face on things, the British seemed unaware of the possible humiliation they piled on their allies. On the day of the defection, Sir Roger Makins had submitted a paper on Anglo-American accord to Sir William Strang with an encouraging view from his recent visit to the USA that relations 'did not seem to be as bad as they looked from London'. That comment was presumably based on the timeline for telling the Cousins what was really going on and for Maclean's interrogation by the jovial Skardon and his permanent pipe, but Moscow Centre had moved at a different pace.

On top of Nunn May, on top of Fuchs, on top of Pontecorvo, this latest episode was made far more damaging by the opacity brought on by a combustible combination of fear and hubris in the weeks leading up to it. The State Department went on the moral offensive on the day the news broke. In a telegram forwarded from the Washington Embassy to the Foreign Office they 'pointed out' that for them 'repeated drunkenness, recurrent nervous breakdowns, sexual deviations and other human frailties are considered security hazards'.* Carey Foster, a year after the disappearance, wrote a secret

---

* It was good news for McCarthy and his followers in their attacks on the State Department that they were now able to equate homosexuality and treachery. They were soon to allege that there were 110 homosexual State Department officers in Taiwan alone.

and spirited cultural attack on this attitude in a memorandum to members of the Foreign Office, saying that while homosexuality was still illegal and therefore open to blackmail, it 'could be said to have almost respectable antecedents in the country of Wilde and Byron'.

*

Sir Percy Sillitoe had anyway been travelling to Washington in mid-June to tell the FBI that Maclean was shortly going to be brought in for questioning. He stuck to his plans even though he was now entering a bitter and less collaborative atmosphere. He had made his name as a senior policeman in Glasgow, scourge of the razor gangs that terrorised the city in the 1930s. That experience could not prepare him for the tough time he had in Washington DC. His telegram to his deputy, Dick White, on 14 June highlighted how tricky it was working for a secret service that chose to keep its secrets from its allies, in this case Walter Bedell Smith and Allen Welsh Dulles, Director and future Director of the CIA. 'Dulles asked me point blank if we had knowledge [of the] activities of Maclean ... from cryptographic sources. I evaded the issue by implying that such sources were not my business ... He immediately changed the subject.' Dulles presented himself as a gentleman, but he harboured a deep mistrust of the British and their clubbiness and inbreeding (as he saw it), which he had already observed at length from the viewpoint of both ruler and ruled when he was teaching in India in the 1920s. Whatever his inner reaction to their evasions, he was anyway not surprisingly most interested in Philby, a more present danger who had been summoned back to London at Bedell Smith's insistence to be questioned by Jim Skardon about his association with Burgess.

Sillitoe was franker about his travails with Lamphere and Hoover in a letter to his colleague James Robertson, in which he admitted to being 'economical with the truth' (as a later civil servant said about a later espionage matter) with them on his first day in the capital: 'I stuck to May 25th as the date on which we had received the new [material about Homer], but threw in that I had heard about the possibility of such a recovery being made a week or two earlier ... I admitted that we had Curzon under surveillance before he skipped, but only in London and that only as part of our investigation of all seven hot suspects.' That 'hot' is giving the impression of an exciting scenario with six more suspects than they had had for some time before the defection.

Sillitoe described his second day with an overwrought British metaphor about the weather: 'the wind blew cold' as he was 'hotly interrogated'. He was asked, quite reasonably, why he had not handed over the names of all of his seven imagined candidates and why he was still not doing so. Lamphere and his FBI colleagues, outraged by the realisation of how much had been withheld from them, 'bombarded' Sillitoe with a 'series of questions which had obviously been prepared and which were calculated to trip me'. He felt he 'had probably made a mess of it' as he emerged from his interrogation 'wringing wet', not an accustomed situation for a man of his standing in the world. Sillitoe was astonished, as well he might be given his service's lackadaisical performance, about the speed and 'thoroughness with which [the Americans] have gone about this task' of investigating Maclean in the previous week since they got the news: they had even found out the name of his French maid in Washington from 1944 with a view to questioning her if she was still in the country. While he might have been embarrassed as his country's emissary and as a security chief, he seemed blithely unaware – or unconcerned – about the intelligence and national security consequences both for his country and for the US: 'I cannot honestly say that I have been working tremendously hard, but it has all been somewhat worrying. However, I am enjoying myself immensely … ' He might have hoped he was running the sweetshop in Eastbourne that had been his retirement plan after his police service.

*

Both 'Lady Curzon' and 'Mrs Curzon' had been interviewed by Skardon, six days after the defection, in Lady Maclean's flat. Melinda happened to be there, awaiting her own mother's arrival in London from Paris. Alan Maclean was also there, having been summoned back from New York, where he was private secretary to Gladwyn Jebb, British Ambassador to the United Nations. He was

grilled by customs at London Airport when they saw his middle
and last names on his passport as if the fugitive might be sneaking
back into the country under a thin disguise. None of these witnesses was able to shed any light on where Donald might have gone.
Sir William Strang had been keen not to involve Melinda until
after she had had her baby, but when Skardon encountered her by
chance in Lady Maclean's flat she was at least able to confirm the
identity of 'Roger Styles' from a photograph of Burgess.

*

The day after the *Express* broke the story, telegrams arrived for Lady
Maclean and Melinda, despatched from the Post Office in the Place
de la Bourse in Paris at ten o'clock the previous night, though obviously they had been kept in hand by Moscow Centre's people in Paris
for several days. Lady Maclean's read 'Am quite all right. Don't worry.
Love to all. Teento.' The childhood nickname, a condensation of
'Teeny Don', was a clear indication that he was behind it; the handwriting and the continental crossing of the numeral '7' in her address
was an equally clear indication that he did not write it. Melinda's telegram was equally anodyne. It had the wrong county given for
Tatsfield and was full of clumsiness as well mistakes in English:

MRS MACLEAN MELINDA. BEACON SHAW. TATSFIELD
NEAR WESTERHAM. SURREY. ENGLAND.
HAD TO LEAV UNEXPECTEDLY. TERRIBLY SORRY.
AM QUITE WELL NOW. DON'T WORRY DARLING.
I LOVE YOU. PLEASE DON'T STOP. LOVING ME.
DONALD

In spite of attempts by MI5 and the FBI to decode this telegram,
dividing the letters up into different groups, trying to find meaning
in the shorter telegram being exactly half the length of the longer,
more verbally padded one; to find the real meanings behind the idio-
syncratic spelling and its pointless assertion that Donald had not
been well before and now was, the only conclusions to be drawn were

that Donald had almost certainly been involved in the telegrams, hence 'Teento', but in the end they had not been written by him.

The telegrams were the final piece of intrigue the newspapers needed to follow up on the Fleet Street bombshell from the day before. The next day's *Daily Telegraph* had three headlines in block capitals:

ALL EUROPE HUNT FOR TWO BRITONS
FOREIGN OFFICE MEN MISSING WITHOUT LEAVE
RIDDLE OF TELEGRAMS FROM PARIS

Around the world, the story made headlines. In New York it was categorically said that the two men had taken 'Hush-Hush Data' with them. That Maclean had worked on the atom bomb itself, the subject of the century, was fertile ground for media fearmongering. This was a story that would keep journalists excited, creative and busy for years to come.

*

Sightings of the fugitives poured in. The *Daily Mail* offered a £10,000 reward for any information that led to a confirmed sighting. Rumours were followed up that the pair were hiding in a chateau outside Paris; or they were in Monte Carlo, Berlin, Naples, Rome, Vienna and Barcelona. They were spotted in a bar in Cannes, identified by 'Gaston, a café caricaturist and an expert in faces', and in a restaurant in Prague. Letters from clairvoyants took up valuable security time if only in the reading and filing. Maclean was recognised in a Greyhound bus station in New York by a woman who managed to identify him by his 'very black hair and protruding front teeth'. Dušan Miljković, a Yugoslav railway guard, was a credible enough witness to be interviewed by the head of Chancery in the Belgrade Embassy to confirm his evidence that two men matching the fugitives' description had travelled from Belgrade to Istanbul, third class, on the early-morning train on 3 June. 'They had little luggage.'

The photographer Humphrey Spender, brother of the poet Stephen and by chance a fellow Greshamian, and the writer Geoffrey Grigson were touring the West Country for *Picture Post* and were arrested in a chemist's shop in Warminster where they had gone to develop some film. Delighted that he had caught the spies pursuing their nefarious tradecraft in Wiltshire, the diligent chemist marched them to the local police station 'wondering which of us was Burgess and which was Maclean' before a call to their editor got them released.

German police arrested two men on a train in Beggendorf who turned out to be SIS 'personalities' on the same hunt. A letter 'From an old pal of Maclean' was hand-delivered to the US Embassy in

London which contained a so-called 'deposition' dictated by Maclean to the author on 24 May in which Maclean stated that as he was 'haunted and burdened' by what he knew of official secrets and in particular 'by the content of high-level Anglo-American conversations' by which the British government had 'betrayed the realm' to the US, he was planning to 'cross the Iron Curtain into the Free World' to deliver up his knowledge to Stalin so that the British people might be alerted in time 'to wrest control of their destiny from the wretches who have stolen it'.

Closer to home, well-wishers spotted the two cleverly disguised men throughout 'the realm'. A chemist in Westerham called in MI5 to tell them about the tall man who came in at weekends to hire his dark room and do his own photographic developing, one time leaving behind a charred piece of paper with the Foreign Office crest on it; he made sure his name got into the newspapers. Goronwy Rees was rung in the middle of the night to be told that Burgess had been seen leaving Reading Station on his way to visit his old friend at his home in Sonning.

What had become of Burgess and Maclean was not known for sure, although it did not take much guesswork among the well-informed and highly educated minds of MI5, the Foreign Office, the State Department, the FBI and the CIA to work out where they had ended up. It was not until a defection on the other side of the world three years later that the truth began to emerge.

*

Vladimir Mikhailovich Petrov was a corpulent, bespectacled man. He had been working in the Maritime Section of the MGB, which became the KGB in 1954, in Moscow. A previous posting in Sweden where he had kept an eye on Soviet merchant seamen on the fringes of the Soviet empire on the lower Danube had given him a taste for Western living. He was pleased to be appointed Third Secretary to the Soviet Embassy in Australia's capital, Canberra, at the start of 1951. He soon came to the notice of the Australian Security Intelligence Organisation (ASIO), who saw through his diplomatic cover role, 'because of his indulgence in good living and heavy drinking', an indulgence to which his rubicund appearance attested. ASIO began 'studying ways and means of organising his defection'. The three-year courtship of Petrov was consummated on 3 April 1954, when he took asylum and £5,000 to hand over all the documents he had.

Although the papers Petrov brought with him were not of great value and he failed to get any of the current cipher books from his Embassy, he did, at last, bring news of Burgess and Maclean now that the trail was three years cold. Also serving in Canberra as Second Secretary was Filip Kislitsyn, who had been working with documents sent out by Maclean and Burgess in Moscow in 1949 after his time in London as a cipher clerk; his section was so full of material that much of it had never been translated. In 1953, when Melinda was once again sensationally in the press, Kislitsyn had told Petrov what he knew about the Maclean case and his know-ledge of the meetings that took place in Moscow. He related a simple plan, which saw the two men safely inside Soviet territory by the time the Foreign Office and security services even realised they were missing.

*

The SS *Falaise* had 200 passengers aboard that Whitsun Bank Holiday weekend, most of whom were safely in their cabins when the last arrivals showed up minutes before the gangplank was raised, their car abandoned on the dockside with the keys still in the ignition. The former diplomats stayed sleepless below decks after the ship had docked in the rain at 9.00 the following morning to ensure that most of their shipmates were disembarked and in the cafés and shops of Saint Malo. They remained on board for their last English breakfast of bacon and eggs, lingering over them so long that they had to take a taxi for the forty-three-mile journey to Rennes to catch up with the Paris train. Or perhaps they assumed Saint Malo station was being watched and so deliberately timed their exit. The taxi driver noted that 'they hardly exchanged a word with me or between themselves' during the drive. He dropped them off in the main square rather than at the railway station in

Rennes: maybe the two tall Englishmen would be less noticeable walking in than being driven to its entrance.

They reached Maclean's beloved Paris in the early afternoon; the men had crossed the city to the Gare d'Austerlitz and from there caught the night train to Bern, the Swiss capital, pulling in at about 6.00 a.m. on Sunday the 27th. Nicholas Elliott, who regarded Kim Philby as one of his greatest friends, even as he was being betrayed time after time, was head of station in Bern, but was made aware of the escape only when it was too late. If only they had got there two days later when the alert had gone out, they might have been slipped the 'decanter of poisoned Scotch' that one of Elliott's fellow spooks had prepared on the grounds that they had been ordered to apprehend the suspects 'at all costs and by all means'. False passports that did not need to be made to the exact British paper specifications as no British customs and immigration officer was going to see them were waiting for them in the Soviet Embassy, and Maclean, possibly the calmer and more psychologically prepared of the pair, picked them up. There was a motor show on in the city: Bern was full of strangers, so two more were not particularly noticed. The watch on the Soviet Embassy was still days away.

The perilous part of the plan was now: it was Sunday and there was no flight out on the route allotted them until Tuesday. The Soviets assumed that Maclean at least would be missed on the Monday, but had not taken into account the near-paranoid British confusion and desire to keep the defections quiet, let alone Melinda's complicit silence. The pair of runaways 'collapsed in a hotel suffering from ... the opposite of euphoria' as the adrenalin wore off. Maclean lay on his bed, calm and focused now that he had no agency in his immediate future, smoking and reading Burgess's edition of Jane Austen. His fellow defector went to look at the cars on display in the city.

On the Tuesday, as the hunt got going from London, they took the Stockholm flight, which touched down briefly in Prague. There Maclean and Burgess were 'immediately taken in hand by KGB agents' and were destined to spend the rest of their lives in Soviet territory. The trail was already stone cold by the time the *Daily*

Express and the British and American authorities learned of Maclean's escape. On 12 June Guy Liddell recorded in his diary that 'GCHQ reported an increase in volume of traffic between London and Moscow as from 25th May ... Two or three days later there was an increase in the traffic from Bern, and about the 4th or 5th June an increase in traffic from Prague,' which corroborates the men's movements as well as the care taken in seeing them to their new home. But the report came too late to be of any use in the hunt for them.

Nobody in the West was to hear of them again for years.

*

Donald Maclean had left the stage and was about to begin the last act in the turbulent drama of his life, for the first time since his early boyhood no longer playing two roles simultaneously. His leading lady was, as always, waiting in the wings.

18

Into the Wilderness

Throughout the febrile months of that summer of 1951 following the defection, Melinda and her children were under siege, enduring their personal agonies as a public drama. Here was a Cold War story that could sell millions of newspapers, and the editors made the most of the wife abandoned in the last days before her confinement and the two young boys left fatherless by the traitor who had had the best Britain had to offer handed to him on a plate. Sir William Strang, mindful of Melinda's pregnancy and the psychological strain she would be suffering, ordered that she should not be questioned for some time after the birth of her child. But when Skardon, under the name of Seddon, went to interview Lady Maclean in her Kensington flat on 30 May, he found Melinda there, waiting for her mother's delayed arrival from Paris at the air terminal in nearby Cromwell Road. 'Mrs Curzon' seemed 'to be very self-contained', 'worried' but 'annoyed rather than disturbed'. He came away with the impression that she believed Donald was on a bender, that all would be explained on his return from his 'escapade', and that meanwhile she was grateful for the 'trouble and kindness shown by the Foreign Office'.

By the time the newspaper story broke on 7 June and her husband was named in the press release, Melinda had much less reason to be calm as her house came under siege from the press. When Mrs Dunbar arrived, she first of all accused the Foreign Office of denying her daughter information and later of abandoning her. In fact, they had no information to offer her, and all they could do was instruct her not to talk to the press. Robert Cecil, now acting head of the American Department, out of concern went to Tatsfield with his wife on 9 June and found the gates locked and the blinds drawn against a throng of reporters and photographers. Fergus finally spotted the visitors from an upstairs window and Melinda let them in. She was 'in a great deal of distress', desperately worried about the birth of her child after the stillbirth and miscarriages, anxious about money now that Donald's salary had stopped coming in and there was the mortgage to be paid, unsure how to cope with the fatherless boys. A few days after this visit she went into hospital and twenty days after her husband disappeared she gave birth to a daughter, Melinda (distinguished within the family as 'Pink Rose' or 'Pinkers' when she was a baby, and 'Mimsie' afterwards), named just as Donald had told Mary Campbell she would be at lunch on his last day. Her mother and sister Harriet were on hand at Tatsfield for the two weeks she was in hospital.

Since the first stillbirth, having children had been risky for Melinda's health, hence her long-planned and lengthy hospital stays. She felt more than usually fatalistic this time and wrote a remarkable letter to Donald which she kept by her until it was found among her effects two years later. He would get to read it at the same time as the rest of the world – when it was published. The letter demonstrated her great courage and the pride she took in their achievements, just as it showed the strength in their relationship at a point where she cannot have known whether he was alive or dead – features that are especially moving in the context of what she had been through in the previous few years. It stands as a powerful tribute to her commitment to Donald, to her generosity, above all to her love and faith in his own courage, and it was a testament to her belief that he would still be a father to the children after she had gone:

My Dearest Donald
If you ever receive this letter it will mean I shan't be here to tell you how much I love you and how really proud of you I am. My only regret is that perhaps you don't know how I feel about you.

I feel I leave behind and have had a wonderful gift in your love and the existence of Fergie and Donald. I am so looking forward to the new baby. It seems strangely like the first time and I think I shall really enjoy this baby completely. I never forget, darling, that you love me and am living for the moment when we shall be together again.

All my deepest love and wishes for a happy life for you and the children.

Melinda

*

During that first summer, and thereafter, Alan Maclean was the reliable conduit between Skardon, the Foreign Office, his mother and Melinda. The comforting policeman became a friend and even solace to Lady Maclean over the ensuing years to the point of enabling her to take pride in her son's notoriety.* He was also was key in providing the moment of comedy that such a tragic drama requires to lighten its impact. Skardon told Alan that now that MI5 had thoroughly investigated the belongings the fugitives had left on the *Falaise* he could go to pick them up from Waterloo Station, and that the office would be sending a car for him and Colonel Bassett, Burgess's stepfather. Lady Maclean insisting on buying her youngest child a new suit for this important expedition, and dug out some of his late father's fermented aftershave to make sure he was presentable. The Colonel was impeccably turned out in his pinstripes and bowler hat, and smelling very expensive. Jim Skardon too was in attendance.

The Waterloo stationmaster himself led them to his enormous office and invited them to sort through the 'various piles of sad-looking objects and clothes' laid out beside two collapsed canvas

---

* Nancy Maclean went to the bank with her mother, and a 'new girl' asked to see her identification. Her mother said 'in a voice loud enough for the whole bank to hear, "Do you mean to say you don't know who I am? I'm Lady Maclean, mother of the Missing Diplomat."'

bags on a table. After a brisk spell in which each man went 'turn and turn about', picking more or less at random, all that was left were 'a pair of really dirty, torn black pyjamas' and a pair of 'revolting socks', full of holes and 'stiff with dried sweat'. Both Alan and the Colonel, who particularly loathed the outing because 'he had never liked Guy and was manifestly upset by his wife's obsessive affection for her son', insisted that the pyjamas had to belong to the 'other's chap', until Alan 'in a moment of inspiration' came up with the line that Donald thought wearing pyjamas was a 'sin against nature' so they could not possibly be his. Even the redoubtable Colonel had to concede defeat in the face of this irrefutable claim, but insisted that the socks had to go to the Macleans in return. On their way out, Alan took heart when he saw a wire-mesh bin on the station concourse. The offending items were no more. As the three men parted on the steps of Colonel Bassett's club, Alan asked Skardon if he had enjoyed his morning. 'I've had a *lovely* time,' said the jovial fellow.

Alan's good nature was needed as it became clear that he would not be given work by the Foreign Office, to the point that he felt he had no option but to resign. This, too, reached the newspapers, hungry for any Maclean-related snippets. The Foreign Office had the grace to say publicly that he was not suspected of sharing the sins of the brother in any way. Over thirty years later Donald was able to explain to Alan that he had wished that his younger brother, who had from a young age looked up to him in the absence of a father, had not wanted to emulate him by entry into the Diplomatic Service, but he could find no way of saying so at the time. Through the establishment friendship with Lady Violet's son, Mark Bonham Carter, Alan went to work for the publisher William Collins before moving to Macmillan and on to a distinguished career as a publisher, in which his diplomatic skills were invaluable and in the course of which he became very close to the Foreign Secretary, Prime Minister and Chairman of the firm, Harold Macmillan.

*

Although by the end of July the environs of Beaconshaw were no longer thronged by reporters, Mrs Dunbar, fully in control by now, decided that the family needed a break and should go away. They made plans to go to Beauvallon, near Saint Tropez in the South of France where Melinda's sister Catherine had rented a house in the middle of August. Just before they set off, the postman knocked on the door with two registered letters addressed to Mrs Dunbar. Both were from St Gall, a town near Zurich, one from the Swiss Bank Corporation and the other from the Union Bank of Switzerland. Each contained a banker's draft for £1,000 from Mr Robert Becker made out to Mrs Melinda Dunbar. The Maclean name was no doubt too explosive to be used. As Mrs Dunbar had lent her daughter and son-in-law £2,000* to buy Beaconshaw, the sum was probably not a coincidence.

Neither Melinda knew of a Robert Becker and they got in touch with MI5 who immediately sent detectives to St Gall where they got the predictable brush-off from a Swiss bank asked to divulge its client's details, other than the confirmation of what was stated on the form accompanying the banker's draft, that Mr Becker had been staying in the Hotel Central in Zurich and had given a New York address. The FBI established that Mr Becker's stated address located him somewhere in the middle of Central Park. Mrs Dunbar was pragmatically advised that she might as well cash the cheques as there was no point in trying to return them.

Two days later Melinda received her own letter, this time signed by her husband. It was undated and had no address but was postmarked Reigate and Redhill, twenty-five miles from Tatsfield. The handwriting was shaky and the somewhat stilted but deeply sensitive and loving letter, establishing Melinda's innocence to official readers, aches with yearning and absence, and a wish to soothe the pain he has caused, while giving away nothing of his whereabouts; it is acknowledging and trying to assuage grief and make things better for the family that he might reasonably expect never to see him again, including his new daughter:

---

* About £75,000 in today's money.

Darling

A friend going to England has said that he will get this to you and I am so happy to be in touch again with your sweet self. I cannot tell you why I left or where I am. I must still lean on the strength of our love to answer for me. Darling, I think of you always and carry you close in my heart and I am sure that you do the same.

I do not know what you must have thought of me leaving you without any money. At my request a friend is now sending you two thousand pounds. It is simpler to send it to your mother's credit, but of course it is meant for you.

Oh what good news about little Melinda! Well done, darling. I was so happy, especially for you. I wonder if she is dark … like all true Melindas; quiet or tempestuous? Perhaps you do not know yourself yet. I can well imagine you two together.

Tell the boys I think of them always. I expect Fergie is helping with the Aga[*] and such things while I am away. I wonder what Donald has in his doctor's bag and whether he practised on himself when they had measles. Please hug him specially from me.

Please give my special love to Mama and tell her that I am close to you all and am sure that, with her great courage, she will not worry or be cast down. I think often, too, of Andy, Nancy and Alan and send them all my affection.

But this letter is for you, darling, and it tries to say that you are so much part of me that I feel that you are always with me and to ask that you will, despite everything, believe in my love. Have faith in me and be of good heart. Be sure that I will write again and that I am well and quite alright.

With all my love, dearest snoop,

Donald

He must have guessed in this personal agony that a drama was being played out in public in England and wanted to bolster

---

[*] The Aga was a stove that needed stoking each day.

Melinda, not least to give her an alibi in case she was to make any confession.

Melinda kept this love letter in her handbag for many years, and her mother noticed that she drew strength from it, panicking when on one occasion more than two years later she thought she had lost it. At a time when doubts about her own future path might have been starting to set in, her husband's words must have gone some way to affirming that she had been right to stand by him, that their lives together had some sort of nobility and purpose that could not have been achieved had she remained an East Coast debutante.

But this final confirmation that her husband was in the pay of a foreign power, as nobody thought for a moment that he could have squirrelled away more than a year's salary in a Swiss bank, caused a turn in MI5's treatment of her: they were enraged that they were not able to locate him. Instead of Skardon, who apparently had a knee injury, a different officer came to talk to her, accusing her of knowing of Maclean's Communism and of having plans to join him. Melinda said that she 'flared up' and said to the policeman that until he proved it to be the case 'I'll never believe he was a traitor to his country.' Nothing of this interview appears in Skardon's friendlier, meticulous and detailed record. Melinda was relieved to leave England for the South of France a few days later against Foreign Office advice. The press pack initally followed the family, but soon the lack of story and spiralling expense accounts meant that their attentions dwindled. They were left to lament that the telephone had been disconnected in the villa, but otherwise stayed away. After a month, the family returned to Tatsfield.

*

A week after his letter to Melinda, an unrepentant Donald wrote to his mother in a hand more like his own. He hoped to see her again soon and 'though I still cannot explain it myself, leaving was the best course and that I have done nothing of which I am ashamed and of which you need be ashamed for me'. Lady Maclean held firm until her death to her conviction that her favourite son was working as a double agent in Moscow (even as Stalin and Beria were exploring that possibility themselves) and was able to derive from this letter the comforting idea that he was still pursuing the path of patriotic righteousness followed by her late husband. Perhaps the solicitous Skardon, once he had realised that she knew nothing of value to his investigation, did little to dissuade her from this view.

*

The next few months were especially tough for the family. After what they now knew of the runaways' political past, the Foreign Office explored ways of preventing other undesirables from joining their ranks through the Cadogan Committee of Enquiry into the affair. But all the office could really do was set up positive vetting in early 1952 for all and that particular attention be paid to peccadilloes which laid anyone open to blackmail. They had little interest in or sympathy for Melinda, nor had the media. She was living off her own small income and what her mother gave her. Fergus and Donald were subjected to some predictable bullying in school, taunted by claims that their treacherous father was dead. Most of all, and seen only by a few, Melinda missed Donald and tried to assess her feelings about him as well as her future as the family marker of Christmas and the start of 1952 went past. She went into hospital in London for a minor operation in the spring and was visited by Clare Hollingworth from her Cairo days. Melinda told Hollingworth that she had decided to move on in life, that she was no longer in love with Donald but in the absence of any news from him did not know how to go about things: to return to America was a big move and for now she felt exhausted by what she had lived through in the past three years and wanted to keep life more or less steady for the children, including her new-born namesake. As Hollingworth's husband Geoffrey Hoare put it, 'She was like a patient after a long and wasting illness who simply could not gather strength again.' Whatever she and Donald had discussed on those last, dreamlike days together the previous May, this exhaustion and uncertainty in her rings true. On the anniversary of the defection the press descended again, and she wrote despairingly to Harriet, 'I don't know whether to be sad or glad: people are asking me out and strangely enough I am in such a state of hyper-sensitivity that almost all social contacts exhaust me to a frightful degree. I really feel nearer to going off my rocker than I ever have.' Melinda seemed to Hoare to be in a 'black depression . . . convinced her marital life was definitely over never to be recommenced'.

Mrs Dunbar put pressure on her to go abroad. Fergus would find life even tougher in the more sophisticated environment of secondary school and eventually she agreed to live in Geneva for a spell from September. With real sadness she left the only home she had ever owned, and in which she had briefly been happy, and rented it to strangers. Before going she gave a last interview to MI5 in which she once again denied any knowledge of her husband's treachery and spoke to the *Daily Express*: 'I have waited for over a year for news of my husband. Now I am starting a new life for my children . . . I may have to come back to this country to wind up my affairs, but I shall never come back to live.'

After leaving England, Melinda first went on a holiday with Harriet in Normandy in which the ceaseless rain did little to lift her spirits. She drove to Geneva on 3 September in her new American Chevrolet car, a gift from her mother and a symbol of her new life.

*

Melinda was therefore out of the country as the ferocious gossip intensified, more particularly among Donald's group of friends. On 21 September 1952, one of those friends, Cyril Connolly, wrote the first of his two long articles for the *Sunday Times*, later published in a book called *The Missing Diplomats*. He was frank (and as stylish as always) about the drinking, Burgess's homosexuality and Maclean's behaviour in his latter days in the Foreign Office, and free with his speculation about the origins and enactment of the men's treachery.

Melinda was out of the Home Office's jurisdiction by this time, but Lady Maclean's telephone was still being tapped against the unlikely event that her son would ring in from wherever he was or that a Russian accent might be contacting her with news. She was as appalled as might be expected of a mother (and a mother brought up in the reign of Queen Victoria at that) who read that 'the child whose craving for love is unsatisfied ... eventually may try to become a revolutionary'. She said on the telephone to her relation Buddy Devitt that the articles 'read as though Connolly was a nasty little boy looking at the world through a dirty window', but the listeners got the overall impression that the family 'seemed to dismiss the articles fairly lightly'. Patrick Leigh Fermor described a lunch party attended by the former Minister of Information and British Ambassador to France Duff Cooper as 'a regular tempest of anger and indignation ... [Duff] grew red in the face until the veins stood out about C's exposing his friends as drunkards, traitors, sadists, Bolsheviks etc. etc., cashing in on friends' failings ... ' Leigh Fermor's was the only voice at this gathering of those of the same ilk as the missing men to speak up for the articles, which although they taught those present nothing new 'rehabilitated them both as human beings ... not the shifty and guilty shadows that have emerged in the press so far'. Connolly's articles were the first, and in many ways the most astute, of the books and articles that were to flood the marketplace over the ensuing years with varying degrees of speculation masquerading as fact, most of which found their way to Russia where they were read and loathed by their subject Maclean for their hyperbole and inaccuracies. At the time, though, he had no idea of the extent to which his and Burgess's story was obsessing the London intelligentsia.

Once Melinda had put the boys into the International School in Geneva she finally explained to them what had happened to their father, reporting to Harriet that 'their worst fear seems to be that I might vanish too ... Fergie is horrified that [Donald] might have done something wrong at the Office and the FO will be very angry when he returns. Little Donald said perhaps he had gone to India ... that would be a good place to hide.' She emphasised the strength and goodness of their father's moral and political beliefs. Fergus announced to some children with whom he was playing a war game that 'My daddy wants to stop all wars.'

The family moved into a small, dark apartment in the rue des Alpes, with a view of the lake, and settled down to make it home. But Melinda remained 'so completely depressed' at this confirmation that she was now bringing up the children alone, an object of pity and fascination, that she could not see how to 'summon up whatever it takes to start a new life'. She went to visit Harriet in Paris, who had never seen her spirits lower. Alan went to Geneva to visit her in early October. They discussed whether Donald was behind the Iron Curtain and whether she would go to join him if she was asked; she said 'firmly' that she would not. She wrote to her sister on New Year's Day 1953 that she 'couldn't have been happier to see 1952 go', but even after a full year in which she had got used to not hearing any news of her husband she 'remained in a dismally unstable state', with the 'horrid feeling that almost anything might push me over the precipice'. It was the first time since the age of twenty-one that, whatever the roller-coaster of their lives together, she had been out of touch with the man who in spite of everything stuck by his commitments, personal as much as political.

*

Stalin died in March 1953. After the *coup d'état* led by Nikita Khrushchev, his sinister security chief Beria was executed (among other charges for being a spy for the British) in December. The temperature of the Cold War rose a couple of degrees. It seemed the Soviet Union would become a more open place without the ruthless control of the two tyrants.

At Stalin's death, Melinda changed. She seemed anxious not to be away from home for too long, as if it had been hoped for or even agreed that Donald would find a way of getting in touch with her when the tyrant had gone. She showed unaccustomed indecisiveness over which destination to choose for the family holiday that year. She told her mother in May that she was going to accept an invitation from some American friends to go to Majorca and bought the tickets on 10 June to leave as soon as the boys finished school on the 30th. She wrote to Harriet that she was 'in a fever of preparation for going away', sorting out clothes, attending to her business affairs and preparing the flat for subletting. On the 30th she suddenly changed her mind, deciding she wanted mountain air, and took the boys to the remote Alpine town of Saanenmöser instead. Five days later she was back, saying that trip had been 'disappointing' and she was going to rebook for Majorca after all. They set off nearly a month late, on 23 July, after their unplanned mountain excursion, an ideal place for an unremarked rendezvous with an emissary from the MGB.

Also staying in Cala Ratjada, Majorca, 'an odd place with a small foreign colony, largely American', was D. A. Wilson, a straitlaced civil servant from the Board of Trade who reported that Melinda's host, 'a very obvious pansy', was an American named Douglas MacKillop, and that it was common knowledge that the family was 'going off somewhere shortly' since Melinda had given MacKillop's maid 'a quite unusually large amount of clothes and cosmetics etc.', that seemed 'exceptional' even by extravagant American standards. Fergus and Beany said to another child they had met on the beach that the photographs their new playmate had taken could not be forwarded to them: 'you can't send them on as we are going away and we don't know where we are going'.

After a few of weeks of sunshine and beach life the family returned to Geneva on Monday 7 September to find that the new term had been postponed a week until the 15th. On Friday the 11th, Melinda came back from the weekly market 'looking elated', according to her mother. She explained that in the market she had bumped into Robin Muir, an old friend from her Cairo days, and he had invited them to stay with him and his wife that very weekend in his villa at Territet, at the other end of Lake Geneva. When her mother asked her if it might not be easiest to leave the children behind with her and their nanny, Melinda airily said that was no problem as Muir had a 'children's nurse'. As the villa was apparently hard to find, Muir had said he would meet her in the lobby of a hotel in Montreux that afternoon. Melinda had also cashed a substantial cheque, for £60, that morning, had bought toddler Melinda some new clothes and had settled an outstanding garage bill. As it was only for a weekend, they took very few clothes with them and when they left at 3.00 the boys got into the Chevrolet in their grey flannel suits and sport shirts. When they had not returned on the Sunday night, Mrs Dunbar started to grow frantic. She notified the British Consul in Geneva at 3.30 on the Monday afternoon.

*

Just as a Swiss taxi driver was the last person identified in the West to see her husband two and a quarter years earlier, an Austrian station porter was the last person to see Melinda and her three children on 11 September 1953. Tickets had been bought for them by a man that afternoon, and luggage had been left in a station locker in Lausanne (it transpired that Melinda had somehow taken most of her wardrobe after all); Melinda left her Chevrolet in the station garage. The boys played with a pop gun on the train and Mimsie had a doll with red hair, or so the conductor noted as he calmed their mother, who was very anxious to know if they would make their connection in Zurich. They did make it, and changed on to a train that took them to Schwarzach in Austria, where a porter, Peter Geiser, took their luggage to a large waiting car with Salzburg number plates which drove off towards Vienna. Halfway there they switched cars and drove to a small airport in the Soviet zone of Austria.* Then they 'boarded a small military-type aircraft' which flew them to Moscow.

*

When they landed, they were reunited with Donald at the Sovetskaya Hotel, near the Dynamo football stadium on the road to the airport. Safely away from sharp journalistic eyes, they were greeted by 'Soviet officials', including Yuri Modin who had come from London and was there to see the reunion in which he had played a leading role. Modin had not met Maclean before and had been introduced to him while they were waiting for the plane to land. He commented on how 'cold' and 'distant' the defector was as

---

* The post-war occupation of Austria did not end until 1955.

they 'chatted about nothing in particular'. After their years apart, after all that Melinda had gone through, the pity and sympathy which she had had to accept and the dissembling she had had to practise, the semi-public meeting was a desperately strained affair. Maclean too was in an unfathomable emotional situation, guilt, love, not knowing where he stood with the sons he hardly recognised and the unknown daughter he had abandoned and not been able to contact. He 'barely embraced his wife'. He had an inkling of the movements of the family in the two years since he had left them, could perhaps imagine some of their path through that time, while they knew absolutely nothing of what had happened to him. The polished diplomat of the American Department, the Travellers Club and Schmidt's and of the evening train to Oxted had gone, to be replaced by a Russian-speaking unknown who had betrayed his own children.

The Macleans travelled on to the city where their father lived and where they were to spend the next two years. 'So it has come off at last!' Filip Kislitsyn exulted in the Soviet Embassy in Canberra when he heard of their arrival, the final part of the 1951 plan – 'to bring out Mrs Maclean' at an unspecified date and in an unspecified manner after her husband's exfiltration – now in place.

*

The news broke at once. Catherine Marling had an American journalist staying with her in Paris when she got the call. In a pre-planned replay of June 1951, a telegram arrived, misspelt, garbled, but with a critical family nickname to authenticate it. It had been handed in at Territet, where Melinda had supposedly been spending the weekend:

TERRIBLY SORRY DELAY IN CONTACTING YOU UNFORESEEN CIRCIONSTANCES HAVE ARISEN AM STAYING HERE LONGER PLEASE ADVISE SCHOOLBOYS RETURNING ABOUT A WEEKS TIME ALL EXTREMELY WELL PINK ROSE IN MARVELLOUS FORM LOVE FROM ALL MELINDA

The press, naturally caring little about their part in her misery of the past two years, turned on Melinda. They no longer pitied the 'pathetic and lonely figure', but conjured a scheming deceiver, and a foreign deceiver at that. 'In her cunning campaign, which fooled many people, Mrs Maclean must have had two objectives: to rejoin her husband and discredit this country as much as possible.'

On 22 October Melinda's traumatised mother received a handwritten letter on cheap, greyish-blue paper of no discernible origin, postmarked Cairo. That was either a poor joke or a hopeless attempt to imply that Melinda might actually have gone back to that city. As with Donald's first letter it gave nothing away, but unlike that it hinted at the possibility of reunion amid the genuine sorrow of departure:

> Darling Mummy
> I know you will be worrying terribly but please believe me that we are all quite alright and well. I hope with all my heart you will understand how deeply I feel the sorrow and worry my leaving will cause you. How much we shall miss you. How much a part of us you are. We shall always think of you.
> Please believe Darling in my heart I could not have done otherwise than I have done.
> All our love to you, Cathy and Harriet.
> Goodbye but-not-forever –
> Melinda

When Mrs Dunbar went miserably to her daughter's flat, feeling that she had profoundly failed her, she found that Melinda had had passport photographs of the three children taken in May under the name of Mrs Smith. One of each of the photographs was now missing. Melinda had also packed her treasured Rolleiflex camera. 'She may have taken it with her into the wilderness,' Jim Skardon noted in a style so much more poetic than his normal police training allowed that it is probably a direct quotation that echoes the bleakness in a mother and grandmother's heart.

After the arrival of this letter (which found its way into the newspapers nine months later) years were to pass before Melinda
Dunbar had any further news of her daughter. The Soviet Union
kept its secrets secure until once again Donald Maclean could be
useful to the Kremlin.

19

Comrade Frazer

Maclean spent very nearly twice as long living and working in Moscow as he did as a spy in the Foreign Office. The great rifts that had fuelled the dramatic outbursts and rampages of recent years were no more; the schisms in which his parents, his marriage, his job, his espionage, his schooling, the events of his times were all swirling in the combustible space between his patriotism and his conscience, his divided duty, were gone. Or they were finally acknowledged, and for being so were no longer a threat to his stability. The dramas of his life were far from over, but the way ahead was now clear. He had some control of his destiny and a greater hold on himself now that he was no longer liable to be buffeted by events that affected his split allegiances to both Britain and the Soviet Union. Unlike some of his fellow defectors, he had now found a version of himself that he could live with.

*

At the end of 1955 Ian Fleming had just published the third of his glamorously implausible James Bond adventures, *Moonraker*. As Foreign Manager of the *Sunday Times* he decided to 'mount a hit-and-run sally into Russia'. 'The new Soviet variety show' of General Secretary Khrushchev and Prime Minister Bulganin had finished a tour of India and Burma and was about to come to Britain. Fleming thought his newspaper should have the first press interview and sent Richard Hughes, star Far East correspondent,*

---

* Hughes is an inspiration for the character of Old Craw in John le Carré's *The Honourable Schoolboy*.

complete with six bottles of whisky in his luggage, to 'net' Khrushchev. After a month without getting any closer to the General Secretary than any other member of the swarming press pack, Fleming cabled Hughes to return in two weeks 'since primary object your assignment appears unattainable'. Five days later the rival *News of the World* scooped them with the Khrushchev interview, in which the premier went as far to deny that Burgess and Maclean were in the Soviet Union. Hughes, fobbed off with an interview with the long-surviving Molotov, sent the leaders a letter via their Foreign Minister which made plain that this 'protracted, futile and absurd policy of silence' about the two defectors would affect the success of their British visit. There had been no sightings of the men since their taxi journey from Saint Malo to Rennes over four years earlier. The news from Petrov in 1954 had filled in some of the gaps in the defection narrative after the astounding and shocking flight of 'pathetic and honest' Melinda and the three children. But the rest of it remained an enigma that spasmodically excited the press and still pained and puzzled their family and friends.

Hughes, comfortably full of vodka, was packing up after his fortnight's grace to catch the flight out on 12 February 1956 when the telephone rang in his room at the Hotel National and he was urgently summoned to come to Room 101. We can only speculate if the choice of room was a subtle piece of Soviet irony a mere seven years after George Orwell's Ministry of Justice in *Nineteen Eighty-Four* had used that number for the place where one's worst fears would be realised. Five men were sitting at 'a white-clothed table, surrounded by Victorian bric-à-brac, a marble clock above the fireplace, and antimacassars'. One of them, 'a tall man in a blue suit and red bow tie' stood up with his hand out. '"I am Donald Maclean," he said with a wooden smile.' Hughes sobered up at once. The interview lasted barely five minutes. Maclean was more or less silent, smoking 'a long Russian cigarette', the much friendlier Burgess said little of interest. This remarkably uninformative newspaper interview was the last one Maclean was to give for nearly three decades. The following day a statement released by the two men announced at British and American breakfast tables that they were alive and revealed their whereabouts after four and a half years of news blackout. Hughes was given a £1,000 bonus by the *Sunday Times*'s owner for his scoop.

The statement, apparently composed by the defectors themselves, had been issued as 'speculation about our past actions' could be getting in the way of 'Anglo-Soviet understanding'. The men had gone to the USSR 'to work for the aim of better understanding between the Soviet Union and the West' as neither the British nor the American government were interested in this aim, which was essential 'if peace was to be safe': the lodestone of Maclean's idealism from the League of Nations at Gresham's to the message Melinda gave his sons about his Communism. The defectors admitted that they had been Communists since Cambridge days but denied, to protect others and themselves in the event of a return home, ever having been 'Communist agents'. They were political refugees, not spies. For Maclean's part, he said it had been impossible to find anyone in authority (presumably he meant among his colleagues in the Foreign Office) who did not speak of 'the menace of Communism' or who understood 'the folly and danger of American policy in the Far East and Europe', with no reference to his last post as head of the American Department in London. When it became clear that 'the Foreign Office and security services had plans of their own' to hamper his future career by bugging and trailing him, he 'therefore decided to come to the Soviet Union to do whatever he could do to further understanding between East and West from there'. That was the work he was getting on with when asked, in a move he could not have welcomed, to break his cover and be reminded of his treachery by speaking to Hughes. Among the half-truths running through the statement, that last point fitted his own sense of his upstanding political and moral conscience at least, and represented how he intended to conduct himself for the rest of his life.

The *Sunday Times* commented in their brief piece that 'the statement leaves many unanswered questions, even for persons who have closely followed the case': such as how the pair had left

England and the whereabouts of Melinda and the children. It thought 'Russian readers may have some difficulty in comprehending the story' as very little had appeared in the Soviet press about the defection.

*

'Understanding' was set back even further during Bulganin and Khrushchev's visit to Britain by Operation Claret. This was the attempt of the heavily decorated Lieutenant Commander Lionel 'Buster' Crabb of the Royal Navy to examine the keel, rudder and propeller of the Soviet cruiser *Ordzhonikidze* while it was in Portsmouth harbour waiting to take the leaders home. Crabb never resurfaced from his dive; his handless and headless body was caught in a fisherman's net some fourteen months later. The following night, at a dinner for the Soviets hosted by Prime Minister Anthony Eden, Khrushchev made a lightly veiled reference to the *Ordzhonikidze* and 'missing or lost property'. *Pravda* reported this less wittily in denouncing 'a shameful operation of underwater espionage directed against those who come to the country on a friendly visit'. Burgess and Maclean's statement did not smooth diplomatic relations much except in clumsily leading the elephant from the room. Operation Claret served only to point to the yawning depths of the Cold War.

*

On their first night in Moscow in June 1951, Maclean and Burgess had dined in style on 'a great hotel balcony on the first floor overlooking the Kremlin'. They got increasingly drunk on vodka until three in the morning. Such a binge was an ideal way for Moscow Centre to handle the traumatised travellers. The next day Maclean recovered from his hangover and tried to comprehend what had transpired, while Burgess went out on his ever-thirsty quest for more drink and more company. But such jovial treatment could not last and from the Soviet point of view the crucial thing was to debrief the two burnt-out agents, find out what they really knew and work out what the future might hold for them, if they had a future.

They were sent to Kuybyshev, the city on the Volga known until 1935 (and after 1991) as Samara, a city closed to foreigners, controlled by the military and Moscow Centre, and accessible to Soviet citizens only with a special pass. The government had been evacuated there in October 1941 when the rapid Nazi advance threatened Moscow, 500 miles away, so it was well provided with secure areas, radio facilities and secret apparatus. It was a depressing, heavily polluted, industrialised place that supplied most of the weaponry for the war. No journalist would run into Burgess or Maclean in its dull streets or joyless bars. 'It was permanently like Glasgow on a Saturday night in the nineteenth century,' Burgess complained to the MP Tom Driberg. The two men, one louche and full of gossip and bile, the other showing more and more of his father's high-mindedness, united for ever by their journey but never destined to be soulmates, shared an apartment.

The back-slapping of that first night in Moscow soon disappeared. They were put in 'a small house guarded night and day by KGB [sic] troops ... to all intents and purposes under house arrest' on Frunze Street with their own minder following them wherever they went. The early debriefing about foreign policy and their contacts soon became closer to a full-on interrogation. To the Soviet mindset, at its most paranoid at that time with the doctors' so-called 'plot' against Stalin and the savage rounding up of the remaining Jewish intellectuals, it was highly likely that the rather derelict pair might even be in Russia as double agents. One of their MGB minders said they had to 'recall a lot, add new information, make comments on different documents, expound on the information the Cambridge Five had given to the Soviet Union'. Maclean was questioned in detail about his career in London, Paris, Cairo and in particular Washington, about the 'issues' and the people he had met. MGB operatives came in relays from Moscow to run through the narrative archive of the previous fifteen years. Between these visits, Maclean trudged around the lowering city, read the classics and started to learn Russian against the day when he might be allowed to start to live his life again.

As Stalin still had his hand ever more crazily and cruelly on the tiller of state, it was by no means obvious that that future would involve being kept alive. The MGB way of doing things made them fearful that if their whereabouts were discovered by the British an assassination squad would appear. Whether they were true Soviet agents or had been turned, death was the only conceivable outcome. A Russian intellectual friend of his later pointed out that Maclean 'was decorated with the Order of the Red Banner. He might equally well have been shot.' Until the death of Stalin in 1953, state security chief Beria pressed for a 'confession' of double-dealing and ruled out giving the exfiltration any sort of propaganda value. That also had the unintended consequence of enraging the British media and public as they poured their speculative fantasies into the news void.

The men had to adopt pseudonyms to prevent leaks about their whereabouts. Maclean was able to start again intellectually, free of despised espionage and the poisonous business of duplicity. He chose to be Mark Petrovich Frazer, after the anthropologist Sir James Frazer, whose *Golden Bough* was a 'sacred text' for intellectuals. T. S. Eliot, the poet Maclean had despised for his politics before the war, referred to 'the hanged god of Frazer' in his notes to *The Waste Land*. Fittingly, Frazer had been awarded an honorary degree at Cambridge in 1920, alongside his fellow Scottish Presbyterian Sir Donald Maclean; as the younger Donald was experienced in psychoanalytic thought, it might not be too much of a stretch to follow his choice of pseudonym from this point to Frazer's most famous volume, *The Dying God*, in which his man-god is slain when he begins to lose his powers to make way for his 'younger and more virile successor', who may even be his own son.

In the greyness of Kuybyshev, such an associative train of thought through his choice of name might have bolstered the intellectually questing Maclean and given him a sense of high purpose, exiled and without his family, friends and standing in the world, facing a very uncertain future. Frazer's 'legend' was that he was a political émigré, a trade union leader persecuted in

England for his political views. He had been born in 1914 in Edinburgh, where his father had been a professor of history until his death in 1932, his mother a housewife, and he had graduated from the university there. His later colleagues, accustomed not to questioning anything strange, knew not to pry further into the erudite intellectual perfectionist's reasons for emigrating. Melinda became Natasha Frazer when she occasionally worked translating Russian stories into English for the weekly English paper *Moscow News* after they had moved to the capital. Even in the mid-1960s a friend had no idea of Frazer's real identity until he became agitated when he spotted a man pointing a camera at him. Not until 1972, when Maclean was an accepted and admired part of Moscow intellectual society and his book was about to be published in Russian under his real name did he write to his employers to say 'Please regard me hereafter as Donald Donaldovich Maclean,' signing the letter 'Frazer'. He looked back to those dangerous days with the stark comment that 'nobody knew why we were there', and was relieved as much for his own safety as for the possibilities for the peaceful flourishing of Communism when the dictator died.

In the less intimidating atmosphere after the deaths of Stalin and Beria and 'the nightmare of [their] persecutions', Maclean was able at last to start living an undivided Russian life. Where Burgess became drunker and roamed Kuybyshev looking for action, on one occasion having his teeth knocked out in a brawl, Maclean made attempts to get sober, eventually undergoing cold turkey in a detoxification clinic. He got himself a job teaching English in a school – exactly what he had been planning to do after he left Cambridge twenty years earlier before his change of heart and application to the Foreign Office. Once Melinda and the children had been sprung from Switzerland for their reunion the family moved to a small apartment on the other side of the hallway from the insalubrious Burgess.

*

Melinda hated Kuybyshev and was by her own admission 'very unhappy' in the 'very primitive and depressing' city. Although Donald had his teaching work, he 'was also very depressed and disillusioned at this point with what he observed as the reality of Soviet Russia'. He was enough of a realist never to have had the roseate vision of those who visited in the 1920s and 1930s and were blind to the misery of the place. While giving up his life of professional acclaim, his Soho restaurants, his mother, his garden at Beaconshaw (which had been sold by Mrs Dunbar after Melinda's escape) and the commuter train from Oxted must have been tough, once he had got more used to Kuybyshev 'he … retained balance and optimism', happy that at least few of those he met in the post-Stalin era 'believed the official ideology any more'. It was a theme that would run through the rest of his time in Russia. The children were put into the local Soviet schools and were already model citizens before the family, deemed fully rehabilitated, moved to Moscow in 1955.

Once in the capital, Maclean could settle into suitable work. He became a magazine correspondent under the pen name of Madzoevsky so that his views could pass for Russian rather than as a voice from the West for those in the know about Frazer. After starting out in a small flat, the family were upgraded to 'a splendid six-room flat on Bolshaya Dorogomilovskaya Street … in the purest Stalin-era style, brand new'. 'The building was a 'massive, heavily ornamented pile' looking out over the Moscow River which the Macleans gradually made more like home with their 'good furniture and western bric-à-brac'. It had 'an unmistakable flavour of SW1'.* Maclean's study was likened to that 'of a Cambridge professor in the '40s or '50s' with copies of the airmail edition of *The Times*, an edition of Trollope and biographies of Gladstone among the English books, prints of the university and 'the upper end of the available furniture'. They had their own pictures and household goods shipped from the Army and Navy Stores Depository outside London where they had been stored after the sale of

---

* SW1 is the postal area of London's smart Knightsbridge and Belgravia.

Beaconshaw. He was able to order new books from Bowes and Bowes in Cambridge, who checked with MI5 who in turn checked with the Bank of England whether they should be supplying him before cashing his cheques. When Kim Philby arrived in Moscow, he too ordered his books from Bowes and Bowes, both men keeping up with new novels by Graham Greene and John le Carré. The exiled spies thus returned to the bookseller in the city where their bookish, youthful idealism had been shaped. Maclean kept in touch with the best of contemporary British fiction as the new generation finally took over from the Edwardians and developed a modern style that he appreciated. He 'Wained, Amised, Brained, Murdoched, Sillitoed'. However, in spite of these reminders and accoutrements of Britishness, his life in the Soviet Union was always characterised by an exceptional absence of nostalgia.

*

In February 1956 the 20th Communist Party Congress continued to blow the breezes of change through the system as Khrushchev made his 'secret speech' denouncing Stalin, and the horrors of his regime, including the Siberian camps, were now openly acknowledged. For the first time in a lifetime of support for the cause, with no need to keep himself hidden, Maclean joined the Communist Party. A telegram arrived at his brother Alan's publishing office in Mayfair asking for Mrs Dunbar's current address (Alan was initially concerned that it was fake because of the sign-off 'Best love to you Old Boy', where his brother was more likely to call him 'Old Fellow') and after five years of silence communications were established with family and friends again. Melinda put the bravest of faces on her situation (while aware of those who might read her letters on both sides of the Iron Curtain) when she wrote to her still grief-stricken mother that she understood the suffering she had caused 'but believe me I did the right thing and don't regret it … Donald is well and happy to be with his family again. This is absolutely the best place for us to be. Life is good here in every way, and for the children their opportunities for education and training in whatever career they choose are unlimited.' She professed herself happy in the flat with its television and part-time maid. Young Melinda's favourite reading was, poignantly, the Beatrix Potter books about Peter Rabbit, that quintessentially English herbivore. Young Donald, aged eight, attached a short note in Russian with the hope that he would soon learn to write in English.

Once in the Party and settled in Moscow, there was no need for Maclean to hide his politics. He maintained a principled, politically open, globally oriented perspective, world peace his consistent leitmotif. He was happily in correspondence within days of his reappearance (via the main post office in Moscow) with his brother Alan about Alan's new job at Macmillan Publishers, and was 'sorry that I missed working under Harold MacM when he was Foreign Secretary', as if he had left the job to go to work for a rival British concern to the Foreign Office. A decade after he had been uncomfortably present and watchful at the AEC meetings, he was able to say, 'it's taken almost ten years for our political leaders to admit that the Russians are not going to attack anybody. Will it be another ten before they say, "Oh, well, why not let's forbid the bomb and disarm."'

In 1956 Philip Toynbee 'wrote a cautious little note asking if [Donald] would like to correspond or not' and added a postscript wondering, 'did Donald see anything of Gordon [his name for the bibulous Donald] in Moscow, by any chance?' He was initially pained to get 'a hectoring, didactic letter' with such propaganda as 'the mighty river of Soviet development is beginning to unfreeze' but was relieved when Maclean's own postscript said that he 'must admit that [Gordon] does come tusking into my room from time to time'. The two of them had a spirited political exchange. Maclean defended the Soviets' brutal crushing of the Hungarian Uprising and, harking back to his early Foreign Office days, regretted that the French and Soviet governments had not intervened in the Spanish Civil War. It was clear to him that 'the better life ... will come to Hungary now'. Toynbee found that letter and its claims (absurd to Western eyes) 'impossible to answer' and their long and eventful friendship withered to nothing. Maclean could once again be freely Communist, and seemed at that early stage of his release to have lost any subtlety of independent thought, echoing the period at Cambridge after his father's death. He had no need to make confessions to the nearest thing he had had to a fellow-traveller, and was now able to blossom in the society he had half chosen, half had forced upon him. If he and Toynbee reflected back over their intense friendship, they would have felt a lot more than twenty years away from the pre-war white-tie debutante ball at which they had met.

Other letters speak of his enjoyment in 'rooting about' in the country around his *dacha* when he had time, a place that is 'wonderful for the children, since there is swimming, fishing, bicycling, mushrooming and cinema all at hand'. The *dacha* was a two-storey country cottage lent to those in favour with the Party in the pine woods twenty miles north-east of Moscow on the River Klyazma at Chkalovskaya. It had limited facilities, with electricity but heated by wood-burning stoves, and water was carried from a communal well in the village. Two generations on from the croft on Tiree, it suited the Macleans after the upheavals, subterfuges and house moves of their lives together. In Moscow they had access to the special shops reserved for the Soviet elite, and were able to import canned goods and drinks from Denmark. For the time and place, they lived well.

Donald fitted his new life so neatly at first that he failed to understand why some friends did not rush to get back in touch now that he was in this idyll, and he assumed that it was for political reasons rather than a result of the depths of the betrayal he had perpetrated on those who had cared for him at his lowest moments. He wondered if the person who had taken him in after his return from Cairo, Mary Campbell, was silent because she was 'disgusted about Hungary' rather than anything else, another sad end to a friendship now that his political beliefs could be given full rein. It is as if once the inner anguish had subsided and the need to dissemble was past, his character had changed; the charm and vulnerability appeared less often. Maybe there was an element of being unable to accept the personal element of his treachery, so certain was he that it was the right thing, so deep was the element of shame. Maclean disliked looking back on his past life: he would say 'we' and 'our' when speaking of the Soviet Union. Unlike Philby, he was not interested in writing his memoirs, and used to say to a friend who was correspondent for the *Morning Star* that he had an 'emotional block' when looking back. 'It was … a different life, a long time ago, and a painful time when everything was viewed "through frosted glass": he had no wish to recall it.' His drinking was now under control as the strain of his double life receded. The time of his destructive alcoholism was in another country, and from another state of mind.

*

After the Petrov evidence had come to light, a White Paper about Burgess and Maclean was published in September 1955. The paper was little better than a whitewash, excusing official myopia in every area relating to the escape of the two men. The *Times* editorial, headlined 'Too Little and Too Late', summed up its impact. Also in reaction to the White Paper, the journalist Henry Fairlie coined the new and still highly relevant usage of the word 'establishment' in *The Spectator* to encapsulate 'the whole matrix of official and social relations within which power is exercised', in this case by 'those who belonged to the same stratum as the two missing men'. Fairlie named Lady Violet Bonham Carter as a 'prominent member of the Establishment', which brought an enraged response from Asquith's daughter alleging that such comments meant that she had used her influence as 'a cloak for treachery' – an illogical position as Fairlie was making the point that the newly dubbed establishment had simply not been open to the idea of treachery. Harold Macmillan, Foreign Secretary at the time, summed up the establishment's emotional position when he said that 'the Foreign Office regards this case as a personal wound, as when something of the kind strikes at a family, or a ship, or a regiment'.

If the establishment hoped to draw a line under the affair with their defensive and disingenuous White Paper and House of Commons debate, immediately followed by overdue changes to the vetting procedure, the reappearance of the men a few months later led to further diplomatic concerns, such as how members of the British Embassy should behave if they saw their two missing colleagues. A directive was sent out that if Burgess or Maclean were encountered at receptions, staff 'should avoid all contact with them, but need not leave simply' because the traitors were present. However, 'if the occasion should be a purely Anglo-Soviet one it should be made plain to the hosts that the staff of the British Embassy will leave' if Maclean or Burgess were there. But, unlike the ubiquitous Burgess, Maclean went out of his way to avoid his fellow countrymen, leaving a concert given by Sir Malcolm Sargent in Moscow in the interval when he realised that he was sitting next to someone from the Embassy. Patrick Reilly, on reporting back to the Foreign Office, hoped that the edict excused leaving public performances if the defectors were spotted as in that case he had twelve seats from his Russian hosts which would have been 'conspicuously empty' if they had departed. The defectors' passports would not be renewed, but even so there was a great kerfuffle when Donald McLean applied to the Embassy for a British visa until it was established that an Australian with that name living in Moscow simply wanted to take his Latvian wife on a trip to London.

The Sargent concert aside, Maclean preferred functions that allowed him to pursue his undimmed interest in foreign policy matters and intellectual debate; he was as uncomfortable as ever with social events. In 1961 he took the job that was to last him the rest of his life, working for the Institute of World Economics and International Relations (IMEMO), the research centre that analyses the economic, foreign, domestic and military policies of overseas countries. He was a researcher and teacher, writing papers for the Institute's magazine which always stressed that if the system which he believed in was to work, the Party had to embrace the intelligentsia, not treat them with suspicion and send them into exile. His perennial teaching course was on the first Labour government in Britain, which was in office shortly before that in which his father had served, and from the Institute he wrote a thesis which later became his book *British Foreign Policy Since Suez*. Throughout his life, he declared, he had got his 'job-satisfaction' from dealing with the 'intellectual problems' of the Foreign Office and 'as an analyst in the Institute', not from either the diplomatic show or the hidden business of espionage which so pained him.

Always on the side of the unjustly treated, Maclean took a close interest in dissidents. He fraternised with like-minded intellectuals, including Alexander Solzhenitsyn, 'united by similar opposition views'. They met 'to discuss the kind of political and literary news you did not find in newspapers'. He remained as true as ever to where his conscience led him, on the intellectual edge of Soviet society as he had wanted to be on British. He learned that a girl whose family he knew slightly had been arrested for distributing 'subversive' leaflets and wrote on his ballot paper in the next Supreme Soviet elections 'While girls like Olga Ioffe are kept in mental institutions, I cannot participate in the elections.'

Although he had supported the suppression of the 1956 Hungarian Uprising, by 1968 his thinking about the Soviets and confidence in speaking out against them had developed to the point where he could voice his opposition to the 1968 Warsaw Pact invasion of Czechoslovakia (an echo of his early days in the Foreign Office and the Munich Agreement that had allowed Hitler to take that territory). He stayed out of trouble in IMEMO only by getting permission to be absent on the day when its members were made to declare support for the Soviet action.

When the dissident historian Roy Medvedev wrote his book *On Stalin and Stalinism* in the 1970s and was looking for 'individual historians, old Bolsheviks and other writers' to read it and add any extra comments, one of those he showed it to suggested that he might like to ask Mark Petrovich Frazer for his opinion. Frazer went on to help Medvedev, who had no English, by translating English texts for him. Raleigh Trevelyan of the London publishers Hutchinson approached him with an idea (which came to nothing) that he should write a book 'on the Russian people' as part of a series to include Doris Lessing on Africa, Kenneth Tynan on America and Lady Diana Cooper on France. Alan Maclean suggested that he might curate a list of the most interesting Russian writing for translation by Macmillan, but, again, with no result.

*

Maclean's own book was published first in Britain and America in 1970, then translated into Russian. It was an extension of his doctoral thesis, very different to the one planned at Cambridge on Calvinism and the bourgeoisie, albeit picking up on many of the same themes that had recurred throughout his intellectual life. He stressed this straight line as an explanation for his current course of study early in the book: 'When, after having spent the first sixteen years of my working life in the Diplomatic Service, I found myself with the necessity of finding a new profession, I decided ... that what I was best qualified to do was to contribute ... by making a continuous study, as objectively as possible, of contemporary British foreign policy.' The first word of the title of his doctorate, 'Problems of British Foreign Policy 1956–1968', gives away his thrust. The book is in three parts: policy towards the other Western powers, towards the Third World and towards the Communist powers. He takes the line that the Anglo-American alliance was now anti-Communist and that Britain was threatening its own destruction by pursuing this course, either by ramping up talk of war when Britain was within range of Russian nuclear weapons or, more likely, in destroying itself economically by overspending recklessly on defence. The country was failing to come to terms with its loss of Empire and the 'rate of error is a function of the particularly rapid change in the post-war balance of forces to the disadvantage of all the imperialist systems, particularly the British'. On the whole, those he had served failed to see Britain's world decline in the same way.

The argument is compelling and the mandarin prose would have been familiar to Maclean's former colleagues as he displayed his mastery of foreign policy from his exile. In his view, consistent with his memoranda as head of the Foreign Office American Department, American economic aggression was more dangerous than Communism and 'the question of policy towards the Communist powers enters into all the main problems of British foreign policy.' The British government could find no reason to ban the book, well researched and tightly argued as it was with its socialist bias much in evidence but not overwhelming (and therefore backing up his publisher's claim that it had not been 'edited' by the Soviet Foreign Ministry). With the respect shown to him within IMEMO, he felt free to criticise the Soviets too for being drawn into the arms race. He called for the conflict between the 'creative' and the 'dark' tendencies within the system to be resolved. With hindsight, it reads like an early plea for the *glasnost* he would not live to see. A decade after the book had been published he wrote to a friend that he felt 'the current leadership' of the USSR were more interested in 'preserving power' for themselves than in 'releasing the energy of the Soviet people', in whom he still placed such faith.

The book was taken seriously in Britain. Maclean even gave a brief, nervy interview to BBC radio to promote his work. Apart from saying he believed Britain's power and influence would increase over at least the next twenty years, most of the four minutes was spent reminding his interviewer that he had an agreement not to answer any questions outside the content of his book. Apart from the sniping prejudice of the *Daily Mail* which blindly dismissed his long-held political views merely as 'Soviet thinking and style', it got respectful reviews applauding his work in a way that would have reminded him of his annual appraisals in the Foreign Office. Donald Cameron Watt in the *Sunday Times* called the work of the 'quondam traitor ... a remarkably clear and objective account of those parts of British foreign policy he has chosen to cover ... impeccably documented'. The completion of his thesis and publication of it as a respectfully received book at the age of fifty-seven seems like a part of the simpler life that he was meant to lead. He expressed his political beliefs with expertise, demonstrated his intellectual curiosity and shared a worldview that for him was consistent and focused.

*

Maclean never became part of the 'twilight brigade community of defectors, down-at-heel, disillusioned and wondering how he had got there'. He did not seek out British company for its own sake unless it could feed his desire for news that would further inform his intellectual interests. He shunned giving interviews where Burgess revelled in them. He had closed the door on that world. When Edward Crankshaw of the *Observer*, a close friend of Alan's, went to Moscow, Burgess was in touch with him within a day and they spent a lot of time together. When Burgess then rang Maclean on Crankshaw's behalf, Melinda was keen to meet him 'but Donald would not hear of it'. The conversation ended with Burgess calling his fellow Communist 'a stuffed shirt' and hanging up on him.

Melinda's mother and sisters came to visit, but Lady Maclean stayed away. She was instead the frequent recipient of letters addressed to 'Dear Queen' or 'Dear Queenie' and signed by his childhood nickname of 'Teento' that detailed her grandchildren's success as model Russian offspring: Fergus spent his summer holiday working on a collective farm, while Beany and Mimsie were going to their respective boy and girl Young Pioneer camps, working the land, playing wholesome games, learning agricultural and horticultural skills, politics in 'black and white ... socialist or capitalist terms', preparing to be good Soviet adults. He portrayed his life as one of contentment intellectually, socially and within the family.

There was a major fluttering in the official hencoops in London in 1962 when it was rumoured that both Burgess and Maclean would soon be returning to Britain, the former because he was suffering from angina and was thought to be wanting to make a farewell visit; the latter because Lady Maclean's health was declining. Although there was no clear evidence for either man's desire to return, a warrant for their arrest was obtained just in case. When the Queen Bee of the family did enter her last days in July of that year, her middle son's telegram of love gave her comfort and Alan reported that 'she was really very *happy* for you and your new life and had no regrets or worries on your behalf'. Six plain-clothes police officers attended the funeral at Penn just in case Maclean chose to return on a false passport. His modest inheritance was sent to him in Moscow.

Burgess's death followed the next summer as a result of his angina, abused liver and the hardening of his arteries. Although

Maclean 'seldom saw Guy, and it gave him a very odd feeling that the names Burgess and Maclean had become as indissolubly linked as Swan's with Edgar's and Debenham's with Freebody's', he gave an address at his funeral. Kim Philby, who had finally made his confession of treachery in Beirut, where he was the *Observer*'s correspondent, and had defected earlier that same year, was not allowed by his minders to attend, in spite of his newly won Soviet citizenship and his inheritance of Burgess's 4,000 books. Maclean was relieved to write at the time of the defection that 'the hounds are baying away again, but I am not the fox, or even half the fox, this time'. Philby would soon give the young Cambridge graduate he had recruited at his Kilburn kitchen table nearly thirty years earlier every reason to regret his arrival in Moscow.

*

Philby was the man who had influenced the course of Donald Maclean's life more than any other. He had recruited him to the Soviet cause, saved him from identification by Volkov, enabled him to reach Russia just ahead of his arrest and interrogation, and now, as he betrayed everyone close to him, did the ultimate double-cross of his fellow agent. Espionage and betrayal, which felt 'like being a lavatory attendant' to Maclean, was a source of thrilling power to Philby, who was now well paid by the KGB as 'an upper-middle-class *apparatchik*'. When Philby's American third wife, Eleanor, joined him in Moscow, the two couples spent two or three nights a week together, at the ballet or just having dinner and playing bridge. Eleanor and Melinda were exiles for whom a discussion about seeing a grapefruit in the market could last five minutes, the men more cerebral and at home with the system. Eleanor Philby found Donald conceited, and Melinda amusing but 'extremely nervous and highly strung, with an annoying habit of repeating herself' and yearning 'for the luxuries of Western capitalism', a yearning only partially fulfilled by the parcels of food and clothes sent by her mother. All the same, Eleanor was pleased to have 'someone new to talk to' in her exile. She sensed that the Macleans' marriage was by now a difficult one again, with Donald on occasion still getting hopelessly drunk; he could be 'unaccountably rude and offensive' to anyone around him, as if he had 'sipped a phial of Dr Jekyll's medicine'. Mrs Dunbar had concurred with this when she reported back after her visit to Moscow in 1959 that 'life in the Maclean *ménage* is not altogether harmonious', the phraseology more Foreign Office than Dunbar. The Macleans were now openly tied together by ideology and geography, and, rather pathetically given Donald's masterful grasp of global foreign affairs, used to talk of the 'good times they would have in Italy and Paris when the Revolution comes'.

When Eleanor went back to America to see her daughter and enjoy a bit of Western luxury for herself in the summer of 1964, she got a stream of letters from her husband in which he described going on holiday with the Macleans to the Baltic countries of the Soviet bloc, staying with them at their *dacha*, dining with them in Moscow and increasingly mentioning Melinda alone. Eleanor's passport was confiscated on her arrival in the US and she was not able to return to Moscow until late in the year; Melinda paid for her enforced stay from the dollar account she still had in her home country. On her return Eleanor found her husband 'restless and uneasy', drinking more than she had ever seen him drink before (although she had generally found him to be most often 'lost in a haze of alcohol' before she left) and no longer on speaking terms with Donald after a 'filthy row' in which Maclean apparently accused Philby of being a double agent working for the British. Christmas and New Year were miserable, spent cross-country skiing with Melinda at the Maclean *dacha* and taken up with Melinda's own complaints about how 'Donald has become quite impossible and I can't live with him any more.'

Eleanor confronted her husband with her suspicions. Philby claimed that he was just 'trying to make [Melinda's] life happier' by spending time with her as she had been miserable for the last fifteen years. And that Donald was impotent. Whether or not this last claim was true, and alcoholism would be a strong factor if it were, the encounter marked the end of the Philbys' marriage. Eleanor was presented with a bunch of tulips by the KGB at the airport before she returned to America. Reflecting on her husband's pathological betrayal of his great 'ideological comrade' as well as herself, she wrote shortly before her death that 'no one can ever truly know another human being'. Melinda moved in with Kim Philby. They lived together for three years, the children remaining with Donald, until Rufina, a half-Polish, half-Russian woman twenty years younger, caught Philby's eye and became his fourth wife. Melinda returned to her husband, who had once again forsworn alcohol in 1968, this time for good, but two years later moved to her own apartment near by. Their extraordinary marriage was finally over.

Maclean made no comment in his letters home about his double desertion, aware as he was of how everything to do with him, Melinda and Philby found its way into the press. In 1968 the *Sunday Times* published a series of articles which became the basis for Phillip Knightley's biography of Philby; no word came from Moscow. In spite of the fulfilment of his work and his attention to the future, as his marriage finally seemed to end, Maclean might have thought back with some regret to Melinda's support after the horror of the Helouan trip and his exit from Cairo the following year, their last days in England and their lives together. Or he might have felt that in his undivided self he no longer had the need for a secret sharer.

Philby's place in the Macleans' expatriate life was taken by George Blake, the spy turned while a prisoner of war in Korea and whose dramatic escape from Wormwood Scrubs (rather than serve the longest prison sentence, forty-two years, ever handed down in a British court) brought him to Moscow in 1969. Maclean saw in Blake a fellow ideologue and found him work at IMEMO, studying the Middle East and the Arab–Israeli conflict. Blake admired the older man's capacity for work and identified with the 'strong Calvinistic streak' that drove that, as well as seeing him as a 'prophet of *perestroika*'. When Blake remarried and had children the families spent Christmas together. Maclean left the younger man his library and his old, stained tweed cap. Among the books in that library were the spy novels of Graham Greene, and *Tinker Tailor Soldier Spy* by John le Carré, whose fictional depictions of ambiguous, divided loyalties in the world of espionage got 'close to the truth imaginatively' for the real-life and deeply ambivalent spy.

*

Maclean was a lifelong smoker, with frequent bouts of bronchitis the price to pay for his addictive habit. In November 1971 he had an operation to remove tumours on his bladder, some of which were found to be malignant. But he worked unceasingly and fulfillingly through his sixties, at one point saying that he had swapped alcoholism for workaholism. That same year, young Donald, 'Beany', his wife Lucy (daughter of the prominent American Communist George Hanna) and their four-month-old son moved into a one-room flat in Moscow, but soon relocated to England the following year. In 1973, his son Fergus left with his wife Olga and son Dmitri and enrolled at University College London, to take a degree in modern history. The governing body debated whether to allow Fergus to matriculate but correctly decided that the sins of his father should not be visited upon him. Donald wrote to his brother Alan expressing his anxiety as to how 'Fergie' would find life in England. That same year Mimsie and her first husband Dmitri Linnik paid a visit to the country of her birth, of which she had no memory at all. The cruellest blow of all was when she too left for good in 1979, taking with her to the US Maclean's adored granddaughter, the fourth Melinda, Melindushka. It is an irony that it was Maclean's high standing in the Soviet hierarchy that enabled his children to get visas in order to leave the country; he used his influence to that end because he felt 'guilt that he had deflected [their lives] from their normal course'. When their spouses and close friends came to visit he made them take a vow not to speak of their experiences to the press or to those outside the tight circle, maintaining the dignity of silence he had created for himself in Russia.

Shortly ahead of their daughter, Melinda senior moved back to the US, taking up residence in Sunnyside, Queens, New York, finally bringing to an end nearly forty years of endurance and sundering, resilience and collapse, outstanding loyalty and betrayal. She lived until 2010, giving carefully guarded interviews when necessary to the FBI but never speaking to anyone who might make anything public. By the time she left Russia, Donald was beginning his final decline, and his last few years were spent in and out of hospital following a diagnosis of cancer. He was looked after by his devoted housekeeper, Nadezhda Petrovna, still seeing students, still writing, lamenting that Khrushchev's reforms had not been continued in the Brezhnev era, expressing strong opinions about British foreign policy and the 1982 Falklands War, wanting to find out from the Reuters bureau chief all he could about the new Prime Minister of Great Britain, Margaret Thatcher, a leader of a type he and his former fellow countrymen had not seen before. When in 1979 Anthony Blunt was exposed by Thatcher in the House of Commons as one of the Cambridge Five after earlier being granted immunity from prosecution and confidentiality in exchange for his co-operation (and no doubt to save embarrassment to the establishment), Maclean refused to make any comment to the press, British or Russian.

His son Fergus visited him in December 1982 and his brother Alan saw him for the first time in over thirty years in early 1983, by which time Donald was being treated for pneumonia. The two men 'held hands rather shyly like children' in the airport and 'talked greedily' for their three days together, 'mostly about our childhoods'. They agreed with each other not to discuss anything which 'Jim [Skardon] and his successors' did not already know.

*

Five days before he died, Donald Maclean gave his only interview to a British newspaper. He greeted Mark Frankland of the *Observer* at his flat wearing a British herringbone tweed jacket and 'incongruous grey pin-striped trousers which might once have been part of a Whitehall suit'. He was composed and calm, fretting that his illness was keeping him from his work at the Institute, not admitting to the pain he must have been in. He did not mention spying, but explained that he was baffled by British foreign policy under

Thatcher, harking back to his days in Whitehall 'when we thought it our job to act as a mediator between the Russians and Americans'. That was how this 'political man of the world' saw himself until mediation proved impossible and he had to make his choice.

In that sense, Maclean was a diplomat until his dying day, working to make the world as he saw it through the lens of his upbringing and time a fairer, more peaceful place. He was also a dissident who held, but could not always voice, his opinions strongly. At the end of his life he believed in 'convergence', confident that 'the Soviet and western systems would eventually find a middle ground and the differences between them would gradually disappear'. Like all good Communists and unlike many of the countrymen he had left behind, he looked to the future, not the past. In the interview he sent his absent family messages from beyond the grave, feeling 'for my poor brother who has suffered so much because of me' and for his children, 'the thing I worry about most in the world'.

*

Donald Maclean died on 6 March 1983 at the age of sixty-nine and his funeral was held in the assembly hall of the Institute, 'of which he was such a distinguished member'. There was a large turn-out for a 'touching farewell to a man who was much loved, admired and respected … not because he was a famous spy, but because he was a good and just man', as his fellow defector George Blake remembered. In his eulogy, Blake spoke about the biblical story of the just men whose presence would persuade God not to destroy a sinful city. Maclean was an atheist, but one of those men. The government newspaper *Izvestia* did not refer to his espionage activities but described him as a man 'of high moral qualities' who had 'devoted all his conscious life to the high ideals of social progress and humanism'.

After the funeral, Maclean's wishes were carried out. His ashes were brought back to Penn by his son Fergus, and interred in his parents' grave, alongside those of his two elder brothers. Accidentally, but fittingly for such a notable spy, they were buried after dark by torchlight, for the mundane and practical reason that Alan Maclean was late and the short service needed to be over before the press got wind of it. The reading was from St Paul's first Letter to the Corinthians:

> Love keeps no score of wrongs, does not gloat over other men's sins, but delights in the truth.
> There is nothing love cannot face, there is no limit to its faith, its hope and its endurance.

*

Donald Maclean's conscience was inspired by his Victorian, church-going parents, and then was forged in the godless atmosphere of the General Strike, the Depression and the rise of fascism. He was dedicated to the pursuit of peace and justice for the largest number, the humanism referred to by *Izvestia*. His conscience and the fulfilment of the secret life enabled him to maintain his core beliefs through the purges and the Nazi–Soviet Pact, and when many others fell away he continued to work for what he still believed in: resistance to the capitalist hegemony and atomic might of his wife's country. There is a purity about this consistency that makes his collapse into alcoholism in Cairo and afterwards all the more painful. His pleas to be removed to Moscow went unheard, leaving him at the time with the torment of feeling that he had betrayed his country to no higher end.

Late in his life he wrote: 'I do not at all regret having done what seemed and still seems to me my duty. I took, and take, no pride in the actual process of carrying out my task' because he disliked the 'deceit and danger' inherent in 'underground work'. Whatever disappointment he felt about aspects of life behind the Iron Curtain, he believed to his death that the USSR and its 'new society has a much better prospect than the old of overcoming the major ills and injustices of our civilisation'. His long-ago best man, Mark Culme-Seymour, had felt deeply betrayed by a man he had loved and trusted but he wrote to Alan Maclean that Donald 'was a victim of our times and I will cling on to the idea that he was a noble victim, no matter how profoundly misguided'.

Had he lived beyond the age of sixty-nine, he would have welcomed the increasing moves towards *glasnost* that he was already detecting, might have felt his was a life less divided than it had seemed by his idealism and his treachery. It was a life that fell into two neat halves: the high-flying and respected British public servant, and the Moscow intellectual. In both cases he ran against the grain of conventional thinking. Had he not been uncovered through the genius and good luck of Meredith Gardner and his team, he might have been able to complete his successful Foreign Office career away from his obligations to Moscow Centre and end up as honoured in his time and as little remembered today as his father.

As it is, the simple, timeless Celtic cross on the edge of a peaceful English country churchyard marks the remains of two men with the same name, both men of their times, of high ideals, optimism and strong consciences. Men with similar but differing beliefs and truths to which they remained firm, perhaps too doggedly firm. Donald Maclean's hope for a better world endured even as his life came full circle and he ended up back in the country he had served and betrayed, next to the father whose edict to follow one's conscience he had obeyed and whose patriotism he had undermined, in obedience to his secular faith.

Afterword

When I heard in early 2015 that a large number of the MI5 and Foreign Office files concerning Donald Maclean were finally due to be released to Britain's National Archives, I realised that he was a figure of national significance who had always been lurking somewhere in the background of my life and whom I would like to explore.

It is a tale that involves both my grandfathers. My maternal grandfather, Roger Makins, features throughout this book. He and Maclean first worked together in Washington and were the two British diplomats on the Atomic Energy Commission there – although Makins did not have the 'access all areas' pass given to his junior. Makins thought highly of Maclean, as did all the Foreign Office chiefs throughout his career, and gave him his last post as head of the American Department. Makins, who knew of Maclean's treachery shortly after he made the appointment and knew that he was soon to be questioned, was the last man from the Foreign Office to see him as they bumped into one another in the courtyard on the evening of 25 May 1951; he sent his regards to Maclean's sister who he thought was staying the weekend. For the rest of his long life it was a source of surprise and minor irritation to him that he had not known the watchers did not work at weekends. Occasional commentators used to imply that the Foreign Office, he in particular, and MI5 had been complicit in letting Maclean defect because the alternative, the trial of such a senior figure, would be too embarrassing for the establishment. Makins was rightly exonerated from any such accusation in Parliament when the White Paper was published in 1955.

My other grandfather was the artist Wogan Philipps. He became a Communist (and was disinherited by his father as a result) after seeing the plight of those working in the East End of London and in the docks when he worked as a mounted policeman during the General Strike of 1926. I quote some of his letters from the Spanish Civil War (where he was an ambulance driver and from which he came back wounded by a shell which obliterated the ambulance parked next to his) to make points about the essential nobility of the left-wing cause to high-minded British converts. Like Maclean, Wogan was a totally committed ideologue who believed that Communism was the only pathway to world peace and a fair society. Like Maclean, he remained a fellow-traveller after the revelations of Stalin's purges and after the Nazi–Soviet Pact had ensured that the Second World War was inevitable. In Maclean's interview with the *Observer,* a few days before he died, he said he did not fear a resurgence of Stalinism and had hopes that Communism could now thrive. Wogan outlived Soviet Communism; he died in 1993. When I asked him after it had ended where he stood on the subject, he said that Stalin had been a disaster for the cause but that the system was still inherently right, would come around again and next time be successful. I think Maclean, with his ideological purity, would have said something similar had he lived another few years.

Finally, Alan Maclean was a family friend and a fellow publisher who retired shortly before I joined the house of Macmillan. My mother worked for him before her marriage. Alan left an impressive legacy of authors there and was remembered with affection and respect.

Acknowledgements

My first and greatest debt is to Ben Macintyre, a matchless friend and brilliant author, who not only first discussed the need for a book about Donald Maclean with me, and raised the prospect of the impending release of documents about him into the British National Archives, but has encouraged and enlightened me with his knowledge and flair throughout the writing of this book.

I would also like to thank in particular Ben Maclean, who allowed me access to the uncatalogued papers of his father, Alan, in Cambridge University Library, lent me the unpublished memoir of his aunt Nancy, and gave up his time which added greatly to my understanding of his uncle. Andrew Lownie, biographer of Guy Burgess and espionage expert, has been unfailingly generous with his contacts and deep understanding of the subject. Geoff Andrews, in his book *The Shadow Man* and in our conversation, was enlightening about Maclean's years at Gresham's School and Cambridge.

No book about Donald Maclean could be written without access to the uncatalogued diaries and papers of Philip Toynbee held in the Bodleian Library, Oxford, and for permission to view these I am very grateful to Jason Toynbee.

The staff of the Bodleian Library, the Cambridge University Library, the British Library and the National Archives have been unfailingly helpful in the writing of this book. As have Liz Larby and Simon Kinder of Gresham's School, Holt, and Alexandra Browne of Trinity Hall, Cambridge, in showing to me and discussing the material in their archives. Rosalind Pulvermacher of the Foreign Office was unfailingly prompt in answering my queries about the history and make-up of that institution. Gleb Uspensky did valiant research in Russia.

I would like to thank the following who generously helped with their time, knowledge, conversation, insights and questions: the late Dame Margaret Anstee; Terry Bushell; Colin Campbell; Nina Campbell; Miranda Carter; George Carey; Teresa Cherfas; Dermot Clinch; Daphne Coburn; David Cornwell; Melissa Cosby; Robert Elphick; Bob Evans; James Fox; the late Jeremy Hutchinson; Josh Ireland; Derek Johns; Linda Kelly; John Lanchester; Deirdre Levi; the late Viscountess Macmillan; Virginia Makins; John Miller; John Morrison; Richard Norton-Taylor; Mollie Norwich; Phyllis Parker; Michael Randle; Mrs Daniel Rodwell; Philip Short; Paul Strudwick; Inigo Thomas; Natasha Walter; Caroline Westmore and Anna Wheatcroft.

Robert McCrum, Ben Macintyre, Giles Milton and John Julius Norwich were kind enough to read the manuscript of the book early on and forthright enough to suggest a great many improvements.

After working as a publisher for so long I believe that I have a strong sense of what good publishing involves. And I have nothing but the highest praise and admiration for my publishers, Stuart Williams of the Bodley Head in London and John Glusman of W. W. Norton in New York. They have been totally supportive from the start, editorially astute and tenacious, collaborative and imaginative. Anna-Sophia Watts and Lydia Brents have been invaluable and tirelessly helpful in steering the book through the publishing process. Chloe Healy and Ceri Maxwell Hughes of the Bodley Head and Rachel Salzman of Norton have been energetic and creative in their marketing and publicity work. It has been a privilege to work with both houses. Peter James is a peerless copy-editor with whom I have worked on many books in the past and it has been a delight and an education to be on the other side of the text from him. Anthony Hippisley's proofreading was rigorous and erudite, and saved me from many pitfalls. Christopher Phipps made an excellent index. Any mistakes remaining are entirely my responsibility, and any criticisms should be addressed to me alone.

Juliet Brightmore is an outstanding picture researcher who left no stone unturned and made that part of the creation of the book very enjoyable.

My agents, Natasha Fairweather of Rogers, Coleridge and White in London and Elyse Cheney in New York, have been encouraging throughout the book's life, from first idea to publication, and I would like to thank them and their teams, especially Max Edwards at Rogers, Coleridge and White, for all their hard and creative work.

Finally and most of all, I would like to thank my wife Felicity and my son Nat for their steadfast support during the writing of this book, as well as in the many years before and to come.

For permission to quote from copyright material, the author and publishers would like to thank: the estate of Cyril Connolly c/o Rogers, Coleridge and White Ltd for permission to quote from *The Missing Diplomats* by Cyril Connolly; the estate of Louis MacNeice c/o David Higham Associates Ltd and Faber and Faber Ltd for permission to quote from *Autumn Journal* and *Letters from Iceland* by Louis MacNeice; Ben Maclean for permission to quote from *No, I Tell a Lie, It was the Tuesday* by Alan Maclean; Patrick Garrett for permission to quote from *The Missing Macleans* by Geoffrey Hoare; Veronica Rodwell for permission to quote from *A Divided Life* by Robert Cecil; Jason Toynbee for permission to quote from the diaries and letters of Philip Toynbee; the Random House Group Limited for permission to quote from *The Climate of Treason* by Andrew Boyle, published by Hutchinson © 1979, 2003.

Bibliography

Archives

Bodleian Library, Oxford
British Library Newspaper Archive, London
Cambridge University Library
FBI Vaults online
Gresham's School
National Archives, Kew
National Archives, Washington DC
Trinity Hall, Cambridge

Books

Aldrich, Richard *The Hidden Hand: Britain, America and Secret Intelligence* (London, 2001)

Andrew, Christopher *The Defence of the Realm: The Authorised History of MI5* (London, 2009)

—— *Secret Service: The Making of the British Intelligence Community* (London, 1985)

Andrew, Christopher and Dilks, David, eds *The Missing Dimension: Governments and Intelligence Communities in the Twentieth Century* (London, 1984)

Andrew, Christopher and Gordievsky, Oleg *KGB: The Inside Story* (London, 1990)

Andrew, Christopher and Mitrokhin, Vasili *The Mitrokhin Archive: The KGB in Europe and the West* (London, 2000)

—— *The Mitrokhin Archive II: The KGB and the World* (London, 2005)

Andrews, Geoff *The Shadow Man* (London, 2015)

Annan, Noel *Our Age: The Generation that Made Post-war Britain* (London, 1990)

Anstee, Margaret *Never Learn to Type* (Chichester, 2004)

Auden, W. H. 'Honour', in Graham Greene, ed., *The Old School* (London, 1934)

Auden, W. H. and MacNeice, Louis *Letters from Iceland* (London, 1937)

Balfour, John, *Not Too Correct an Aureole* (Wilton, 1983)

Banville, John *The Untouchable* (London, 1998)

Beckett, Francis *Enemy Within: The Rise and Fall of the British Communist Party* (Woodbridge, 1998)

Bennett, Alan *Single Spies* (New York, 1998)

Berlin, Isaiah *Affirming: Letters 1975–1997, ed.* Henry Hardy and Mark Pottle (London, 2015)

Bew, John *Citizen Clem: A Biography of Attlee* (London, 2016)

Blake, George *No Other Choice* (London, 1990)

Blunt, Wilfrid Scawen *My Diaries 1888–1914* (New York, 1923)

Blythe, Ronald *The Age of Illusion* (London, 1963)

Bohlen, Charles *Witness to History 1929–1969* (New York, 1973)

Bonham Carter, Violet *Champion Redoubtable: The Diaries and Letters 1914–45*, ed. Mark Pottle (London, 1998)

Borovik, Genrikh *The Philby Files: The Secret Life of the Master Spy* (New York, 1994)

Bower, Tom *The Perfect English Spy: Sir Dick White and the Secret War* (London, 1995)

Boyle, Andrew *The Climate of Treason: Five Who Spied for Russia* (London, 1979)

Brendon, Piers *The Dark Valley: A Panorama of the 1930s* (London, 2000)

Bruce-Lockhart, Logie *Now and Then, This and That* (Dereham, 2013)

Bullock, Alan *Hitler and Stalin: Parallel Lives* (London, 1991)

Bushell, Terry *Marriage of Inconvenience: An Anglo-Soviet Alliance* (London, 1985)

Cairncross, John *The Enigma Spy: An Autobiography* (London, 1997)

Campbell, William *Villi the Clown* (London, 1981)

Carpenter, Humphrey *Benjamin Britten* (London, 1992)

Carter, Miranda *Anthony Blunt: His Lives* (London, 2001)

Cave Brown, Anthony *Treason in the Blood* (London, 1995)

Cecil, Robert *A Divided Life: A Biography of Donald Maclean* (London, 1988)

Christiansen, Arthur *Headlines All my Life* (London, 1961)

Churchill, Winston *The Second World War: The Gathering Storm* (London, 1948)

—— *The Second World War: The Hinge of Fate* (London, 1951)

—— *The Second World War: Closing the Ring* (London, 1952)

—— *The Second World War: Triumph and Tragedy* (London, 1954)

CIA *A Fixation on Moles: James J. Angleton, Anatoly Golitsyn and the 'Monster Plot': Their Impact on CIA Personnel and Relations* (Washington DC, 2013)

Conant, Janet *The Irregulars: Roald Dahl and the British Spy Ring in Wartime Washington* (New York, 2008)

Connell, John *The Office* (London, 1958)

Connolly, Cyril *The Missing Diplomats* (London, 1952)

Costello, John *Mask of Treachery: The First Documented Dossier on Blunt, MI5 and Soviet Subversion* (London, 1988)

Costello, John and Tsarev, Oleg *Deadly Illusions* (London, 1993)

Damaskin, Igor and Elliott, Geoffrey *Kitty Harris: The Spy with Seventeen Names* (London, 2001)

Davenport-Hines, Richard *An English Affair: Sex, Class and Power in the Age of Profumo* (London, 2012)

Deacon, Richard *The Greatest Treason* (London, 1989)

Deakin, Nicholas, ed. *Radiant Illusion: Middle-Class Recruits to Communism in the 1930s* (Edenbridge, 2015)

Deighton, Anne, ed. *Britain and the First Cold War* (London, 1990)

Driberg, Tom *Guy Burgess: A Portrait with Background* (London, 1956)

Fahmy, Isis *Around the World with Isis* (London, 2003)

Fisher, John *Burgess and Maclean* (London, 1977)

Frankland, Mark *Child of my Time* (London, 1999)

Gardiner, Juliet *The Thirties: An Intimate History* (London, 2010)

Garrett, Patrick *Of Fortunes and War: Clare Hollingworth, First of the Female War Correspondents* (London, 2016)

Gentry, Curt *J. Edgar Hoover: The Man and the Secrets* (New York, 1991)

Gillies, Donald *Radical Diplomat: The Life of Lord Inverchapel* (London, 1999)

Gladwyn, Lord *Memoirs* (London, 1972)

Glees, Anthony *The Secrets of the Service* (London, 1987)

Gordievsky, Oleg *Next Stop Execution* (London, 1995)

Gore-Booth, Paul *With Great Truth and Respect* (London, 1974)

Gouzenko, Igor *This Was my Choice* (London, 1948)

Greene, Graham, ed. *The Old School: Essays* (Oxford, 1984)

Hamilton, Ian *Keepers of the Flame: Literary Estates and the Rise of Biography* (London, 1992)

Hamrick, S. J. *Deceiving the Deceivers* (New Haven, 2004)

Haslam, Jonathan *Near and Distant Neighbours: A New History of Soviet Intelligence* (Oxford, 2015)

Hastings, Max *The Korean War* (London, 1987)

Hastings, Selina *Rosamond Lehmann* (London, 2002)

Haynes, John Earl and Klehr, Harvey *Venona: Decoding Soviet Espionage in America* (New Haven, 1999)

Haynes, John Earl, Klehr, Harvey and Vassiliev, Alexander *Spies: The Rise and Fall of the KGB in America* (New Haven and London, 2009)

Henderson, Nicholas *New Friends and Modern Instances* (London, 2000)

Hennessy, Peter *Having It So Good: Britain in the Fifties* (London, 2006)

—— *Never Again: Britain 1945–1951* (London 1993)

—— *The Secret State: Preparing for the Worst 1945–2010* (London, 2010)

Herken, Gregg *The Brotherhood of the Bomb* (New York, 2002)

—— *The Winning Weapon: The Atomic Bomb in the Cold War 1945–1950* (Princeton, 1981)

Herman, Arthur *Joseph McCarthy* (New York, 2000)

Hermiston, Roger *The Greatest Traitor: The Secret Lives of Agent George Blake* (London, 2013)

Hoare, Geoffrey *The Missing Macleans* (London, 1955)

Hobsbawm, Eric *Age of Extremes: The Short Twentieth Century 1914–1991* (London, 1995)

—— *Interesting Times: A Twentieth-Century Life* (London, 2001)

Holzman, Michael *Donald and Melinda Maclean: Idealism and Espionage* (New York, 2014)

—— *James Jesus Angleton* (Amherst, 2008)

Howarth, T. E. B. *Cambridge between Two Wars* (London, 1978)

Hughes, Richard *Foreign Devil: Thirty Years of Reporting from the Far East* (Warwick, NY, 2008)

Ireland, Josh *The Traitors* (London, 2017)

Isaacs, Jeremy and Downing, Taylor *Cold War* (London, 1998)

Jeffery, Keith *MI6: The History of the Secret Intelligence Service 1909–1949* (London, 2011)

Kennedy, David M. *Freedom From Fear: The American People in Depression and War 1929–1945* (Oxford, 1999)

Kern, Gary *A Death in Washington: Walter G. Krivitsky and the Stalin Terror* (New York, 2004)

Knight, Amy *How the Cold War Began* (New York, 2006)

Knightley, Phillip *Philby: KGB Masterspy* (London, 1998)

—— *The Second Oldest Profession: The Spy as Bureaucrat, Patriot, Fantasist and Whore* (London, 1986)

Koestler, Arthur *Darkness at Noon* (London, 1940)

—— *Scum of the Earth* (London, 1941)

Krivitsky, W. G. *In Stalin's Secret Service* (New York, 2000)

Lamphere, Robert J. and Schachtman, Tom *The FBI–KGB War: A Special Agent's Story* (New York, 1986)

Lawford, Valentine *Bound for Diplomacy* (London, 1963)

Lehmann, John *I Am my Brother* (London, 1960)

—— *The Whispering Gallery* (London, 1955)

Leigh Fermor, Patrick *Dashing for the Post: Letters* ed. Adam Sisman (London, 2016)

Lewis, Jeremy *Cyril Connolly: A Life* (London, 1997)

Liddell, Guy *The Guy Liddell Diaries*, vols 1 and 2, ed. Nigel West (Abingdon, 2005)

Lownie, Andrew *Stalin's Englishman: The Lives of Guy Burgess* (London, 2015)

Luke, Michael *David Tennant and the Gargoyle Years* (London, 1991)

Macintyre, Ben *A Spy Among Friends: Kim Philby and the Great Betrayal* (London, 2014)

McKinstry, Leo *Operation Sealion* (London, 2014)

Maclean, Alan *No, I Tell a Lie, It Was the Tuesday: A Trudge through his Life and Times* (London, 1997)

Maclean, Donald *British Foreign Policy Since Suez* (London, 1970)

Maclean, Fitzroy *Take Nine Spies* (London, 1978)

Macmillan, Harold *The Macmillan Diaries: The Cabinet Years 1950–1957* ed. Peter Catterall, (London, 2003)

MacNeice, Louis *Selected Poems* ed. Michael Longley (London, 1998)

Maisky, Ivan *Diaries* ed. Gabriel Gorodetsky (New Haven and London, 2015)

Martin, David C. *Wilderness of Mirrors* (New York, 1980)

Marton, Kati *True Believer: Stalin's Last American Spy* (New York, 2016)

Mather, John, ed. *The Great Spy Scandal* (London, 1955)

Mayall, Lees *Fireflies in Amber* (Wilton, 1989)

Miller, John *All Them Cornfields and Ballet in the Evening* (Kingston-upon-Thames, 2010)

Milne, Tim *Kim Philby: A Story of Friendship and Betrayal* (London, 2014)

Modin, Yuri *My Five Cambridge Friends* (New York, 1994)

Montefiore, Simon Sebag *Stalin: The Court of the Red Tsar* (London, 2003)

Moorehead, Alan *The Traitors: The Double Life of Fuchs, Pontecorvo and Nunn May* (London, 1952)

Morgan, Kevin *Ramsay MacDonald* (London, 2006)

Motion, Andrew *The Lamberts* (London, 1986)

Mount, Ferdinand *Cold Cream: My Early Life and Other Mistakes* (London, 2008)

Newton, Verne W. *The Cambridge Spies: The Untold Story of Maclean, Philby and Burgess in America* (published in the UK as *The Butcher's Embrace*) (New York, 1991)

Orwell, George *Coming Up for Air* (London, 1939)

Overy, Richard *The Morbid Age: Britain between the Wars* (London, 2009)

Page, Bruce, Leitch, David and Knightley, Phillip *Philby: The Spy Who Betrayed a Generation* (London, 1968)

Partridge, Frances *Everything to Lose: Diaries 1945–1960* (London, 1985)

—— *Julia: A Portrait of Julia Strachey* (London, 1983)

Pearce, Martin *Spymaster: A Life of Maurice Oldfield* (London, 2016)

Penrose, Barrie and Freeman, Simon *Conspiracy of Silence: The Secret Life of Anthony Blunt* (London, 1986)

Perkins, Anne *A Very British Strike: 3–12 May 1926* (London, 2006)

Perry, Roland *Last of the Cold War Spies: The Life of Michael Straight* (Boston, 2005)

Petrov, Vladimir and Evdokia *Empire of Fear* (London, 1956)

Philby, Eleanor *Kim Philby: The Spy I Loved* (London, 1968)

Philby, Kim *My Silent War: The Autobiography of a Spy* (London, 1968)

Philby, Rufina *The Private Life of Kim Philby: The Moscow Years* (London, 1999)

Pincher, Chapman *Their Trade is Treachery* (London, 2014)

—— *Treachery: The True Story of MI5* (Edinburgh, 2012)

Plokhy, S. M. *Yalta: The Price of Peace* (New York, 2010)

Powell, Anthony *To Keep the Ball Rolling: Memoirs* (London, 1983)

Purdy, Antony and Sutherland, Douglas *Burgess and Maclean* (London, 1963)

Purvis, Stewart and Hulbert, Jeff *Guy Burgess: The Spy Who Knew Everyone* (London, 2016)

Ranelagh, John *The Agency: The Rise and Decline of the CIA* (London, 1987)

Read, Anthony and Fisher, David *The Deadly Embrace: Hitler, Stalin and the Nazi–Soviet Pact* (London, 1988)

Rees, Goronwy *A Chapter of Accidents* (London, 1971)

Reynolds, David *From World War to Cold War* (Oxford, 2006)

Riordan, Jim *Comrade Jim: The Spy Who Played for Spartak* (London, 2009)

Roberts, Andrew 'The Holy Fox': The Life of Lord Halifax* (London, 1991)

Robertson, K. G., ed. *War, Resistance and Intelligence* (Barnsley, 1999)

Romerstein, Herbert and Breindel, Eric *The Venona Secrets: Exposing Soviet Espionage and America's Traitors* (New York, 2000)

Rose, Kenneth *Elusive Rothschild: The Life of Victor, Third Baron* (London, 2003)

—— *King George V* (London, 1983)

Sandbrook, Dominic *Never Had It So Good: A History of Britain from Suez to the Beatles* (London, 2005)

Sansom, Major A. W. *I Spied Spies* (London, 1965)

Shirer, William L. *The Collapse of the Third Republic: An Enquiry into the Fall of France in 1940* (New York, 1969)

Sinclair, Andrew *The Red and the Blue: Intelligence, Treason and the Universities* (London, 1986)

Skelton, Barbara *Tears before Bedtime* (London, 1993)

Skidelsky, Robert *John Maynard Keynes: The Economist as Saviour 1920–1937* (London, 1992)

—— *Oswald Mosley* (London, 1990)

Smith, Michael *The Spying Game: The Secret History of British Espionage* (London, 2004)

Spender, Stephen *Journals 1939–1983* (London, 1985)

Stansky, Peter and Abrahams, William *Julian Bell* (Stanford, 2012)

Straight, Michael *After Long Silence* (London, 1983)

Strauss, Lewis L. *Men and Decisions* (New York, 1962)

Sudoplatov, Pavel *Special Tasks: Memoirs of an Unwanted Witness* (New York, 1994)

Thomas, Gordon *Secret Wars: One Hundred Years of British Intelligence Inside MI5 and MI6* (New York, 2009)

Trevor-Roper, Hugh *The Secret World* (London, 2014)

Tusa, Ann and John *The Berlin Blockade* (London, 1988)

US Department of Energy *The New World: A History of the United States Atomic Energy Commission vol. 1: 1939–1946* (Washington DC, 2013)

Vansittart, Lord *Lessons of my Life* (London, 1943)

Walter, Natasha *A Quiet Life* (London, 2016)

Weinstein, Allen and Vassiliev, Alexander *The Haunted Wood: Soviet Espionage in America in the Stalin Era* (New York, 1999)

West, Nigel *Manhunt: Searching for Soviet Spies in British Intelligence* (London, 1989)

—— *Venona: The Greatest Secret of the Cold War* (London, 1999)

West, Nigel and Tsarev, Oleg *Crown Jewels: The British Secrets Exposed by the KGB Archives* (London, 1998)

West, Rebecca *The New Meaning of Treason* (London, 1964)

Wevill, Richard *Diplomacy, Roger Makins and the Anglo-American Relationship* (Ashford, 2014)

Wheen, Francis *Tom Driberg: His Life and Indiscretions* (London, 1990)

White, G. Edward *Alger Hiss's Looking-Glass Wars* (New York, 2004)

Wright, Peter *Spycatcher: The Candid Autobiography of a Senior Intelligence Officer* (New York, 1987)

Ziegler, Philip *London at War 1939–1945* (London, 2002)

Unpublished Papers

Blunt, Anthony, memoirs (British Library, London)

Maclean, Alan (Cambridge University Library)

Maclean, Sir Donald (Bodleian Library, Oxford)

Maclean, Nancy Jean, memoirs 'Past Imperfect' (1997)

Makins, Roger (Lord Sherfield), memoirs (Bodleian Library, Oxford)

Reilly, Patrick (Bodleian Library, Oxford)

Toynbee, Philip, letters and diaries (Bodleian Library, Oxford)

Articles

Cecil, Robert 'Legends Spies Tell', *Encounter*, April 1978

Fluegel, Dr Edna 'The Burgess–Maclean Case', *American Mercury*, February, March and April 1957

Hennessy, Peter and Townsend, Katherine 'The Documentary Spoor of Burgess and Maclean', *Intelligence and National Security*, April 1987

Kerr, Sheila 'Investigating Soviet Espionage and Subversion: The Case of Donald Maclean', *Intelligence and National Security*, Spring 2002

—— 'Oleg Tsarev's Synthetic KGB Gems', *International Journal of Intelligence and Counterintelligence* vol. 14, 2001

Thesis

Kerr, Sheila 'An Assessment of a Soviet Agent: Donald Maclean 1940–1951' (PhD dissertation, London School of Economics, 1996)

Notes

TNA – The National Archives, Kew, London. Citations marked KV refer to Security
Service files, FCO to Foreign Office files, PREM to Prime Minister's Office files,
CAB to Cabinet Office files, CSC to Civil Service Commission
FBI – Federal Bureau of Investigation, Washington DC
USNA – United States National Archives, Washington DC

Prologue

p. 1   watered the cyclamen – Fisher, *Burgess and Maclean* p. 120
p. 2   branches above him – Cecil, *A Divided Life* p. 113
p. 2   'in a tunnel' – Connolly, *The Missing Diplomats* p. 29
p. 3   'calm and genial' – *ibid.* p. 35
p. 4   hired that afternoon – Lownie, *Stalin's Englishman* pp. 237–8
p. 4   a 'special dinner' – Hoare, *The Missing Macleans* p. 5
p. 4   'be back soon' – *ibid.* p. 6
p. 5   'to talk to' – TNA KV 2/4143
p. 5   'for it on Monday!' – Cecil *op. cit.* p. 143
p. 5   and some 'disorder' – TNA KV 2/4140
p. 5   the Prime Minister – Hoare *op. cit.* p. 10

Chapter 1: Purity in Thought

p. 7   'ahead of others' – Gerald Holtom memoir, 1985, Gresham's School archives
p. 7   as 'exceptionally good' – 1935 Foreign Office reference, Gresham's School
         archives
p. 7   'let you down' – Holtom *op. cit.*
p. 7   'that walked alone' – Wansbrough-Jones, TNA KV 2/4140
p. 7   'betray one's friends' – Alan Maclean obituary, *Daily Telegraph* 2.10.06

p. 8   among his papers – papers of Sir Donald Maclean, Bodleian Library, Oxford

p. 9   'where he was born' – *ibid.*

p. 9   'in his hand' – *The Times* 17.6.32

p. 9   as well as … trade – Philip Williamson, *Dictionary of National Biography*

p. 9   'in his bones' – *ibid.*

p. 10   'loved by another' – J. M. Barrie, *The Times* 17.6.32

p. 10   'sincerity and industry' – *The Times* 16.6.32

p. 10   'difficult to live with' – Nancy Maclean, unpublished memoirs, 'Past Imperfect'

p. 10   'of episodic drinkers' – TNA FCO 158/186

p. 10   'and glittering eyes' – Cecil *op. cit.* p. 10, quoting from Asquith's diaries

p. 11   was 'that traitor' – Alan Maclean, *No, I Tell a Lie …* p. 3

p. 11   nanny and nursery-maid – *ibid.*

p. 11   a bicycle race – *ibid.* p. 7

p. 11   'soundly and sweet-temperedly' – *The Times* 16.6.32

p. 12   'at its best' – *The Times* 17.6.32

p. 12   Donald's strongest memories – Hoare *op. cit.* p. 42

p. 12   'middled-aged martinet' – *ibid.*

p. 12   'a harsh man' – interview Viscountess Macmillan 18.11.15

p. 12   the 'teetotal fold' – A. Maclean *op. cit.* p. 9

p. 12   'doting old parent' – N. Maclean *op. cit.*

p. 12   'genuine political animal' – A. Maclean *op. cit.* p. 2

p. 13   'sense of rectitude' – Page, Leitch and Knightley, *Philby* p. 33

p. 13   'It's their country' – *ibid.* pp. 33–4

p. 13   'a healthy basis' – Auden, *The Old School* ed. G. Greene p. 9

p. 15   twenty-one to Oxford – interview Simon Kinder, Gresham's 28.9.15

p. 15   three or four miles – correspondence Liz Larby, Gresham's School, 2015

p. 15   'impressed the boys …' – Howarth, *Cambridge between Two Wars* p. 142

p. 16   'and honest work' – J. R. Eccles, *Cooperation in School Life*, quoted Cecil *op. cit.* p. 14

p. 16   'refrain from smoking' – Bruce-Lockhart, *op. cit.* p. 110

p. 16   'talk or masturbation' – *ibid.*

p. 16   'founded upon trust' – J. R. Eccles, *My Life as a Public School Master*, quoted *ibid.*

p. 17   'trust and honour' – Berthoud to Patrick Dean 18.10.55, TNA FCO 158/8

p. 17   'for years afterwards' – *ibid.*

p. 18   'upon the Government' – *Daily Mail* 3.5.26

p. 18   'steel-helmeted clubmen' – Osbert Sitwell, quoted Perkins, *A Very British Strike* p. 121

p. 18   loans for Soviet Russia – Newton, *The Cambridge Spies* p. 61

p. 18   'new revolutionary era' – Rajani Palme Dutt, *Communist International*, June 1926, quoted Perkins *op. cit.* p. 243

p. 19   'supercilious and reserved' – Page, Leitch and Knightley *op. cit.* p. 33

p. 19   'never would like' – quoted Andrews, *The Shadow Man* p. 15

p. 19   'the common good' – *ibid.* p. 10

p. 20   'influence over people' – Deutsch report, quoted West and Tsarev, *The Crown Jewels* p. 207

p. 20   demonstrations and marches – TNA KV 3/442

p. 20   'a father figure' – J. Bridgen, 'Frank McEachran 1900–1975' in K. Bucknell and N. Jenkins, eds, *W. H. Auden: The Map of All my Youth*, quoted Andrews *op. cit.* p. 21

p. 20   'still at Gresham's' – *ibid.*

p. 20   'of human civilisation' – McEachran, *The Unity of Europe*, quoted Andrews *op. cit.* p. 21

p. 21   'liberalism and languages' – Boyle interview with Klugmann 23.8.77, quoted Andrews *op. cit.* p. 22

p. 21   'and historical materialism' – *ibid.* p. 24

p. 21   'liberty and justice' – *The Gresham* 28.3.31

p. 22   with 'Number Seven' – *The Grasshopper*, 1931, Gresham's School Archives

p. 22   'clever oddity' – Boyle interview with Klugmann, quoted Boyle *op. cit.* p. 59

p. 22   'hopeless at games' – Andrews *op. cit.* p. 25

p. 23   school's 'Fascist state' – Auden, memoir, Gresham's School Archives

p. 23   fn. 'promises from me' – 'Last Will and Testament', from Auden and MacNeice, *Letters from Iceland* p. 235

p. 23   'grief and anger' – interview John Lanchester 4.11.15

p. 23   'in social service' – debate of 11.10.30, *The Gresham* 18.10.30

Chapter 2: Dared to Question

p. 24   'of the theory' – *Granta* 18.10.33

p. 25   'Cambridge is annoyed' – *Granta* 8.11.33

p. 26   'of the British Empire' – Howarth *op. cit.* p. 142

p. 26   buses and soup kitchens – Andrews *op. cit.* p. 28

p. 26   'the writer and the dog' – Howarth *op. cit.* p. 143

p. 27   'or almost Communists' – *New Statesman* 9.12.33, quoted Skidelsky, *Keynes: The Economist as Saviour* p. 515

p. 27   'literally transformed overnight' – A. Blunt, 'From Bloomsbury to Marxism', quoted Andrew and Gordievsky, *KGB* p. 166

p. 27   'countries still civilised' – Bensusan-Butt obituary, *Independent* 23.10.11

p. 27   'and political order' – quoted Andrew and Gordievsky *op. cit.* p. 145

p. 28   'and of civilisation' – Skidelsky, *Oswald Mosley* pp. 37–8

p. 28   'infectious, warm personality' – Penrose and Freeman, *Conspiracy of Silence* p. 47

p. 28   'mysteries appear logical' – Costello, *Mask of Treachery* p. 165

p. 28   'as never before' – Howarth *op. cit.* p. 147

p. 28	to indoctrinate undergraduates – Rose, *King George V* p. 369
p. 29	'not very far off' – Klugmann, introduction to J. Clark, ed., *Culture and Crisis in Britain in the 30s*, quoted Andrews *op. cit.* p. 36
p. 29	'wonders of the age' – Clark *op. cit.* p. 146
p. 29	peak of three million – 'Labour Market Trends', Government Statistical Service, January 1996
p. 29	16,000 in 1939 – statistics from CPGB website
p. 31	'head and manner' – Straight, *After Long Silence* p. 61
p. 31	'perfidy of their leader' – Cecil *op. cit.* pp. 20–1
p. 31	'all the answers' – Leonard Forster, quoted Boyle *op. cit.* p. 62
p. 31	'the international bourgeoisie' – *Communist International*, March 1919
p. 32	'the universal provider' – quoted Boyle *op. cit.* p. 69
p. 32	'and debonair manner' – *ibid.* p. 22
p. 32	'other songs vociferously' – TNA KV 3/442
p. 32	members of the Communist Party – Lownie *op. cit.* p. 41
p. 32	'bread and jam' – Penrose and Freeman *op. cit.* p. 89
p. 32	'the capitalist system' – TNA KV 3/442
p. 33	'Helmets rolled' – Cecil *op. cit.* p. 23
p. 33	'the propertyless classes' – *Granta* 20.5.32
p. 34	'and moral decline' – Page, Leitch and Knightley *op. cit.* p. 35
p. 34	'overtly rebellious' – Lownie *op. cit.* p. 30
p. 35	'feckless undergraduate' – Connolly *op. cit.* p. 18
p. 35	'sordid sexual life' – TNA FCO 158/184
p. 35	'frustrations and inhibitions' – *ibid.*
p. 35	'whale-like body' – Boyle *op. cit.* p. 107
p. 36	'few renegade Socialists' – *ibid.* p. 66
p. 36	'worry and overwork' – *ibid.* p. 67
p. 36	'impenitent Free Trader' – *Spectator* 17.6.32
p. 36	'tawdry and meaningless' – Boyle *op. cit.* p. 67
p. 36	could move off – N. Maclean *op. cit.*
p. 37	'as he saw it' – Boyle interview with Christopher Gillie, quoted Boyle *op. cit.* pp. 67–8
p. 37	'the straight course' – papers of Sir Donald Maclean, Bodleian Library, Oxford
p. 37	'the Communist cause' – Klugmann, quoted Costello and Tsarev, *Deadly Illusions* p. 184
p. 38	'as regards his fingernails' – TNA KV 2/4157
p. 39	'manner, marched back' – Pat Sloan, ed. *John Cornford: A Memoir*, quoted Penrose and Freeman *op. cit.* p. 94
p. 39	'crimes of imperialism' – Lownie *op. cit.* p. 43
p. 39	barricade outside Peterhouse – Skidelsky, *Keynes* p. 496
p. 40	'the losing side' – *Silver Crescent* Michaelmas 1933
p. 40	his 'monastic existence' – Hobsbawm, *Interesting Times* p. 123

p. 41   'ruling-class culture' – *Cambridge Left* Winter 1933–4

p. 41   'revolutions and wars' – *Silver Crescent* Lent 1934

p. 42   'of tutorial fees' – *Granta* 7.3.34

p. 42   'it is the cause!' – Boyle interview with Christopher Gillie, quoted Boyle *op. cit.* p. 113

p. 42   'books and tracts' – *ibid.* p. 107

p. 42   'any particular significance' – TNA KV 2/4140

pp. 42–3   'enjoyed social activities' – TNA KV 2/4141

p. 43   'revolutionaries of the intelligentsia' – Hoare *op. cit.* pp. 135–6

p. 44   'the English language' – Modin, *My Five Cambridge Friends* p. 95

p. 44   'something in Communism' – TNA KV 2/4141

p. 44   'into his confidence' – *ibid.*

p. 44   'newish creed, Communism' – *ibid.*

p. 44   'the Diplomatic Service' – *ibid.*

p. 44   'well-earned holiday' – TNA KV 2/4150

p. 44   'the married sister' – *ibid.*

p. 45   'always doing that' – *ibid.*

p. 45   to make love – *ibid.*

p. 45   'and possibly satisfaction' – *ibid.*

p. 45   'in that direction' – letter in Trinity Hall archive, Cambridge

p. 46   'his own mind' – TNA KV 2/4141

p. 46   'all that lately' – Cecil *op. cit.* p. 37

Chapter 3: Orphan

p. 47   'devoted to Communism' – Andrew and Mitrokhin, *The Mitrokhin Archive* p. 76

p. 47   'tremendous little sexpot' – Cave Brown, *Treason in the Blood* p. 159

p. 47   'got used to it' – quoted Page, Leitch and Knightley *op. cit.* p. 58

p. 48   'an elite force' – K. Philby, *My Silent War* p. xxxii

p. 48   'light curly hair' – Kim Philby, quoted Andrew, *MI5* p. 169

p. 48   Russian and English – Lownie *op. cit.* p. 52

p. 48   'exploitation and alienation' – Andrew and Mitrokhin *op. cit.* p. 73

p. 48   'the better orgasm' – Andrew *op. cit.* p. 170

pp. 48–9   'led him to fascism' – Cave Brown *op. cit.* p. 63

p. 49   'the Magnificent Five' – Andrew and Mitrokhin *op. cit.* p. 75

p. 49   'scions of the bourgeoisie' – *ibid.* p. 74

p. 50   'cosmopolitan ways' – Cairncross, *The Enigma Spy* p. 63

p. 50   'at that moment' – quoted Borovik, *The Philby Files* pp. 29–30

p. 50   'Heil Hitler Brigade' – quoted Andrew and Mitrokhin *op. cit.* p. 87

p. 51   'righteousness of socialism' – Borovik *op. cit.* p. 42

p. 51   in the don's view – quoted Haslam, *Near and Distant Neighbours* p. 72

p. 51   'the Communist party' – F. Maclean, *Take Nine Spies* p. 237

p. 51   'dear father was' – *ibid.*

p. 51   'for rejecting Maclean' – Borovik *op. cit.* p. 42

p. 52   'points of view' – Maclean tutorial file, Trinity Hall archive, Cambridge

p. 52   cricket and hockey – TNA KV 2/4140

p. 52   'pecuniary embarrassment' – TNA CSC 11/171

p. 53   his 'modest table' – Borovik *op. cit.* p. 45

p. 53   'work there for us' – Philby, memoir in KGB files, quoted Tsarev and
          Costello *op. cit.* p. 186

p. 53   'international Soviet republic' – *Communist International*, March 1919

p. 53   'international proletarian revolution' – Cecil *op. cit.* p.34

p. 53   'tied to Moscow' – Borovik *op. cit.* p. 46

p. 54   fn. 'KGB the following year' – Andrew *op. cit.* p. 174

p. 54   'contact with us' – Maclean KGB file 83791, quoted Costello and Tsarev
          op. cit. p. 187

p. 54   'praise and reassurance' – Costello and Tsarev *op. cit.* p. 94

p. 55   'useful for us' – Deutsch KGB file 32826, quoted Costello and Tsarev *op. cit.*
          pp. 193–4

p. 56   'imposing but distant' – Macintyre, *A Spy among Friends* p. 25

p. 56   'intimacy between us' – Cairncross *op. cit.* p. 26

p. 56   fn. 'to all polygamists' – quoted Andrew *op. cit.* p. 174

p. 56   'instilled in him' – Carter, *Anthony Blunt* p. 3

p. 57   'last three centuries' – *Glasgow Herald* 26.3.40

p. 57   'it was doomed' – Cecil *op. cit.* p. 39

p. 57   'public-school *gaucherie*' – Page, Leitch and Knightley *op. cit.* p. 90

p. 57   'sense of humour' – interview Viscountess Macmillan 18.11.15

p. 58   'just too unformed' – Connolly *op. cit.* p. 17

p. 58   of 'Liberal stock' – interview Viscountess Macmillan 18.11.15

p. 58   'very independent' – interview Lord Hutchinson 19.7.16

p. 58   'make *proper* marriages' – *ibid.*

p. 59   'extraordinarily formidable' – *ibid.*

p. 59   'good-looking and Liberal' – *ibid.*

p. 59   'wild and warm' – Mount, *Cold Cream* p. 47

p. 59   'to my fury' – Toynbee diary 20.12.35, papers of Philip Toynbee, Bodleian
          Library, Oxford

p. 59   'possibility of happiness' – *ibid.* 14.4.35

p. 59   'I didn't argue' – *ibid.* 21.7.36

p. 59   'the ruling classes' – Philip Toynbee, 'Maclean and I', *Observer* 15.10.67

p. 60   'poor bugger' – Toynbee diary 21.7.36

p. 60   'sophisticated good humour' – Toynbee, 'Maclean and I' *op. cit.*

p. 60   coming up at all – Page, Knightley and Leitch *op. cit.* p. 82

p. 60   'master-class in mendacity' – Macintyre *op. cit.* p. 190

p. 61   'than the oppressed' – Connolly *op. cit.* p. 19

p. 61   'for Soviet Russia' – quoted Newton *op. cit.* p. 64

p. 61   'a boring companion' – conversation quoted Boyle *op. cit.* p. 127

p. 61　　　　'of his parents' – TNA KV 2/4157

p. 61　　　　'the Liberal Party' – interview Viscountess Macmillan

p. 61　　　　'at the same time' – A. Maclean *op. cit.* pp. 18–19

p. 62　　　　'Soviet special service' – Cave Brown *op. cit.* p. 171

p. 62　　　　'to London prostitutes' – Carter *op. cit.* p. 161

p. 63　　　　'had gone down' – Hobsbawm *op. cit.* p. 102

p. 63　　　　'its sole decoration' – Lawford, *Bound for Diplomacy* pp. 191–2

p. 63　　　　'250-ft. gas-holder' – *ibid.* p. 189

p. 64　　　　'be all, Mr Maclean' – quoted Boyle *op. cit.* p. 114

p. 65　　　　'modest Scottish shopkeeper' – Cairncross *op. cit.* p. 65

p. 65　　　　the rest scored 220 – TNA FCO 158/209

p. 65　　　　'and quiet. Attractive' – TNA KV 6/144

p. 65　　　　'Rather weak face' – TNA FCO 158/186

Chapter 4: Lyric

p. 66　　　　as a 'sleeper' – Modin *op. cit.* p. 97

p. 66　　　　'and striped trousers' – F. Maclean *op. cit.* p. 237

p. 67　　　　'the Andaman Islands' – Lawford *op. cit.* p. 235

p. 68　　　　meant by that – A. J. P. Taylor, *English History 1914–45*, quoted Holzman, *Donald and Melinda Maclean* p. 85

p. 68　　　　'eagles fall out' – quoted *New Histories* online 26.4.2012

p. 68　　　　question of war – Brendon, *The Dark Valley* p. 354

p. 68　　　　'attitude towards Germany' – A. Blunt interview, *The Times* 21.11.79

p. 69　　　　fn. 'to Comrade Stalin' – Andrew *op. cit.* p. 174

p. 69　　　　return to the office – K. Philby, Stasi training video, BBC News 4.4.16

p. 69　　　　'remoter open spaces' – K. Philby, *My Silent War* p. xxix

p. 70　　　　Copenhagen diplomatic pouch – Andrew and Mitrokhin *op. cit.* pp. 81–2

p. 70　　　　'the Three Musketeers' – *ibid.*

p. 70　　　　'extremely pressing' – Maclean KGB file 83791, quoted Costello and Tsarev *op. cit.* p. 199

p. 70　　　　'Russians and Germans' – TNA KV 2/1008

p. 71　　　　Paul and Lydia Hardt – TNA KV 2/1009

p. 71　　　　'before February 1936' – TNA KV 2/1008

p. 71　　　　'event of war' – Haslam *op. cit.* p. 71

p. 71　　　　frenetic diplomat 'patience' – Modin *op. cit.* p. 97

p. 72　　　　'succeed in doing this' – Maclean KGB file, quoted Costello and Tsarev *op. cit.* p. 200

p. 72　　　　'and the Soviet Union' – *ibid.*

p. 72　　　　'serious political complications' – *ibid.* pp. 200–1

p. 72　　　　'the number required' – TNA FCO 158/253

p. 73　　　　'hands of the Soviet Union' – Maclean KGB file, quoted Costello and Tsarev *op. cit.* p. 201

p. 73　　　　'problems and liabilities' – TNA FCO 158/25

p. 73   by Marxist texts – Brendon *op. cit.* p. 309

p. 74   'friendly – just children' – Wogan Philipps to Rosamond Lehmann 27.4.37, possession of the author

p. 74   and community centres – Ian Jack, *Independent* 21.11.15

p. 75   'very sordid surroundings' – quoted Gardiner, *The Thirties* p. 64

p. 75   'under our eyes' – Cecil *op. cit.* p. 45

p. 75   'size of the military' – N. Maclean *op. cit.*

p. 75   'irredeemably heterosexual' – Carter op. cit. photograph caption

p. 75   'the Spanish front' – MacNeice, *Autumn Journal* vi, in his *Collected Poems*

p. 76   'horrible development' – *Documents on British Foreign Policy*, quoted Cecil *op. cit.* p. 46

p. 76   'official humbug' – Brendon *op. cit.* p. 332

p. 76   'prolonging the war' – quoted Gardiner *op. cit.* p. 392

p. 76   'fear of ideas' – Ireland, *Traitors* p. 9

p. 76   'so much the better' – Gardiner *op. cit.* p. 393

p. 76   'Non-Intervention agreement' – Taylor, *English History 1914–45*, quoted Holzman *op. cit.* p. 89

p. 76   'a true gentleman' – Brendon *op. cit.* p. 331

p. 77   'the International Brigade' – to Dennis Ogden, 1980, A. Maclean papers *op. cit.*

p. 77   'confidence in himself' – TNA FCO 158/186

p. 77   'and ticklish work' – *ibid.*

p. 77   'with cigarette ends' – quoted Cecil *op. cit.* p. 46

p. 77   'efficiently and zealously' – Brendon *op. cit.* p. 332

p. 77   'the right background' – Cairncross *op. cit.* pp. 56–7

p. 78   'brains in the Foreign Office' – West and Tsarev *op. cit.* p. 208

p. 78   'lack of social graces' – Andrew and Mitrokhin *op. cit.* p. 108

p. 78   'amiability and weakness' – Connolly *op. cit.* p. 17

p. 78   'morally and physically' – *ibid.* p. 20

p. 78   'of view simultaneously' – *ibid.* p. 21

p. 79   'this wish isn't unhelpful' – TNA FCO 158/186

p. 79   'sound political judgement' – *ibid.*

p. 79   fn. died in the gulag – Andrew and Gordievsky *op. cit.* p. 106

p. 79   153 executed – Damaskin and Elliott, *Kitty Harris* p. 153

p. 79   'in their teeth' – Brendon *op. cit.* p. 403

p. 80   'become a clod' – Walter Krivitsky, Spartacus-educational.com

p. 80   'real spy after all' – Andrew and Mitrokhin *op. cit.* p. 102

p. 80   sleep all he liked – Michael Voslensky, *Nomenklatura*, quoted in Kern, *A Death in Washington* p. 101

p. 81   'met the case' – TNA KV 2/1022

p. 81   'bumptious in manner' – TNA KV 2/2008, quoted Andrew *op. cit.* p. 180

p. 81   'shrapnel samples from G.' – Damaskin and Elliott *op. cit.* p. 185

p. 82   'destroy his idealism' – *ibid.* p. 148

p. 82   'preached by Christianity' – quoted Hermiston, *The Greatest Traitor* p. 126

p. 83   'the working classes' – TNA KV 2/805

p. 84   'out for a walk' – Andrew and Mitrokhin *op. cit.* p. 107

p. 84   'Wilson's surgery hours' – Damaskin and Elliott *op. cit.* p. 151

p. 84   on 7 January – *ibid.* p. 162

p. 85   be of use again – *ibid.* p. 163

p. 85   'Otto and Theo' – undated letter in Maclean KGB file, quoted Costello and Tsarev *op. cit.* pp. 211–12

p. 86   she loved him – Costello and Tsarev *op. cit.* p. 210

p. 86   'as far as possible' – *ibid.* p. 211

p. 86   from his destination – Damaskin and Elliott *op. cit.* p. 171

p. 86   their private schools – Orlov, *Handbook* (1963), quoted Costello and Tsarev *op. cit.* p. 210

p. 87   and made love – *ibid.* p. 177

p. 87   'of his own class' – Deutsch KGB file 32826, quoted Costello and Tsarev *op. cit.* pp. 193–4

p. 87   'Fancy-Pants' Maclean – F. Maclean *op. cit.* p. 237

p. 88   'an odd taste' – TNA FCO 158/186

p. 88   'work point of view' – *ibid.*

p. 88   'naturally delighted' – TNA KV 2/4140

p. 88   straight to Moscow – Damaskin and Elliott *op. cit.* p. 182

p. 88   'is non-existent' – Andrew *op. cit.* p. 185

Chapter 5: City of Light

p. 89   'an emotive subject' – D. Maclean, *British Foreign Policy since Suez* p. 9

p. 89   'his diplomatic debut' – Lawford *op. cit.* p. 289

p. 89   'Napoleon were feeble' –Shirer, *The Collapse of the Third Republic*, p. 339

p. 89   seventeen air brigades – Hugh Ragsdale, *The Soviets, the Munich Crisis and the Coming of World War Two*, quoted Holzman *op. cit.* p. 105

p. 90   'action with France' – *Foreign Relations of the United States (FRUS)* 1938, vol. 1, quoted *ibid.* p. 106

p. 90   'in acid terms' – Cecil *op. cit.* p. 51

p. 90   'almost any price' – Phipps telegram 24.9.38, *ibid.*

p. 90   'without any culture' – quoted Brendon *op. cit.* p. 461

p. 90   'and without fighting' – MacNeice *op. cit.* vii

p. 90   'the aggressor's appetite' – quoted Brendon *op. cit.* p. 577

p. 90   'betrayal of Czechoslovakia' – post-1976 to Dennis Ogden, A. Maclean papers, Cambridge University Library

p. 91   'corruption of Stalinism' – Lehmann, *The Whispering Gallery* p. 282

p. 91   'of German power' – TNA KV 4/16

p. 92   'to be abandoned' – Read and Fisher, *The Deadly Embrace* p. 30

p. 92   'to leave early' – Lawford to Cecil, quoted Cecil *op. cit.* p. 54

p. 92   'de la République' – Borovik *op. cit.* p. 143

p. 93   'with us anymore' – Damaskin and Elliott *op. cit.* p. 183

p. 93   'loyalty to us' – *ibid.* p. 186

p. 93   'hates this atmosphere' – Maclean KGB file 83791, quoted Costello and Tsarev *op. cit.* pp. 215–16

p. 93   'was doing little' – obituary, *Independent* 29.9.96

p. 94   'in the Communist system' – *ibid.*

p. 94   'for technical matters' – Damaskin and Elliott *op. cit.* p. 184

p. 94   blocking the drain – *ibid.* p. 185

p. 95   rather gloomy apartment' – Cecil *op. cit.* p. 53

p. 95   'sofas of orange-crates' – *ibid.*

p. 95   'Left Book Club' – *ibid.*

p. 95   'but definitely *ordinaire*' – Lawford to Cecil, *ibid.*

p. 95   on the Paris Metro – papers of Patrick Reilly, Bodleian Library, Oxford

p. 96   'to say good-night' – Cecil *op. cit.* p. 53

p. 96   'and ill at ease' – Cecil in Andrew and Dilks (eds), *The Missing Dimension* p. 174

p. 96   'state of anxiety' – Cecil, 'Legends Spies Tell', *Encounter*, April 1978

p. 96   'few curt answers' – Cecil, *A Divided Life* p. 53

p. 97   'Germany and Italy' – Maisky, *Diaries* p. 57

p. 97   'ideas of liberty …' – quoted Boyle *op. cit.* p. 178

p. 97   'entirely different mentality!' – Maisky *op. cit.* p. 192

p. 98   'with its contents' – *FRUS* 1939 vol. 1, quoted Holzman *op. cit.* p. 117

p. 98   code-named 'the Baron' – Jeffery, *MI6* p. 312

p. 98   fn. translate as 'washtub' – Brendon *op. cit.* p. 580

p. 98   'such tactful manners!' – Maisky *op. cit.* p. 212

p. 99   'reaching an agreement' – *ibid.* p. 216

p. 99   thirty-two 'attendants' – *ibid.* p. 219

p. 100   It was a 'bombshell' – Modin *op. cit.* p. 81

p. 100   'nearly destroyed' it – to Dennis Ogden 26.1.80, A. Maclean papers *op. cit.*

p. 100   '200 years earlier' – Cairncross *op. cit.* pp. 79–80

p. 100   'whatever the consequences' – *ibid.* p. 82

p. 100   'against fascism now?' – quoted Macintyre *op. cit.* p. 48

p. 100   'made war inevitable' – Rees, *A Chapter of Accidents* p. 149

p. 100   'one of their agents' – Andrew and Mitrokhin *op. cit.* p. 150

p. 100   a 'ticking bomb' – Lownie *op. cit.* p. 103

p. 100   Moscow Centre wisely refused – Andrew and Mitrokhin *op. cit.* p. 113

p. 101   'falls into pattern' – quoted Fisher *op. cit.* p. 67

p. 101   'are fighting for' – Koestler, *Scum of the Earth* pp. 30–1

p. 101   'going to happen' – *The Times* 21.11.79, quoted Carter *op. cit.* p. 241

p. 102   'term than lover' – Gardiner *op. cit.* p. 186

p. 102   'come out at last' – MacNeice *op. cit.* xxiv

p. 102   'and laughed uproariously' – Cecil, *A Divided Life* p. 55

p. 103   'hostilities with Russia' – TNA CAB/65/5/26, quoted Holzman *op. cit.* p. 125

p. 103   'campaign in Britain' – Maisky *op. cit.* p. 244

p. 103   'its downward path' – *ibid.* p. 252

p. 103   'in the Caucasus' – *ibid.*

pp. 103–4 'small man, a Pole' – TNA KV 2/802

p. 104   'menacing blue eyes' – Newton *op. cit.* p. xviii

p. 104   'Western European countries' – TNA KV 2/802

p. 104   as Walter Scott – Andrew and Mitrokhin *op. cit.* p. 981

p. 104   'general in the army' – TNA KV 2/805

p. 105   'our other information' – FO minutes 24.5.39, 25.5.39, 26.5.39, quoted Kern *op. cit.* p. 192

p. 105   'a theatre of war' – memorandum by Mallet, TNA KV 2/802

p. 105   'also a sculptor' – TNA KV 2/802

p. 105   'in artistic circles' – FBI WFO 65–5648

p. 106   'interests of the State' – TNA KV 2/815

p. 106   'a real ordeal' – Andrew and Mitrokhin *op. cit.* p. 65

p. 106   'ugly unsolved puzzle' – TNA KV 2/816

p. 106   *Gone with the Wind* – Newton *op. cit.* p. 19

p. 106   'citizens of the USSR' – TNA KV 2/805

p. 106   it was poison – Andrew *op. cit.* p. 264

p. 106   'out of his shell' – Liddell, *The Guy Liddell Diaries* vol. 1, p. 62

p. 107   'chiefs of the Foreign Office' – TNA KV 2/805

p. 108   'have tried before' – quoted in Martin, *Wilderness of Mirrors* p. 6

Chapter 6: Left Bank

p. 109   'of Melinda Marling' – Cecil, *A Divided Life* p. 58

p. 109   a different setting – Fisher *op. cit.* p. 70

p. 109   the 'heterogeneous society' – Hoare *op. cit.* p. 45

p. 110   had been published – Neil Pearson Rare Books website

p. 111   'a problem child' – TNA KV 6/144

p. 111   'lazy, carefree life' – Hoare *op. cit.* p. 33

p. 111   'be quite dominant' – *ibid.* p. 36

p. 111   'hard little nut' – TNA FCO 158/191

p. 112   'a bit prim' – Natasha Walter, 'Spies and Lovers', *Guardian* 10.5.03

p. 112   'her eyes shine' – Cecil, *A Divided Life* p. 59

p. 113   'relating to the cinema' – TNA KV 2/4150

p. 113   'practically no friends' – TNA KV 2/4143

p. 113   'interested by him' – Hoare *op. cit.* p. 47

p. 113   'severe and distinguished' – Connolly *op. cit.* p. 21

p. 114   'demolishing your apartment' – quoted Cecil, *A Divided Life* p. 60

p. 114   'and English artists' – Toynbee, 'Maclean and I' *op. cit.*

p. 114   'gossamer-thin nightdress' – Damaskin and Elliott *op. cit.* p. 191

p. 114   'the same language' – *ibid.* p. 192

p. 115   'than she thought' – *ibid.*

p. 115   'and with enthusiasm' – Maclean KGB file 83791, quoted Costello and Tsarev *op. cit.* p. 217

p. 116   'together ever since' – *ibid.* p. 215

p. 116   'I have only one' – TNA KV 2/4150

p. 117   'place and password' – Borovik *op. cit.* p. 151

p. 117   'good and brave comrade' – Damaskin and Elliott *op. cit.* p. 196

p. 118   processed and despatched – *ibid.* p. 197

p. 118   'gas-mask cases' – *ibid.* p. 190

p. 119   'months or days . . .' – TNA FCO 158/186

p. 119   'something of a weakling' – Sir John Balfour to Boyle, quoted Boyle p. 300

p. 120   'to leave France' – Hoare *op. cit.* p. 49

p. 120   'wonderful, Mummy!?' – *ibid.*

p. 120   the best man – TNA KV 2/4150

p. 120   'surrealist goulash' – Koestler *op. cit.* p. 166

p. 120   a refugee committee – Page, Leitch and Knightley *op. cit.* p. 100

p. 121   best Parisian meals – Cecil, *A Divided Life* pp. 49–50

Chapter 7: Blitz and Barbarossa

p. 122   'their finest hour' – Gilbert, *Finest Hour* pp. 568–71

p. 122   fn. 'his impromptu remarks' – quoted *New York Times Magazine* 3.7.60 p. 31

p. 122   to see them – Cecil, *A Divided Life* p. 63

p. 123   preferably in church – Fisher *op. cit.* p. 81

p. 123   mother in Surrey – N. Maclean *op. cit.*

p. 123   'by air raids' – Maisky *op. cit.* p. 289

p. 124   finished much later – Fisher *op. cit.* pp. 80–1

p. 124   evacuation to Bordeaux – Cecil, *A Divided Life* p. 65

p. 124   of what wolfram – *ibid.*

p. 124   'the word "immature" recurs' – TNA KV 2/4140

p. 125   'should be broken' – quoted Andrew and Mitrokhin *op. cit.* p. 109

p. 126   'flattery and hypocrisy' – Andrew and Gordievsky *op. cit.* p. 130

p. 126   'moonlike bespectacled face' – Cairncross *op. cit.* p. 90

p. 126   'angry eyebrows' – Vladimir Borkovsky, quoted Costello and Tsarev *op. cit.* p. 218

p. 126   'business-like manner' – *ibid.*

p. 126   'most general terms' – Borovik *op. cit.* p. 135

p. 126   'including the leaders' – Churchill, *The Second World War: Their Finest Hour*, quoted Boyle *op. cit.* pp. 187–8

p. 127   'young and so lost' – letter to Cecil, quoted Cecil, *A Divided Life* p. 65

p. 127 'would not have missed' – Hoare *op. cit.* p. 50

p. 127 'destroyers around a battleship' – Colin Perry, quoted Ziegler, *London at War* p. 112

p. 127 'blown to bits' – Lehmann, *I Am my Brother* pp. 80–1

p. 128 'fell in love' – TNA KV 2/4143

p. 128 'an inconsolable child' – Boyle *op. cit.* p. 201

p. 128 'relieved of it' – Maclean KGB file 83791, quoted Costello and Tsarev *op. cit.* p. 219

p. 129 three and a half years – Carter *op. cit.* p. 268

p. 129 Walter Krivitsky – West and Tsarev *op. cit.* p. 145

p. 129 could be carried out – Cairncross *op. cit.* pp. 80–1

p. 129 following morning – *ibid.* p. 92

p. 129 4,419 documents – Andrew and Mitrokhin *op. cit.* p. 120

p. 130 'possibilities of peace' – Rees *op. cit.* p. 155

p. 130 'intellectual challenge' – Luke *op. cit.* p. ix

p. 131 'familiar territory' – *ibid.* p. 145

p. 131 white-coated waiters – Holzman *op. cit.* p. 153 and n.

p. 131 'of stubborn loyalties' – Hoare *op. cit.* p. 51

p. 131 claustrophobia of the shelters – *ibid.* p. 51

p. 131 'reached ambassadorial level!' – Andrew and Gordievsky *op. cit.* p. 212

p. 132 'clumsy propaganda manoeuvre' – Bullock, *Hitler and Stalin* p. 786

p. 132 'attack … seemed improbable' – Maisky *op. cit.* p. 365

p. 132 'sense of relief' – A. Blunt, unpublished memoirs

p. 133 'incomprehensible risk' – KGB files, quoted Andrew *op. cit.* p. 273

p. 133 'coming to England' – Andrew and Mitrokhin *op. cit.* p. 157

p. 133 'Blue-Eyed Gretchen' – Bower, *The Perfect English Spy* p. 83

p. 134 'aristocrats' at that – quoted Haslam *op. cit.* p. 127

p. 134 'Britain been exposed'? – Tsarev and West *op. cit.* p. 161

p. 134 British Embassy in Moscow – *ibid.*

p. 135 one-time pad – Haynes and Klehr, *Venona* pp. 25–8

p. 136 thousands of pads – *ibid.* p. 29

p. 136 solving crossword puzzles – *ibid.* p. 30

p. 137 emphasis on cryptography – N. West, *Venona* pp. 3–4

p. 137 Berlin and Helsinki – Haynes and Klehr *op. cit.* p. 31

p. 137 'general characteristics' – *ibid.*

p. 137 Secretary of State Stettinius – Lamphere and Schachtman, *The FBI–KGB War* p. 84

p. 138 'tired and worn' – Cecil, *A Divided Life* p. 67

p. 138 'drank too much' – Hoare *op. cit.* p. 51

p. 138 'reeking of whisky' – Boyle *op. cit.* p. 251

p. 138 'sweetness and understanding' – Connolly *op. cit.* p. 25

p. 138 'say what it is' – Boyle *op. cit.* p. 251

p. 138 'Within reason' – TNA FCO 158/186

p. 138   'a trifle immature' – TNA FCO 158/186
p. 139   'admirably clear assessments' – TNA FO 371/42556, quoted Kerr *op. cit.* p. 95
p. 139   'any British subject' – Winston Churchill, *Blood, Sweat and Tears*, quoted Newton *op. cit.* p. 66

Chapter 8: Homer

p. 141   George VI had eaten his – Roberts, *'The Holy Fox'* pp. 380–1
p. 141   'of British diplomacy' – *ibid.*
p. 141   his 'visceral aversion' – Modin *op. cit.* p. 101
p. 142   'supercilious and ineffective' – Fisher *op. cit.* p. 82
p. 142   'bad, decayed teeth' – FBI interview with Hal Dunbar, FBI WFO 65–5648
p. 142   'passionate but unsatisfied' – Fisher *op. cit.* p. 83
p. 142   Park Avenue as hers – Newton *op. cit.* p. 82
p. 142   the 'problem child' – TNA KV 6/144
p. 142   did not give her any – Hoare *op. cit.* p. 52
p. 143   'at the time' – TNA KV 6/143
p. 143   the Dunbar farm – TNA KV 2/4143
p. 143   602,000 in 2010 – *Washington Post* 22.12.10
p. 144   Kalorama Road – TNA KV 6/143
p. 144 $250 (furnished) respectively – TNA FO 115/3610, quoted Holzman *op. cit.* p. 162
p. 144   to San Francisco – Andrew and Mitrokhin *op. cit.* p. 165
p. 145   'in case of need' – NSA files, quoted Holzman *op. cit.* p. 169
p. 145   'work was based' – A. Maclean papers *op. cit.*
p. 145   'unravel complex issues' – Andrew and Gordievsky *op. cit.* p. 260
p. 146   'all the sessions' – NSA files, quoted Holzman *op. cit.* p. 171
p. 146   'Boar with Captain' – Venona 1105–1110 2/3.8.44, quoted Haynes and Klehr *op. cit.* p. 54
p. 146   'with this plan' – *ibid.*
p. 147   'in European politics ...' – *ibid.* p. 172
p. 147   'for bigger coins' – Djilas, *Conversations with Stalin*, quoted Bullock, *op. cit.* p. 942
p. 147   'change in the plans' – Haynes and Klehr *op. cit.* p. 54
p. 147   'The budding paragon' – Balfour, *Not Too Correct an Aureole* p. 260
p. 147   'particular ideological bias' – *ibid.*
p. 148   'showed through at times' – conversation with Boyle, quoted Boyle *op. cit.* p. 300
p. 148   taken of his family – Boyle *op. cit.* pp. 290–1
p. 148   'not of this century' – quoted Conant, *The Irregulars* p. 25
p. 148   'Could you invite some?' – Michael Ignatieff, *Isaiah Berlin*, quoted Holzman *op. cit.* p. 165
p. 149   'liberal young people' – *ibid.* p. 166

p. 149　　'stupid and reactionary Alice' – Berlin to Boyle, quoted Boyle *op. cit.* p. 292

p. 149　　'thick and thin' – Holzman *op. cit.* p. 165

p. 149　　'pulled off him' – Berlin to Boyle, quoted Boyle *op. cit.* p. 292

p. 149　　'and her family' – Berlin, *Affirming* p. 121

p. 149　　'unreconstructed liberal reformer' – Kennedy, *Freedom from Fear* p. 457

p. 149　　'unable to forgive him' – Holzman *op. cit.* p. 166

p. 150　　'so impeccably organised' – R. West, *The New Meaning of Treason* p. 222

p. 150　　'any of his colleagues' – R. West *op. cit.* p. 222

p. 150　　'occupation of Germany' – Holzman *op. cit.* p. 175

p. 151　　'plans of the British' – Venona 1271–4, 7.9.44, quoted Haynes and Klehr *op. cit.* p. 53

p. 151　　influence in Greece – Bullock *op. cit.* p. 939

p. 151　　Cunard's shipping lines – FBI WFO 65–5648

p. 151　　'to be unsatisfactory' – *ibid.*

p. 152　　sort things out – Hoare *op. cit.* p. 54

p. 152　　to be deported – Cecil, 'Legends Spies Tell'

p. 152　　by Marie Morvan – TNA KV 6/144

p. 152　　bring fresh ones – interview Phyllis Parker 27.10.16

p. 152　　'American social life' – FBI *op. cit.*

p. 152　　'their instinctive vulgarity' – Boyle interview with Hoare, quoted Boyle *op. cit.* p. 292

p. 152　　'with perfect manners' – FBI *op. cit.*

p. 152　　'the coming man' – Cecil, *A Divided Life* p. 73

p. 153　　'a pre-lunch drink' – TNA FCO 158/186

p. 153　　the Patriotic War – Holzman *op. cit.* p. 182

p. 153　　'had been obtained' – Newton *op. cit.* pp. 67–8

p. 154　　Chinese–British–American Committee – *ibid.*

p. 154　　even suggested Melinda – KGB file 43173, quoted Weinstein and Vassiliev, *The Haunted Wood* p. 230

p. 154　　'a timely way' – KGB file 35118, quoted *ibid.*

Chapter 9: Iron Curtain

p. 155　　'a bad effect' – Montefiore, *Stalin* p. 424

p. 156　　respective grand residences – Andrew and Mitrokhin *op. cit.* p. 173

p. 156　　well with caviar – *ibid.*

p. 156　　'growing in the hall' – Churchill, *Triumph and Tragedy* p. 303

p. 156　　receive a knighthood – Andrew and Gordievsky *op. cit.* p. 274

p. 156　　would raise them – Plokhy, *Yalta* p. 78

p. 157　　'boozy, womanising' – Montefiore *op. cit.* p. 428

p. 157　　'after our bodies' – *ibid.*

p. 157　　'wrong about Stalin' – Andrew and Mitrokhin *op. cit.* p. 176

p. 157　　'toilet is over there' – Andrew and Gordievsky *op. cit.* p. 277

p. 157   eight plenary sessions – Bullock *op. cit.* p. 956

p. 157   'the state of Europe' – USNA Leahy file, quoted Newton *op. cit.* p. 74

p. 158   'watchmaker's mind' – R. West, *op. cit.* pp. 221–2

p. 158   'behalf of the Poles' – TNA FCO 850/185, quoted Newton *op. cit.* p. 75

p. 158   'differences of tactics' – Venona 1815 30.3.45, quoted Hamrick, *Deceiving the Deceivers* p. 75

p. 158   'his last word' – Venona 714 8.3.45, quoted N. West *op. cit.* p. 128

p. 158   'collision with the Russians' – Venona 1517 7.3.45, quoted *ibid.* p. 130

p. 158   'Molotov remain adamant' – *ibid.* p. 134

p. 159   'certain foreign targets' – Hamrick *op. cit.* p. 35

p. 159   had been transcribed – David Stout, *New York Times* 18.8.02

p. 160   'of photographic memories' – K. Philby *op. cit.* p. 68

p. 160   'on sound ground' – TNA KV 4/196

p. 160   'sums of money' – Burgess KGB file, quoted N. West, *Crown Jewels* p. 171

p. 160   'sturdily built' car – Modin *op. cit.* p. 156

p. 161   'has to do it' – Cecil interview with Robin Denniston, quoted Cecil, *A Divided Life* p. 77

p. 161   Greek and Iranian regimes – Newton *op. cit.* p. 87

p. 161   'against socialist states' – A. Maclean papers *op. cit.*

p. 162   'lackadaisical in manner' – TNA FCO 158/186

p. 162   'Ambassador to Washington' – Newton interview with Alsop, quoted Newton *op. cit.* p. 68

p. 162   'comments grossly offensive' – *ibid.* p. 89

p. 163   'sent me Maclean' – Newton interview with Hickerson, quoted *ibid.*

p. 163   'confidence to Donald' – Gore-Booth, *With Great Truth and Respect* pp. 374–5

p. 163   'partner within it' – D. Maclean *op. cit.* p. 54

p. 163   'nations of the world' – quoted Holzman *op. cit.* p. 218

p. 164   'of personalities altogether' – quoted Hoare *op. cit.* p. 142

p. 164   'did so with hatred' – Hoare *op. cit.* p. 147

p. 164   'sensible walking-shoes' – Cecil, *A Divided Life* p. 73

p. 164   'been twice divorced' – TNA KV 2/4141

p. 164   'and conscienceless talker' – undated post-1956 letter to Alan Maclean, A. Maclean papers *op. cit.*

p. 164   'painful and comic' – TNA FCO 158/186

p. 165   he might behave – Hoare *op. cit.* p. 54

Chapter 10: Distant Thunder

p. 167   'far from rock steady' – K. Philby *op. cit.* p. 119

p. 167   Pera Palace Hotel – Macintyre *op. cit.* p. 95

p. 167   'with Soviet activities' – TNA FCO 158/193

p. 167   in a few days – *ibid.*

p. 168   'the greatest importance' – K. Philby *op. cit.* p. 119

p. 168   not have to do so – Macintyre *op. cit.* p. 98

p. 168   two 'diplomatic couriers' – Andrew *op. cit.* p. 344

p. 169   'not worth including' – K. Philby *op. cit.* p. 128

p. 169   'narrow squeak indeed' – Andrew *op. cit.* p. 113

p. 169   'arouse undue interest' – Gouzenko, *This Was my Choice* p. 306

p. 170   fn. material for blackmail – Andrew and Mitrokhin *op. cit.* p. 181

p. 171   of false passports – Lamphere *op. cit.* p. 83

p. 171   'most closely concerned' – Newton *op. cit.* p. 94

p. 171   'suburban bank clerk' – Moorehead, *The Traitors* p. 19

p. 171   'support of the left' – *ibid.* p. 21

p. 172   was highly 'agitated' – Andrew *op. cit.* p. 344

p. 172   in Eastern Europe – *ibid.* p. 343

p. 173   'kept in the picture' – Liddell Diary, TNA KV 4/467

p. 173   'former fighting allies' – quoted Romerstein and Breindel, *The Venona Secrets* p. 13

p. 173   'somewhat squalid case' – Moorehead *op. cit.* p. 43.

p. 173   'an empty theatre' – *ibid.* p. 46

p. 173   'wickedness … and degradation' – quoted Newton *op. cit.* p. 125

p. 173   'safety of mankind' – Report of Royal Commission, Ottawa, quoted Cecil, *A Divided Life* p. 77

p. 173   of importance anyway – H. Montgomery Hyde, *Atom Bomb Spies*, quoted Andrew *op. cit.* p. 348

p. 173   'sense of shame' – Andrew *op. cit.* p. 203

p. 174   'have to counter' – TNA KV 4/158, quoted *ibid.* p. 351

p. 174   'give him a password' – TNA CAB 130/20, quoted Hennessy, *The Secret State* p. 90

p. 174   'spoken of with respect' – K. Philby *op. cit.* p. 167

p. 174   'svelte and striking blonde' – *World-Telegram*, quoted *New Yorker* 13.10.48

p. 174   'Nutmeg Mata Hari' – A. J. Liebling, *ibid.*

p. 174   on the *Mayflower* – Weinstein and Vassiliev *op. cit.* p. 88

p. 175   outlet in the US – *Time* 9.8.48

p. 175   'about each other' – Elizabeth Bentley, *Out of Bondage*, quoted Andrew and Gordievsky *op. cit.* p. 228–9

p. 175   her knitting bag – *ibid.* p. 283

p. 176   'than anything else' – Akhmerov to Moscow 25.6.44, Venona files, quoted Weinstein and Vassiliev *op. cit.* p. 98

p. 176   'her natural needs' – *ibid.* p. 100

p. 176   'not given Stephenson' – KGB file 75405, quoted Weinstein and Vassiliev *op. cit.* p. 104

p. 177   'a future meeting' – *ibid.*

p. 177   'safeguarded from failure' – Haynes, Klehr and Vassiliev, *Spies* p. 400

p. 177   'too well lately' – KGB file 75405, quoted Weinstein and Vassiliev *op. cit.* p. 108

p. 177   'Ambassador look into' – FBI Vaults

p. 178   'leak like sieves' – Hennessy and Townsend, 'The Documentary Spoor of Burgess and Maclean'

p. 178   the merest outline – Newton *op. cit.* p. 123

p. 178   'my own colleagues' – *ibid.* p. 125

p. 179   1,000 million to one – N. West *op. cit.* p. 17

p. 180   peace with Berlin – Haynes and Klehr *op. cit.* p. 8

p. 180   each telegram decipherable – Wright, *Spycatcher* p. 180

p. 181   'language is "the"' – *Daily Telegraph* 20.8.02

p. 181   'they were doing' – David Stout, *New York Times* 18.8.02

p. 181   1.5 per cent was cracked – Romerstein and Breindel *op. cit.* pp. 10–11

p. 181   'Tsars before him' – Newton *op. cit.* p. 101

p. 182   'on excellent authority' – quoted *ibid.* p. 103

p. 182   'about this double-cross' – Modin *op. cit.* p. 120

p. 182   'consultations with the British' – Dept of State, Press Conferences, quoted Newton *op. cit.* pp. 103–4

p. 183   'would be taken' – *FRUS* 1945 vol. 8 quoted *ibid.* p. 104

p. 183   'anathema to the USSR' – Modin *op. cit.* p. 120

p. 184   'bitterness and hostility' – USNA 767.68119, quoted Newton *op. cit.* pp. 106–7

p. 184   'to the Turkish Government' – TNA FCO 371/48699, *ibid.* p. 107

p. 184   'Soviet naval base' – Modin *op. cit.* p. 120

p. 184   'thoughts with us' – TNA FCO 371/48699, quoted Newton *op. cit.* p. 107

p. 184   'tell him the result' – *ibid.*

Chapter 11: Access All Areas

p. 186   fn. only in 1957 – Herken, *The Brotherhood of the Bomb* p. 62

p. 186   'against the Japanese' – Truman, *Year of Decision*, quoted Cecil *op. cit.* p. 71

p. 186   get a move on – Bohlen, *Witness to History* p. 237

p. 186   'of total destruction' – Truman, *Years of Trial and Hope*, quoted Boyle *op. cit.* p. 297

p. 187   'actual use basis' – Herken, *op. cit.* p. 103

p. 187   'to the War Cabinet' – Costello and Tsarev *op. cit.* p. 218

p. 187   'on that basis' – Herken *op. cit.* p. 106

p. 187   'dealt with atomic energy' – Makins, unpublished memoirs

p. 188   'in security matters' – *ibid.*

p. 188   Field Marshal Lord Wilson – Holzman *op. cit.* pp. 238–9

p. 188   'for the Americans' – Modin *op. cit.* p. 199

p. 189   'arrested as and when' – Newton *op. cit.* p. 134

p. 189   'areas to pursue' – TNA FCO 115/4313, quoted *ibid.* p. 180

p. 190   made in 1948 – Hennessy, *Never Again* p. 353

p. 190   'through the building' – Strauss, *Men and Decisions* p. 256

p. 190	'in agreeable circumstances' – Newton *op. cit.* p. 149
p. 190	with 'heavy responsibilities' – FBI WFO 65–5648
p. 190	met in the building – Holzman *op. cit.* p. 248
p. 191	most 'comradely' occasion – Cecil, *A Divided Life* p. 84
p. 191	a year later – Holzman *op. cit.* p. 240
p. 191	the Cairo–Suez region – Cecil, *A Divided Life* p. 83
p. 191	'on Truman's face' – Newton *op. cit.* p. 168
p. 191	'until about 1955–60' – TNA CAB 81/132, quoted Hennessy, *The Secret State* p. 33
p. 192	'to the Manhattan Project' – Newton *op. cit.* p. 134
p. 192	'I do for Roger Makins' – TNA KV 2/4140
p. 192	two retired admirals – FBI WFO 65–5648
p. 192	'and sleep there' – *ibid.*
p. 193	'strongly he felt' – quoted Boyle *op. cit.* p. 301
p. 193	'became unstable' – TNA KV 2/4143
p. 193	an 'awful swine' – *ibid.*
p. 193	'attitude of hatred' – *ibid.*
p. 194	'all our troubles!' – Cecil, *A Divided Life* p. 79
p. 194	'great deal indeed' – R. West *op. cit.* p. 227
p. 194	'akin to skittles' – Gillies, *Radical Diplomat* p. 188
p. 194	fn. their 1950 edition – Gillies *op. cit.* p. 183
p. 195	'new policy decisions' – Boyle *op. cit.* p. 302
p. 195	'a sweetie' – Cecil, *A Divided Life* p. 79
p. 195	'to me by Stalin' – *ibid.*
p. 195	'including the Registry' – Boyle *op. cit.* p. 301
p. 195	'left the room' – Boyle *op. cit.* p. 80
p. 196	modest dresses instead – Hoare *op. cit.* pp. 48–9
p. 196	he became 'dissipated' – TNA KV 2/4143
p. 196	'the homosexual streak' – Cecil, 'Legends Spies Tell'
p. 197	teenage girl's discomfort – interview Phyllis Parker 27.10.16
p. 197	empty of families – *ibid.*
p. 198	'disappears in sweat' – Hoare *op. cit.* p. 59
p. 198	New York Consulate – Cecil, *A Divided Life* p. 78
p. 198	'tension was palpable' – *ibid.* pp. 78–9
p. 199	dead letter drops – KGB file 43173, quoted Weinstein and Vassiliev *op. cit.* pp. 290–1
p. 199	fn. 'Marshall will do' – Isaacs and Downing, *Cold War* p. 45
p. 200	'to sinking men' – quoted *ibid.* p. 52
p. 200	'State Department with joy' – TNA FCO 115/4359
p. 201	'stop at exhortation' – TNA FCO 115/4348, quoted Newton *op. cit.* p. 195
p. 201	'held in Washington' – *ibid.* p. 196
p. 201	'was in Whitehall' – Cecil, *A Divided Life* p. 85
p. 201	'any predatory animal' – TNA FCO 115/4348, quoted Newton *op. cit.* p. 196

p. 202   'of Soviet expansion' – quoted Martin *op. cit.* p. 51

p. 203   'to other members' – TNA FCO 158/186

p. 203   'his young family' – *ibid.*

p. 204   'good old jokes' – quoted Newton *op. cit.* p. 22

p. 204   'was contemplating suicide' – FBI WFO 65–5648

Chapter 12: Chaos on the Nile

p. 205   'Kennedy's favourite diplomat' – quoted Newton *op. cit.* p. 159

p. 205   'calibre and attainment' – *ibid.* p. 218

p. 206   'life in general' – *ibid.*.

p. 206   'able to acquire!' – TNA FCO 158/85

p. 206   'a shocking state' – TNA KV 4/470

p. 207   and British embassies – Newton *op. cit.* p. 225

p. 208   'a harmonious couple' – Hoare *op. cit.* p. 55

p. 208   'not an expert' – Connolly *op. cit.* p. 27

p. 209   'rather pretty, well off' – Holzman *op. cit.* p. 273

p. 209   'diplomats as amateurs' – Newton *op. cit.* p. 226

p. 209   at his own elbow – *ibid.*

p. 209   'in the Middle East' – TNA FCO 141/1377

p. 210   'champion of the underdog' – Hamilton, *Keepers of the Flame* p. 127

p. 210   'sympathy with the Nationalist cause' – W. S. Blunt, *My Diaries* p. 12

p. 210   with ivory pieces – Fisher *op. cit.* p. 87

p. 210   'to their parents' – interview Colin Campbell 8.9.15

p. 211   the night before – Fisher *op. cit.* p. 88

p. 211   'Middle East cosmopolitans' – *ibid.*

p. 211   her 'American housekeeping' – FBI summary report, quoted Newton *op. cit.* p. 237

p. 211   'with gold trim' – N. Maclean *op. cit.*

p. 211   'shyness and diffidence' – Hoare *op. cit.* p. 58

p. 212   'young people's evening' – Cecil, *A Divided Life* p. 95

p. 212   'and simpler people' – quoted Newton *op. cit.* p. 229

p. 212   'of Cairo parties' – Hoare *op. cit.* p. 57

p. 212   'rather intense efficiency' – *ibid.* p. 58

p. 212   'independent minds' – K. Philby *op. cit.* p. 171

p. 212   'covenanting conscience' – *Sunday Times* Insight 8.10.67

p. 212   'country from Communism' – Hoare *op. cit.* pp. 57–8

p. 213   'and even contempt' – interview Colin Campbell 8.9.15

p. 213   'capital in 1940' – TNA FCO 158/186

p. 213   'and political problems' – Hoare *op. cit.* p. 58

p. 214   'relations with him' – Modin *op. cit.* pp. 163–4

p. 214   'even read it' – *ibid.*

p. 214   Tel Aviv and Jerusalem – Holzman *op. cit.* p. 277

p. 214   'chances of peace' – *FRUS* 1949 vol. 6, quoted Holzman *op. cit.* p. 278

p. 215   2.7 million lives – *ibid.* p. 288

p. 215   'position in the Middle East' – quoted Newton *op. cit.* p. 226

p. 215   'insensitive handling' – Andrew and Mitrokhin *op. cit.* p. 202

p. 215   'swan among geese' – Modin *op. cit.* p. 164

p. 215   a 'skulking informer' – *ibid.*

p. 216   'expected of him' – Andrew and Mitrokhin *op. cit.* p. 202

p. 216   in the hairdresser – Modin *op. cit.* p. 164

p. 217   end of his life – conversation Derek Johns 11.5.16

p. 217   'and very nosy' – quoted Andrew *op. cit.* p. 377

p. 217   'of Soviet institutions' – KGB file 43173, quoted Weinstein and Vassiliev *op. cit.* pp. 291–2

p. 217   'of any importance' – Haynes and Klehr *op. cit.* p. 49

p. 218   'Siberia time' – Lamphere and Schachtman, *op. cit.* p. 19

p. 218   'to three weeks' – *ibid.* p. 82

p. 219   'appalling blunder' – Modin *op. cit.* p. 192

p. 219   'skilful horse traders' – Lamphere and Schachtman, *op. cit.* p. 127

p. 219   'persona non grata' – TNA KV 4/470

p. 219   'classic flanking maneuver' – Lamphere and Schachtman *op. cit.* p. 129

p. 220   'in quick succession' – Fahmy, *Around the World with Isis* p. 27

p. 220   'the same people' – *ibid.* p. 27

p. 220   'sleep than most' – TNA KV 2/4141

p. 220   'almost daily basis' – Fahmy *op. cit.* p. 27

p. 220   with her servants – TNA FCO 158/186

p. 221   ended in 1948 – E. Philby, *Kim Philby* p. 158

p. 221   'a bad cold' – TNA FCO 158/186

p. 221   'betray his country' – Balfour *op. cit.* p. 114

p. 221   'of secret documents' – Sansom, *I Spied Spies* p. 234

p. 222   'Head of Chancery' – *ibid.*

p. 222   'the place up' – *ibid.* p. 236

p. 222   a security risk – Page, Leitch and Knightley *op. cit.* p. 203

p. 222   'officer like Maclean' – Cecil *op. cit.* p. 100

p. 223   'of other work' – TNA FCO 158/237

p. 223   'was a dear' – N. Maclean *op. cit.*

p. 223   'very difficult' – interview Viscountess Macmillan 18.11.15

p. 223   'cold American bitch' – TNA FCO 158/186

p. 223   'permanent affection' – letter to Alan Maclean 10.7.76, A. Maclean papers, Cambridge

p. 223   'an excellent talker' – Mayall, *Fireflies in Amber* p. 81

p. 223   'was absolutely infantile' – TNA FCO 158/186

p. 223   'no practical solutions' – *ibid.*

p. 224   'in the moonlight' – Mayall *op. cit.* p. 77

p. 224   version of arak – Page, Leitch and Knightley *op. cit.* p. 205

p. 225   'ugly excited murmur' – Mayall *op. cit.* p. 79
p. 225   'like very much' – *ibid.* p. 81
p. 226   'maudlin and contrite' – Page, Leitch and Knightley *op. cit.* p. 205
p. 226   'a rough ride' – *ibid.*
p. 226   'lives of his staff' – interview Colin Campbell 8.9.15
p. 226   'with proven fact' – information Nina Campbell 21.7.16
p. 226   'an adequate report' – Reilly papers, Bodleian
p. 226   'left-wing opinions' – TNA KV 2/4143
p. 227   'the British bulldogs' – Lamphere and Schachtman *op. cit.* p. 129
p. 227   the 'real story' – TNA FCO 158/1
p. 227   'nervous breakdowns' – TNA FCO 158/1
p. 227   'permanent nervous wreck' – TNA KV 6/141
p. 227   'entry-and-exit lists' – Lamphere and Schachtman *op. cit.* p. 129
p. 228   'at the facts' – TNA KV 4/470
p. 228   'information from us' – TNA FCO 158/1
p. 228   'Alexander Halpern's secretary' – TNA KV 4/471
p. 229   'ever been recruited' – TNA KV 6/141
p. 229   'views at the time' – *ibid.*
p. 229   'be a traitor' – Bower interview with Carey Foster, quoted Bower *op. cit.* p. 91
p. 229   'waste-paper baskets' – K. Philby *op. cit.* p. 167

Chapter 13: Collapse

p. 231   'pressing attention' – Cecil, quoted Andrew and Dilks *op. cit.* p. 188
p. 232   'and shabby clothes' – Lamphere and Schachtman *op. cit.* p. 130
p. 232   'wanted to do' – quoted Andrew *op. cit.* p. 378
p. 233   'as enquiries proceed' – TNA KV 6/141
p. 233   his Soviet 'colleagues' – K. Philby *op. cit.* p. 145
p. 233   'the British Embassy' – *ibid.* p. 147
p. 233   'of a problem' – *ibid.* p. 165
p. 234   'isotopes of Enormoz' – quoted N. West *op. cit.* p. 147
p. 234   'even cosy man' – A. Maclean *op. cit.* p. 100
p. 234   'a subject's story' – Lamphere *op. cit.* p. 135
p. 234   'the atomic bomb' – TNA KV 2/2146, quoted Andrew *op. cit.* p. 388
p. 235   'Dear Old Klaus' – A. Maclean *op. cit.* p. 101
p. 235   of 'disclosing myself' – Moorehead *op. cit.* p. 119
p. 235   'are doing wrongly' – *ibid.* p. 120
p. 236   US State Department – Lamphere and Schachtman *op. cit.* p. 136
p. 236   'history of nations' – quoted Newton *op. cit.* p. 235
p. 236   'their historic homeland' – Borovik *op. cit.* p. 272
p. 237   'A big zero' – *ibid.* p. 273
p. 237   'go by him' – FBI interviews, quoted Newton *op. cit.* pp. 237–8

p. 237   'was completely loaded' – *ibid.*

p. 237   'put in writing' – TNA FCO 158/186

p. 238   'amongst the friends' – Andrew *op. cit.* p. 267

p. 238   'draw to your attention' – TNA FCO 158/2

p. 238   'Krivetsky's [*sic*] interrogation report' – *ibid.*

p. 239   'itself out endlessly' – K. Philby *op. cit.* p. 167

p. 240   'Western imperialism' – Modin *op. cit.* p. 164

p. 240   'prepared to go' – *ibid.*

p. 240   'behaviour filtered through' – *ibid.*

p. 240   'looked at' the letter – *ibid.*

p. 241   read as well – Andrew and Mitrokhin *op. cit.* p. 202

p. 241   'decadent and effete' – quoted Cecil, *A Divided Life* p. 170

p. 241   'the Arabs here' – TNA FCO 158/157

p. 242   a 'leading Communist' – TNA KV 6/140

p. 242   'put him off altogether' – TNA KV 2/4140

p. 242   'definitely anti-Communist' – *ibid.*

p. 242   'not unbalanced, temperament' – *ibid.*

p. 242   'drinking difficulty' – *ibid.*

p. 243   'antique tropical suit' – Toynbee, 'Maclean and I' *op. cit.*

p. 243   'end-of-Empire gathering' – Toynbee diary 14.4.50

p. 243   'late for everything' – TNA FCO 158/186

p. 243   'two-day trough together' – Toynbee diary 22.4.50

p. 244   'or democratic ideas' – TNA KV 2/4143

p. 244   'almost equally' – Toynbee diary 26.5.50

p. 244   'it came from' – Toynbee, 'Maclean and I' *op. cit.*

p. 244   'I get drunk' – *ibid.*

p. 245   'be shut up' – Toynbee diary, quoted Holzman *op. cit.* pp. 300–1

p. 246   'had gone before' – Toynbee, 'Maclean and I' *op. cit.*

p. 246   'would pass out' – TNA FCO 158/186

p. 246   'and his wife' – FBI WFO 65–5648

p. 246   'astonished *suffragi*' – Hoare *op. cit.* p. 62

p. 246   'miasma of destruction' – Toynbee, 'Maclean and I' *op. cit.*

p. 246   into the bathtub – FBI WFO 65–5648

p. 247   'down the lavatory' – Hoare *op. cit.* p. 62

p. 247   'mirror remains intact' – Toynbee, 'Maclean and I' *op. cit.*

p. 247   'we might fall' – Toynbee diary 9.5.50

p. 247   had been 'gnawing' – TNA FCO 158/186

p. 247   'into their car' – Hoare *op. cit.* p. 62

p. 247   'serpent in Eden' – Toynbee, 'Maclean and I' *op. cit.*

p. 247   'show for it' – quoted Mount *op. cit.* p. 48

p. 247   'Donald went amok' – TNA KV 6/143

p. 247   'the Marling sisters' – Toynbee diary 10.5.50

p. 248   'state of mind' – TNA FCO 158/186

p. 248   'and somewhat offensive' – Newton *op. cit.* p. 240

p. 249   'a third country' – *ibid.*

p. 249   'a vicious circle' – *ibid.*

p. 250   'have been suffering' – TNA KV 2/4140

p. 250   'silent than usual' – Hoare *op. cit.* p. 63

Chapter 14: Reconciliation

p. 251   'break at home' – TNA FCO 158/186

p. 252   'known to me' – *ibid.*

p. 252   'a rapid cure' – *ibid.*

p. 252   'out for Cairo' – *ibid.*

p. 253   'overwhelmed with sadness' – quoted Hoare *op. cit.* pp. 64–5

p. 253   'missed a beat' – *ibid.*

p. 253   'in the war' – TNA FCO 158/186

p. 253   'psychiatric emergencies' – Fisher *op. cit.* p. 97

p. 254   'doesn't look good' – *ibid.*

p. 254   'most favourable treatment' – TNA FCO 158/186

p. 254   'slow and retarded' – *ibid.*

p. 255   'difficulties with his wife' – TNA KV 2/4140

p. 255   'ideal married life' – TNA KV 2/4143

p. 255   'of American wives' – TNA KV 2/4141

p. 255   'any point in it' – Hoare *op. cit.* p. 65

p. 255   'drug as "pentothal"' – TNA KV 2/4143

p. 256   'a family background' – TNA KV 2/4140

p. 256   'charm and intelligence' – Fisher *op. cit.* p. 98

p. 256   'is really desirable' – TNA FCO 158/186

p. 256   'be a quack' – Andrew *op. cit.* p. 421

p. 256   'Nothing Recorded Against' – Cecil, *A Divided Life* p. 110

p. 256   'help very much' – TNA KV 2/4140

p. 257   'a journalist friend' – *Daily Express* 17.5.50

p. 257   'of his condition' – TNA FCO 158/186

p. 257   of his 'trouble' – *ibid.*

p. 257   'shouldn't be concealed' – Toynbee diary 10.5.50

p. 258   'of your staff' – TNA FCO 158/186

p. 258   'with Philip Toynbee' – Partridge, *Everything to Lose* p. 121

p. 258   'some new thing' – TNA KV 2/4140

p. 258   'again in Cairo' – TNA FCO 158/186

p. 259   'between my eyes' – Sansom *op. cit.* p. 237

p. 259   'never coming back' – Hoare *op. cit.* p. 68

p. 260   'begin to operate' – Jung, *Memories, Dreams, Reflections*, quoted Cecil,
            A Divided Life p. 109

p. 260   'fighting her hard' – TNA FCO 158/4

p. 260   'from nervous exhaustion' – TNA KV 2/4140
p. 260   'no means normal' – *ibid.*
p. 260   'to people generally' – TNA KV 2/4141
p. 261   'and intellectual challenge' – Luke *op. cit.* p. ix
p. 261   'staff in Cairo' – Cecil, *A Divided Life* p. 112
p. 262   'The Russians!' – *ibid.* p. 113
p. 262   'of the DTs' – TNA KV 2/4143
p. 262   'his clinical condition' – Cecil, *A Divided Life* p. 113
p. 262   'Communism was right' – Robin Campbell, quoted Page, Leitch and
           Knightley *op. cit.* p. 217
p. 264   'Communists in Italy' – R. West *op. cit.* p. 207
p. 264   'No Trace Against' – Andrew *op. cit.* p. 391
p. 264   to an 'explosion' – TNA KV 6/144
p. 264   'happened to be drinking' – Rees *op. cit.* p. 180
p. 264   their local favourites – Lownie *op. cit.* p. 190
p. 265   'can't mean goats?' – *ibid.* p. 196
p. 265   'trail of havoc' – Rees *op. cit.* p. 195
p. 265   'points outside Washington' – K. Philby *op. cit.* p. 166
p. 266   'knock them out' – TNA KV 2/4140
p. 266   'Are they after me?' – quoted Page, Leitch and Knightley *op. cit.* p. 217
p. 267   'through front doors' – TNA FCO 158/186
p. 267   'as his bedroom' – Connolly *op. cit.* p. 29
p. 267   'return to him' – Hoare *op. cit.* p. 69
p. 268   'foundation for happiness' – *ibid.* p. 70
p. 268   'that at all' – *ibid.* p. 71
p. 268   'publicity is primary' – Cecil, *A Divided Life* p. 111
p. 268   'and quiet industry' – Connolly *op. cit.* p. 29
p. 269   'work something out' – Hoare *op. cit.* p. 71
p. 269   'poor lamb!' – *ibid.*
p. 270   'in general to women' – *ibid.*
p. 270   'homosexual spree' – Cecil, 'Legends Spies Tell'
p. 270   'men than women' – TNA FCO 158/186
p. 270   'mentioned homosexual tendencies' – TNA FCO 158/177
pp. 270–1 'repulsed his advances' – Fisher *op. cit.* p. 101
p. 271   'inclined to … perversion' – TNA KV 2/4150
p. 271   bed with Maclean – Partridge, *op. cit.* p. 182
p. 271   'positively no' – TNA KV 2/4141
p. 271   'blazoning' his conquests – A. Blunt *op. cit.*
p. 271   'by November 1' – TNA FCO 158/237
p. 271   'away from realities' – *ibid.*
p. 272   'of any officer' – TNA FCO 158/186
p. 272   'Toynbee in Cairo' – TNA KV 6/142
p. 272   'argument' about it – TNA FCO 158/237

p. 272	'and South America' – quoted Connell, *The Office* p. 327
p. 273	'sense of humour' – Modin *op. cit.* p. 182
p. 273	'out of his life' – TNA FCO 158/186
p. 273	early months of 1951 – TNA FCO 158/189
pp. 273–4	'much more anonymous' – letter to Alan Maclean 29.11.50, A. Maclean papers *op. cit.*

Chapter 15: Curzon

p. 275	'long as possible' – K. Philby *op. cit.* p. 168
p. 275	'leave him alone' – Modin *op. cit.* p. 181
p. 276	'the Distribution Room' – TNA FCO 158/1
p. 276	'as enquiries proceed' – TNA FCO 158/2
p. 276	pre-war 'Communist connections' – TNA FCO 158/1
p. 276	'an expensive house' – TNA KV 6/140
p. 277	'the letter G' – TNA KV 6/141
p. 278	'occupied another storey' – Anstee, *Never Learn to Type* p. 78
p. 278	'sleepy, almost drugged' – Cairncross *op. cit.* pp. 129–30
p. 278	'the Mogul Empire' – Anstee *op. cit.* p. 78
p. 278	'I must go' – *ibid.* p. 72
p. 278	'and become unreliable' – *ibid.* p. 69
p. 279	'control of everything' – *ibid.* p. 77
p. 279	'state of mind' – *ibid.*
p. 279	'pale pink liberal' – *ibid.*
p. 279	'very popular' – interview Daphne Coburn, November 2015
p. 280	'[the atom bomb's] use' – Hastings, *The Korean War* p. 214
p. 280	'to the bone' – TNA FCO 158/24
p. 281	'with military equipment' – Bullock *op. cit.* p. 1037
p. 281	'troops in Korea' – Hastings *op. cit.* p. 219
p. 281	'made argument impossible' – TNA KV 2/4143
p. 281	their own 'prestige' – Connolly *op. cit.* p. 30
p. 282	'about his Minute' – TNA KV 2/4143
p. 282	'a pointless war' – Modin *op. cit.* p. 184
p. 282	'later to [Gorsky]' – TNA KV 6/142
p. 283	vetted before 'indoctrination' – TNA KV 6/140
p. 283	'on the whole' – *ibid.*
p. 284	'[her] married life' – Hoare *op. cit.* p. 72
p. 285	'been for years!' – TNA KV 2/4140
p. 285	'in his cups' – *ibid.*
p. 286	'you at breakfast' – Rees *op. cit.* p. 190
p. 286	'and stumbled away' – Rees, *Sunday Times* 16.1.72
p. 287	'to conceal them' – *ibid.*
p. 287	'a violent form' – TNA KV 2/4143

p. 287	'Go on, report me' – Connolly *op. cit.* p. 31
p. 288	'high alcoholic content' – *ibid.*
p. 288	'he was talking' – TNA KV 2/4143
p. 288	'bitterly rejected Communism' – Toynbee, 'Maclean and I' *op. cit.*
p. 288	'change of heart' – Toynbee, 'Alger Hiss and his Friends', *Observer* 18.3.51
p. 289	'the English Hiss' – Connolly *op. cit.* p. 33
p. 289	'have much admiration' – TNA KV 2/4143
p. 290	'it happens' – *ibid.*
p. 290	evening as a 'disaster' – *ibid.*
p. 291	'a responsible position' – TNA KV 6/142
p. 291	'a moment's hesitation' – *ibid.*
p. 291	fn. 'falling to pieces' – Gore-Booth *op. cit.* p. 375
p. 292	'to premature conclusions' – TNA KV 6/142
p. 292	'anti-administration politicians' – *ibid.*
p. 293	'and a teetotaller' – K. Philby *op. cit.* pp. 170–1
p. 293	'were old ones' – TNA KV 6/142
p. 293	'initials on telegrams' – *ibid.*
p. 294	'blown sky-high' – *ibid.*
p. 294	'Soviet intelligence system' – TNA KV 6/144
p. 294	'ifs and buts' – *ibid.*
p. 295	'depressingly conformist' – K. Philby *op. cit.* p. 171
p. 295	'Partner for Peace' – Lownie *op. cit.* p. 219
p. 295	'Don't you go, too' – K. Philby *op. cit.* p. 171
p. 296	'direct security significance' – TNA KV 6/142
p. 297	'numerous counter suggestions' – *ibid.*
p. 297	on Erna Rosenbaum's – TNA KV 2/4140
p. 297	'would be otherwise' – *ibid.*
p. 297	'in the picture' – TNA KV 6/142
p. 298	'lower-middle-class family' – *ibid.*
p. 298	'while awaiting confinement' – quoted N. West *op. cit.* p. 132
p. 299	'and studying philology' – BBC Radio 4 18.3.98
p. 299	'can't believe it' – Cecil, *A Divided Life* p. 117
p. 299	'pale green car' – TNA KV 2/4140

Chapter 16: Endgame

p. 300	'love to Mother!' – TNA KV 2/4140
p. 300	'drinking quite heavily' – *ibid.*
p. 301	philosopher Freddie Ayer – TNA FCO 158/189
p. 301	'be of value' – TNA KV 2/4143
p. 301	'sort of person' – TNA KV 2/4141
p. 302	'was a Communist' – Hoare *op. cit.* p. 73
p. 302	'to be "cut adrift"' – *ibid.*

p. 302   'was forgotten' – *ibid*. p. 74

p. 302   'his shoulders hunched' – Cecil, *A Divided Life* p. 139

p. 303   'now, perhaps hours' – Modin *op. cit*. p. 200

p. 303   'they question him' – *ibid*.

p. 303   'through with it' – *ibid*. p. 201

p. 304   'not fit in' – TNA KV 6/142

p. 304   'has been interrogated' – *ibid*.

p. 304   and three women – Macintyre *op. cit*. p. 148

p. 304   'policeman as possible' – Harry Hunter, quoted Andrew *op. cit*. p. 335

p. 305   from street corners – Macintyre *op. cit*. p. 148

p. 305   'good little functionaries' – Modin *op. cit*. p. 207

p. 305   'trusting foreign criminal' – R. West *op. cit*. p. 238

p. 305   'a fixed distance' – Cecil, *A Divided Life* p. 139

p. 305   'fairly easily identified' – Reilly papers, Bodleian

p. 306   fn. 'with your hands!' – Gordievsky, *Next Stop Execution* p. 140

p. 306   'topline agent' – TNA FCO 158/7

p. 306   'about his relatives' – TNA KV 2/4151

p. 306   'forward and rejected' – Petrov and Petrov, *Empire of Fear* p. 272

p. 306   'right fibre content' – Gordievsky *op. cit*. p. 140

p. 307   'about Donald's escape' – A. Blunt *op. cit*.

p. 307   'like a tramp' – Lownie *op. cit*. p. 228

p. 307   'with great vigour' – *ibid*.

p. 307   'policeman-like manner' – Page, Leitch and Knightley *op. cit*. p. 224

p. 307   'denying everything' – Modin *op. cit*. p. 202

p. 308   'agree to defect' – *ibid*.

p. 308   'with assiduous bohemianism' – Motion, *The Lamberts* p. 235

p. 309   'a word was spoken' – Connolly *op. cit*. p. 34

p. 310   'to the scrap-heap' – K. Philby *op. cit*. p. 172

p. 310   'anti-British feeling' – quoted Cecil, *A Divided Life* p. 124

p. 310   'only by a lie' – TNA KV 6/142

p. 310   *'very* hot' that summer – Bower *op. cit*. p. 110

p. 311   'brighter than he was' – TNA KV 6/142

p. 311   'beginning of the war' – TNA KV 4/473

p. 311   'down for a night' – TNA KV 2/4143

p. 312   'fold very rapidly' – Modin *op. cit*. p. 203

p. 312   'independently identify Maclean' – TNA KV 6/142

p. 312   lack of 'action' – *ibid*.

p. 313   'on our hands' – Andrew *op. cit*. p. 424

p. 313   'along the coast' – Modin *op. cit*. p. 205

p. 314   'and civil servants' – *ibid*.

p. 314   'when they are together' – Andrew *op. cit*. p. 425

p. 315   'was very real' – TNA KV 6/143

p. 315   'breach of faith' – *ibid*.

p. 316   'without arousing suspicion' – *ibid.*

p. 316   'requiring special keys' – Cecil, *A Divided Life* p. 139

p. 316   Friday the 25th – TNA KV 6/143

p. 316   'of running away' – TNA KV 2/4150

p. 317   from 'going off' – TNA KV 2/4141

p. 317   'a languid glance' – Cecil, *A Divided Life* p. 140

p. 317   'with kid gloves' – Page, Leitch and Knightley *op. cit.* p. 214

p. 318   was 'completely himself' – TNA KV 2/4143

p. 318   'with Maclean again' – *ibid.*

p. 318   'mellow and confidential' – Connolly *op. cit.* p. 35

p. 318   some 'garbled explanation' – Cecil, *A Divided Life* p. 142

p. 318   'steady on his feet' – TNA KV 2/4140

p. 319   in the Americas – Anstee *op. cit.* p. 81

p. 319   'raising an alarm' – Makins *op. cit.*

p. 319   '6.10 p.m. train' – TNA KV 2/4140

p. 320   around 6.00 – Lownie *op. cit.* pp. 237–8

p. 320   'old green Penguins' – A. Maclean *op. cit.* p. 108

p. 320   at around 8.00 – TNA KV 6/143

p. 320   'casually and amicably' – Hoare *op. cit.* p. 7

p. 321   'a special ham' – Driberg, *Guy Burgess* p. 96

p. 321   'mainly about books' – TNA KV 2/4140

p. 321   'night accessories' – *ibid.*

p. 321   'conduct pretty outrageous' – TNA KV 2/4143

p. 321   went to bed – Hoare *op. cit.* p. 7

p. 321   'her young women' – TNA KV 2/4143

p. 321   had been laid – N. Maclean *op. cit.*

p. 322   berths to Bern – Driberg *op. cit.* p. 97

p. 322   not at Tatsfield – TNA KV 2/4143

p. 322   'as soon as possible' – N. Maclean *op. cit.*

p. 322   could 'kick herself' – *ibid.*

p. 323   'a day off' – TNA KV 2/4140

p. 323   Monday off as well – private information

p. 323   'great search started' – TNA KV 2/4143

Chapter 17: Establishment

p. 324   'a political escape' – Mather, ed. *The Great Spy Scandal* pp. 11–15

p. 325   'So it's out' – *ibid.*

p. 325   'their idealistic purposes' – *Daily Express* 7.6.51

p. 325   'out of his world' – Boyle *op. cit.* p. 382

p. 326   'from June 1' – FO press release 7.6.51

p. 326   'in the Seine' – Cecil, *A Divided Life* p. 1

p. 326   'done a Pontecorvo' – Anstee *op. cit.* p. 82

p. 326   'betray his country' – *ibid*.

p. 327   friends' representative – TNA KV 6/144

p. 327   'interests of secrecy' – *ibid*.

p. 328   'express an opinion' – Lownie *op. cit*. p. 251

p. 328   typed them up – Newton *op. cit*. p. 325

p. 328   'manhunt in history' – *ibid*. p. 326

p. 328   'he knew everything!' – quoted Purdy and Sutherland, *Burgess and Maclean* p. 100

p. 329   'the radio report' – TNA FCO 371/90931

p. 329   'was no pretence' – K. Philby *op. cit*. p. 172

p. 329   'taking French leave' – TNA KV 2/4146

p. 329   'for a few days' – *ibid*.

p. 329   'rather uncomfortable meeting' – Lamphere and Schachtman *op. cit*. p. 231

p. 330   '"tipped off Maclean"' – Newton *op. cit*. p. 333

p. 330   'looked from London' – quoted Cecil, *A Divided Life* p. 147

p. 330   'considered security hazards' – TNA PREM 8/1524

p. 330   fn. in Taiwan alone – Ranelagh, *The Agency* p. 235

p. 331   'of Wilde and Byron' – TNA FCO 158/254

p. 331   'changed the subject' – TNA KV 6/144

p. 332   'seven hot suspects' – *ibid*.

p. 332   'enjoying myself immensely' – *ibid*.

p. 334   'LOVING ME. DONALD' – Mather *op. cit*. p. 83

p. 334   'TELEGRAMS FROM PARIS' – *Daily Telegraph* 8.6.51

p. 335   'Hush-Hush Data' – *New York Daily News* 7.6.51

p. 335   'expert in faces' – *Daily Mail* 8.8.51

p. 335   'protruding front teeth' – FBI, quoted Cecil, *A Divided Life* p. 151

p. 335   'had little luggage' – TNA FCO 158/211

p. 335   'which was Maclean' – H. Spender, *London Review of Books* 3.5.81

p. 335   SIS 'personalities' – Aldrich, *The Hidden Hand* p. 422

p. 335   'have stolen it' – FBI Vaults

p. 335   Foreign Office crest – Purdy and Sutherland *op. cit*. p. 175

p. 337   'organising his defection' – TNA FCO 158/7

p. 337   never been translated – Andrew and Gordievsky *op. cit*. p. 323

p. 337   'or between themselves' – *The Times* 8.6.51

p. 338   'by all means' – Cave Brown *op. cit*. p. 430

p. 338   'opposite of euphoria' – Driberg *op. cit*. p. 98

p. 338   'by KGB agents' – Modin *op. cit*. p. 209

p. 339   'traffic from Prague' – TNA KV 4/473

Chapter 18: Into the Wilderness

p. 340   'the Foreign Office' – TNA KV 2/4140

p. 342   'the children. Melinda' – Hoare *op. cit*. pp. 16–17

p. 342   fn. 'the Missing Diplomat' – N. Maclean, *op. cit.*

p. 343   'for her son' – A. Blunt *op. cit.*

p. 343   'a *lovely* time' – A. Maclean *op. cit.* pp. 102–3

p. 343   so at the time – Cecil, *A Divided Life* p. 156

p. 345   'dearest snoop, Donald' – TNA KV 2/4145

p. 346   'to his country' – Hoare *op. cit.* p. 27

p. 346   'ashamed for me' – TNA FCO 158/4

p. 346   working as a double agent – interview Viscountess Macmillan 18.11.15

p. 347   'gather strength again' – Hoare *op. cit.* p. 80

p. 348   'than I ever have' – *ibid.*

p. 348   'to be recommenced' – *ibid.*

p. 348   'back to live' – Mather *op. cit.* pp. 99–100

p. 349   'become a revolutionary' – Connolly *op. cit.* pp. 15–16

p. 349   'articles fairly lightly' – TNA KV 2/3426

p. 349   'press so far' – Leigh Fermor letters, *Dashing for the Post* p. 66

p. 349   'place to hide' – quoted Hoare *op. cit.* p. 87

p. 349   'stop all wars' – TNA KV 2/4150

p. 350   'a new life' – *ibid.*

p. 350   she would not – TNA FCO 158/191

p. 350   'over the precipice' – quoted Hoare *op. cit.* p. 89

p. 350   'for going away' – quoted *ibid.* p. 90

p. 351   'colony, largely American' – TNA FCO 158/7

p. 351   'we are going' – *ibid.*

p. 351   a 'children's nurse' – TNA FCO 158/90

p. 352   'military-type aircraft' – *ibid.*

p. 353   'embraced his wife' – Modin *op. cit.* p. 246

p. 353   next two years – FBI 1250859–1

p. 353   'come off at last!' – Petrov and Petrov *op. cit.* p. 271

p. 353   'bring out Mrs Maclean' – *ibid.* p. 273

p. 353   'FROM ALL MELINDA' – Mather *op. cit.* p. 119

p. 354   'much as possible' – *Spectator* 14.10.55

p. 354   'but-not-forever' – TNA FCO 158/191

p. 354   'into the wilderness' – TNA KV 2/4150

Chapter 19: Comrade Frazer

p. 356   'sally into Russia' – Hughes, *Foreign Devil* p. 107

p. 356   'Soviet variety show' – *ibid.*

p. 357   'policy of silence' – *ibid.*

p. 357   'a wooden smile' – *ibid.* p. 121

p. 358   'West from there' – Driberg *op. cit.* pp. 121–4

p. 359   'comprehending the story' – *Sunday Times* 13.2.56

p. 359   'or lost property' – Macintyre *op. cit.* p. 199

p. 359	'a friendly visit' – *ibid*.
p. 359	'overlooking the Kremlin' –Penrose and Freeman *op. cit.* pp. 351–2, from Nigel Burgess on being shown Moscow by Maclean following his uncle's funeral
p. 360	'the nineteenth century' – Driberg *op. cit.* p. 100
p. 360	'under house arrest' – Miller, *All Them Cornfields* p. 53
p. 360	'to the Soviet Union' – Lownie *op. cit.* p. 284
p. 361	'have been shot' – Roy Medvedev, *The Times* 31.5.83
p. 361	'confession' of double-dealing – Miller *op. cit.* p. 53
p. 361	a 'sacred text' – Cecil, *A Divided Life* p. 165
p. 361	'more virile successor' – *ibid*.
p. 362	pointing a camera – Campbell, *Villi the Clown* p. 232
p. 362	the letter 'Frazer' – Piotr Cherkasov, 'Homer's Second Life', *Izvestia* 25.5.03
p. 362	'we were there' – Cecil, *A Divided Life* p. 164
p. 362	'of [their] persecutions' – TNA KV 2/4154
p. 363	'of Soviet Russia' – FBI interview with Melinda Maclean, FBI 1250859–1
p. 363	'official ideology any more' – Bushell, *Marriage of Inconvenience* p. 17
p. 363	'style, brand new' – Modin *op. cit.* p. 246
p. 363	'flavour of SW1' – E. Philby *op. cit.* p. 81
p. 363	'the available furniture' – interview Bob Evans 18.12.15
p. 364	'Brained, Murdoched, Sillitoed' – Toynbee papers, Bodleian
p. 364	'Old Fellow' – TNA KV 2/4154
p. 364	'choose are unlimited' – *ibid*.
p. 365	'bomb and disarm' – TNA FCO 158/11
p. 365	'time to time' – *Observer* 15.10.67
p. 365	'to Hungary now' – TNA FCO 158/11
p. 365	'impossible to answer' – *Observer* 15.10.67
p. 366	'all at hand' – Toynbee papers, Bodleian
p. 366	'disgusted about Hungary' – *ibid*.
p. 367	an 'emotional block' – Bushell *op. cit.* p. 18
p. 367	'to recall it' – *ibid*.
p. 367	'two missing men' – *Spectator* 23.9.55
p. 367	'cloak for treachery' – *Spectator* 30.9.55
p. 367	'or a regiment' – Hansard 7.11.55
p. 368	'conspicuously empty' – TNA FCO 158/11
p. 368	trip to London – *Daily Express* 11.10.60
p. 368	'analyst in the Institute' – to Dennis Ogden 16.3.76, A. Maclean papers *op. cit.*
p. 369	'find in newspapers' – Medvedev, *The Times* 31.5.83
p. 369	'in the elections' – Medvedev, *Washington Post* 19.6.83
p. 369	support for the Soviet action – Frankland, *Child of my Time* p. 174
p. 369	'and other writers' – *ibid*.
p. 369	'the Russian people' – TNA KV 2/4161

p. 370   'contemporary British foreign policy' – D. Maclean *op. cit.* p. 9

p. 370   'particularly the British' – *ibid.* p. 220

p. 370   'problems of British foreign policy' – *ibid.* p. 253

p. 371   'the Soviet people' – to Dennis Ogden, 1980, A. Maclean papers *op. cit.*

p. 371   'thinking and style' – *Daily Mail* 4.5.70

p. 371   'impeccably documented' – *Sunday Times* 3.5.70

p. 371   'had got there' – interview Bob Evans 18.12.15

p. 372   'a stuffed shirt' – TNA KV 2/4130

p. 372   'or capitalist terms' – Gordievsky *op. cit.* p. 61

p. 372   'on your behalf' – TNA KV 2/4158

p. 373   'Debenham's with Freebody's – Toynbee papers, Bodleian

p. 373   'fox, this time' – to Alan Maclean 13.7.63, A. Maclean papers *op. cit.*

p. 373   'upper-middle-class *apparatchik*' – Cave Brown *op. cit.* p. 537

p. 373   'of Western capitalism' – E. Philby *op. cit.* p. 82

p. 374   'Dr Jekyll's medicine' – Riordan, *Comrade Jim* p. 171

p. 374   'not altogether harmonious' – TNA KV 2/4161

p. 374   'the Revolution comes' – E. Philby *op. cit.* p. 83

p. 374   'haze of alcohol' – Cave Brown *op. cit.* p. 545

p. 374   'him any more' – E. Philby *op. cit.* p. 119

p. 374   '[Melinda's] life happier' – *ibid.* p. 169

p. 375   'another human being' – Macintyre *op. cit.* p. 279

p. 375   'prophet of *perestroika*' – Blake, *No Other Choice* p. 268

p. 376   'the truth imaginatively' – Bushell *op. cit.* p. 18

p. 376   'their normal course' – Blake *op. cit.* p. 271

p. 377   Margaret Thatcher – interview John Morrison 9.11.15

p. 377   'about our childhoods' – A. Maclean *op. cit.* p. 108

p. 377   'and his successors' – *ibid.*

p. 378   'political man of the world' – *Observer* 13.3.83

p. 378   'would gradually disappear' – interview Philip Short 4.1.16

p. 378   'most in the world' – *Observer* 13.3.83

p. 378   'a distinguished member' – Blake *op. cit.* p. 272

p. 378   'good and just man' – *ibid.*

p. 378   'progress and humanism' – *Washington Post* 12.3.83

p. 379   'and its endurance' – 1 Corinthians 13:5

p. 379   'of our civilisation' – to Dennis Ogden 16.3.76, A. Maclean papers *op. cit.*

p. 379   'how profoundly misguided' – Culme–Seymour to Alan Maclean 13.3.83,
          ibid.

List of Illustrations

Section One

The Maclean family: *Private Collection*. Donald Maclean's parents: *Victor Console / Associated Newspapers / REX / Shutterstock*. Lady Bonham Carter: *TopFoto.co.uk*. School photograph: *Courtesy of Gresham's School*. James Klugmann library card: *Marx Memorial Library*. Cambridge Armistice Day March: *Private Collection*. The 'Magnificent Five', in clockwise order: *Ramsey and Muspratt*; *Private Collection*; *Keystone / Staff*; *Keystone / Staff*; *Photo © Tallandier / Bridgeman Images*. Arnold Deustch, Theodor Maly and Kitty Harris: *Private Collection*. British Embassy staff, Paris: *Private Collection, as per* The Missing Macleans *by Geoffrey Hoare (Cassell & Co Ltd, London, 1955)*. Anatoly Gorsky: *Private Collection*. Melinda Marling: *TopFoto.co.uk*. Sir Roger Makins: *Bettmann / Contributor*. Yalta conference: *INTERFOTO / Alamy Stock Photo*. British Embassy, Washington: *Popperfoto / Contributor*. Walter Krivitsky: *AP / Rex / Shutterstock*. Meredith Gardner: *National Security Agency*. Robert Lamphere: *Bettmann / Contributor*. Arlington Hall: *U.S. Army Intelligence and Security Command*.

Section Two

Donald and Melinda: *AP / Rex / Shutterstock*. Philip Toynbee: *© National Portrait Gallery, London*. Donald, Melinda and Harriet Marling: *Private Collection, as per* A Divided Life *by Robert Cecil (The Bodley Head, London, 1988)*. Donald in pin-stripes: *Bridgeman Images*. Beaconshaw: *Evening Standard / Stringer*. Maclean family: *Keystone-France*. Moscow Centre: *Courtesy of SVR Archives*. Foreign Office: *Trinity Mirror / Mirrorpix / Alamy Stock Photo*. Yuri Modin: *Private Collection*. The Falaise: *Science & Society Picture Library / Contributor*. Wanted posters: *AP / Rex / Shutterstock*. Melinda and children: *Keystone Pictures USA / Alamy Stock Photo*. Alan Maclean and mother: *TopFoto.co.uk*. Jim Skardon: *Popperfoto / Contributor*. Melinda and boys in Geneva: *Private Collection as per* The Missing Macleans *by Geoffrey Hoare*. Vladimir Petrov: *Keystone Pictures USA / Alamy Stock Photo*. Melinda Marling: *AP / TopFoto.co.uk*. Bugress funeral: *AP / Rex / Shutterstock*. Philby and Melinda: *Photograph by John Philby, Camera Press London*. Maclean's funeral: *AP / Rex / Shutterstock*. Tomb of Sir Donald and his son: *Private Collection*.

Other

Telegram on page 334: *Levy/AP/REX/Shutterstock*

INDEX

147–8, 237; diffidence, 34, 42, 57–8, 77; dress, 1, 38, 57, 66, 317, 377; drinking and alcoholism, 2, 12, 17, 22, 34–5, 95, 113–14, 138, 152, 161–2, 197–8, 205, 220–21, 237, 243, 255–6, 266, 284–6, 289, 374; effeminacy, 23, 113; evasiveness, 24–5; fatherhood, 145, 284, 301, 311; handwriting, 204, 266, 344; idealism, 34–5, 358; immaturity, 55, 124, 128, 138–9, 223; industriousness, 37, 42, 77, 79, 92; introversion, 34, 78; language skills, 30, 57, 360; memory, 86, 145; morality, 12–13, 19, 22, 23, 34, 37, 188, 212; need for praise and reassurance, 55–6, 110, 125, 128, 216, 262–3; outsider, 26, 42–3; patriotism, 53, 132, 188, 215, 380; preference for bohemian lifestyle, 109, 212, 308; relations with parents, 12–13, 22, 31, 49, 56; relations with women, 45–6, 55, 57–9, 87, 113; secrecy, 14, 17, 125; sexuality, 17, 35, 44, 60, 196–7, 270–71; smoking, 77, 376; solitariness, 42–3; sporting prowess, 7, 25, 37, 42, 52, 141; support for underdog, 37–8, 212–13, 223, 369; temper, 193–4

Maclean, Donald ('Beany'; DM's son): birth, 196; childhood, 197, 210, 243, 267, 269, 284, 299, 347; and father's defection, 1, 4, 317; family moves to Geneva, 348, 349–50, 351; holiday in Majorca, 350–51; family joins DM in Soviet Union, 351–3, 362; life in Soviet Union, 363, 365, 372; marriage and later life, 376

Maclean, Sir Ewen (DM's uncle), 9

Maclean, Fergus (DM's son): birth, 143; childhood, 151, 197, 210, 267, 269, 284, 299, 347; and father's defection, 1, 4, 317, 341; family moves to Geneva, 348, 349–50, 351; holiday in Majorca, 350–51; family joins DM in Soviet Union, 351–3, 362; life in Soviet

Union, 363, 372; marriage and later life, 376, 377; interment of DM's ashes, 378–9

Maclean, Sir Fitzroy, 1st Baronet, 51, 87–8

Maclean, Sir Fitzroy, 26th Clan Chief, 8

Maclean, Gwendolen, Lady (*née* Devitt; DM's mother): family background, 10, 123; appearance and character, 10–11, 123; marriage and family life, 10–11, 14; and DM's student life, 33, 42–3, 44; and DM's politics and post-university career options, 44, 45–6, 51, 61; widowhood, 45–6, 123; visits DM in Paris, 95; and DM's marriage, 122–3, 268, 269; visits DM and family in Washington and Cairo, 164, 220; DM visits on return to England, 251; and DM's treatment for breakdown, 255; phone tapped by security services, 297, 348–9; during DM's last days in England, 300, 301, 321; learns of DM's disappearance, 322–3; in months following DM's disappearance, 341, 342; interviewed by Jim Skardon, 332–3, 340, 342; receives telegram from Paris, 333–4; reaction to DM's espionage and defection, 10–11, 56, 346–7, 348–9; later life and death, 372

Maclean, Ian (DM's brother), 11, 12, 14, 18; death, 137

Maclean, John (DM's grandfather), 9

Maclean, Lucy (*née* Hanna; DM's daughter-in-law), 376

Maclean, Melinda (*née* Marling; DM's wife): background and early life, 110–111, 298; appearance and character, 109, 110, 111–12, 207–8, 298; first meets DM in Paris, 109; their courtship, 110, 112–14, 118; knowledge of DM's espionage, 115–16, 138, 154; marriage and honeymoon, 118–21; first pregnancy, 119, 127, 128; couple

Scott's restaurant, Mayfair, 311
Second World War: outbreak, 99, 207;
    Soviet–Finnish Winter War, 102–3,
    137; Nazi occupation of Low
    Countries and France, 116, 117, 118;
    Battle of Britain, 122; Blitz, 127–8, 130;
    Nazi invasion of Soviet Union,
    129–30, 131–2, 134–5, 360; US entry,
    129, 136; Battle of Kursk, 133; D-Day
    landings, 134, 139, 277; Soviet advance
    on Berlin, 155, 185; end of, 161, 185
Sereni, Emilio, 264
'sex-pol' movement, 48–9, 56n, 82
Shakespeare, William, Othello, 42
Shawcross, Sir Hartley (later Baron
    Shawcross), 173
Sheers, Harriet see Marling, Harriet
Sheers, Jay, 301–2
Shipping, Ministry of, 124
Shrubb, Sylvia, 273
Sillitoe, Alan, 364
Sillitoe, Sir Percy, 264, 315, 330, 331–2
Silver Crescent (Trinity Hall magazine),
    39–40, 41
Simon, Ernest (later 1st Baron Simon of
    Wythenshawe), 14
Simon, Jocelyn (later Baron Simon of
    Glaisdale), 37–8, 61
Skardon, William 'Jim', 234–5, 239, 260,
    287, 330, 342–3, 354, 377; questioning
    of family and associates following
    DM's disappearance, 311, 320, 331,
    332–3, 340, 342, 346, 347
Slater, Humphrey, 285, 296, 318
Smith, Phyllis, 197
Smith, Sally (later Toynbee), 285
Smith, Walter Bedell, 331
Society of Analytical Psychology, 256
SOE (Special Operations Executive), 137
Solly-Flood, Peter, 193, 253
Solon, Larry, 324–5
Solzhenitsyn, Alexander, 369
Sonning, Berkshire, 336

Sorbonne, 111
South Egremont, Massachusetts,
    111, 143, 197
Southampton, 5, 303
Soviet Union: Western diplomatic
    recognition of, 26; under Stalin, 29,
    79–80, 82, 360–61; Five Year Plans, 29;
    Western visitors to, 29, 363; Western
    communists' views on, 33; purges,
    79–80, 82–3, 312; Second World War,
    118, 131–2, 134–7, 155, 360; and post-war
    division of Europe, 146–7, 150–51,
    155–9, 199; Berlin blockade, 202;
    atomic weapons development, 173,
    189, 191–2, 231–2, 235–6; and Korean
    War, 263; 'Doctors' plot' against
    Stalin, 360; death of Stalin, 350, 361,
    362; under Khrushchev, 350, 356–7,
    362, 364, 377; under Brezhnev, 377;
    glasnost and perestroika, 371, 375, 380;
    see also Nazi–Soviet Pact
Spanish Civil War, 73–7, 90, 91, 101, 365, 382
Spectator, The (magazine), 367
Speers, Ellen, 246
Spence School, New York, 111
Spender, Humphrey, 14, 335
Spender, Sir Stephen, 14
Spurgeon, Ernest, 90
Stalin, Joseph: Five Year Plans, 29; purges,
    79–80, 82–3, 312; and Munich
    Agreement, 90–91, 96; Second World
    War, 118, 130, 131, 133, 135; and post-war
    division of Europe, 146–7, 150–51,
    155–9, 199; and Iranian oilfields, 162;
    and Churchill's Iron Curtain speech,
    163; and Turkish Straits crisis, 181–2;
    and atomic weapons development,
    186, 202; and Marshall Plan, 199–200;
    and Berlin blockade, 202; 'Doctors'
    plot' against, 360; and threat of
    nuclear war, 281; death, 350, 361, 362;
    denounced by Khrushchev, 364; see
    also Nazi–Soviet Pact

penguin.co.uk/vintage